The Many Faces
of Communism

The Many Faces
of Communism

Edited by
Morton A. Kaplan

THE FREE PRESS
A Division of Macmillan Publishing Co., Inc.
NEW YORK

Collier Macmillan Publishers
LONDON

The Free Press
A Division of Macmillan Publishing Co., Inc.
866 Third Avenue, New York, N.Y. 10022

Collier Macmillan Canada, Ltd.

Library of Congress Catalog Card Number: 77-99096

Printed in the United States of America

printing number

1   2   3   4   5   6   7   8   9   10

Library of Congress Cataloging in Publication Data

    Main entry under title:

    The Many faces of communism.

    Includes bibliographical references and index.
    1. Communism—1945-   —Addresses, essays, lectures. 2. Com-
munist parties—Addresses, essays, lectures. I. Kaplan, Morton A.
II. Chicago. University. Center for Strategic and Foreign Policy
Studies. HX44.M317   335.43'09'047   77-99096
ISBN 0-02-917230-6

Contents

Preface

The Center for Strategic and Foreign Policy Studies of the University of Chicago has its primary mission in that area in which academic scholarship and important issues of public policy coalesce. It draws on expertise from academia, government, and the professions in its effort to elucidate important issues of public policy. In turn, the Center seeks to disseminate the results of these efforts to the educated public, to students, and to government agencies.

The subjects the Center investigates are controversial and it seeks the assistance of those who have informed and definite opinions. Where possible, it seeks a range of opinion in the belief that dialogue advances knowledge and permits better public policy. It attempts to avoid that type of judicious blandness that escapes controversy at the price of obscurantism.

The Center for Strategic and Foreign Policy Studies is part of the University of Chicago. It takes seriously the academic mission of the University and its institutional neutrality on public issues. On the other hand, universities cannot be entirely insulated from the societies that permit them to operate as the types of institutions that they are. Moreover, the University of Chicago is a private university in the Midwest. We take seriously a specific Midwestern mission, although we hope we do not do so in a parochial fashion. Although our conferences usually have wide attendance from official agencies in Washington and often from scholars or public officials from abroad, our major effort is devoted to establishing our links to Midwestern academics, students, businessmen, and professionals. The widest thrust of the Center's public educational activities are toward the Midwest. For this reason, we make a particular effort to secure a number of small grants from Midwestern institutions or individuals. During the academic year 1976-1977, we were particularly fortunate in receiving modest grants, for which we are very grateful, from the First National Bank of Chicago, the Relm Foundation, the International Cultural Foundation, the Exchange National Bank of Chicago, Arthur Andersen & Company, the American Bar Association, and the Denoyer-Geppert Company. We also received generous individual assistance from Sydney Stein, Jr., Huntington Harris, Eli Coplan, and Kenneth Lipper. Although not all grants were from the Midwest, the bulk of them were.

The chapters in this book were written by a distinguished international panel of experts on the various European and Asian communist parties. I believe that the chapters have benefited greatly from discussions that were held at the conference on this topic at the University of Chicago, April 7- 9, 1977. We did not permit the papers to be given at the conference. Instead, the writers of the chapters participated in a number of panels with other invited guests on specified functional issues such as "Eastern European Alternatives to Soviet Policy," "Soviet Options with Respect to Eurocommunism," and "Implications of Eurocommunism for NATO." Other panels dealt with the organizational structure of different communist parties. Thus, the individual analyses in the papers were subjected to comparative analysis during the discussions. This approach, I believe, was very useful to the volume contributors in drafting their final versions. Had we been sufficiently funded, the discussions would have been very useful to me in deciding how to provide experts with funds to carry out research vital to answering the important questions concerning changes in communist parties and their implications that were raised at the conference. These are questions that policy-makers in all major nations will have to face in the near future. Even in the absence of such additional research, I believe that this volume will make an important contribution to public consideration of the key issues involved in the evolution of communist parties: hence our title, *The Many Faces of Communism*.

I should like to include an apology. By the time we began thinking about transliteration, footnote styles, and reference standards, our authors were scattered all over the world. We did the best we could under the circumstances, but we hope the substance of the book will compensate for the lack of uniformity in style.

Morton A. Kaplan

Contributors

Mikhail Agursky was born in the Soviet Union, graduated from the University of Marxism-Leninism, and received his Ph.D. from the Academy of Sciences of the USSR. Agursky is now a senior lecturer in the Soviet and East European Research Center of the Hebrew University of Jerusalem.

Franco Ferrarotti is director of the Institute of Sociology at the University of Rome. He has been an independent deputy in the Italian Parliament. He was among the founders of the European Council of Municipalities and head of the Social Factors Division at the Organization for European Economic Cooperation. Ferrarotti is widely published in the field of sociological theory and is editor of *La critica sociologica*.

Haruhiro Fukui was born in Japan and received his undergraduate and master's degrees from Tokyo University. He is now an associate professor at the Santa Barbara campus of the University of California and has written widely on Japanese politics.

Morton A. Kaplan is director of the Center for Strategic and Foreign Policy Studies at the University of Chicago.

Pavel Machala was born in Czechoslovakia and did undergraduate work in the School of Economics of Charles University, Prague. He is now assistant professor in the Department of Political Science, Amherst College.

Eusebio M. Mujal-León was born in Cuba and is completing his doctoral thesis at the Massachusetts Institute of Technology. He has published several articles on the Chilean Communist party, Spanish communism, and Portugal.

Nenad D. Popovic was born in Yugoslavia. He was vice-president of the State Planning Commission of Serbia and vice-president of the State Economic Council of Serbia. He then became an executive director of the International Monetary Fund and later a plenipotentiary minister in the Ministry of Foreign Affairs. Subsequently, Popovic was a professor at the Maxwell Graduate School of Citizenship and Public Affairs at Syracuse University. He has published widely on Yugoslav problems.

Jean Victor Poulard was born in France and received his Ph.D. from the University of Chicago. He teaches political science at Indiana University at Gary.

Teresa Rakowska-Harmstone was born in Poland and is now a professor in the Department of Political Science at Carleton University in Canada. She has been employed in the Ministry of Foreign

Affairs of Poland and has written widely on the Soviet Union and Eastern Europe.

Tang Tsou is a professor of Political Science at the University of Chicago. He has written the definitive study of American Far Eastern policy: *America's Failure in China.* He has also written extensively on Chinese domestic politics and foreign policy.

The Many Faces
of Communism

Introduction:
What Is Communism?

Morton A. Kaplan

One of the most fascinating, perplexing, and controversial aspects of contemporary political life is the metamorphosis of communist parties—especially, but not limited to, the Western European ones—that Santiago Carrillo, the secretary of the Spanish Communist party, has likened to the breaking up of Christianity during the Protestant Reformation. Many have referred to this phenomenon as Eurocommunism, a term that blurs the major distinctions among Western European communist parties, neglects Asia entirely, and slights the interactions among the Western and Eastern European parties. Coincidentally, these communist parties are the ones whose policies will have the greatest impact on global politics.

This book represents a major, but preliminary effort to understand the metamorphosis in contemporary communism and to place it in context. The chapters that follow seek to elucidate the situations of the major communist parties. My introduction merely sets the stage for their expert testimony.

The Mythos of the Party

The death of Stalin in 1953 and Khrushchev's "secret speech" to the twentieth party congress in 1956 triggered what may turn out to be a cataclysmic chain of effects for international communism. The set of circumstances that permitted this trigger to operate, however, has a longer history.

It is difficult to recapture the mind set that supported the mythic significance of Soviet communism and that, in my opinion, could not long have survived Stalin's death, at least in its early form, in any event. Its spirit, however, is captured in the title of a book, published by former communists before World War II, that sought to explain their disillusionment: *The God That Failed*.

Marxian theory was believed by its communist adherents to be a science—in this case a historical science, but almost or equally as much a science as physics—that predicted the inevitability of a new social, economic, and political order that would produce freedom and justice for all for the first time in human history.

Marxian doctrine, like its Hegelian antecedent, was more complex than this in its treatment of inevitability; and its complexities, or more accurately a misunderstanding of them, led to the famous prerevolutionary dispute in Russia between those Marxians who emphasized human will and those who emphasized material necessity. This debate was fueled by the weakness of the revolutionary movement in the developed West, for that weakness constituted a theoretical problem for Marxian thought.

Under Lenin's leadership, the Bolsheviks were the inheritors of that strand of the tradition that believed that the revolution would inevitably result from the self-conscious activities of the revolutionary vanguard, that is, the leadership of the Communist party, the legitimacy of which rested on its ability correctly to interpret history and to act effectively upon this understanding. This vanguard would recognize the correct historical moment and would seize it to introduce a new scientific regime in which, in Lenin's phrase, administration would be replaced by accountancy, meaning that politics or discretion would be replaced by addition or logic. It would bring to pass scientifically first socialism and then communism. History, in effect, was God and the party its pope, or at least its authorized accountant.

Assimilating the Russian Revolution to Marxian theory, however, was not a simple matter. Lenin had hesitated before leading the Bolsheviks in the successful November Revolution. Even after its success Lenin at first believed that communism in the Soviet Union was an aberrant exception to Marx's prediction that communism would come first to the most advanced societies. He continued to believe, at least for a time, that revolution in Western Europe was required if Soviet communism were to survive. But these doubts were soon suppressed—and theory eventually received a new orthodox interpretation—as revolution failed in Germany, as communism,

Soviet style, planted itself firmly in the USSR, and as Stalin expounded his thesis of communism in one country.

By the late 1920s the important dissenters had been delegitimized by the Soviet steamroller. The success of the Soviet led movement that survived as the Third International legitimized the belief—and the parties' survival, especially in the USSR, depended upon the claim—that the Soviet party was the historical avatar of communist practice and communist science. Within the party, the politburo was the fount of authority. And, shortly, the general secretary became the sole source of legitimate writ—a situation later formalized by Stalin's authorship of the orthodox texts and party positions on linguistics, economics, politics, philosophy, physics, and biology.

A failure to remain loyal to the party was equivalent "objectively" to treason or, even worse, to meaninglessness for the party was the objectively self-chosen, and the only possible, instrumentality and interpreter of history and thus the only connection to a meaningful life with an "inner" relationship to historical truth. To leave the party was to abandon progress and the future, to be relegated to the garbage pail of history. Scientific socialism filled the vacuum left by disbelief in religion. Truth, as Georg Lukàcs, who recognized the tyranny of Stalin, plaintively observed, was preferable to meaninglessness. Truth was what the party, that is, Stalin, decreed. The mythos of communism, not its actuality, was the essential Truth for this tortured generation. Thus, the actual course of events in the Soviet Union was secondary to "inner Truth." And the transformation of the regime—a transformation dialectically entailed by Lenin's methods—escaped serious analysis among the faithful.

Lenin had imposed the same techniques of democratic centralism on the Third International that he had imposed on the Bolshevik faction and that had been outlined in his famous pamphlet *What Is to Be Done?* What became predominant, however, was dictatorship rather than party or doctrine. Lenin had suffered his eventually fatal stroke in the very birth pangs of the new regime for by 1923 the civil war had barely ended. Within a few short years Stalin had used Lenin's control mechanisms to vitiate both party and doctrine. By 1927 Stalin had outmaneuvered his serious opponents. By 1934, with the assassination of his former collaborator Serge Kirov (the Leningrad leader with whom Stalin had replaced Zinoviev, Stalin's former opponent—after Kirov mounted a central committee majority against Stalin's demand for the execution of former party comrades), a radical transformation had occurred in the Soviet regime. Both the Communist party of the Soviet Union and the Comintern were virtually dismantled as Stalin exercised control over the Soviet Union and the international communist movement through three basic agencies: his personal secretariat; the secret police, which was itself divided; and divisions between as well as within governmental agencies and party sections in the Soviet Union and within factionalized foreign parties. Moreover, the process was necessary. Because reality and practice falsified prior theory, party legitimacy could not have survived scrutiny. Control would have been lost if the party had not suppressed opposition outside the party and, if later, Stalin had not suppressed opposition within the party. The choice was between factual or formal loss of the party's primacy—and that of Marxian theory—in the Soviet system. And formal loss of the party's primacy would have brought down all the incumbent leaders, including Stalin. It might, however, have restored that type of Marxian theory that Marx preferred as represented in his avowal, "Je ne suis pas Marxiste."

These developments in the Soviet system were not entirely unnoticed although not all who noticed them understood their significance. Some in the West contrasted the good nationalist Stalin with the wild revolutionary Trotsky. Occasional communists in the West did become disillusioned as they observed how their parties were sacrificed to the interests of the Soviet Union. As Mikhail Agursky points out in Chapter 4, these events helped persuade some of the reactionary emigres to support Stalin as a Russian patriot and gave rise to a (rarely simple) national bolshevist orientation within the Soviet Union that was at least in partial conflict with ideological communism, particularly as represented within the ideological apparatus of the party. This is a very complex phenomenon that I merely note except to add that even the current Soviet opposition to the Communist regime is permeated by similar complex and contradictory tendencies, as one can see in some of the reactionary and racist portions of the Samizdat papers.

Despite some necessary qualifications, by the late 1930s Stalin was the communist movement and the communist movement was Stalin. The identity had become so deep because the revolution had occurred in Russia and had become the embodiment of scientific socialism. Because Stalin was the *vozd* (boss) of the Soviet Union, to deny Stalin's identity with the party and communism was virtually to deny scientific socialism and/or hope for the future. Moreover, so monstrous were Stalin's crimes against ordinary moral standards that no justification could be offered for them except in terms of historical necessity as interpreted by legitimate authority—a road that had been paved by Lenin's earlier strictures against bourgeois morality. But why did not foreign communists reject this criminal regime?

The cadre of the 1930s was the first revolutionary generation. Its members were not and could not have been expected to be prepared to deny the legitimacy of the 1917 Revolution. The Revolution of 1917 represented their adolescent hopes; its victory, the fulfillment of their dreams; its promises, their gift to humanity; and its organization, an essential element in their sense of identity. Even when they became aware of Stalin's crimes, very few were capable of splitting with the Soviet dominated International and of joining normal political parties. Most who left joined organizations such as the Trotskyite that at least asserted the eventual triumph of the October Revolution over Stalin's "Thermidorean" reaction. How could they deny the greatest experience of their lives, an experience essential to their own sense of identity?

Those who remained in the party had to suppress doubt. Doubt would have forced them to defect and to denounce Stalin's crimes. Doubt was "objective" treason, as testimony in the "show" trials reveals that some of the victims of the purges themselves felt. Doubt was incompatible with preservation of the party's and Stalin's dictatorship. The entire structure of legitimacy would have collapsed if doubt were allowed, at least during the generation of true believers.

Of course, the picture I have painted is done in broad strokes. The world was not exactly like that. In Chapter 1 Franco Ferrarotti points out clearly how even the very early history of the Italian party under leaders such as Gramsci and Togliatti, as opposed to those such as Terracini, laid the foundations for the current posture of the party. Yet even the Italian Communist party (PCI) was dominated from Moscow in this period. How could it have been otherwise? The present course of the PCI, which we can see foreshadowed in the early positions of Gramsci and Togliatti, in the Salerno position, and in the *partito nuovo*, were then merely minor themes not fully integrated in the dominant intellectual and organizational structure of the PCI. Today, under new circumstances, these minor themes are becoming dominant, but the other themes have not entirely been dissipated. This contributes to the current ambiguity.

Major changes are occurring throughout Western European communism. These include the "historic compromise" with the Christian Democrats in Italy, the Common Program with the Socialist party in France, and the democratic communism of Santiago Carrillo in Spain. Some commentators, in an effort to debunk recent trends in Western European communism, assimilate these new developments to the old popular fronts of the 1920s and thirties. The popular fronts from below of the late 1920s and the popular fronts from above of the 1930s, as these critics point out correctly, were both directed by Stalin. They were turned on and off by order of the Soviet Union to serve the purposes of Soviet foreign policy. This, however, is not true of the historic compromise in Italy and the front between the Communists and Socialists in France. These popular fronts spring from indigenous conditions and reflect both social and organizational transformations in the parties that have removed them from the control of Moscow. There is abundant evidence of a debate within the Soviet Union concerning these developments that is reactive and not directive. We can understand this development best by seeing it as part of a historical process in which new phenomena that are superficially similar to past phenomena have been transformed dialectically by new circumstances. There are false identities as well as false opposites, and contemporary popular fronts are not truly identical to those of the prewar period. The mythos and the organizational conditions that permitted Stalin's control of the international movement in the prewar period are too attenuated to be operative in the postwar period.

Factors Making for Change

Although post-World War II events are rooted in a deeper past, the Second World War served as a breakwater for the international communist movement. Stalin was forced to turn to extreme nationalism internally in order to rally support during the war. In the meantime, his communications with partisan resistance movements were intermittent at best. And his control over foreign parties, including clandestine networks and GPU control mechanisms, was badly damaged. Thus, the organizational instruments of control he had exercised in the 1930s had been shattered and only his charismatic personality, his organizational position, his great longevity in office, and the Red Army in Eastern Europe permitted him to retain control of international communism.

However, the equilibrium in the communist movement had become unstable. Tito had taken over Yugoslavia with more help from the West than from the Soviet Union. And under his secret police chief, Rankovic, his party had been unified and in 1948 was in a position successfully to resist Stalin. Even Tito, however, had been enthralled by the mythos of communism. Before the rupture of 1948 he had spoken of Yugoslavia's becoming a state within the Soviet Union. As Nenad D. Popovic (see Chapter 7) told me over lunch, when he had been in charge of economic planning in Serbia, he tried to follow the Soviet model religiously from Soviet books and only learned later that the books had little to do with reality. But not even mythos could overcome organizational reality in 1948 in the absence of the Red Army.

In Italy, a new generation of Communists, who as adolescents had served as partisan leaders, came to prominence in the PCI. Their memories and character were forged in these experiences as well as within the tradition of Gramsci. They became the lieutenants of Togliatti in opposition to the militants. And Mao eventually came to control in China as a consequence of Stalin's errors in 1927; furthermore, he did so contrary to Stalin's desire and with a different theory for Communist strategy in China.

Our generational account is not a simple one, however, for the French party (PCF), despite the activities of its members in the resistance, remained the most sclerotic and Stalinist of all parties, at least until Waldeck Rochat. Changes were occurring beneath the surface in the PCF, but they were less visible and less pervasive.

Nonetheless the situation was ripe for major changes in perspective, even in France. We must remember that the Russian Revolution was barely twenty years old when World War II broke out. By Stalin's death it was nearly forty years old. And today it is more than sixty years since the Russian Revolution. In the meantime Mao had provided an alternative mythos, the very existence of which is inconsistent with exclusiveness and which, with his death, is being modified by Chinese bureaucraticism. While these historical events have been transpiring, a second and third revolutionary generation have been moving into positions of prominence and a fourth post-revolutionary generation is coming to political consciousness. The perspectives of the third generation—its historical memories, its organizational experience, and its motivations—are massively different from the perspectives of the first generation. What was once true belief is now mostly ritual and formal legitimation, even where insisted upon as in the Soviet Union and parts of Eastern Europe. In Western Europe and Japan even ritual is fading. The beliefs of the fourth generation likely will be even further removed from contemporary beliefs.

There were factors, however, that slowed down the process of change. In particular, at the close of World War II the Eastern European model was viewed widely as a formula for rapid development and modernization. But an increasingly fragile equilibrium in international communism could be sustained only for so long. Today, there is widespread cynicism inside the Soviet Union concerning the backwardness of its political and economic systems. The leadership cannot entirely surrender communist ideology, however, for it still conveys some degree of legitimacy both abroad and at home: neither real elections nor divine providence is available to it, after all. Yet force seldom is or can be far from the surface as Soviet leaders first loosen up the system to let steam off and then tighten it up in an effort to manage a potentially unstable system in which the ability to control is the ultimate arbiter.

There are too many vested interests at top and intermediate levels of the Soviet system to accept its collapse. Yet it cannot be reformed in any substantial sense without threatening these interests. This is no longer a mythos that can function external to the Soviet Union except in relation to direct major interests of other parties— e.g., regime maintenance in Eastern Europe—or force. Communism in the Soviet Union is primarily, although not exclusively, an embattled control system in which its beneficiaries are struggling for political survival.

Cynicism is far greater in Eastern Europe. And it will increase in China as noncharismatic leaders attempt to restore stability, economic growth, and military strength. The French and Italian party papers and journals no longer attempt to portray the Soviet system as progressive economically. Their readers are aware of hidden unemployment in the Soviet Union, of inequalities in income, of failures in production, and of excessive bureaucracy. Furthermore, their electoral interests support this recognition and their search for solutions different from the Soviet.

The fourth revolutionary generation in France and Italy is attacking the two Communist parties from the Left and denounces the Soviet Union for its bureaucratic state capitalism. No communist party can tolerate too vigorous a challenge from the Left, even if it is not highly organized, and therefore some of the challenge must be absorbed. In Italy, the challenge from the Left is also a threat to the labor unions allied with the Communist party. Moreover, if many in the PCI agree with the extreme Left that the Soviet Union is a bureaucratic state—although Reichlin, the editor in chief of *L'Unità*, the party newspaper, stated that the Italian party is not prepared to *say* (italics added) that the Soviet Union is not a socialist state—they can hardly argue for Eastern European models. In fact, the PCI explicitly rejects the latter. Furthermore, several PCI leaders have said that nationalizations have gone too far in Italy. The French party, on the other hand (which is largely restricted to a worker base and is dominated by its Socialist partner), favors extensive nationalizations, partly to strengthen its political base through control of the nationalized companies. The risk that this stand may lead to the defeat of the Left is deemed acceptable because in any event the next French government will have to impose austerity measures that will be unpopular with PCF supporters. (Toward the end of this introduction I will further account for some of the factors that may explain these differences.)

If observers in the West had been sufficiently alert during the immediate postwar period, we would have noticed the incubation of these tendencies. We did not see the Balkan concerns that led Tito and Dmitrov to support the Greek civil war to Stalin's annoyance. We did not fully appreciate Togliatti's attempt to support the Marshall Plan in 1948 nor do we fully understand even today the intraparty struggle that kept Togliatti in Italy in that year despite Stalin's attempt to remove him to Moscow. Moreover, in that very same year Togliatti gave support to Tito during his break with Moscow, a stand that may have reflected the close collaboration between the PCI and the Tito partisans during the war. Even the old war-horse Georgi Dmitrov of Bulgaria gave behind-the-scenes support to Tito during his break with the Kremlin. We did not pay much attention to the fact that in China only the Soviet embassy moved to Canton with the fleeing Nationalists, a decision that was probably related to negotiations over Singkiang, poor intelligence, and a desire by Stalin that the Chinese Communists (CCP) not take all of China. We did note, but perhaps not sufficiently, the length of the negotiations between Stalin and Mao after the CCP victory. And perhaps we should not be blamed for this astigmatic view of international communism, for as long as Stalin lived he did dominate the communist movement and did exercise, if not monolithic, at least real control. Nor did this control entirely disappear with his death or even after Khrushchev's secret speech. Following that speech only Togliatti among the major European communist figures advanced the cause of polycentrism and asserted that the fault that produced Stalinism lay not merely in Stalin but in the Soviet system as well. We still await public recognition by communist leaders that the fault lies also in their apocalyptic view of history.

The breakup of the communist movement in 1956 would have been too great a shock, for this was still the second postrevolutionary generation. Moreover, the cold war was still on; the myths about imperialism were extremely strong; and there was no wish to renounce the Soviet Union entirely, as is still true for many within communist movements. Very few countries are Switzerlands or Swedens. Indeed, many on the Left perceive even a tyrannical Soviet Union as a barrier to reaction at home. They may be mistaken, but these fears are part of political reality.

Changes in such movements occur only slowly as personalities, memories, frameworks of experience, and real alternatives change—usually at a glacial speed. These changes (of a democratic nature) in Western European communism are not inevitable and what happens will depend upon particular histories and particular circumstances.

It is a human fault to oversimplify and to insist upon neat categories. Either these changes are genuine or they are not. If they are genuine, the parties will break with Moscow, and so forth. However, politics is not a unity. Coalitions, parties, and individual minds are at least partly inconsistent complexes and even the elements function inconsistently in different settings. Political situations usually change only at the margin. Statesmen recognize this fact and attempt to use these margins for their ends. What can be done depends upon the right moves at the right times.

Just as fruits should be eaten only when ripe—and neither before nor after—so some political situations should be allowed to develop without untimely interference. If Eastern Europe had been excluded from the original Marshall Plan proposal, neither Italy nor France, with their coalition governments, which included Communists—and where there was considerable public acclaim over Communist resistance activities—could have joined the plan. On the other hand, if the USSR had remained within the plan, it never could have been gotten through Congress. Only when Molotov's proposals at Paris were so palpably unacceptable were noncommunist governments in France and Italy able to join the Marshall Plan without Soviet and East European participation. Henry Kissinger nearly lost Portugal to communism by great overt hostility to a government in which Communists participated. And unlike the PCI, the Portuguese party is Leninistic and antidemocratic. However, even the Portuguese moderates, except for those around Spinola, who were soon discredited, were unwilling and unable to break the antifascist coalition until the Portuguese Communists behaved in an outrageous fashion. If it had not been for the activities of European social democrats and our perceptive ambassador in Lisbon and his intervention through the secretary of defense, we might have had a political disaster.

For these reasons, I must disagree with the otherwise excellent chapter by Pavel Machala (Chapter 6) when he states that we must not become open to Western European communists until they break with Moscow. We should not demand, for instance, that the Italian Communists make a clean break with Moscow and Eastern Europe. They still have militants within the party. Such insistence easily could force the party either into unified resistance to the demand or to a split that I do not believe would assist anyone in the West. The PCI is not without influence in Eastern Europe, and although I do not wish to overestimate this influence, it is not valueless. Moreover, as Ferrarotti points out, the PCI's charisma, with its electorate as well with its membership, to a considerable extent depends on its perceived resistance to *transformismo*. Too clean a break with its past would have a disillusioning effect, especially at a time when the PCI is under severe attack from the unorganized Left. Furthermore, there are approximately 1.5 million armed militants on the Right who might attempt to stage a coup if the Communists came to power. The PCI cannot afford to cut off all lines of retreat to its own militants.

The situation is simply not ripe for the PCI to make a clean break with the East, and perhaps it never will be ripe. We do not yet know whether a split in the PCI or a break with the East necessarily will be desirable. Furthermore, I doubt that we should wish *transformismo* upon the PCI. It already has made many concessions to the immobilism of an Italian system that is unjust and reactionary.

Unlike the French party, with its history of Stalinist scleroticism, the PCI has a sufficient historical basis to its newly democratic aspects to reinforce their plausibility. The PCI rejects both Russian and Eastern European models. Some in the leadership regard the Allende regime in Chile as largely, if not entirely, responsible for its own downfall. And many of its leaders have no respect for the position of the Portuguese Communist party. This transformation is supported by changes in membership composition and organization, a subject to which this introduction will return and which is elucidated in Chapter 1.

But there is ambiguity. The leaders of the PCI differ from each other and probably cannot predict what they will do under undefined circumstances, e.g., a flight of capital, a coup attempt against them, antagonistic American policies, and so forth. The ambiguity is both practical and intellectual for only the course of events can permit clarification. There is not and cannot be any single or simple answer to the questions that are being raised.

On the whole, however, I view the present situation of the PCI as a healthy development, particularly if it permits us to break the widely, although inaccurately, perceived intimate connection between defense of the NATO area and of capitalism. There is no need for us to carry that intellectual and political burden.

NATO and the Soviet Union

Much of the disquiet over the position of the communist parties in European governments stems from the situation of NATO and their attitudes toward it. I agree that this is a perilous situation but not because the Soviet regime is eager for new territorial gain. Agursky probably is correct concerning the essentially conservative nature of the Soviet regime. The Soviet regime, and particularly the so-called national Bolshevik element within it, probably is more concerned with maintaining its stability than it is with expansion. However, the Soviet regime is sitting on a powder keg. Agursky points out the demographic aspect of the powder keg—the differential birthrates between the Great Russians and the other nationalities. This disparity, as he indicates, is a major reason why the leadership is resistant to an expansion that in many ways would exacerbate Soviet nationality problems. The regime is also weak economically. It requires transfusions of capital, credit, and technology, and even these may not overcome the bureaucratic constipation of the Soviet economic system. The USSR has numerous problems with its Eastern European allies, as they have with their own populations.

It is the political and economic weakness of the Soviet Union that, combined with its vast military strength, makes it a serious danger to the West. The Soviet Union might face a crisis either internal or within the bloc so threatening to the regime that grave pressure, threats, or perhaps even overt violence against Western Europe would appear as the least unattractive of its alternatives. However, it would be foolhardy entirely to neglect the possibility that a future Soviet leadership with a more secure economic base might attempt to Finlandize Western Europe, a result that would avoid worsening the Soviet nationality problem and that would reduce the potential of its Warsaw Treaty (WTO) allies for some degree of autonomy.

The General Strategic Situation

I shall attempt to place in perspective the impact of communist parties on world politics by discussing the general strategic problem that the democratic camp faces. Until after World War II, world politics was really the politics of Europe. The rest of the world played a peripheral role despite the decisive intervention of the United States in both world wars. The various regional systems that did exist did not function as integrated parts of the whole.

In both world wars, Germany was the central power with interior lines of communication. However, Germany lacked manpower, resources, and space. Therefore, unless it could gain access to the resources of Russia and the Middle East, it could not win without taking command of the oceans from the United States and Great Britain. Fortunately, it succeeded in neither task.

However, the growth of the Soviet Union into a superpower has created a new situation in which the world and its affairs are almost, if not totally, interdependent. For the first time in history, there is a heartland power on what Sir Hjalford MacKinder called the world island. Its area of control stretches from the border between the two Germanies to the Bering Strait. And—except for the policies of the United States—it would dominate Western Europe, East Asia, South Asia, and the Middle East. The growth of this superpower coincides with several revolutions in military technology that transform

Western Europe from a military space to a thin skin. The distance from the East German frontier to Paris is roughly 300 miles, or less than the width of the state of Pennsylvania. Soviet operational manuals call for rapid penetrations of more than sixty miles a day.

The situation is equally perilous in the Far East. The distance between Japan and South Korea is about 120 miles, not much greater than the ninety-mile distance between Philadelphia and New York. Roughly twenty miles separates northern Japan from Soviet territory. Japan depends upon an independent South Korean government to protect its southern flank while it maintains its weak defense forces in Hokkaido as a delaying force to provide time for American intervention if the Soviet Union should attack. If South Korea fell to the North and came under Soviet influence, the Japanese situation would become so critical that Japan would be tempted strongly either to Finlandize itself or to go nuclear. A collapse of the Western position in either Europe or Asia would permit the mobilization of overwhelming Soviet pressure on the other periphery. And the United States then likely would be forced back into an uncomfortable "Fortress America" posture.

On the other hand, the peripheral powers in Western Europe and Asia—Japan, China, and India are the major ones—are even more dependent on the United States than it is on them: the U.S. is the only significant barrier to Soviet dominance on the world island.

The situation, however, is much more complex than it was at the height of bipolarity. In that era (roughly the 1950s and the early 1960s) Japan and Western Europe were so clearly dependent on U.S. support, and the Soviet Union seemed to them so aggressive, that they became mere tails on American policy (France under De Gaulle was an exception). The United States obversely saw itself as the only power that could halt Soviet aggression and thus it engaged in almost automatic responses to perceived Soviet threats. Moreover, the U.S. failed to understand the appropriate role for uncommitted states and the United Nations (a universal actor) in a loose bipolar system, an understanding that an adequate theory of bipolarity would have provided for policy.

The reinvigoration of Western Europe and Japan, the split between China and the Soviet Union, Gaullism, restlessness in Eastern Europe, and détente have complicated the picture. The peripheral powers to some extent now are playing off one superpower against the other, somewhat as the uncommitted states did earlier. They do this sometimes on calculations of international politics and sometimes for domestic reasons. This is true to a degree within Eastern Europe, too, except perhaps for East Germany, where the internal consensus is relatively weak. The East European states do require a strong Soviet Union to maintain internal control. However, if the Soviet

Union were to dominate Western Europe, local autonomy would become endangered. Even the Rumanians, whose highly authoritarian political system might be corroded by Eurocommunism, are willing to support Eurocommunism and to risk this corrosion because it strengthens their autonomy. On the other hand, because the strength of the Rumanian regime is the best guarantee against Soviet control—and the population understands this—the risks of Eurocommunism are reduced for it. Thus, the Soviet Union cannot expect automatic or wholehearted support for its policies from its Eastern European allies except in situations in which it is willing to pay the very high price of resort to the use, or the credible threat, of naked force.

This situation has both advantages and dangers. Its complexity reduces the potential for a head-on collision between the United States and the Soviet Union. This complexity also opens the way for solutions to problems that bipolarity normally would close off. However, because it confuses responsibility for decisive intervention where this may be essential and encourages Gaullist policies in the hope that others will be responsible, or greater concern for domestic political requirements than for international policy needs, it may produce an unnecessary crisis or inadequate policy in a crisis. In that ultimate situation—of low but not negligible probability—the concrete military-geopolitical situation would come to the fore.

The Soviets have bought a military force that permits them to neutralize American strength although they are weak politically and economically and to win a war if war becomes necessary. This requires a nuclear strategic force that at the least can immobilize the American force and that at best can achieve forms of superiority that permit local counterforce use. On the seas, the Soviet Union does not require either superiority or equality. Because it is not dependent on command of the seas, as is the case with the United States—the position of which is utterly dependent upon U.S. ability to maintain consistent communications with and support for its allies off the coasts, and on the periphery, of Europe and Asia—the Soviet Union requires only the ability to prevent the United States from retaining command of the seas. As the United States has already voluntarily surrendered to a great extent its ability to maintain this form of command (and at best has only a very modest and insufficient base at Diego Garcia with which to maintain global lines that minimize its horrendous two-front tasks) the Soviet naval buildup assumes even more menacing proportions than it otherwise would. If one adds to this the overwhelming advantage that the Soviet Union has built up in ground forces in the WTO area, the vulnerability of NATO bases, and the vulnerability of its small number of entrance points—a result of French withdrawal from combined plans—the military picture looks so threatening that only political, economic, and technological factors, in addition to the Chinese flank, prevent the sheer weight of the Soviet presence in Europe from Finlandizing Western Europe through voluntary accommodation and without excessive use of overt threat.

Communists in Government and World Politics

For reasons given in the prior strategic analysis, we have reason to be concerned about the impact that communists in coalition governments either in Western Europe or in Japan might have on the strategic balance. And we must take into account the policies of the other communist giant, China. Italy is the most critical political area of all with respect to a coalition because the PCI, unlike the PCF, dominates the Left. PCI leaders, however, are not unaware of the potentially unstable strategic situation in Europe. They privately call attention to Yugoslavia as the critical issue in Europe, particularly for Italy. If, after Tito's death, Yugoslavia were to succumb to Soviet influence, the PCI probably would feel forced to accommodate to Soviet power even though this likely would mean the destruction of the present leadership of the party. However, this does not necessarily distinguish the Communists from other Italians, for whom the price would be lower, or even from other Western Europeans. If the United States proves so weak or so inept as to permit the Soviet Union to gain hegemony over Yugoslavia, the impact of this development upon all of Western Europe, with the possible exception of Western Germany, will be mind-boggling.

Questions are raised about the real extent of PCI support for NATO. It is true that the Italian Communists are not prepared to support major increases in the Italian military budget, but neither is any major Italian party. Furthermore, both Christian Democrats and the PCI wish to develop a sophisticated arms industry in Italy using American models, the output of which, on the order of roughly $1 billion a year, would be used to equip Italian forces and to support itself in part by selling arms abroad. This is a very constructive opportunity that as of August 1977 the United States is managing industriously to do nothing about. It is quite true that certain sections of the PCI would strongly resist any efforts in support of NATO that did not involve a Warsaw Pact attack on Italy itself. And the PCI, as well as the French and even the Spanish party, has joined the USSR in attacking American development of neutron bombs. There is ambiguity here also. On the other hand, this sentiment, though unhelpful in terms of the military balance, is widely shared within the European Left. Thus, the PCI position on the neutron bomb may be a cheap concession to popular opinion by the leadership rather than a sure indicator of future behavior. This is a genuine handicap for NATO, although I would suggest that the militants are not likely to carry the day in a really serious affair.

In one respect, although this is highly debatable, PCI cabinet responsibility might be an advantage. One of the most severe NATO problems is mobilization. NATO strategy calls for meeting a prospective Warsaw Pact attack on the basis of a forty- to sixty-day mobilization. This depends upon warning. Senator Nunn doubts that there would be such warning time, and he likely is right, for the Soviet Union can mobilize and transport its troops in less time. Perhaps there nonetheless would be strategic warning because of a preceding political crisis. We did have strategic warning of the Soviet attacks on the Nagy government in Hungary in 1956 and on Czechoslovakia in 1968 although the Soviet Union produced tactical surprise in each case. However, democratic governments cannot normally take serious mobilization measures during such crises for almost all crises are ambiguous. During the Czechoslovak crisis of 1968, NATO maneuvers near the East German border were canceled to avoid even an appearance of provocation. If a crisis should occur in the future, it is most likely that democratic governments in the NATO area would be unable to mobilize because they would be under domestic pressure to show that they had made every effort to preserve peace, including the avoidance of all moves that the public might perceive as provocative, such as mobilization. However, if there is PCI participation in such decisions and at least shared PCI cabinet responsibility for military matters in general, NATO might be able to order mobilization in Western Europe in such situations. The partial openness of the PCI to the Soviet Union would be a possible warrant for the defensive nature of the arrangement, thus likely reducing the appearance of provocative behavior. The presence of a Communist minister of defense, for instance, in Italy, under some circumstances, might permit NATO to mobilize in a crisis, thereby maintaining assurance in the West and inhibiting any tendency toward excessive accommodation or self-Finlandization.

The French Communist party could not be expected to act as responsibly as the PCI. It has a long history of Stalinism and remains militant although changes in its third generation leadership may be making real its nationalism and perhaps even its support for formal democracy. However, the PCF is more Gaullist than the Gaullists and now supports an independent nuclear force and a *tous azimuts* policy. Given the encapsulated political situation of the Communist electorate in France, even if the French Communist party participates in a Left coalition it is likely that the Socialist party will control defense. Mitterrand and the people around him appear reasonably dependable on defense issues despite the influence of the CERES group. And, if a crisis occurs that invokes French defense interests and the Communists resist action, this might be the incident that would give rise to a centrist coalition between the Mitterrand and Giscard forces. Even in mid-1977 the Socialists are concerned that PCF defense policy might prohibit French participation in anything short of a central nuclear war, a policy Mitterrand feels is so deficient that it may split the Left or lead to its defeat.

Although the metamorphosis of communist parties in their program and outlook on internal affairs has gone furthest in Western Europe, the most drastic transformation of outlook and program in international affairs—one that poses the most serious challenge to the Soviet Union in global politics and within the communist movement—has taken place in China. In Chapter 9 Tang Tsou renders a new interpretation of the rejection of the theory of the two camps by the Chinese and their adoption of the doctrine of "three worlds" in its place. He analyzes the doctrine of three worlds in terms of the impact on Chinese thinking of their experiences both in the revolutionary civil war and in global politics after 1949. He sees that doctrine as a synthesis of the Chinese theory and practice of the united front with a new understanding of the advantage of occupying the middle position in a series of triangular relationships in international affairs. This doctrine limits China's conflict with the United States and sharpens its challenge to the Soviet Union while it makes Chinese policies more flexible and moderate. To the extent that China adopts policies paralleling those of the United States toward Western Europe, the Soviet military threat and the danger of Finlandization decrease.

Japanese Communist policy is still unhelpful, particularly with respect to Korea and defense policy, although the Japanese Communist party (JCP) is trying to stake out an independent nationalist position on foreign policy. There are some signs, however, as Haruhiro Fukui points out in Chapter 8, of potential favorable changes in the foreign policy of the JCP.

U.S. Policy toward Communist Governmental Participation

The only areas in which U.S. policy is relevant to communist governmental participation now are in Western Europe. My prior analysis of the possible favorable aspects of such participation clearly is hypothetical. Perhaps cautious observers would not care to rely upon it. Then they should take into account the fact that the United States can do little, if anything, to prevent the emergence of a winning Left coalition in France in 1978, although the increasingly bitter attacks by the PCF on the Socialists may damage the unity of Left. Overt American opposition to a Left victory may even glue the Left coalition together, generate nationalist sentiment in its favor, and make it difficult for Mitterrand in office to pursue the mildly pro-NATO policies that he evidently prefers.

Today the Christian Democrats in Italy are dependent upon Communist support within the Parliament, without which they cannot adopt a government program or undertake military effort in any event. The greater risk is that even the moderate resistance of the Carter administration to PCI governmental participation may strengthen the militants in the PCI, reduce the prospects for a constructive evolution within the party, and produce a self-fulfilling prophecy by inspiring a flight of capital.

There is, however, another possible motive for resistance to the Western European communist parties' participation in government. Their installation in office in a form so divergent from, or even hostile toward, Soviet communism might be such a threat to the Soviet Union that détente would collapse.

The fear that so-called Eurocommunism—so-called because the various Western European parties, their histories, and their positions on both domestic and international issues are so divergent that the term has little genuine meaning—in power would threaten détente cannot be simply dismissed. The harshness of Soviet reviews (at least one of which represented the highest party circles) of Santiago Carrillo's *Eurocommunism and the State* (1977) provides a glimpse into the problems of the Soviet Union with respect to democratic communism. Nor has the Soviet Union likely failed to observe the support given to Carrillo *after* the Soviet reviews by Rumanian and Hungarian leaderships (for different reasons, of course). Although there are no signs in Eastern Europe of anything so radical as a new Czech spring, the Kremlin cannot have failed to note the extent to which political participation is developing at the local level in Hungary and to which disagreement is permitted at top policy levels. The need of the Polish government to consult the opposition and the church in some respects may seem even more dangerous to the Soviet leadership. Eurocommunism is a threat, moreover, to the safest allies of the Soviets. Czechoslovak conservatives such as Vasil Bilak, for instance, who are dependent on Soviet support and most vulnerable to Eurocommunism, bitterly denounce Eurocommunism as anti communism.

If the Soviet regime, as Agursky's thesis suggests, is deeply conservative and committed primarily to regime maintenance, it

cannot fail to recognize the likely corrosive influences already resulting from Eurocommunism or the likely much greater impact of
communist participation in Western European governments. Successful participation in Western European governments by communist
parties within states that are nonideological and pluralistic would
relegate the Soviet political and economic systems to the category of
a backward development model, and a relatively unsuccessful one at
that. It would gravely weaken the vestiges of the legitimacy of the
party's monopoly of political power and might produce an ideological crisis. Furthermore, it would disturb the tenuous relationship
between the Soviet party (CPSU) and the Soviet armed forces.
Communist participation in West European governments, by debunk-
ing the imperialist menace to socialism, would remove even the
lingering semblance of legitimacy for the massive Soviet military
preparations in Europe and the stationing of so many Soviet divisions
in the territory of its Warsaw Treaty Organization allies.

Soviet embarrassment has been progressing geometrically ever
since the twenty-fifth CPSU meeting in March 1976 and the June
1976 congress of communist parties in Berlin. At the twenty-fifth
CPSU meeting in Moscow, Secretary Enrico Berlinguer stated that
the PCI stood for "a Socialist society that guaranteed individual as
well as collective rights, and religious freedom, as well as cultural,
artistic, and scientific freedom."

At the Berlin meeting in June 1976 Berlinguer said that

> there is not and cannot be any leading party or leading state. . . . It is
> our opinion that the respect for the principle of noninterference cannot
> exclude freedom of judgment on theoretical or political positions taken
> by other parties, as well as on particular events in international life and
> in the workers' movement. Everyone knows, for example, that while we
> have always stressed the great advances made by the Socialist countries,
> we Italian Communists have more than once expressed critical judg-
> ment both on certain events and situations (for example, toward
> Czechoslovakia) and on more general problems relative to the relation-
> ship between democracy and Socialism in various Socialist countries.[1]

Berlinguer also denied the existence of an international communist
body.

> After all, this meeting of ours is not the meeting of an international
> Communist body, which does not exist and could not exist in any
> form, on either the world or the European level. Ours is a free meeting
> among autonomous and equal parties, which does not seek to lay down
> guidelines for, or to bind, any of our parties. And it is important that
> this debate be *open and public* [italics added]. In the course of it each
> Party expresses its own point of view, since we are all aware that on
> various questions, *including some important ones* [italics added], our
> positions are different, *and not only because of the diversity of the
> objective conditions in which each party works* [italics added].[2]

Even Georges Marchais argued that

> the Socialism for which we are fighting will be profoundly demo-
> cratic . . . . not only because it will create the essential conditions for
> freedom by ending exploitation, but also because it will guarantee,
> develop, and broaden all the freedoms which the people want. This
> refers to the freedom of thought and expression, of creation and
> publication, the freedom to demonstrate, to hold meetings and to
> assemble, the freedom of movement within the country and abroad, the
> freedom of religion and the right to strike. It is also a question of the
> recognition of the results of the general elections—which includes the
> possibility of democratic alternation [of government]—recognition of
> the right of political parties to exist and carry out their activities, the
> independence of the system of justice and the rejection of any official
> philosophy.[3]

The words of both Berlinguer and Marchais, let alone those of
Carrillo, must have grated upon the ears of Secretary Brezhnev,
especially since Berlinguer was not even willing to grant that the
underdeveloped conditions of the Soviet Union objectively justified
the forms of party control. True, his statements were oblique, but no
one present was likely to mistake the implications.

Many in the West at the time of the Berlin congress interpreted
Berlinguer's insistence upon a democratic process in Italy as a Machiavellian tactic decided upon in concert with the Soviet Union to increase
the PCI's chances for an electoral success in Italy. Since then events
have made it clear beyond any reasonable doubt that Brezhnev was
forced to pay a very high price for holding that meeting, in the absence
of which, however, he would have had to admit that he had failed
totally to convene a congress that the USSR had been proposing for
years—and this would have been a severe blow to the figleaf of
respectability that the oppressive Soviet system still retains.

Some observers welcome this particular type of impact by Eurocommunism on the ground that it will weaken the Soviet Union and
produce attrition within the bloc. They differ less with the analysis
of those who oppose Eurocommunism for fear that it may injure
détente than with their evaluation of its costs and benefits. Although
détente is merely a term and has been overinterpreted in the West, at
least in my opinion—for the structure of the present international
system forces both the Soviet Union and the United States toward
various kinds of cooperative activities—the dangers inherent in Eurocommunism for the Soviet Union are very real. Under some circumstances this could impact unfavorably on the prospects for peace. If
the Soviet Union were less strong militarily, or if the men in the
Kremlin were less determined to hold on to power, or if they were in
a position to learn from Western communism and to carry through
pervasive reforms within the Soviet Union, these dangers would be

more manageable. But none of these conditions holds, and the dangers, if far from inevitable, are too real for comfort.

However, these dangers do not justify a resistance to participation in Western governments by communist parties of the democratic type. In Italy, for instance, I do not believe that reform is possible without the cooperation of the Italian Communist party. If the PCI is kept indefinitely within a political ghetto, the present leadership may be discredited. It is quite true that the present leadership, for a variety of reasons, is in no hurry to obtain power. But if the road is clearly foreclosed, and if American influence plays a considerable role in this closure, the militants may regain control of the party. In any event, such a foreclosure would run a serious risk of thrusting Italy toward chaos and of insuring rule by authoritarians of either the Left or Right. In France, the encapsulated Communist party can become a serious threat only if we insure a true union of the Left by opposing its participation in a cabinet. Mitterrand, moreover, cannot afford to incur the wrath of the CERES group within the Socialist party in the absence of PCF provocation and a suitable situation. In Spain, the Communist party is constructive, far from power, and we would be ill-advised to interfere in Spanish politics over this issue. Furthermore, it would place us in a very awkward position both morally and politically to oppose Western European communist parties, which have a democratic right to participate in Western European governments, for fear of developments in the Soviet Union or Eastern Europe: that would be to carry Machiavellianism in politics too far and would damage our own political process, our image of ourselves, and our sense of national and political identity. This is not the nineteenth century, and an attempt to play such clever games in a democratic age is far more likely to be self-defeating than even slightly beneficial.

In short, the United States must be open to communist participation in Western European governments. We should neither encourage nor discourage this process. We should allow the European social democrats to take the lead as they did so ably in Portugal for they are more knowledgeable than we are and will not be resented. There should be neither the reality nor the appearance of American pressure for any reasons domestic or international. Although the Carter administration is showing somewhat more flexibility in this respect than did Henry Kissinger, it still suffers from undersophistication and rigidity on these issues.

If the communists do come to participate in Western European governments, we should be ready to engage their cooperation in activities designed to improve human and economic conditions throughout Western Europe. Although it should be clear that we would expect these communist parties to support the NATO alliance for the defense of Western Europe, we should not ask them to take anti-Soviet stands or to attempt to undermine the Soviet position in Eastern Europe except perhaps as the natural consequence of their own examples or their natural and spontaneous support for dissidents. We must avoid, if possible, the appearance of attempting to create instability in the Soviet Union or Eastern Europe lest we cause political dissension in Western Europe that is damaging to NATO or make more likely a rash Soviet act. Whereas it is proper and desirable to express support for our own ideals or to criticize offensive denials of human rights in the Soviet Union, we must remember that a letter from President Carter to André Sakharov in the Soviet Union is more threatening (and seems to be more threatening) than would be a letter from Brezhnev to Angela Davis. Formally the actions would be similar. Practically, they would be quite different for a vulnerable Soviet political system and a fearful leadership resonate to breezes that would not be noticed in the American system.

The Soviet system is paradoxically weak and strong simultaneously. Unlike traditionally oriented authoritarian systems that sit loosely upon the societies they exploit and that rarely sink their roots below the surface or break up traditional social institutions, the Soviet system—in its fully developed form as in the USSR—fragments and destroys traditional social organizations, prevents the emergence of more modern ones, and extends its control apparatus into every block, every factory, and every form of activity. In effect, it creates a "comprador" class that is a significant fraction of the population while destroying the cohesion of the rest of the society. It also provides this comprador class with a justificatory ideology, in Marx's sense of the term, that is both a strength and a potential weakness of the system. That is why, for instance, it is so difficult to mount guerrilla movements against communist governments. However, once the system begins to weaken under pressure, it tends to collapse even more quickly and completely than traditional authoritarian systems, as in Hungary in 1956 and Czechoslovakia in 1968; the greater integration of the system and its lack of real support tend to have tumultuous national repercussions rather than merely localized effects in the capital. And that is why dissent that can be easily tolerated in democratic systems responsive to popular control and marked by organic social cohesion becomes such a threat to the parasitic Soviet type authoritarian regime.

For these reasons, the United States cannot afford to weaken its military forces. It has already permitted the Soviet Union to gain a dangerous strategic advantage, dangerous not because of clear expansionist intentions on the part of the Soviet Union but because of its political rigidity and economic weakness. American military weakness may persuade the Soviet Union that it is safe to apply strong pressure against Western Europe to contain the corrosive poisons circulating within the Soviet Union and the Eastern bloc should they appear dangerous to the regime's stability.

Because we may prefer to slow down the arms race rather than to compete with the huge and steadily increasing Soviet arms budget, it may be advisable to think through the possibility of proposing major force reductions on both sides of the European divide. I am reluctant to write at great length about this subject because I trust no proposals of this kind unless they are carefully thought through in detail. In any event, what is required is comparable strength and yet friendliness and openness toward the Soviet Union. We must attempt to avoid sudden crises or explosive situations.

Socialism and Capitalism

"What Is Communism?" is the title of this introduction. It is really a defect of English that it facilitates questions in this form for the form posits the existence of an entity called communism and subjective conceptions that copy this concept. John Kenneth Galbraith has argued on television that Marx said that communism would come first to the most advanced countries. Because Vietnam did not have a developed economy, according to Galbraith, the North Vietnamese leaders could not be communists. By this standard, Lenin, Stalin, and Mao could not have been communists. And by the standards of American television perhaps they are not. I am afraid, however, that we will have to make do with less flashy standards in our effort to come to terms with this question.

Although there is a chain of intellectual descent from Marx to Lenin, their concepts of communism are not identical. What for Marx was a system that could develop only in an advanced economy and with the enfranchisement of the entire working class in a substantive as well as a formal sense—which is what Marx apparently meant by dictatorship by the proletariat—became for Lenin a system that could be developed out of a backward economy and on the basis of a conspiratorial party that became the vanguard of the people and that operated on the basis of democratic centralism. Lenin's system, not Marx's, was what communism became under Soviet, and general world, conditions in the aftermath of World War I. It became something different as it developed in China.

The differences among various types of communist parties (whether in or aspiring to power) are sufficiently clear that contemporary communists insist upon at least different roads to communism that are responsive to different concrete national conditions while they maintain the fiction of a single goal. However, the roads are becoming so diverse that the commonness of the goal is questionable.

We live in an age in which very few economists, even in communist countries, take the concept of surplus value seriously. Nationalization is ceasing to be regarded as socialization by at least some communists. Yugoslavia calls workers' management socialism, but disillusionment is setting in as it becomes clear that the workers do not really manage in any event and that other difficulties beset the Yugoslav system. Even the concept of equal pay is coming to be seen as excessively abstract for it denies the different meanings of either dollars or products to different people in different situations. Whether the various types of communism will have enough in common with each other and with the traditional meaning of the concept for it to retain any significant meaning cannot be known with any degree of assurance at this time. However, the direction of transformation with respect to such concepts as communism and socialism is so broad that perhaps we should speak not of direction but of directions. At some point we may question whether the directions are sufficiently close for their intermediate—let alone "end"—states to be included within a single rubric such as communism.

There has been a similar evolution of the concept of capitalism. Certainly we no longer have either a mercantilist system or its successor, the Manchesterian economy. Today we accept state intervention with respect to the supply of money, environmental standards, and conditions of work. In France, Italy, and Japan, the very direction of the economy is determined by the state. Marx, who predicted the growth of monopolies that would exclude small corporations, and thus a self-socialization of industry, perhaps would be shocked by the extent to which huge multinational corporations coexist with government regulation, with giant state owned or managed corporations, with smaller, but still very large, corporations, and with much smaller businesses throughout the economy.

Today we know that "ownership by the whole people" is a fiction that obscures conflicting interests and power contests among workers, managers, political leaders, bureaucrats, and professionals and that it is more antagonistic to and inconsistent with human dignity than capitalism. The identification of the working class with governmental decisions made by political leaders in a socialist society is now understood by many as the theoretical error that justified Stalinism. Although national (and international) and organizational interests are real, they can never be identical. Nor can individual interests be identical with any of them.[4] No political system that fails to recognize these distinctions and to give them adequate weight in its operation can be consistent with human dignity.

One of the ambiguities in the current situation of Western communist parties lies in the fact that they have broken only partly with the ideology that produces oppression in the Soviet Union. Their break is primarily programmatic rather than radically philosophical. Yet even some Soviet leaders implicitly recognize that their philosophical dogmas do not really stand the test of practical experience. In the Soviet sphere, decentralization and market type solutions are opposed primarily because of their impact on party control rather than primarily for economic and/or ideological reasons.

Thus, we are living in a period in which crucial definitions are subject to flux and ambiguity. It is no wonder that Western communist and socialist parties are subject to enormous doubts and perplexities. We are searching for new forms of organization consistent with production and human dignity. But we do not know how to find them. We know little about how the patterns of economic organization within societies or across them affect motivation, family structure, value systems, or political organization. We know practically nothing of the impact of government regulation upon the motivational structure of business or the rationality of its organization. In part, this is the fault of the universities for they have failed on the whole to investigate the most important features of contemporary society. Whatever the failures of Marxian analysis, at least Marx's methodology pointed to important problems that current professional social scientists tend to ignore.

The Chinese in their different way are facing similar problems. With the defeat of the "gang of four," it appears that Maoism in its pristine, revolutionary form is on the wane. Chapter 9 is instructive here. This should surprise no one. The charismatic revolutionary leader might maintain some minimal degree of order while periodically shaking up the system. Mao, after all, was even more identified with the Chinese Revolution than Stalin with the Russian. No successor leadership could attempt this without dismal failures involving the economy, political control, and relations with the Soviet Union across the border.

In Japan, the Communist party faces a system that we call capitalistic but in which the control of capital lies with the state—a state in which the bureaucratic leadership spills over into the political party system and that controls the direction of the entire economy. There is competition and a market system. There is even ruthless discarding of inefficient industries. But is this capitalism? The system operates according to parliamentary conceptions of national goals and standards. Meanwhile, the Japan Communist party, which contemplates "radical" changes, represents in fact the elite of the working class; whereas those workers who do not have permanent jobs are largely unrepresented. In addition, those workers the Communist party represents have lifetime occupations, including often secondary occupations after retirement and cradle-to-grave security.

How long will it take us to understand that the typical terms of the debate between socialism and capitalism have lost significant meaning and that future debates will turn on conditions of life, relationships between organizations and motivation, and debates over the nature and potential of man? I believe that we are witnessing not merely a transformation of communist parties throughout the world but an outmoding of political ideas and criteria. Different communist parties are in different stages of transition. This process could halt or even reverse, if we permit a major war or the Finlandization of Western Europe by the Soviet Union, if some other catastrophe occurs, or if our obdurate resistance to democratic communism closes the door to it. Otherwise I believe that we have seen merely the first steps in an ideological revolution.

Those of us who are setting the terms of the debate today are responding to the third revolutionary generation but are doing so in terms of nineteenth-century concepts. I do not believe that these concepts can survive two additional generations of transition. Therefore, "What is communism?" may be a question that we cannot even begin to answer for we really need to conduct an inquiry for which we do not yet have an adequate vocabulary. Nor do we yet comprehend the conditions of choice adequately. However, we can know that our political responses to those developments will require great statesmanship and prudence in the best sense of those words.

The Key Research Questions

How can we begin to analyze the problem of in what directions the communism of parties that call themselves communist is likely to develop? The chapters in this book, I believe, open up these questions in a useful fashion. In my opinion, they give a better portrayal of the various communist parties and of their positions than any other set of analyses I have seen. However, they merely open up the subject. They point in the direction that research should take. I should like briefly to indicate the key areas in which research on the communist parties outside the Soviet Union, Eastern Europe, and China is needed. The key questions—as the individual chapters reveal—involve the organization, program, class base, and electoral tactics and strategies of these communist parties.

The recent development of democratic or pluralistic communism in Western Europe involves first of all an increasingly direct relationship among the Western European communist parties outside of and even against any relationships they may have with the Soviet Union. This is quite different from the situation of the 1920s and thirties, when relationships among the parties were mediated primarily through Moscow. The strategy of the Western European communist parties involves their extensive presence in a wide variety of institutions in civil society and, where possible, outside of the proletariat (France and Portugal are partial exceptions here, at least in practice). Chapter 1 documents the bourgeois and professional penetration of the PCI, for instance, and the decline of working class influence in the Italian Communist party.

This new strategy accepts compromise as a mode of procedure and both functional and territorial organization. This is particularly so for the Spanish and Italian parties (Portugal is an exception). Communist parties in Western Europe today accept aspiration to power in combination with other parties as something other than a mere tactic (Portugal is an exception). They respect the bourgeois aspect of the political system and its practices. They include a program base that may or may not involve some additional degree of nationalization. In France, the PCF carries this rather far, whereas private conversations have disclosed that important figures in the PCI believe that nationalization has already gone too far in Italy.

The communist parties of Western Europe (perhaps with the single exception of the Portuguese party) are attempting to extend the strength of the entire Left, including the moderate Left. They are looking for a change in the social base of the Left vote. Nationalism has become a signal aspect of the parties' programs. This is less true, for instance, of the Portuguese party than of the Spanish party, and the Portuguese party is much weaker if not in electoral strength as such then at least in terms of its social base and its closeness to the centers of power. The internal organization of the party has become noncellular in Spain and Italy and is closer to normal political organization. These developments may be playing major roles in the moderation of the Spanish and Italian parties. The Portuguese party has not changed in this respect, however, and the French and Japanese parties are still considerably backward. The parties, again with the exception of the Portuguese, also appear to be European oriented rather than merely nationalistic, although there are individual differences among them.

With the exception of the Portuguese party, the Western European communist parties do not have to compete against an extreme Left in any serious sense. For instance, when the Portuguese Communists ran against local extreme leftists, the extreme Left received 15% of the vote and the Communists only 7.5% of the vote. This may account to some extent for the militancy of the Portuguese party. The Spanish party, on the other hand, faces a basically conservative electorate, even to the right of the German electorate, and thus faces circumstances of an electoral nature almost diametrically opposed to those of the Portuguese party.

In theory, the communist parties practice democratic centralism and factionalism is outlawed even in Italy. However, in fact in Italy the 1977 movement of unemployed workers and students against the party resulted in the formation of three different party factions, with three different positions and three different interpretations of what the party is and should become, as Ferrarotti points out in Chapter 1. The French party is more problematic in this respect, as Jean V. Poulard so vividly documents in Chapter 2. And the internationalist history of the leadership of the JCP, as Fukui contends in Chapter 8, leaves much room for doubt concerning its democratic pretensions. In any event, all communist parties show much greater discipline than normal bourgeois parties despite their increasing—but still very limited—acceptance of dissent and factionalism. This is clearly a source of danger under some circumstances, particularly those in which the party may be beleaguered, fighting off armed opposition, or unable to cope with problems that have arisen. We need to know much more than we now do about what factors support communist discipline and tend to suppress factionalism and under what conditions party discipline will or will not be effective.

What sort of social and economic system will result if the communists come to serious power in any of the states except Portugal? It is too early for us to know but in attempting to answer this question we must discard all clichés.

A Practical Reason

In addition to the reasons previously offered for accepting transformed, democratic communist parties (particularly the Spanish and Italian parties) at least tentatively as normal parts of the political process, I should like to add one important reason. Those communists who have returned to the humanistic elements that always have been present in Marx—albeit along with others that contain dangerous implications—are essential to a dialogue that has not yet begun and without which a new and humane society is not likely to emerge. If 20% in France, 35-40% in Italy, and 15% in Spain and Portugal are excluded from dialogue, the moderate center may become the prisoner of a political Right that is corrupt and/or authoritarian and that lacks incentive to change.

If we are to conserve what was best in the past, we must begin to understand how its potential can be realized under modern conditions. It will be difficult enough to midwife a humane future without excluding any constructive political force. Although we must alertly guard against the possibility that communism in power in Western Europe may prove undemocratic—and possess the courage, will, and strength to protect democratic institutions in Europe if they come under serious threat—it is also important to avoid the risks involved in attempting to exclude a large proportion of the European public from significant dialogue. Our policies should be framed by concrete situations as they develop and not by preconceived dogmas. The future in large part will be what we make of the present and not a mechanical *déroulement* of today's situation.

We live in an age in which prudence, virtue, and openness are needed. Overly clever and closed minds are hazards to be avoided.

Notes

1. *New York Times*, 1 July 1976, p. 12.
2. Ibid.
3. Ibid.
4. See Morton A. Kaplan, *Macropolitics* (Chicago: Aldine, 1969), pp. 29–33, on the reality of organizations and of what this means with respect to individuals. Classes are not real in this sense but are merely qualitative attributes of individuals. See also idem, *Justice, Human Nature, and Political Obligation* (New York: Free Press, 1976), and *Alienation and Identification* (New York: Free Press, 1976), for a discussion of the problems of justice and the sociology of knowledge that are resolved by this approach.

1

The Italian
Communist Party and
Eurocommunism

Franco Ferrarotti

There can be little doubt that at least for the time being Eurocommunism is more a catch-phrase than a definite political and ideological reality. Nevertheless, a profound political malaise affects the European communist parties, East and West, and it would be light-minded not to take notice of this state simply because it does not fit the prevailing interpretations of past experience. Whether for tactical or for strategic reasons, it is a fact that the relationships between Western European communist parties, especially French, Spanish, and Italian, and the Communist (Bolshevik) party of the Soviet Union have never been so strained. Moreover, there are at the present time crucial theoretical problems that seriously impinge on the official ideology of the Western European communist parties and that are interwoven with organizational issues concerning the internal structure and the day-to-day functioning of the parties themselves. For the first time, perhaps, the "party" is in question and what used to be an ideological issue is turning into a problem of organizational sociology. At the heart of this issue is the concept of pluralism.

Pluralism

The meanings attached to "pluralism" in the current Italian political debate are diffuse. In its most traditional meaning, pluralism indicates a social and political situation in which various and contrasting political parties are competing to achieve power. In this respect, Western European societies are all pluralistic because there is in all of them more than one party at work. Eastern European "socialist" countries and especially the Soviet Union cannot be regarded as pluralistic because in them there is either a single party or a variety of parties under the paramount leadership of the communist party. Another meaning of pluralism that has been recently gaining ground in Italy centers on a notion of mass democracy of a plebiscitary type in which the role and function of the traditional parties would be taken over and fulfilled by a nationwide network of grass-root organizations, thus insuring broad social participation. In this case, the question of political opposition would be left open as an irrelevant problem.

The debate over pluralism directly affects the Italian Communist party (PCI), its internal structure, and in particular Lenin's notion of "democratic centralism." This becomes apparent in the interesting debate on pluralism that has developed in Italy during 1976 and 1977. Independently of the merits of the various contending positions and of the final results of the discussion, a preliminary question must be put forward: Why now? Why is a debate on "pluralism in Italian society" appealing at the present time?

The answer is not too difficult: because of the growing electoral strength of the Italian Communist party. During the past thirty years, the PCI vote has grown from 15% to about 35% of the total vote while other political parties of the historical Left, the Italian Socialist party (PSI), for example, have constantly declined. In the political elections of June 20, 1976, the PCI succeeded in doing what to many observers of the Italian scene appeared for years an impossible feat: it monopolized the Left. In that year the PSI received a meager 10% of the vote. The extreme leftist groups have been virtually smashed while the radical party seems unable to go beyond a vocal but in the long run stultifying and self-defeating battle for individual rights, which are usually asserted as if they were metaphysical principles that are irrelevant to the state of the economy and of the actual political scenario.

As the PCI approaches national political power, the question of its democratic legitimacy becomes urgent. The PCI has recognized this issue and party leaders have discussed it with a sincerity that verges almost on candor. Enrico Berlinguer in Moscow has asserted that the PCI does not renounce socialism as its ultimate goal but that it insists upon a "pluralistic" society. *Pravda* mistranslated "pluralistic" as "multiple" or "multigroup"—a defective construal because it indicates variety in a given society without, however, making it clear whether or not basic dissent would be tolerated.

The major elements of the debate on pluralism in Italy are the following:

1. The Marxist concept of the state.
2. Pluralism as a plurality" of opinions and organized political forces.
3. Pluralism as a "plebiscitary democracy" that turns itself into a Caesaristic regime.
4. The way to legitimacy for the PCI through the "historic compromise" between the PCI and Christian Democracy (CD).

As a result of the general elections of 1976, there was an agreement between the PCI and the CD whereby the CD would have the chairmanship of the Senate (Amintore Fanfani) and the PCI would have the chairmanship of the Chamber of Deputies (Pietro Ingrao). Many political observers have seen in this agreement the first practical consequence of the still secret historic compromise. It is a fact that Ingrao has been very active in reviving the role, and in restoring the image, of the Italian Parliament. Paradoxical as it might sound, the Italian Communists are at present the best parliamentarians in Italian history. They rarely miss a session; they abide by the rules; and their at least formal respect for the bodies of traditional representative democracy could not possibly be greater. From a theoretical point of view, the picture is less bright. The Marxist theory of the state is too meager to offer valid materials to fill the ideological lacunae. For the time being, Ingrao has simply recalled the necessity of modernizing the house committee bylaws in order to cut red tape and excessively formalistic procedures. But no problem of substance has been faced yet, and the guarantees of democratic freedom and individual rights in a future socialist state remain vague.

It seems clear that the Italian Communists themselves are reluctant to go to the logical extreme conclusions. They refrain from full-scale discussion of the nature of the democratic state. They assert that they accept the democratic rules of "bourgeois democracy" because they do not see anything better at hand. At the same time, they cling to a distinction between "formal" and "real" democracy and hope for a polity in which formal rights will be given economic substance. This debate is not very inspiring. The simple fact is that as regards the state not much can be learned from Marx and even less from Engels's idea of a "vanishing state."

This problem is recognized by the leaders of the PCI, as can be seen in the works of PCI philosopher Galvano della Volpe or in Pietro Ingrao's *Masse e potere* (*Masses and Power*). It has been aptly observed that Della Volpe's book nicely illustrates the importance of going beyond the "either Kant or Rousseau" alternatives of abstract universalism or concrete justice. Furthermore, Della Volpe asserts that if a socialist society is classless, its state cannot at the same time justify its political philosophy in class terms. Socialist society is legitimated not because it is proletarian but because it is not.

The discussion of the state and of bourgeois democratic rules has been spurred in the PCI by the trauma of 1956. Perhaps in no other communist party around the world has the problem of Stalinism been more thoroughly debated. Stalinism for the PCI was not merely a deviation from socialist legal norms that resulted from the attributes of a single personality. It called into question the Soviet system as such, a system that the majority of present-day PCI leaders would hardly regard as socialist.

The view that Stalinism was a structural and not merely a psychological deviation had been expressed immediately after Khrushchev's "secret speech" in 1956 by Palmiro Togliatti, although with the usual prudence. The so-called Yalta Memorandum, written a short time before his death, has been neglected for years but it deserves careful consideration. It stands out as one of the few profound reflections on Stalinism, on the problem of socialist legality, and on the issue of national autonomy for the various communist parties. In fact, Togliatti's "polycentrism" laid the foundations, as it were, for "pluralism" and for "Eurocommunism."

Hegemony

However, pluralism is strictly connected for the PCI with Gramsci's concept of "social hegemony" or "hegemony of the working class." Two Gramscis have been distinguished and differentiated: the Gramsci of the Ordine nuovo and the 1920 factory occupation and the Gramsci of the *Prison Notebooks*. I personally feel that such a differentiation, although philologically accurate, cannot be maintained. It seems to me that the whole of Gramsci's thinking centers around the idea that substantial legitimacy comes "from below" and that it is essential to master society first in order to master the state. For some commentators such as Louis Althusser, when Gramsci uses the formula "working class hegemony" he means actually "dictatorship of the proletariat." The term "hegemony," Althusser has argued, was used by Gramsci to escape the strictures of jail censorship. It is true that Gramsci, like Lenin, uses "hegemony" in the sense of a "working class direction of society" that is capable of transforming the society and at the same time transforms the mode of thinking, that is, the prevailing social consciousness.

There is certainly a close relationship between dictatorship and hegemony. But in Gramsci the two terms indicate two distinct social processes and political situations. When Lenin writes about "proletarian dictatorship" he never once mentions the term "hegemony." It is hard to deny that between Lenin and Gramsci there is a qualitative difference here. For Lenin "hegemony" refers essentially to a "directive function"; any interpretation of "hegemony" as a broadly based social process would smell for Lenin of "anarchism." Gramsci, on the contrary, conceives of "hegemony" as including both a "directive function" and "generalized social power and influence," not necessarily formally codified, exercised by consensus over the whole society, and that develops from below as well as from above. The contrast between Lenin and Gramsci in this respect becomes especially apparent when we deal with the concept of the political party. For Lenin the Revolutionary party is the "vanguard, organized and conscious, of the working class", that is, the party is an "organized minority" interested in the seizure of central political power even if its ideology has not developed a hegemony over the global society. According to Gramsci, the seizure of central political power by an organized revolutionary minority might be necessary in some cases, but it cannot be sufficient for socialism. It is always necessary to bring pressure and to work from below, at the grass-roots level. Working and pressing from below is for Gramsci essential in order to muster true, genuine social consensus; for Gramsci, power can never be simply seized. For Lenin, Gramsci's concept of hegemony would imply dangerous concessions to anarchism and spontaneity.

From a liberal democratic point of view, the inadequacy of the concept of hegemony—even as differentiated from the concept of dictatorship of the proletariat—concerns directly the concrete possibility of rotation in government. In fact, hegemony for Gramsci and the PCI refers to a broadly based social democracy in which a plurality of opinions is guaranteed and permitted, if not stimulated. But there is no assurance that such a radical questioning of the existing political regime as Gramsci and the PCI advocate will ever be possible. This latter factor is the key to the notion of a historic compromise between the PCI and the CD.

Political Enigma

To understand the idea of historic compromise one has to take a critical look at recent Italian political history. Unlike other European countries, Italy during the past thirty years has been ruled by the same political elite, a group belonging to the Christian Democratic party. Until recently, this party has been receiving 35–40% of the popular vote. But with this relative majority of almost 40% it has managed to control 80% of the power positions. The political stability of this group, until recently, has been something of a political masterpiece. From the standpoint of self-perpetuation, it is a unique performance. In France the MRP (Mouvement républicain populaire) has vanished. In Germany the CDU (Christian Democratic Union) has been forced out of government. In Italy the same group is still going strong. Only after the elections at the local level of June 5, 1975, and after the general elections of June 20, 1976, have things started to change. But so far, the Christian Democrats have assimilated or "digested," as it were, their close allies: the Liberals, the Republicans, the Social Democrats, and at least some of the Socialists. Who is next? The Communists perhaps? A tough bone, to be sure.

Italy has purchased this political stability at a fairly high price. The social and economic structure of the country has changed dramatically. Since 1952, agriculture has lost half of its workers and industry has increased its employees by more than 2 million, while tertiary occupations have added 2.5 million. New contradictions have emerged; new needs are more widely felt. Choices have to be made but the political elite does not act lest it lose its electoral base. Its stability is slowly changing into stagnation and the party seems to be a captive of its supporting interests. Major political support comes from a hypertrophic and inefficient public administrative bureaucracy that is tied up with huge state owned industry sheltered from competition by government subsidy.

On the other hand, government posts become lifelong professions for many members of the political elite. But even political heroes grow old. The Italian political elite has been so stable over the past thirty years that Italian democracy is in danger of becoming a gerontocracy, a frozen regime. As long as the economy was booming, things seemed to go reasonably well: mass migration, urbanization, industrialization. Two hundred years after England, Italy had her own homemade industrial revolution. At the present time, however, with economic depression threatening massive unemployment, the top leadership of the political elite does not seem to be in a position to make the necessary changes because its supporters are the natural beneficiaries of the existing situation and change would threaten their base of support. To implement such changes, the only force available seems to be the Italian Communist party, but it is clear to everyone (and to the Communists themselves) that its rise to national power would create internal tensions and international complications as regards the East-West balance of power.

Moreover, Italian politics are less sanguine and dynamic than European politics generally—perhaps because Italian politicians, rightist and leftist alike, do not feel free from another, "secret" power. A "higher authority" reigns in Italy and although not directly involved in the political scene it is constantly referred to: the Catholic church. Being universal and based in Italy, the church is the single most powerful factor and it skews the Italian power structure. The Italian ruling class, if we use this approximate formula, does not find its proper justification only in its acceptance from below, that is to say, from the underlying population. There is a higher authority, deprived of any democratic justification but charismatic and authoritative nevertheless, that must be taken into account. The church cannot be overlooked. This is considered obvious when moral or ideological issues are at stake. But in Italy even when a public building is inaugurated or a civic ceremony takes place a preliminary blessing from some church dignitary is a must. This is certainly true for Catholic Action or the Christian Democratic party or the ACLI (Association of Italian Christian Workers) or the CISL (Italian Christian Labor Union). Equally important, however, is the fact that the attitude of at least formal subservience toward the church is common among the nonconfessional political groups, including the Communists.

The secret of Catholic power in Italy is linked to the primary socialization process whereby all Italians, irrespective of their adult political choices, seem to internalize in their early years a basically identical "structure of sentiment" that transcends ideological differences and class positions. Hence, it is fairly easy to understand the meaning of the historic compromise that the Italian Communists have offered the Christian Democrats. This offer reveals the profound belief that no change can come about in Italy without at least a temporary truce with the Catholic church.

Reflections on Chile

What happened in Chile in September 1973, with the violent death of President Allende and the downfall of Unidad popular, has been a cause of deep concern for the Italian Communist leaders. Basically, Unidad popular is seen as a formula far too advanced politically and ideologically not to raise strong resistance both internationally and domestically. Allende is considered by the PCI to have been politically unwise; some of his supporters, especially the Socialists and the MIR (Revolutionary Left Movement) leaders, are considered to have been politically impatient and unstable. The PCI calls attention to the fact that events in Chile demonstrated that "imperialism" is still aggressive. At the same time, Vietnam shows that imperialism can be beaten only if not attacked frontally. The PCI counts on "international détente and peaceful negotiations among states." Berlinguer has remarked that

> recognition of the underlying trend emerging in the world historical
> process—a trend that in the last analysis is progressively shrinking the
> area of imperialist domination—does not prevent us from seeing . . .
> that international imperialism and the reactionary forces in many
> countries are still in a position to contain the emancipating struggle of
> the peoples and, in certain cases, to inflict crushing setbacks on the
> forces that animate this struggle.[1]

Détente and coexistence do not imply, according to Berlinguer, an era of absolute tranquility. But in order to effect substantial political and economic changes one has to analyze carefully the actual power relations among the various social groups. Ideological "dreams" are not per se sufficient to bring about revolutionary change. As regards Italy, Berlinguer pointed out that

> there is, first of all, the problem posed by the presence in Italy of the
> Catholic Church and its relations with the State and civil society. . . .
> But it is impossible to escape the other big problem represented by the
> existence and strength of a political party such as the Christian Demo-
> cratic Party which, quite aside [from the fact] that it calls itself
> "Christian," gathers in its ranks or under its influence a large part of the
> working and popular masses of Catholic orientation.[2]

It seems that the political mistake made by the leaders of Unidad popular in Chile, according to Berlinguer, consisted in underestimating the strength of Catholic opposition both in Parliament and in the country at large, especially among the urban middle classes. On the basis of the Chilean experience, Berlinguer asks himself:

> What can we do? In what direction should we try to push things? From
> the summary recapitulation of the Christian Democratic Party's social
> composition and political conduct . . . it is clear that this party is not
> only a varied, but also a changeable reality. And it is clear that these
> changes are determined both by its dialectics and, even more, by the
> struggles and force relations among the classes and parties, by the
> weight exerted on the situation by the working class movement and the
> PCI. . . . This being the reality of the Christian Democratic Party and
> the point it has reached today, it is clear that the duty of a Party such
> as ours can only be to isolate and drastically defeat those tendencies
> that aim . . . at contraposition and splitting the country in two.[3]

In the eyes of the PCI leadership Unidad popular seemed to have made not only a tactical mistake. It also has been responsible mainly through the influence of the Socialist party, of a Trotskyite orienta- tion, and through that of the MIR, a radical, extreme, left-wing group, of a doctrinaire, abstract approach. There was a loss of contact at a certain point between the Chilean government of Allende and the bulk of the rank and file, not to mention the Santiago middle classes. In this sense, and using Gramsci's categories, Unidad popular occupied a "dictatorial," not "hegemonic," position vis-à-vis Chilean society.

Reflections on the events in Chile lead the PCI to the conclusion that in a country such as Italy it would be impossible to rule even if the PCI could get 51% of the popular vote. An alliance with the other mass party, the Christian Democratic party, is therefore necessary; some sort of compromise must be sought and worked out.

The PCI on the Defensive

The idea of a compromise with noncommunist and nonsocialist political forces in Italy to preserve national unity did not have to wait, however, for the Chilean experience and tragedy. As soon as he reached Salerno in 1943, Togliatti initiated a dramatic change in PCI policy by calling for cooperation with the Italian monarchy and unity among all antifascist forces for the liberation of the country. This call for unity is a constant of Italian Communist policy. It indicates great self-reliance on the part of the PCI. However, the political climate has recently changed. Since February 1977, despite the victory of June 20, 1976 (a mixed victory because with one-third of the total vote it can no longer simply stay in the opposition but at the same time it does not have enough strength to take hold of government), the PCI is, perhaps for the first time, on the defensive. It is being seriously challenged and attacked from the left. PCI leaders are called "revisionists." Attacks and critiques had been leveled before, notably in 1968 and afterward, but they were the product of fairly small intellectual groups such as the so-called Manifesto. At the present time, masses of students, unemployed youths, and "organized unemployed" are bitterly attacking the PCI. They denounce it as part and parcel, if not the main pillar, of the establishment.

Before the elections of June 20, 1976, the PCI had tried to absorb completely and to monopolize the representation of the Left in order to be safe from that side; the electoral returns prove that the operation was successful. The economic depression in the meantime has created a new situation. As long as the PCI was the center of anti-Christian Democracy opposition, the far Left had no base. Now the Left rises again in a myriad of small groups as the PCI, in its long march toward democratic legitimation and national power, abstains in the confidence votes and therefore supports, although indirectly, the present government headed by Christian Democrat Andreotti.

Recent developments put the PCI in an uncomfortable position. Attacks from the left cannot be ignored or simply dismissed. They have the function of putting the PCI on the spot. What kind of party is it? Has it become part of the establishment or not? Has it given up its struggle for socialism or not? What value should be attached to the idea of historic compromise with the Christian Democrats? Is it a tactical move or is it part of a strategic design aimed at freeing completely the PCI from Soviet tutelage? If it is a bona fide part of an overall project, are the PCI leaders going to revise their ideological heritage or not? Can they afford to do that or should they proceed cautiously along the lines of ideological revisionism lest they fall into the contradictions and weaknesses of traditional social democratic parties? In other words, why do they act as social democrats but reject the label of "reformists" and keep stating that they "will never go to Bad Godesberg?"

Berlinguer's admission in January 1977 that "we are *not* in a stage of transition to socialism; only some socialist elements will emerge as a direct consequence of a democratic renovation of Italian society"[4] seems to point to a spirit of gradualism that could be called "Fabian." Napolitano, an important PCI leader, has officially stated that "we are not seeking a new model of economic development (in a global sense), but a new type of development, that is, a different orientation of investments *within* the framework of the present (capitalistic) model of development."[5] It seems that PCI leaders are groping for something new, quite apart from Soviet collectivism and from laissez-faire capitalism, something that perhaps could be labeled "oriented capitalism."

These uncertainties are not merely a matter of idle intellectual speculation. On the contrary, they reflect with great precision the social and economic contradictions of Italian society. The PCI reflects these in an almost mirrorlike fashion. During the past thirty years Italian society has undergone profound changes. In particular, as a consequence of a fairly widespread process of industrialization, new middle classes have arisen in Italy. The PCI has been generally successful in securing their political representation in Parliament and at the municipal level. But the present-day depression has again underlined the *dual* nature of Italian economy and society. With emigration falling to a minimum—actually, with emigrants from Italy being forced to return to their hometowns (notably from Germany, Switzerland, etc.)—the gap between the regularly employed and the structurally unemployed is bound to become wider and wider. There is a trend toward an increasingly sharp polarization between "haves" and "have-nots." People who are "in," as in the past, will be effectively protected by the PCI and Communist oriented trade unions, but there will be little hope for the people who are "out." Furthermore, effective protection of people already employed (for instance, firings are not permitted even if productivity becomes unreasonably low and absenteeism high) has the usual effect of discouraging new job-creating investments.

Under these conditions the issue in Italy today does not seem to be whether the PCI is "democratic enough" to become part of a national government. Rather, it seems to be: will the PCI resist the temptation, or the pressure from its rank and file, to return to the opposition? Or, in a broader framework but quite real for Italy: can a country such as present-day Italy afford not having a rational, politically wise, and consistent opposition? If the PCI keeps moving toward the center, who is going to take over the role of left-wing opposition?

The PCI leaders themselves are, of course, fully aware of these difficulties. As Napolitano stated, "The vote of June 20, 1976, was for the PCI a great success, but not a victory."[6] Polling one-third of the total popular vote puts a political party in an uncomfortable position: it lacks sufficient strength to get hold of the national government but it constitutes a relevant political force without which or against which nothing important can be done. On the other hand, can the PCI realistically go back to a role of pure and simple opposition in the style of the 1950s? It is not only a matter of ideological choice. The fact is that the PCI is now a government party capable of mobilizing huge resources and well rooted in Italian society in the sense that it attracts voters from practically all social classes. It is no longer, if it ever was, a purely proletarian or working class party such as, for instance, the French Communist party.

I do not think the social composition of a political party's leadership should be considered an independent variable per se that produces mechanically a given policy and a given ideological orientation. The relationship between social group and policy, however, should be carefully explored. What seems to some to be the extemporaneous expression of political expediency—the shift in the ideology of the PCI—might then acquire a different image. Sociologically, the leadership group of the PCI, and especially the middle echelon party executives, has changed from predominantly working class to predominantly middle-class. Moreover, ideologically the notion of a compromise with Catholic forces in Italy has a history. Not sufficient attention has been paid to political and ideological statements that have been made by responsible PCI leaders throughout the last three decades. During the fifth PCI national convention (December 1945-January 1946), for instance, the party was described as "a-ideological." Catholics were invited to join without giving up their religious beliefs. Subsequently, Togliatti's Yalta Memorandum came to be ignored, but therein the idea of an Italian, that is, nationally autonomous, way to socialism was already fully developed.

The Internal Evolution of the PCI

As the PCI approaches a governmental role by its parliamentary cooperation with the cabinet or even by the projected inclusion in the cabinet of some independent deputies elected on its ticket on June 20, 1976, a question that in Europe is considered important but one that in the United States would hardly make sense is heard: is the PCI still a working class party or is it becoming a bourgeois, middle-class political organization? Is the PCI still a revolutionary party or is it becoming a purely electoral machine?

I submit that to answer such questions a purely ideological analysis, that is to say, an analysis based on ideological declarations and policy statements, important as it is, is far from adequate. I think it is important also to explore the social and professional origins, including present-day life-styles, of the leadership group of the PCI as they seem to affect its ideological evolution and its current political choices. The following discussion should be considered only as a preliminary step in this research project. The problems are varied and complex. In the first place, as regards the internal evolution of the party, especially since the end of the clandestine phase (approximately 1925–1943), there is a problem of periodization to be resolved.

The interval from 1943 to the present is a complex one that spans more than thirty years, during which Italy has undergone, as mentioned previously, its own industrial revolution. In a little more than a generation Italy was transformed from a predominantly agricultural country into an industrial economy. This transformation has deeply affected all the political parties, including the PCI. A criterion based on the different stages of the Italian economic postwar development would then seem plausible. One might select the low points of industrial production and investment of specific economic cycles as major turning points in the overall evolution of the country (1952, 1958, 1964, and 1971). According to this criterion, three major phases could easily be identified: (1) the phase of postwar reconstruction (approximately 1945–1952); (2) the phase of the so-called economic miracle, that is, the phase of laissez-faire capitalistic development during which the transformation of the country was achieved, despite failures with respect to the relationship between north and south, the establishment of basic social services, and the imbalanced nature of the Italian class structure (approximately 1952–1964); and (3) the phase of economic restructuring as a consequence of the worldwide business slowdown and the domestically required rationalization of the Italian system of production vis-à-vis the demands of organized labor, no longer as cheap as it used to be, and the more severe international competition (approximately 1965–1968 to the present).

This economic criterion, plausible as it sounds, does not take into account, however, critical events, such as the April 18, 1948, great electoral victory of Christian Democracy and the defeat of the Popular Democratic Front (resulting from the electoral alliance between the PSI and PCI); the ensuing crisis of the Communist organization during the fifties; the fateful year 1956, when Stalin's crimes were disclosed by Khrushchev's secret report and the Polish uprising and Hungarian revolt occurred; the student movement of 1968; and the so-called hot fall and the wildcat strikes of 1968–1969. Different criteria have been proposed by PCI leader Giorgio Amendola and by political commentator Giorgio Galli, but they do not seem adequate. Amendola concentrates on electoral returns and Galli sees the middle echelon party executives in the Communist party hierarchy as an independent variable subject only to the varying position of the PCI with respect to the Soviet leaders. To describe and interpret the internal evolution of the PCI, I propose six phases.

1. 1944–1948: The *partito nuovo* as a permanent feature of the Italian political system and not, therefore, as a merely tactical "trick."

2. 1948–1953: The *partito nuovo* reacts to the offensive of the cold war, in particular against Premier de Gasperi and the minister of the interior, Scelba;

3. 1953–1960: A phase of internal crisis for the PCI. Its unity is preserved only nominally; there are seriously contrasting views among leaders as regards neocapitalism, on the one hand, and the crisis of the international communist movement following the twentieth Soviet Communist party convention, on the other.

4. 1960–1968: Attempt on the part of Premier Tambroni (CD) to form a government with the votes of neofascist deputies. Immediate reaction on the part of all antifascist political organizations led by the PCI; through militant antifascism, the PCI succeeds in getting out of the political "ghetto" in which it was confined for years. Center-Left governments.

5. 1968–1976: Crisis of the capitalistic system. Growth of the Left in Italy and particularly of its Communist component. June 20,

1976, marks an important electoral success for the PCI, which gains political control of major Italian cities (Turin, Rome, and Naples, among others), but Christian Democracy remains the leading national party, polling approximately 38% of the total popular vote.

6. 1977: Expectations are great as regards the PCI, but the PCI cannot "deliver the goods" because although it has achieved an important success, it still is the "second party" and cannot reach final, decisive governmental power. It has to share power with the Christian Democratic party and come to terms with it. The Left, both inside but especially outside the PCI, becomes increasingly restless and dissatisfied. PCI leaders are publicly denounced as "revisionists"; at times they are called disparagingly "reformist" and "opportunist." The student movement and the "organized unemployed," the latter especially strong in and around Naples, are mounting a powerful protest against Communist dominated municipal and regional administrations and against Communist oriented trade unions. More and more the PCI is pushed to the right. It is difficult to see any substantial difference between the PCI and the traditional social democratic policies and stands. But the PCI seems perplexed and hesitant. It asserts its autonomy vis-à-vis the Soviet comrades but at the same time it refuses any ideological revision or any clear-cut break. When Santiago Carrillo is attacked by the Soviet leaders (June–July 1977), a PCI delegation in Moscow tries to ease the dispute in the name of international working class solidarity just as Togliatti, years earlier, had tried to bridge the conflict between Stalin and Mao. The PCI leaders have been the inventors, as it were, of Eurocommunism, but their overcautious attitude makes their position at the present time somewhat ambiguous.

The Partito Nuovo

THE PERIOD 1944–1948

For decades charges have been leveled against Togliatti for duplicity. Was he serious when he was writing or making speeches about the *partito nuovo* ("new party")? What did he really have in mind? It seems that according to Togliatti the *partito nuovo* was new in the sense that it was a mass party in which ideological unity was not required. As noted previously, at the fifth national convention of the PCI the party was officially described in the preamble of its by-laws as an "a-ideological party" for which Marxism-Leninism constitutes only a cultural heritage. To join this new party it was not essential to be a Marxist or a Leninist. It was necessary only to agree with its present-day platform and its actual, day-to-day policies, based on antifascism and concerned with the preservation and strengthening of democracy. But what kind of democracy? Liberal, or bourgeois, democracy with its individual freedoms was not considered sufficient. Until about 1950 Communist leaders and Togliatti especially continued to speak of "progressive democracy," meaning a type of democratic regime in which individual freedoms would not be abstract legal principles only but on the contrary would acquire definite social substance through basic, or "structural," economic reforms aimed at achieving social equality. The adjective "structural" was deemed important insofar as it marked the qualitative difference between real reforms, linked with basic changes in the capitalistic system, and piecemeal, social democratic reforms that would not be capable of modifying essentially the capitalistic mode of production but would rather contribute to its perpetuation.

The word "progressive" was dropped after 1950. It is interesting to observe that since that time the concept of the PCI as a new party has been understood mostly as indicative of the movement of the PCI away from a revolutionary, leftist position toward a more moderate stand that abides by the democratic rules of the game. Although one might locate the origins of this development as early as the Lyon convention of the PCI in France, after the party was exiled by fascism and the need for national autonomy for the party was already felt, I think that the concept of the *partito nuovo* was Togliatti's most brilliant and original contribution, even more so than the famous Salerno switch of 1943, when Togliatti, newly arrived from the Soviet Union, convinced the antifascist parties, especially the Action party and the Socialist party, to forget for the time being their antimonarchist principles and to unite in order to liberate the country. Georg Lukàcs's evaluation then of Togliatti as "the greatest tactician of the Third International" was both unsatisfactory and restrictive because it clouded the most significant "Italian moment," that is, the inventive adaptation to the Italian situation in 1943. Similarly inadequate seem to me the evaluations by Paolo Spriano in his *Storia del partito comunista italiano*, who has offered, however, the most penetrating treatment of the *partito nuovo*, and by Ernesto Ragionieri in the *Storia d'Italia*, in which the *partito nuovo* is rather ambiguously described as a mass political organization within which social struggles and political objectives have been variously combined.[7]

The question is sometimes dramatically asked: was Togliatti acting in good or bad faith? These moral categories do not carry the analysis very far. I do not think it is a matter of good or bad faith. Togliatti was an able politician who had been capable of surviving the darkest and most cruel years of Stalin's rule. As a policymaker he practiced in the first place the virtues of "prudence" in Edmund Burke's sense. As he reentered Italy after years of exile in the Soviet

Union, he knew two things: first, that Italy belonged to the sphere of influence of the United States; and second, that fascism had not been just a bad dream and that the Catholic church was a formidable social and political reality.

Not much could be done about the first objective condition. But as regards fascism and the Catholic church the PCI could develop a new, flexible approach. The interpretation of fascism could not be confined to the doctrinaire idea of fascism as the armed protection of the big bourgeois vested interests. Fascism was also something more. It was a social movement with a solid mass base made up of small functionaries, schoolteachers, World War I veterans, unemployed workers, nationalist intellectuals, and anarcho-syndicalist trade union organizers. All these people had to be reorganized into the PCI irrespective of their own personal preferences or ideological bent. Although fascism was a reactionary political movement, it represented a reaction of a new type: no longer of a reactionary, small, elite group, such as was the establishment in the prefascist liberal democracy, but of a large, middle-class and worker supported, state directed, and socially conscious reactionary regime.

The profound political insight of Togliatti is remarkably shown in one of his speeches in March 1944:

> On July 25 [1943] the whole political system collapsed; not only 20 years of Fascism, but all the preceding years. . . . All that which made up the Italian nation was in ruin. . . . The people suffered; men were needed who would be near them and understand them. How many comrades were needed in the Party? No closed doors, but open doors: recruit! Take into the Party all the active elements; houses cannot be built with bricks that are perfectly equal and smooth. They will be improved in the great school which is our Party or they will be ousted. . . . It is not enough to establish a good policy; it is also necessary to bring this policy to the masses and this cannot be done without an organization.

The need for an organization sounds very Leninistic. It was in fact Lenin who insisted on the party as a weapon, as a tightly organized group. But Lenin demanded a small, vanguard party in a conspiratorial vein, whereas Togliatti opted for a mass party. The party Togliatti had in mind was not a small, elite group passing instructions to the masses, but the masses themselves in organized form: a position he shared with Gramsci and that is more reminiscent of Rosa Luxemburg than of Lenin. In fact, in this speech Togliatti is very clear on this very point:

> An order to be followed by the masses is not sufficient. We must have in our ranks all those elements who are necessary to be present everywhere. The Party organization is not a sum, a meeting of comrades, but the means to make the Party work. There is a tendency to

want statutes; but there are no fixed, legalistic organizational formulas. Organization means: to know men, to study comrades, to discover enemies, to utilize comrades.

It is clear now that through the concept of the *partito nuovo* Togliatti was trying to capture the mass aspects of the Fascist experience. The Fascist regime in Italy had been capable of important mass linkages as well as of a particular relationship with the Catholic church. Togliatti had a keen appreciation of the stabilizing effect in favor of fascism that had been the result of the "conciliation pact" between Mussolini and the Pope on February 11, 1929. Interestingly enough, when that pact came under discussion during the drafting of the constitution in 1946, the PCI voted in favor of the inclusion of the former in the new fundamental law of the country. (This is the famous issue of article 7.) The present-day historic compromise between the PCI and the CD has a long history indeed.

Under the direction of Togliatti, the PCI has never failed to realize the true nature of the Christian Democratic party even when immediately after World War II this party had not yet been selected by the church hierarchy as its exclusive representative as far as the Italian domestic political scene was concerned. Togliatti was always keenly conscious that many semipolitical organizations, more or less attached to the CD, had been able to survive during fascism and that now, after fascism had collapsed, they were in a position to contribute human and organizational resources to a Catholic party. Speaking to the Florence Communists in September 1944, Togliatti called attention to the fact that the CD and PCI were the two strongest parties in Italy even if the CD had not yet received a specific mandate from the church. "There are, however," Togliatti specified, "already some converging trends between the CD and the many Catholic organizations which were able to exist legally for twenty years under Fascism; thus, they have already a number of cadres who will now reenter political life and who can work rapidly for the organization of a large party." The character of the CD as a popular party was thus recognized despite its conservative orientation.

Later, an effort was made by some Communist leaders, notably Pietro Ingrao, to talk directly to the Catholic masses and to win them away from their conservative leadership group. When this attempt failed, the PCI started realistically to deal directly with the Catholic leaders. Ingrao contends in *Masses and Power* that the Christian Democratic party not only has a popular base but that through the years, especially since its great electoral victory on April 18, 1948, it has become a "state party," that is to say, a party so well rooted in the government machinery at the local and at the national level as to have become almost completely identified with the state itself.[8]

Since the end of fascism Italy has been uninterruptedly governed by a Christian Democratic premier. This political predominance has been aptly reinforced through the apparatus of state owned and state operated industry. Approximately 50% of Italian industry is under public ownership. Most presidents of the boards of administration, chairmen, top managers, and middle echelon executives are political appointees. Roughly 80% of them are Christian Democrats with a handful of Republican party and Socialist party members. This network of alliances, supervision prerogatives, and expected subservience has given rise to a neofeudal structure that entitles, in my opinion, the Italian industrial system to be rightly regarded as a "dynastic capitalism."

The *partito nuovo* idea had some recognizable organizational repercussions. The dropping of Marxism-Leninism as an official ideology was followed by organizational practices that were severely criticized by the party traditionalist faction, in particular, the lack of expansion of work-place party organizations such as factory cells; the obsolescence of nonclass, general social pressure groups such as street cells, neighborhood cells, and women's cells; and the increased role conferred on the territorial section as the central political coordinator and promoter of cell initiatives.

It is a fact, however, that despite the concept of *partito nuovo* not much has changed in terms of who has the power and who makes the relevant decisions. As Giorgio Bocca puts it in his book *Palmiro Togliatti*: "The old guard was always at the top of the hierarchy. The party remained in the faithful hands of the elders who knew the 'holy history' and whose faith was beyond discussion."[9] What Bocca does not seem to understand is that the permanence of the old guard was to the rank and file members of the PCI the supreme guarantee that their party would not fall victim to the traditional Italian political practice of *transformismo*, that is to say, of petty corruption and ideological indifference resulting in systematic opportunism.

It would be an interesting subject for further research to discover whether, despite the dropping of Marxism-Leninism and of any other official ideology, the PCI has not fallen into the trap of widespread opportunism as has been the case with many European social democratic parties. It is sufficient here to observe that the "new party" found its important test in the electoral defeat of April 18, 1948, and in the subsequent attempt on the life of Togliatti. Yet, it survived fairly well.

AT THE HEIGHT OF THE COLD WAR, 1948-1953

Usually the electoral defeat of April 1948 of the PCI has been blamed on the alliance with the PSI: the Partito socialista di unità proletaria (Socialist Party for Proletarian Unity) in a single electoral organization called the Popular Democratic Front. People got scared, it is generally maintained. Actually, the single most important factor behind the PCI defeat was the explicit and vocal support given by the United States and by the Catholic church to the Christian Democratic party. I think that the PCI learned its lesson from that defeat; for the PSI a gentle decline began that is reaching its lowest point at the present time. In a sense, the PCI was little by little moving in on the PSI, taking away from it its traditional passwords, its idea of gradual transformation of the country ("social justice with political freedom"), and, last but not least, its electoral base. Was the PCI becoming a bourgeois, middle-class party? Any conclusion on this subject would be premature.

The fact is that the impact of the April 18, 1948, defeat was experienced deeply by the PCI and its mass membership and cadres: the attempted assassination of Togliatti; the general strike and the upheaval that followed; the trade union schism motivated by the "politicization" of the strike, which, however, was called unanimously by all the members of the general secretariat of the CGIL (General Trade Union Confederation). Out of this schism the CISL (of Christian Democratic orientation) and the UIL (Italian Labor Unions—of Social Democratic orientation) came into existence, and labor unity, which had been achieved in the common struggle against fascism during the resistance, was dissolved. After the profoundly experienced unity of the people under Fascist and Nazi oppression, especially from 1943 through 1945, the Italian polity again appeared fragmented and divided. Card-carrying Communists were publicly denounced and officially excommunicated by Pope Pius XII. Rumors that the Red Army would be moving toward the West and invade Italy were widespread. Unemployment was high. The war was not yet felt to be completely over.

It is understandable that under such circumstances the *partito nuovo* idea could not be developed with the expected coherence. Pietro Secchia, an old guardsman generally considered to be a tough organizer, was fast reaching the top of the PCI. If Luigi Longo was and continued to be after Togliatti the person around whom the unity of the *partito nuovo* was achieved, in Secchia was felt the hand of one who transformed the great mass of members into an organized force. Indeed, he ruled the PCI central organization until 1954, when he was replaced. His personality was among the dominant ones from the sixth to the seventh congress. The party needed obviously to streamline its organization in order to protect itself against the vast offensive of its political enemies.

It is amazing to observe how the PCI was able to capitalize on a difficult situation and turn it to its own advantage. Secchia divided the membership into "groups of ten," each with individual leaders. Such an internal organizational change was justified by the necessity of involving a greater number of militants and of extending the party's social penetration. This penetration was certainly helped by the new organization, but the formation of the groups of ten introduced qualitative changes into the life of the rank and file organization that were not necessarily positive. Internal political debate was broken up into too many pieces, and it was therefore weakened. It lost momentum and required repeated and minute connections among a myriad of small, self-enclosed groups, fixed in their membership. The PCI organization in effect became a defensive structure. This might be regarded as a negative feature now, but at the time defense was a vital necessity. De Gasperi, the Christian Democratic premier, and Scelba, his minister of the interior, were trying to make the most of the electoral victory of April 1948. A certain amount of red scare and witch-hunting was going on in the country at large.

Moreover, the events in Poland and Czechoslovakia were certainly not encouraging. The militant anticommunism of Pope Pius XII proved to be an important obstacle to Communist expansion in Italy. The PCI could rely only on its good record during the years of the resistance and the struggle against fascism. In this respect one should notice that in Italy, contrary to other European countries, the Communist party never lost its social respectability and basic acceptance within the framework of democratic, postfascist Italy thanks to its magnificent contribution to the antifascist cause since its foundation in 1921. But this social respectability, which had been earned the hard way, could be used, as the PCI leaders well realized even at that time, only to the extent to which the PCI could free itself from too much pressure from Moscow and finally embark upon an Italian, that is, national, road to socialism.

Among the rank and file the organizational line of the groups of ten encountered much opposition, but some opposition to it came also from the top of the party. In general one may say that the successful resistance of the young *partito nuovo* to De Gasperi's offensive could not be entirely credited to this organizational reform. This reform, at any rate, was never fully implemented. The cells never completely disappeared although people would no longer talk about them. Organizational traditionalism has always been very strong within the PCI just as in any other mass organization. One important consequence, however, of that organizational reform was that the PCI began slowly to lose its conspiratorial, clandestine nature, and its official image came increasingly to coincide with its real outlines.

It is true that for some years after 1945, groups of young activists who had been in the resistance movement and in the underground against Fascist and Nazi troops kept alive the idea of a miniature Red Army within the PCI. Rumors about a secret armed group within the party or at least with PCI support were heard now and then, but no substantial evidence for this has ever surfaced.

There has been a certain amount of talk about Stalin's attempt to remove Togliatti from Italy especially at the time when the Marshall Plan was under discussion and when Togliatti and Longo were not seeing eye to eye on this specific issue. As cautious as ever, Togliatti was quite consistent in trying to make the PCI relatively independent of Moscow. He never missed a chance to criticize the double standard that was not uncommon among the rank and file and even the middle echelon cadres: lip service acceptance of the democratic regime to appease naive fellow travelers and political enemies while they waited consciously for the great occasion for insurrection and violent conquest of central national power.

This was obviously the reflection of an even stronger conflict at the top of the PCI. It was known that Secchia and Longo favored a purely instrumental use of the democratic regime in order to await and to prepare for a good opportunity to seize power through revolution. In the past both leaders had been organizers of the clandestine armed struggle against fascism. Longo's role in the Spanish Civil War had been prominent. Neither was ever considered an "intellectual," whereas Togliatti was the typical humanities professor turned to politics. Not much is known about this inner struggle around contrasting concepts of and attitudes toward democracy—as something to believe in or as a temporary regime to take advantage of. For some time two models seemed to coexist: the party of clandestine cadres, that is, the Leninist model, and, superimposed on it, the new party of the masses, taking advantage of the democratic rules but being at the same time a kind of "democracy on the march."

THE TRYING YEARS BEFORE THE END
OF THE "GHETTO," 1953-1960

This double standard necessarily resulted in widespread confusion among party members. The program of the party was clear and definite only in its negative dimensions: the fight against the Christian Democratic monopoly of all power decisions and government posts. But to be successful, such a program still required, first, a positive platform about what to do once the power positions were changed or even reversed and, second, some allies, both politically and trade union oriented, in order to dispel the suspicion that the Communist party, while demanding a more articulate democratic regime, was in fact pursuing only its narrow partisan interests. The second condition especially was important, and for a while the Communist leadership was earnestly searching for some common national objectives that would attract the minor parties (Republicans, Social Democrats, and Socialists).

In the meantime the CD party was quite conscious that its quasi-absolute rule was being threatened. With the help of the Republicans and the Social Democrats (PRI and PSDI) it approved an electoral law for the general political elections of 1953 that would award a majority premium to the winning tickets. The justification for such a law was the avowed necessity to correct the "evil effects" of purely proportional representation, which would make for an excess of political fragmentation and general political instability. The fact is that the CD majority was realizing that it was being eroded day by day and that the time was nearing when it would have to have resort to the PSI (Nenni's Socialists) because of the narrowing margins offered by the PRI and PSDI. In topographical parliamentary terms, from the center the government would have had to move to the left of center (a coalition of the CD, PRI, PSDI, *and* PSI).

The majority premium electoral law did not succeed because the majority parties failed to reach, in 1953, a relative majority of the total popular vote. But the PCI could not at that time exploit to the full its electoral success because of international difficulties.

In 1954 Giorgio Amendola replaced Pietro Secchia in the directorate of the organization commission of the party. This was a clear sign that PCI "moderates" were on the winning side. Amendola had always been considered a "social democrat" among PCI leaders. The son of a prominent Liberal party member, Giovanni Amendola, who was killed by the Fascists, Amendola has always favored the integration of Italy within the Common Market, an open dialogue with the Catholics, and total acceptance of democratic rules as a fundamental historical heritage for a Western European country such as Italy.

The ascent of Amendola in the party hierarchy meant that the PCI was taking good notice of the evolution of Italian society. In the fifties Italy was escaping from the category of poor agricultural countries to which it had belonged for centuries. Its class structure was becoming more articulated. The mythology of class warfare was less and less attractive. It was necessary for a mass party such as the PCI to renovate its cadres and to update its propaganda. Italian society was following fairly closely the pattern of the more developed regions of Western Europe.

The years 1953 through approximately 1962-1963 represented a decade of unprecedented economic development in Italian history, comparable only to the first decade of this century. The entrance of the Italian economy into a worldwide market after the autarchic economy of fascism gave a tremendous impetus to industrial production and urbanization. Perhaps more attention should have been paid to basic social services and to the still missing infrastructures; yet it is a fact that the average yearly growth rate of the gross national product in real terms was 5.3% during the period 1951-1958 and 6.6% during the period 1958-1963, reaching a peak of 8.3% in 1960 and 1961, and that between 1951 and 1963 the added value contributed by the industrial sector to the Italian economy as a whole rose from 33.7% to 43.8%.

The long awaited crisis of the capitalistic system simply had not materialized. The PCI leaders were quite realistic: they did not try to hide this fact. They realized that they could not rely on the model of the Eastern European economy—using the justification that capitalism does not work—without jeopardizing their credibility among their working class followers, who by now were driving around in Fiat 500s all over the country.

But this period of readjustment, ideologically as well as organizationally, was not painless. During the fifties the PCI was in serious trouble. Its collateral organizations, such as Communist dominated unions and clubs, were in danger. The CGIL (Communist oriented Confederazione generale italiana del lavoro) suffered a grave defeat at Fiat international elections for shop stewards. An impressive wave of self-criticism was immediately started that took note of their lack of knowledge about the actual changes that had occurred in the factories, in the organization of the work place, and in the wage structure. Although capitalism had been pronounced dead, neocapitalism was arising as a system with its own ideology founded on the notion of mass production, mass distribution, high ages and salaries, mass consumption, scientific management, sociological know-how, and human relations.

The PCI was baffled and shocked. At the same time, on the international scene, labor riots in Poznan, Warsaw, and Budapest were taking place. They were curbed by the police: Communist police against Communist workers, a bewildering paradox. Anticommunists, in Italy as well as all over the world, took advantage of such difficulties. The repercussions of the anti-Stalin report by Khrushchev were perhaps more profound than the Soviet leaders had anticipated. In Italy a major effort was made to isolate the PCI, to force it again, and for good, inside a political ghetto. The defensive reaction on the part of the PCI was slow and uneven. It followed three main lines:

1. Revision of the party history in terms of renouncing defense of the indefensible, that is, defense of its entire past; the early party rift between Terracini and Amadeo Bordiga, on one hand, and Gramsci and Togliatti,

on the other, came finally to the fore; the old guard was no longer presented and interpreted as a monolithic, cohesive group; dissensions and contrasting views were expressed and set in the open.

2. Conceptual elaboration of an "autonomous, national way to socialism" in a mature capitalistic economy, for which neither the Soviet Union nor any Eastern European country could be regarded as an example.

3. Internal reorganization through the gradual renewal of the party cadres, especially at the middle echelon.

The third point is of special importance. Unfortunately, data and analytical support are still lacking. The most enlightening account of the "1958 switch" is Pietro Ingrao's January 21, 1977, interview in *Rinascita*. In it Ingrao asserted that "the importance of the original effort was to integrate the [changed] outlook on Stalin with the development of a new strategy."[10] He then emphasized the rich and positive nature of the debate, which was dramatic at the level of the masses and in which the clash over ideological principles was intertwined with a political initiative for the definition and organization of a new power bloc to be led by the working class in a socialist direction. In this perspective, Ingrao was confirming the exceptional nature of the eighth PCI congress, which was comparable in importance to the founding congress, at Leghorn in January 1921, and to the Lyons congress. Avoiding the pitfalls of hagiography, Ingrao evaluated as essential the response of the eighth congress regarding the "forms of socialist power" and the expansion of "political democracy" as a "qualifying element of a socialist society." However, at the same time he dismissed the analyses of the structural changes in Italian society as too general and thus judged the "strategy of reform" as defective.

In contrast with this interpretative line, Galli inaptly has insisted on specifying the recovery of Soviet prestige as the solution to the crisis: "The USSR is ahead in the space race which was alleged as a proof of the superiority of the Soviet system. On this basis, the Communist militant felt himself part of a positive reality and confirmed his activist commitment." No doubt a kind of Sputnik mythology did exist and Gagarin's flight carried a definite amount of pro-Soviet propaganda value, but the inner state of the PCI was not fundamentally affected by such exploits. The difficulties and the wear and tear on the party framework are manifest in the fact that obvious signs of weakness appeared in the organizational and mass character of the party in the years since 1953, although, from an electoral standpoint, the period was one of growth. Something strange, from a traditional Communist standpoint, was happening. The PCI was losing members and at the same time gaining votes. Why? Was it becoming a purely electoral machine like any other "bourgeois party"?

In ten years beginning in 1954, the PCI lost 25% of its organizational strength. Its youth organization, the FGCI (Federazione giovanile comunista italiana), lost 60% of its members. In the 1970s this tendency was reversed and membership increased but not at a rate sufficient to reach the two million level of 1954-1955. It seems clear that the PCI, both organizationally and ideologically, was not keeping pace with tremendous changes in Italian society during those years. A research effort was made by the PCI leadership group to detect what was new in the Italian economy, to identify and explain the basic trends of Italian capitalism, especially its ambiguous nature as a system based on private enterprise and free initiative and at the same time characterized by huge state owned and state operated industry.

TRYING TO WIN RESPECTABILITY AND CREDIBILITY, 1960-1968

The PCI was able to reestablish its unity and to gain political credibility and electoral support not because its analysis of the changes in Italian society was particularly brilliant and its policy coherent with the analysis but because of a serious political mistake made by a faction of the CD. At the beginning of the third legislature (1958-1963) it became evident that a parliamentary majority for a center government no longer existed. When the Liberal party determined the fall of the Segni government, there only remained one way to revive a center government in the De Gasperi tradition: because of the withdrawal of the minor parties of the center-Left (the PRI and PSDI), it was necessary to resort to neofascist votes. This had occurred before, but it had not previously been planned as a deliberate political operation. Now, however, the time seemed ripe. The end of the war and the collapse of fascism seemed far enough in the past not to excite the imagination and the passion of the people. At the suggestion of the then president of the Republic, Giovanni Gronchi, Prime Minister Tambroni tried a center-Right solution that required neofascist votes.

The move was a typical case of miscalculation. Political repercussions were immediate and violent. All over the country antifascist organizations set up demonstrations against the Tambroni administration. The CD was clearly isolated. Trade unions went on strike. The PCI emerged as the leader of a national antifascist unity that evoked the political climate of the resistance movement against Fascists and Nazis during the war. In building this new antifascist unity the PCI played a major role. Once again, just as after the Salerno switch, the theme of the *partito nuovo*, without ideological requirements, became dominant, and at the same time it served the purpose of getting the PCI out of the political ghetto in which for years it had been confined and of making it the leader of the new antifascist and anti-Tambroni movement.

The CD was internally divided, but some of its leaders, especially Fanfani and Moro, immediately realized the danger of being in their turn isolated from Italian society as a whole and started to maneuver to bring down Tambroni and to establish a center- Left government. The strategic goal of such a government would still have been the same as that of the Tambroni government, that is, the isolation of the PCI. The main tactical step toward this goal was the political divorce of the PSI from the PCI. The overall purpose of this complex political operation in the eyes of the CD was the isolation and eventually the disappearance of the PCI as an important political force. By the mid-1960s it was clear that the center- Left operation had failed in terms of making the PCI "politically superfluous" and that its net political result instead had been the weakening of the PSI as the electoral strength of the PCI continually increased.

On the other hand, for the PCI there was danger in its electoral successes. It was, in fact, true that far from being isolated from the Italian society the PCI could count on such a vast electoral following that the government could not fail to consider all PCI stands. One could see in this situation, as most PCI leaders saw and some CD leaders realized, a foreshadowing of the historical compromise, as Berlinguer would later term it.

Where, then, was the danger? From a traditional Communist point of view, or to use the old-fashioned phraseology, from "a revolutionary party point of view," the danger concerned the very nature of the Communist party. The PCI had been able to emerge as the most vocal exponent of the antifascist protest against Tambroni and his attempt to use neofascist votes. It was a mass democratic movement of a liberal character that would again express itself, a year later, in May 1975, in the divorce referendum. The PCI was becoming more and more like the other democratic parties: an electoral machine rather than a revolutionary apparatus.

The ratio of members to voters indicates such a change. In 1953 the ratio was 2.8 votes per member; in 1958 it was 3.6; and in 1963 it was 4.8 In the 1976 electoral campaign that ratio was seven votes per member. According to Berlinguer, this kind of ratio indicates certain difficulties on the part of the PCI, both organizationally and "psychologically," in adapting to the profound changes in Italian society during recent years. In my opinion, it is not only a matter of adaptation and of psychological acceptance of a changed social milieu. I view the constant increase of the voter-member ratio as an important indication of the internal qualitative modification of the *partito nuovo*. The more electorally successful the PCI becomes, the less attractive it seems to be to militant revolutionary members. In other words, and to put it bluntly, the PCI is becoming more and more similar to a social democratic party. Popular insurrection and armed revolution are considered by the PCI to be relics of the past. The principle of the "dictatorship of the proletariat" has become obsolete, to be admired perhaps under certain past historical circumstances but certainly not to be used at the present time.

My point is that these new attitudes and developments on the part of the PCI are not the product of a conscious ideological revisionism—which clearly has not yet occurred—but rather are the necessary consequences of an internal evolution of the party in terms of its sociological composition. Sociologically speaking, the PCI is becoming more and more bourgeois; its leadership groups (that is, the national directorate and the central committee) are increasingly composed of middle- and upper middle-class members; representatives with a working class background are fewer and fewer and their rotation is much faster than that of their middle-class "comrades." (For data on the internal structure of the PCI see the chapter appendix.)

MODERATION PAYS AND THE PCI ENTERS
THE GOVERNMENT ARENA, 1968–1976

The years 1968–1969 were in Italy, as in France, a period of mass uprisings against traditional institutions and economic potentates. These movements, made up of students, marginal workers, and disgruntled intellectuals, did not spare the political parties and trade unions of what they would call "the official, or institutionalized, Left." They called themselves the "New Left" and asserted that they were working toward a radical change of capitalistic societies on the basis of an extra-parliamentary approach. These movements were very vocal in their demands but rather weak in terms of tactics and strategy. As far as Italy is concerned, a paradox must be pointed out. The greatest single beneficiary of these huge and loosely organized mass movements was their greatest enemy, the PCI. The PSI could not take advantage of the general push to the left simply because it appeared too "compromised" with the CD through its participation in the center–Left governments. All the extremist movements—the students' movement, the feminists, the wildcat strikes in the "hot fall," the divorce referendum—despite their strong reservations about the cautious attitude of the PCI, "objectively" seemed to have been working for it. In fact, as a result of those years of extra-parliamentary struggles and demonstrations, anticommunism as an ideologically well established presupposition of Italian political life, since at least 1947, became less respectable and less acceptable than ever.

As a major consequence of this new political climate, a different relationship was established between parties and trade unions. A trade union federation was organized among the most important Italian trade unions, including trade unions of Communist, Socialist, and Christian Democratic orientation. Autonomy of trade union organization and activity was asserted. The principle of incompatibility between being a trade union officer and a leader of a political party was reintroduced and implemented. Accordingly, many union officers, both Communist and Socialist, abandoned their seats in Parliament.

There are many indications that the PCI is slowly becoming a middle-class party. Annual membership in the PCI has always fluctuated considerably. The PCI has generally tried to compensate for membership losses with new recruits. This effort repeatedly failed, however, until the 1970s, when the number of new members began to increase again. Total membership as well has been increasing in this decade. Fluctuation seems to be drastically reduced. Why?

The annual membership fluctuation has generally been attributed to political reasons and practical reasons (such as changes in residence or work place, migratory flows, commuting, etc.). It is clear that the second set of reasons would affect especially unskilled and marginal laborers. Equally clear seems the fact that the increased number of middle-class persons gravitating into the party constitutes a bloc characterized by greater stability and generally more free time to devote to party work and organizational drives. More open and regular ways of calling and holding meetings and engaging in propaganda have been introduced. One notices a certain respect for and implementation of formal parliamentary procedures and especially for rank and file rights to intervene in the discussions and to vote. Middle-class participation in grass-roots and intermediary party organs is very apparent. Also great are the numbers of middle-class members in delegations that are nominated or elected in schools, ward committees, management sections of social and cultural services, and so on. The numbers of young people (generally students) in Communist sections have also grown markedly. Among active women members housewives have tended to decrease, although it should be noted that housewives of proletarian and working class families have traditionally been a very strong presence in the PCI. A whole series of intermediate social groups are on the rise within the PCI. This is bound to have important political repercussions once the PCI is part of the government or at least, as is the case at present (July 1977), part of the government supporting majority. (It is interesting to note that already the PCI occasionally seems to find itself to the right of the PSI, especially on issues such as the public financing of private—Catholic—schools, movie censorship, and so on.)

As far as the feminist movement is concerned, PCI positions are certainly more conservative than those expressed and defended by the PSI and the PR (Radical party). Middle-class women as well as students have more time on their hands to devote to political activities than their working class counterparts. At the May 1977 congress of the PCI Rome federation, out of ninety-six women delegates only three were workers and only twelve were housewives. An important point, however, needs to be kept in mind. The bulk of the "liberated" middle-class women and students are not with the PCI but tend rather to belong to the other political organizations of the Left, namely, the Italian Socialist party, the Radical party, and Democrazia proletaria (DP). A libertarian orientation is common to these organizations that puts a priority on individual rights and freedoms over traditional objectives of class struggle in the economic sense. When the percentage of middle-class women and students is on the rise within the PCI, as is the case in 1977, the emphasis on class struggle issues tends to be blurred; the party becomes cautious and less militant as far as collective economic issues are concerned; and human rights issues tend to prevail. Hence, there is a conservative, no longer strictly proletarian or "revolutionary," emphasis within the party as well as in party initiatives.

In a sense, it would be fair to say that the PCI has been pushed forward on the path toward democracy and the rediscovery of democratic individual freedoms *malgré lui*. But this is the price to be paid, the old guard would admit, if the party is to get out of its political ghetto and finally to win political respectability. The PCI has never been enthusiastic about the divorce law referendum. In fact, it tried to avoid the referendum through a parliamentary agreement with the CD that failed simply because the CD could not avoid the battle against divorce as a result of pressure from the Vatican. At present, the PCI and especially those left-wing Catholics who were elected as independents on its ticket on June 20, 1976, are trying to slow down proceedings and to avoid a referendum on abortion whereas PSI, PR, and DP members are quite eager to have it.

The constant growing strength of the middle classes within the PCI does not necessarily mean that "internal democracy" is on its way to victory as far as the decisionmaking mechanism of the party is concerned. The basic organizational principle as regards major political decisions remains Lenin's principle of "democratic centralism," which is, of course, a contradiction in terms from the point of view of liberal democratic practice. Moreover, no "organized" internal dissension is allowed: it would be condemned as factionalism. The case of the group centering around the weekly *Il Mani-*

festo, now a daily paper, is illustrative of the dogmatic method followed by the PCI leadership whenever it feels seriously threatened in its exclusive prerogatives.

The PCI has won democratic recognition although democratic practice is not yet one of its basic features as far as party internal life is concerned. There is no plausible reason, however, to doubt that Togliatti and the major PCI leaders made a basic choice in the direction of democracy when they set up and tried to develop the theory of the *partito nuovo*. I do not think this theory, since its formulation in 1943, can be viewed as a merely tactical expedient. It was clear to Togliatti that in order to avoid the political mistake of 1922, when Communists and Socialists were isolated and defeated by fascism, the PCI could not remain a self-enclosed, sectarian organization and had to face the reality of a relatively developed society such as was to be found in postwar Italy. Only an open, nondogmatic, and broadly based political party could hope, in a Catholic country with a developing capitalistic system, some day to enter the government arena without basic violent disruptions. The idea of the *partito nuovo* was not intended to deceive naive Italian democrats but rather to bring the Italian working class inside the Italian state, making it part of the national community not only in formal but also in substantial terms.

However, internal democracy as regards the inner life of the party is still more of a promise than an everyday reality. General instructions still stem from the center and it is doubtful whether local conventions have an impact on policy decisions. Rather, they function as a sounding board and a means for popularizing policies set by top leadership. On the other hand, PCI leaders have been undeniably sensitive to the changing mood and needs of Italian society. The great challenge that is at present confronting this leadership concerns the ability to keep such a huge party going without turning it into a purely electoral machine and a well-lubricated organization. In this respect, benevolent paternalism will probably prove to be inadequate.

The Importance of Eurocommunism

Why is the Italian experience so relevant? Why has Enrico Berlinguer, an otherwise rather grey type of bureaucrat, emerged as an inspiring, if not charismatic, leader when compared with Georges Marchais, Santiago Carrillo, and, to some extent, Alvaro Cunhal? Naturally there is more than one single answer. It is, however, an established fact that Eurocommunism is the only way—barring an armed insurrection or a direct intervention in Western Europe by the Red Army—that is open for communist parties in southern Europe to get out of the political ghetto of permanent opposition and to enter eventually into government.

According to the Soviet magazine *Novoe vremya* (*New Times*), in a review of Santiago Carrillo's *Eurocommunism and the State*, "the concept of Eurocommunism is erroneous. There is only one communism. Its foundations were laid by Marx, Engels, and Lenin and its principles are adhered to by the present-day communist movement." Santiago Carrillo promptly replied that the Kremlin was not different from the Inquisition. In the Catholic countries of Europe there can be no greater condemnation than that. This means that Eurocommunists do not accept Brezhnev's theory of interdependence and limited sovereignty. They consider that in each country each communist party can and in fact should have its own way of building socialism. This claim is not based primarily on intellectual grounds or pure theory. It is based rather on actual historical conditions. The Italian Communists especially go to great pains to point out that the Soviet model is not practicable in southern Europe because the economic and social structure is so very different. It would be anti-Marxist, they say, to apply mechanically the Soviet model in Western Europe, where there are political and cultural traditions that should be safeguarded. These traditions make it compulsory and politically wise to build socialism through democratic means and on a democratic ground. In Western Europe, they say, socialism should include democratic freedoms, parliamentary institutions, local autonomy, political and cultural pluralism, and autonomy of the trade unions vis-à-vis the state and the communist party.

In a sense, Eurocommunism is a misleading term. It ignores the Communist party of Japan. This is quite startling given the fact that the Japanese Communists were the first to take the path now called Eurocommunism. Moreover, Eurocommunism is less a positive program of action than a convergence of negative reactions against the Soviet Union. Any positive definition of Eurocommunism is bound, therefore, to be unsatisfactory. What binds together the various Eurocommunist parties is a twofold desire for substantial, if not total, independence from the Soviet Union and the acquisition of a separate and different image from that of the Soviet Union.

In this respect it becomes clear that it is essential for Eurocommunist parties to free themselves from the tutelage of the Soviet Union. Two facts have helped in this connection: (1) the rift between the Soviet Union and China; and (2) the anti-Stalin disclosures by Khrushchev in 1956. Basically, however, Eurocommunism depends on two major factors—the first, of an international nature, and the second, having to do with the economic, social, and cultural realities of Europe and Japan.

The first international factor that made it possible for Eurocommunism to come into existence was détente. It was détente that brought about a clear perception of contrasting economic and political interests between the Soviet Union on the one hand and the Western communist parties on the other. These parties were bound to become fearful of any dealings between Moscow and Washington over their heads. Moreover, with détente it became imaginable for each communist party to be able to participate in the government of its own country, sharing power prerogatives and making therefore— more or less historic—political compromises with the other political parties. To implement such a national policy it is clear that the communist party in each country has to get rid, first of all, of the old label that would depict it as the *longa manus* of Moscow and, second, that each must develop policies in an autonomous way without awaiting Moscow's approval.

These autonomous policies to be meaningful must be developed on the basis not of obedience to Soviet dogmatic models but of a Marxist analysis of the social realities of Western European countries, especially in southern Europe.

This analysis can be termed Marxist in the sense that it is intended to offer a realistic picture of the economy of these countries in connection with the other major aspects of social, political, and cultural life so as to yield a global, dialectical view of the interaction of each social element. In particular, this analysis is centered on the problems of how the capitalistic system has been able to survive its main crises after World War II, on the role and function of the state in an advanced capitalistic system, and on the future of parliamentary democracy. It is a basic principle of Eurocommunism—and an important departure from classical Marxist and Leninist teaching—that parliamentary democracy is here to stay and that for Western European countries the adoption of an Eastern European type regime would be a big step backward.

Therefore, the first important theoretical consequence of Eurocommunism is a new doctrine and practice of the relationship of party, government, and state. In particular, according to this doctrine, it is necessary to drop the principle of the dictatorship of the proletariat and the connected idea that the communist party must be the only party, a party so identified with the government and the state that alternation of governments becomes inconceivable. Hence, the lesson to be derived from the Soviet experience is a negative one as far as Eurocommunism is concerned. Obviously, this negative evaluation concerns Stalinism as a structural and not only a psychological deviation from socialist ideals. Moreover, the lesson is negative with respect to the present-day structure of the Soviet state and the so-called popular democracies of Eastern Europe.

It is then no wonder that Gramsci's theories have become so popular with the Eurocommunists. His concept of social hegemony insofar as it is possible to oppose this to Lenin's concept of proletarian dictatorship is an invaluable contribution. In fact, if this differentiation with regard to Lenin could be plausibly confirmed, it seems clear that this would open the road for an autonomous European elaboration of Marxism that would not have to depend on or to be concerned with the official Soviet version of Marxism. This is the reason why Eurocommunist theorists insist so much both on the convergence and at the same time on the essential difference between Lenin and Gramsci when it comes to the relationship between dictatorship of the proletariat and social hegemony.

When Gramsci writes about hegemony with reference to Lenin he has in mind its contrast with the dictatorship of the proletariat. In 1926 Gramsci indited his oft quoted passage: "Turinese Communists had faced in concrete terms the question of the hegemony of the proletariat, that is to say, of the social basis of the proletarian dictatorship and of the workers' state."[11] In Gramsci's analysis at that time a strict and necessary link between hegemony and dictatorship of the proletariat becomes evident. The proletarian dictatorship is the purely political form in which the process and the progress of social hegemony are expressed. Dictatorship of the proletariat without social hegemony is blind and purely dogmatic; hegemony without dictatorship is powerless.[12]

Social hegemony is then the ability to be authoritatively present in civil society, to direct social alliances including various social classes, and to offer a concrete social base to the workers' state. In this sense, hegemony has a definite priority in Gramsci's mind insofar as it provides the social content and basic consensus that is expressed at the political level by the proletarian dictatorship. In Gramsci we therefore find two clearly differentiated concepts: the concept of dictatorship and the concept of hegemony. In Lenin, on the contrary, although we may have the substance of the notion of hegemony, it is never spelled out clearly as an autonomous concept. At best, one may contend that the concept of hegemony in Lenin is implicit. He uses it only when he deals with the Revolution of 1905, which he considers a purely democratic, bourgeois revolution. But his concept of hegemony is a reductive one; he conceives of hegemony only in the sense that the organized vanguard of the working class must direct the political action and social initiative of the masses. In other words, hegemony has for Lenin a purely instrumental value and it is not connected with the issue of social consensus as a basic democratic prerequisite. What is most important for Lenin is the conquest of political power and of its central locus, the state machine. And this conquest is the business of professional revolutionists. Social consensus is, of course, of some value, but it is discounted. The professional revolutionists have it, as it were, in their bones.

The problem presents itself in more elaborate terms in Gramsci. According to Gramsci, the supremacy, or the domineering position, or the ruling function of a social group manifests itself in two ways, that is, as a "domination" and as an "intellectual and moral direction." The domination aspect of a social group, or social class, concerns primarily its social "enemies," that is, those rival groups, or classes, whose interests are so sectorial as to be contradictory to the general interest as represented by the working class, or proletariat. These groups are tendentially to be liquidated even with armed force if in the end this is necessary. The hegemonic function concerns, on the contrary, those social groups, or classes, that do not contradict the general interest and with which political alliances and compromises can be made on the way to power. When central political power is finally achieved, the two functions will still be there, that is to say, the workers party will still have to rule, with force when necessary; yet at the same time it will have to direct, that is, to exercise an influence, moral as well as broadly cultural, upon the civil society outside the strictly political institutions. It is important to observe that for Gramsci no basis for legitimation would exist for a proletarian dictatorship unless social hegemony over the society at large already existed. Pure force is for Gramsci unacceptable. Lenin's position is quite different in this respect.

Summing up Gramsci's position we could say: (1) a social group, or class, exercises a function of domination (is in a ruling position); (2) a social group, or class, exercises a directive function or has a broad social influence; and (3) in its social relationships this group, or class, behaves differently depending on whether it deals with socially homogeneous groups, or classes, that do not have contradictory interests or whether it faces groups, or classes, that can be regarded as social enemies in the sense that they have class interests that contradict general, or working class, interests. The test for the historical maturity and the ability of a revolutionary leadership is for Gramsci given by its ability to muster sufficient democratic consensus to isolate in a minority position the social enemies and to get the workers party out of the political ghetto and into a position of social prominence and prestige as a prerequisite for the advent to power. The "small steps" policy in this perspective cannot be equated with the traditional social democratic reformist policy, based on a piecemeal approach. It is, on the contrary, a clearly defined strategy because although the steps, individually taken, might be small once they have been achieved they will never be abandoned; they will function like stepping-stones for the next stages until central power is conquered. In this respect, one might also appreciate the reason why Italian Communists, for instance, have been so eager to secure and administer local municipalities and regional bodies despite their apparent lack of true political power when relevant political decisions have to be made.

Step by Step: To Where?

It is a fact that Italian Communists are very cautious in their political demands. They have organized meetings to study and protect small and middle size enterprises, not to mention the stock exchange. They are moderate and flexible. From the point of view of actual policy, it would be difficult to distinguish them from social democrats. They feel, however, that they are not social democrats because they have not given up their ideology. They might implement the same reformistic pragmatic policies on a day-to-day basis but always with a view toward a grand design of total social change—change that will not come about as the result of a sudden radical move but rather as the cumulative effect of many small steps.

This approach in itself is something quite new in the history of communist parties, but many questions are still open. The present-day position of Eurocommunists might just be the simple recognition that France, Italy, and Spain are in the West, not in the East. Moreover, the Catholic church has deep roots in these societies and the values of the bourgeois revolution cannot be light-mindedly obliterated. If Eurocommunism is going to be something different from pure opportunism, however, theoretical changes and not only adaptations based on expediency seem necessary.

In a few words, are the Western European communist parties ready to complete their "practical revisionism" with a "theoretical correction" of Marxist principles, especially as regards private property, the functioning of the free market, the principle of profit as an indicator of sound management, and the acceptance of NATO? There is room for doubt that Gramsci's teaching can by itself play a decisive role in this "correction," given its ambiguous nature. As Salvadori has pointed out:

> What has happened to Gramsci is that he has become a fountain from which everyone takes whatever water he needs: for some, he is the father of the conception of authentic proletarian democracy; for others, he is a strict Stalinist; for still others, he is a Social-Democrat,

maybe even of a right-wing variety; there are those who consider him an orthodox Marxist-Leninist; while in the eyes of others, to conclude, he is an incorrigible idealist who has never understood anything of Marxism—or just about.[13]

At present, Eurocommunists display a great amount of political realism. In France, they beat the nationalist drum more loudly than anybody else, and they are thus likely to attract former Gaullists. But it should not be forgotten that the reason why the Soviets liked General de Gaulle was his isolationist position within the Atlantic alliance. No Eurocommunist would doubt that NATO constitutes a real problem. The Carter administration essentially shares Kissinger's idea that the entry of communists into the cabinets of Western Europe would have disastrous effects on NATO, if only for the reason that this would greatly rouse suspicions in the United States and especially in the U.S. Congress and this would bring into question the American commitment to NATO.

Italian Communists reply that they are not fighting for a one-party government or even for a two-party government with the Socialist party; they are fighting for a broad coalition government including a party that still is stronger than the PCI, that is, the Christian Democratic party. They feel that this is a rather important guarantee for people who are afraid of what the PCI might decide once in power.

It is clear, however, that with Communists approaching central power in Western European countries NATO is going to have problems. But problems cannot be solved without political change; their solution is possible only if change is skillfully managed. The key issues will probably be the national defense budget, defense policy, and European cooperation in arms procurement and in the organization of defense—in one word, in how to maintain a strategic balance as far as the Mediterranean area is concerned. A new framework of stability for the Mediterranean must be worked out. Eurocommunists could cooperate in establishing this framework.

But does Eurocommunism really exist as a unified practical and theoretical project? Any consideration of Eurocommunism must in the end face this question. What really exists for the time being is a variety of European countries with strong national communist parties that face similar problems. These parties are close to government position and responsibility. This means that they must adjust to a new situation. Their conversion to democratic ways is dictated by the history of their countries and seems now irreversible. But practical expediency does not automatically result in a conscious choice. It is more than ever necessary to press upon these parties the obligation of coherence in order to force them to revise theory in accordance with practice.

Appendix: Data and Remarks on the Rotation and Social Background of Central Committee and Party Directorate Members

1. Of the seventy members of the central committee (CC) elected from the fifth congress (1946), eleven still serve on the two leadership organs: the central committee and the central control commission (CCC). Of these eleven, those who have served continuously since 1946 on the PCI directorate are Longo, Amendola, Pajetta, Berlinguer, and Terracini. In 1946 Berlinguer entered as a full member of the directorate in his capacity as secretary of the youth organization. Columbi no longer serves as CCC president.

2. At the eighth congress two distinct leadership organs were filled (CC and CCC). The quantitative dimension assumed different proportions after the sixth and seventh congresses from that of the fifth. At the eighth congress 110 members were elected to the CC and 45 to the CCC. At every congress the effort to reduce numerically the size of the organs was complicated by the dual difficulty of welcoming the new elements and excluding those elected previously. At the last congress (the fourteenth), 177 members were elected to the CC and 52 to the CCC.

3. Between the thirteenth and the fourteenth congresses the following trade unionists left the CC: Lama, Scheda, Trentin, Garavini, Novella, Donatella, Turtura (the agricultural day laborer trade unionist), Canullo (Rome chamber of labor), Mola (Naples chamber of labor), Pugno (Turin chamber of labor), Francisconi (Inca Foundation), Nella Marcellino (food workers trade unionist), Giunti (CGIL secretary), Scalia (external office), and Rossitto (agricultural day laborer trade unionist). Perhaps even more have left recently.

Trade union leaders had left the directorate even earlier. Novella (who had replaced Di Vittorio when the problem of incompatibility was raised between his trade union and party duties) left the CGIL secretariat but remained in the party and in the directorate until his death. Lama and Scheda, on the other hand, opted for their trade union positions and left the directorate though they remained in the CC. They departed from the CC together with all the other trade unionists when the single CGIL-CISL-UIL federation was formed and they were forced to apply the congress rule against dual roles. The first congress to elect a CC without trade union members was the fourteenth in 1975.

4. The directorate that emerged from the CC of the fifth congress was formed by Communists of the 1920s. They were founding party members: Togliatti, Longo, Roasio, Terracini, Secchia, Noce, Negarville, Montagnana, Colombi, Massola, D'Onofrio,

Scoccimarro, and Roveda. Just a few years after 1921 Li Causi, Giancarlo Pajetta, Spano, Di Vittorio, Grieco, and Novella joined the PCI. Later additions included Sereni, who joined the party in 1927, Amendola in 1929, and Giuliano Pajetta in 1930. Berlinguer represented the FGCI; he joined in 1943.

In the directorate of the fifth Congress, workers and farm day laborers were fairly numerous: nine out of twenty-three. In addition, there were thirty-two out of seventy in the CC. However, the designation "worker" recalls their professional status twenty years earlier. The Fascist repression changed their course of life; they became party functionaries with all the risks that this entailed but also with the probability of cultural advancement. The CC of the 5th congress was also practically closed to those who joined party ranks during the 1930s. It is believed that those few who joined the party since 1930 were Banfi, Concetto Marchesi, Alicata, Reale, Pesenti, Di Benedetto (Palermo), and Di Donato (Bari). Only two members of the CC joined during the 1940s: Berlinguer, who represented the youth organization, and Boldrini, who joined in 1943 and who had acquired political leadership at the 1946 congress on the basis of his role in the organization of the partisan resistance. This was a different path than that followed by the more prestigious Communist leaders who were in a strong political position and who became exponents of the CLN (national liberation committee) and of the armed units.

A very large group of those elected to the CC at the fifth congress had party seniority dating back to the 1920s and were selected for their role in international struggles as well as in the difficult life of clandestineness and emigration. They were internally differentiated according to the influence and varying weight of formative elements that the Communist old guard considered important: work experience with Gramsci, the Turin experience of Ordine nuovo, and the occupation of the factories, direct acquaintance with members of the Communist International, and participation in legal or illegal mass organization in Italy, France, Spain, the U.S., and Africa.

5. The generation of members enrolled in the 1930s began to enter the directorate only at the eighth congress after the Khrushchev report. This includes Ingrao and Alicata. With them entered Romagnoli, who joined only in 1942, but he headed the CGIL together with Di Vittorio. Of the comrades of the 1920s only sixteen remained in the directorate. In addition to these three recruits, two other comrades—Dozza (mayor of Bologna) and Pellegrini (who ran the Veneto), both of whom belonged to the preceding political generation—entered the directorate. Alicata was head of the cultural commission. Ingrao was director of the press and propaganda com-

mission. Of those who had been elected to the fifth congress, some no longer belonged to the directorate: Grieco was dead; Massola left, staying only in the CC; Rita Montagnana stayed only in the CC at first, then in the CCC; and Teresa Noce, secretary of the textile union, continued in the CC when she left the directorate after the sixth congress. Giuliano Pajetta left at the seventh congress and since then has remained in the CC. At the eighth congress Pietro Secchia also left the directorate; in 1954 he had left the organization commission.

In this way the internal struggle between the moderates and the militants within the ruling group was concluded, a struggle that was dealt with summarily in outlining the 1953–1960 period. In the directorate elected by the CC at the eighth congress, workers held five of twenty-one places, all from the original group of nine previously mentioned. It can be concluded that the change at the directorate level after the eighth congress was characterized more by exclusion from it than by new entries into it. Without underrating the personalities of Ingrao and Alicata, it was the reduced weight of Secchia that was the most significant fact. Secchia, however, would remain in the CC until his death.

6. The directorate derived from the ninth congress displayed some novel elements. Several Communists of the 1920s generation departed: Li Causi, Spano, D'Onofrio, Pellegrini, and Dozza. They all would stay in the CC, but with their exclusion from the directorate only eleven of the twenty-three elected to the fifth congress would remain in the national executive organ. Di Vittorio was dead. Romagnoli, who stayed in the directorate, would go on to direct the agrarian commission after leaving the CGIL. The trade unions were now represented by Novella and Scheda. Together with Scheda four new members were elected who were linked to large organizations: Bufalini (Rome), Cossutta (Milan), Alinovi (Campania), and Macaluso (Sicily). Of the newly elected members Scheda was a construction worker. The total number of workers was four out of nineteen.

7. The tenth congress confirmed the previous directorate with few exceptions. These involved Roasio and Alinovi from the crisis ridden Piedmont and Campania organizations. Indeed, Pecchioli, PCI secretary in Turin, took Roasio's post, and Napolitano, PCI secretary in Naples, assumed Alinovi's position. After twelve years a woman returned to the directorate in the person of Jotti, who for some time had directed the women's commission. Worker representation decreased to three out of twenty-one.

8. The eleventh congress of 1966 was held after the death of Togliatti and shortly after the demise of Alicata. Longo, the new secretary general, resolved the problem that preoccupied him by dividing his power with a large number of leaders, making them

comanagers of the party. This move was not toward the old group that had been elected at the fifth congress but rather to the new recruits. The directorate increased to thirty-one members; of these only eight had party seniority dating from the 1920s. Entering the directorate were Chiaramonte (Naples), Di Giulio (central mass work commission), Fanti (Bologna), Lina Fibbi (FIOT [blue-collar workers] Secretary), Galetti (Bologna secretary), Lama (CGIL secretary), La Torre (Sicily), Miana (Emilia region), Natta (cultural commission), Serri (Veneto region), Reichlin, and Tortorella. The workers numbered three out of thirty-one. Occetto entered the directorate as FGCI delegate.

9. Three years later Longo confirmed his method of direction and even argued (it must be remembered) the utility of a certain rotation. But this measure interested the comrades working in organizations on the periphery of the party, not the group that directed the apparat. Thus, several persons left the directorate: Lina Fibbi, Galetti, La Torre, Miana, and Serri. Those who entered were Cavini (Emilia), Galluzzi (Tuscany), Minucci (Turin federation), Romeo (Puglia), Seroni (who had replaced Jotti in the women's commission), and Borghini as FGCI delegate. Lama and Scheda left on the basis of the agreements among trade union organizations to observe the rule on incompatibility. Workers were reduced to three out of thirty.

10. Following Longo's illness, Berlinguer, who had become secretary general, repeated the tactic of involving Communists who worked in important sectors and organizations in the responsibilities of party leadership. At the thirteenth congress thirty members of the directorate were elected by the CC. Of those elected at the previous congress the only one who was not included was Scoccimarro, who had died. All the others were reconfirmed including Galetti and Serri, who had not been confirmed at the earlier congress. Those newly elected were Barca (economic commission), Ceravolo (Liguria), Petroselli (Rome), Quercioli (Lombardy), and Perna (vice-president of the Senate). With the dissolution of the PSIUP, Vecchietti and Valori entered the directorate. Imbeni represented the FGCI in the directorate; Occhetto was a regional secretary in Sicily. Workers numbered five out of thirty-nine.

11. Finally, at the fourteenth and last congress, the original 1946 group was again reduced. Sereni was not reconfirmed, and Novella had died. Likewise not reappointed were Galetti, who went on to the directorate of the League of Cooperatives, Cavina, Galluzzi, Romeo, and Cerevolo. In their places were elected Cervetti (organization commission), Carossino (Liguria region), and Conti (Umbria region president). Imbeni became Bologna secretary; D'Alema was assigned to the FGCI. Workers numbered two out of thirty-three.

In general it will be noted that the directorate tends to have a stable character. Membership in the directorate means (with few exceptions) an operative role in the management of the party. Thus, its real power is very substantial, and the permanent tendency of the directorate is to bypass the CC.

The low representation of workers is generally seen as a serious matter. At the 1969 congress with the "hot fall" still at the gates, the congress agreed to a proposal by Longo to add a group of workers. But this was abortive. During the last eight years, which has seen a new Italian working class identity emerge, there has been little success in the formation of a worker cadre at the top of the PCI. If in the CC a strong turnover has characterized the congresses, in the party directorate the tendency has been toward the disappearance of workers cadres. There has never been adequate research carried out to explain these results.

If the category of worker is taken to include agricultural day laborer, peasant, and sharecropper, from the fifth to the fourteenth congress out of sixty-eight leaders who were members of the directorate, only sixteen belonged to the worker category. The average tenure of the sixteen members of the Communist directorate of worker, peasant, or proletarian origin was 2.6 congresses. The average tenure of the 52 directorate members of intermediary social class extraction was four congresses.

Reliable data are very scarce regarding the presence of workers in the party as members. Tables 1 and 2 are based upon data furnished

TABLE 1. PCI members according to professional status.

STATUS	YEAR* 1954	1962	1972
Workers	40.0%	39.5%	39.5%
Salaried employees	17.8	12.7	8.0
Peasants, sharecroppers	16.1	16.3	9.6
Commercial artisans, small entrepreneurs	5.2	5.2	7.6
Professionals, teachers	0.5	0.6	0.9
Clerks, technicians	2.2	2.2	3.4
Students	0.3	0.5	1.2
Housewives	13.5	12.5	12.6
Others (pensioners, unemployed, domestic workers, etc.)	4.4	9.8	17.2
Rank and file	2,145,312	1,630,550	1,584,147

Source: Enrico Berlinguer, Critica marxista, nos. 5 and 6 (1963); Organization Commission.
*The lowest point in PCI membership occurred in 1969 (1,503,816). Thereafter, a reverse tendency has been seen.

by a study by Enrico Berlinguer and on data provided by the organization commission.

TABLE 2. Social composition of the directorate of the Italian Communist party: Summary table.

CONGRESS	YEAR	WORKERS AND PEASANTS	OTHERS	TOTAL	% WORKERS AND PEASANTS
Fifth	1946	9	14	23	39.13
Eighth	1956	5	16	21	23.81
Ninth	1960	4	15	19	21.05
Tenth	1962	3	18	21	14.29
Eleventh	1966	6*	25	31	19.35*
Twelfth	1969	3	27	30	10.00
Thirteenth	1972	5	34	39	12.82
Fourteenth	1975	2	33	35	5.71

Source: Same as Table 1.

*The social origin of one of the members of the directorate elected to the ninth congress is uncertain. If there is an error, the number of workers would decrease to five and the percentage to 16.12%.

Notes

1. Enrico Berlinguer, *Democrazia e sicurezza in Europa* (Rome: Editori Riuniti, 1973), pp. 5-6.
2. Ibid.
3. Enrico Berlinguer, *Rinascita*, no. 40 (1973).
4. Speech delivered at 1 January 1977 meeting of CPI on the mid-term project for the Italian society in Rome.
5. Ibid.
6. Ibid.
7. Paolo Spriano, *Storia del partito comunista italiano* (Turin: Einaudi, 1973), 5: chap. 15; and Ernesto Ragionieri, *Storia d'Italia* (Turin: Einaudi, 1970).
8. Pietro Ingrao, *Masse e potere* (Rome: Editori Riuniti, 1977).
9. Giorgio Bocca, *Palmiro Togliatti* (Bari: LaPerza, 1967).
10. Interview with Pietro Ingrao, *Rinascita*, 21 January 1977.
11. Cf. Antonio Gramsci, *La questione meridionale* (Rome: Editori Riuniti, 1966), p. 13.
12. Cf. Franco Ferrarotti, "Il principio dell'egemonia sociale," *Giorni presenti*, February 1970, pp. 9-15.
13. M. L. Salvadori, *Gramsci e il problema storico della democrazia* (Turin: 1970), p. 164.

2

The French Communist
Party and the
Popular Union

Jean V. Poulard

The French Communist party (PCF) is the best organized and, in terms of its electoral strength, the largest of all French political parties. For this reason, all analyses of the French political system, more often than not, deal extensively with the problem that this particular party poses. Indeed, no analysis of French politics can avoid attempting to explain not only the presence of what is often called a totalitarian party in that democratic system but also its size, its electoral support.

Whereas most studies of French politics often view the PCF as simply the product of historical events of both an international and a national nature, it has been argued by others that the PCF's existence is to a great extent the result of the French political culture, or of the political, social, and economic cleavages in France, or of the lack of a consensus about the legitimacy of the regime, or, again, of the French class struggle.

Alfred Grosser argues that opposition in France is a way of life. He calls it "a principle of political life"[1] fostered by a centralized system of education. Although Grosser's argument applies primarily to the multiplicity of oppositions in France, this point certainly helps to elucidate the phenomenon of the PCF. For until recently, the PCF has represented paradoxically a certain fusion of authoritarianism and rebellion. Of all the French parties, the PCF, which has shared power for less than two years of its fifty-five-year history, has been the epitome of rigid organization and discipline and of opposition: opposition to governments, opposition to policies, opposition to the regime and the society.

Many analysts have noted quite rightly that the PCF is the focus of a large number of French protest votes. For example, Mattei Dogan contends that although it can be demonstrated that about 49% of French workers vote for the PCF, many among them vote for the party simply to protest.[2] The relative stability of the PCF's electoral support (20- 25% of the French electorate since World War II) can thus be viewed as the result of the continuing effect of the French political culture whose major characteristic is this propensity for opposition, for protest.

In his study of political party systems in Western democracies, Giovanni Sartori finds three different types of party systems in democracies and defines them as (1) simple pluralism; (2) moderate pluralism; and (3) extreme pluralism.[3] It is this third type that is exemplified by France and Italy. Systems of this kind are characterized by a large amount of "irresponsible opposition."[4] In France, the PCF is the largest such irresponsible opposition. The implication of Sartori's study, as far as the PCF is concerned, is quite clear: large communist parties are likely to be fostered by party systems of the extreme pluralism type.

Gabriel Almond, in his extensive study of the appeals of communism in Western democracies, seems to come to the conclusion that political and social cleavages more than economic cleavages explain the presence of a large Communist party in France.

> The Communism of [Western Europe] has often been referred to as "stomach" Communism. If one has to locate it in an organ of the body, it would be more appropriate to call it "heart" Communism, since what is involved in most cases is not so much hunger, as feelings of rejection and neglect at the hand of a society which gives everything to some and very little to the rest.[5]

Suzanne Berger explains the presence of the PCF in France and particularly its size in terms of the French class struggle.

> The imperviousness of the Communist party vote to changes in the fortunes of the international Communist movement and in domestic politics may reflect still another factor: that Communist voters see politics as class conflict and consider their votes primarily as instruments for affecting the balance of social and economic power. One-third of the working class votes Communist, and half of the Communist voters call themselves members of the working class—although only 46 percent of them would be so defined by objective criteria. In fact a Communist voter is more likely than any other voter to define himself in terms of class.[6]

Perhaps the most renowned student of French communism, Annie Kriegel, suggests that the explanation of the PCF must be found in the analysis of international politics: "The centrality of the problem of power is such that it explains why contemporary history is in the first place dominated by the international relations system, its givens, its variables, its virtues and its hazards."[7] To Kriegel, the presence of the PCF in the French political system is above all the result of the creation of the Soviet Union and, later, of Soviet policy. She underlines this point in her monumental work on the origins of communism in France.[8]

It is difficult to say which of these theories or explanations of the PCF's existence is the most accurate. Probably all variables of the French political system plus the international dimension have played a role in the rise and development of the PCF. One thing is certain: any analysis of French politics, as Grosser so aptly put it, "should reserve to the Communists a special place . . . because the behavior of the voters and of the non-Communist parties is in large measure determined by" the party's "existence: because its very presence contributes a certain number of particular characteristics to the political game in France."[9] For this reason, any significant change in the PCF might also change the characteristics of the French political game. If indeed the French Communist party is becoming or, as some have proclaimed, has become "a party like the others," then the characteristics of French politics must be in the process of change.

Has Change Occurred?

The French Communists are unequivocal. On the front page of L'Humanité of August 3, 1971, Laurent Salini wrote: "The French Communist party changes. It has changed. It will change. Precisely where formerly we were accused of sclerosis, of incapacity to adapt, of obsolescence, one must acknowledge that we are evolving. This evolution is in the nature of our party."[10] If this last statement is true, then indeed the nature of the PCF must have changed, for reliable observers and scholars have characterized the PCF for many years, as Salini notes in his article, as a party either incapable of altering or unwilling to change its views and its methods, whether in its internal life or in the French political system. But a note of skepticism is immediately introduced as to the truthfulness of Salini's statement not simply because it comes from a member of the PCF but because of what follows: "[The PCF] would not be the instrument of revolutionary struggle that it is, in its long battle for socialism, if it did not know how to proceed in 'the concrete analysis of the concrete situation.' "[11] The phrase in single quotation marks is an old slogan of the PCF—a slogan that can be found in many reports presented at practically every party congress the PCF has ever held. Nevertheless, it is interesting to note here that the French Communists are now acknowledging in their own daily newspaper that their party can evolve. This is certainly in contrast with the party's steadfastness, which PCF leaders have often professed in the past.

According to public opinion surveys in the 1960s and 1970s, a significant portion of the French people thinks more and more that the PCF has changed.[12] The first important survey on the attitude of the French public toward the PCF appeared in 1964 in the weekly *L'Express*. Then, the conclusion was that the French no longer feared communism.[13] Early in 1966, another French weekly, *Le Nouvel Observateur*, reported the results of a new survey in an article entitled "The Communists Have Changed."[14] Encouraged by these results, the PCF itself engaged in the polling of the French public on its attitude toward the party. And in January 1967, *France nouvelle*, the French Communist weekly, published the PCF's results and an analysis by the Communist sociologist Michel Simon.[15] Simon later collaborated with three other sociologists—Monique Fichelet, Raymond Fichelet, and Guy Michelat—in a survey the results of which were published in the French Communist review *Cahiers du communisme* in December 1967 and January 1968, as well as in a separate pamphlet.[16] This survey indicated that 56% of the respondents felt that the PCF had changed in the past ten years. Another survey published in *L'Express* in March 1968 indicated that 32% of the respondents thought that the PCF was now "a party like the others"—like the other French political parties.[17] A similar survey made by the Société française d'enquêtes par sondage (SOFRES) in late July 1971, again published in *L'Express* in August 1971 and commented upon in *L'Humanité*, indicated that 33% of the respondents believed that the PCF had "changed rather for the better"; 12% responded that the PCF had changed but "for the worse."[18] Many more such surveys were made by different polling agencies. In 1974 a SOFRES poll found that 45% of the French (against 36%) considered the PCF henceforth to be a democratic party that would respect freedom of expression and private property if it came to power.[19]

All these polls are interesting in themselves. However, many of their results are ambiguous or ambiguously stated. This is sometimes the result of the ambiguity of questions,[20] sometimes the result of lack of clarity on the part of data analysts.[21] Much has been made about the results of these surveys—by the French Communists themselves, of course, but also by others who have perceived some signs of change within the party. It is very tempting, indeed, following the saying "Where there's smoke, there's fire," to see in these data a clear implication that the PCF has in fact changed. However, although the results of these surveys have significance, they certainly do not demonstrate that the PCF has changed and even less to what degree it may have changed. They simply demonstrate that the *image* of the French Communist party has changed in the eyes of a significant number of the French people.[22] And it must be added that the polls do not indicate whether their respondents have perceived real changes or have been seduced by a skillful and successful advertising campaign.

Because the public opinion surveys do not really demonstrate change within the PCF, their results are dismissed as unimportant by experienced and serious students of the party, such as Annie Kriegel.[23] This eminent scholar, who was at one time a member of the party, has further concluded that "the PCF can change without changing anything" or that "the PCF changes and changes but remains the same."[24] Moreover, she has explained that the party may introduce changes at its exposed or public level—such as changes in strategy and tactics, acting like a social democratic party, or making "concessions" in the creation of a "program of government" in alliance with the French Socialist party—but at its hidden level, its soul, as she calls it, remain the same.[25]

Many anticommunist observers of French communism have reached similar conclusions. Louis Terrenoire wrote in the Gaullist newspaper *La Nation*: "The Communists . . . remain essentially faithful to themselves. I do not doubt that they would establish a strong state that would appropriate to itself the ways and means of political and economic power and that would revise totally the social contract."[26] And many scholars who have analyzed mostly the exposed level of the PCF affirm the unchanging nature of the party. To be sure, they have looked often at a very telling public side of the party—its relationship with the Soviet Union or the Soviet Communist party. On this particular subject, François Fejtö wrote in 1967: "The PCF is no longer . . . the party of unconditional fidelity, but nobody is asking it to be. It has merely had to adjust its positions to a more subtle comprehensive strategy, which is now determined by the general interests of the Soviet Union and the CPSU."[27] In other words, nothing has changed; the PCF still is *fundamentally* subservient to Moscow as it was forty, thirty, or even twenty years ago. Fejtö reinforces this point by stating another conclusion specifically about the hidden level of the party.

> On the internal plane, the PCF is pursuing . . . two primary and apparently contradictory aims: First, the preservation of the decision-making power and of the totalitarian structures of the party apparatus; and

second, greater participation in the national political game under the auspices of the *"unité de la gauche."*[28]

This point of view about the internal life of the party is confirmed by some former PCF members. After his exclusion from the party at the nineteenth congress of the PCF in February 1970, Roger Garaudy, at one time *the* theoretician of French communism, pointed out that "it is necessary that [the PCF] change not its objectives or its program but its methods of thinking and of acting . . . that its conception of 'democratic centralism' not reduce itself only to one of its components: 'centralism' . . . but that it reestablishes the balance with the other component: 'democracy.' "[29] Thus, as far as Garaudy is concerned, the PCF, fourteen years after Khrushchev's "secret speech," has remained true to the shape it took and the methods it adopted under the aegis of its famous leader Maurice Thorez, one of the most loyal followers of Stalin. And in that sense, the PCF remains what has been called a "Stalinist" party. This is definitely the opinion of Charles Tillon, a longtime party member expelled in 1970: "I believe it to be my duty to say that, despite its new language, the P.C.F. remains Stalinist in its structure as well as in its political strategy."[30]

Following these conclusions, Jean-Francois Revel, the "liberal" political editorialist of *L'Express* (a magazine of the center of the French political spectrum), derides those who think that the PCF has changed: "Because a Communist intellectual, Roger Garaudy, has maintained that the working class is no longer made up sociologically in the same manner as a century ago, he is expelled from the P.C.F.; and we are reduced to welcome as progress the fact that he was able to express himself in a congress before being eliminated."[31]

This lack of progress and change is well suggested again by Kriegel. She states that all one has to do to check the veracity of this point is to look at the background of the new members elected to the PCF central committee at the nineteenth congress of January-February 1970.

Of 95 incumbent members of the central committee . . . 85, that is, 90 percent, were reelected. As to the group composed of the 22 newly elected alternate members of the central committee, not only is its average age 39.7 years . . . which is an extremely high average for entry in the directing organ of a party of militants, but, particularly, it is composed of 85 percent (19 of 22) of men and women who joined the party *before 1953*, that is, before the death of Stalin. . . . Among them, the newly elected member whose *seniority* . . . is the least is nevertheless the holder of a seniority of 12 years. . . . One could not show in a clearer manner that the French Communist party continues to draw its leading cadres from the purest Stalinist generation, that its formation is placed exactly between two time limits: *after* the resistance [World War II] and *before* the XXth congress [of the CPSU].[32]

That is the generation of Georges Marchais, the new secretary general of the PCF.

In *Esprit* of June 1971, the Socialist J.-M. Domenach seems to tackle this problem by asking: "Has the French Communist party changed?" At first glance, he answers that one could say "yes"; but (as Kriegel noted the retention and the election of "Stalinists" to the central committee), he also notes the retention of "Stalinist" methods. On this point he is referring specifically to Tillon's expulsion from the party. Domenach sees in this event a parallel with the elimination of the old Bolsheviks by Stalin in Russia.[33]

In the debate over the evolution of the PCF, this first group, of which only a sample is presented here, often includes people who might be prepared to see some signs of change within the party. On this side of the debate, there are very few who make this claim categorically and without reservation. Kriegel, the contributors to *Le Crapouillot*, and most writers of *Est et ouest* are among the few who assert that the PCF cannot possibly change because that would mean, for all practical purposes, its disappearance from the French political system.

Notwithstanding the sometimes very convincing arguments and documentation offered by the first group of analysts, a certain number of observers and scholars believe, as do many of the French people interviewed by the pollsters, that the PCF has changed.

Harvey Waterman in his book on political change in contemporary France points out what he considers as the most conspicuous changes that one can plainly detect about the PCF:

There have been some changes in party doctrine, as well as in the party's willingness to tolerate disagreement and dilution of the current line. Thus, since World War Two the party has decided that there are separate roads to socialism, found that France will take a peaceful one (considered impossible before the war), accepted the plurality of parties (though those which try to reestablish capitalism after socialism is achieved will not be allowed), and defined the beneficiaries of socialism to include practically everybody: The working class, the non-proletarian salariat, artisans and small businessmen, peasants, . . . even small capitalists.[34]

Waterman's observations about the PCF are sober. For him, the PCF has changed in many ways, as other things have changed. His firmest assertion is that the "French Communist Party has undoubtedly lost its revolutionary fervor and has gradually adapted to the growing consensus in French politics." However, he reminds us that the PCF's "ideological basis remains."

François Borella, a French political scientist, agrees somewhat with Waterman but emphasizes the place of the PCF in the French political system and concludes that "a spectacular evolution took place under the Vth Republic. From 1958-1959, when the P.C. places itself outside of the political system, and against it, to 1971, when the P.C. adopts a program of government, the party has passed from absolute, metaphysical opposition to a functional opposition with nuances."[35] In other words, Borella interprets the evolution of the PCF as its greater and greater "integration" into, or useful participation in, the French political system.

Some scholars go much further in their assessment of the evolution of the PCF. Some go even so far as to state that the party is no longer of the Bolshevik type but has become something akin to a social democratic party.[36] What is meant by a social democratic party is not always very clear. Most analysts of the PCF who use this term do not bother to define it. However, one can assume that what they have in mind when they speak about a social democratic party is a political party that tends to be Marxist in doctrine but quite open to public scrutiny, whose intraparty elections provide a choice of candidates (or of opinions), and whose dissidents are not necessarily expelled from the party or even forbidden to display publicly their divergent views.[37] Domenach, mentioned earlier, is ambivalent in his analysis of the PCF: "One has difficulty imagining a PCF becoming social democratic while remaining Stalinist, and yet it is this feat that it is now accomplishing. Why not? The others hinder it so little."[38] One indeed has difficulty imagining a Stalinist social democratic party! It would certainly be a different kind of social democratic party.[39] Domenach and others, as we shall see later, apparently think it is a possibility.[40] For example, Fejtö, also quoted earlier, seems to believe that the PCF can follow this optional course: "The future is uncertain for the PCF, depending on changes in internal and external circumstances. It could be pushed either into becoming a party of a social democratic type or on the contrary (in the case of radical mass activity) toward the left."[41]

Among the scholars who believe that the PCF has taken a turn toward becoming a social democratic party, the most renowned is Georges Lavau. His theory is presented in a lengthy article that he wrote for a colloquium on French and Italian communism in March 1968. In this article, although Lavau begins by saying that his "study does not pretend . . . to advance an explicit answer to the question: Has the Communist party changed?"[42] he clearly argues that the PCF has indeed changed. The purpose of 'Lavau's essay is to show that the party, far from wanting to destroy the French political system, has in fact integrated itself very well in that system to the extent that it provides some support for it.[43] The party accomplished this by performing the function of *tribune of the plebeians*—a function that "is principally to organize and to defend some plebeian social categories, . . . and to give them a feeling of strength and confidence."[44] Lavau states that the turning point in the PCF's evolution from a revolutionary party to a "tribune" party was the period 1934-1936. He argues further: "Our hypothesis is not that the P.C.F. today has arrived at the same point as the social democratic parties but that since 1936 it has been engaged on the same road."[45] Lavau does not conclude explicitly that the PCF will ever become a social democratic party "like the others," but he clearly implies that it is plausible and probable.

In this debate over the evolution of the PCF, one can distinguish a third position that consists of arguments that the PCF will change or that it is bound to change. More often than not, exponents of this view could be included among those taking the second position, just as the latter are often led to the conclusion that the PCF will change some more. However, it is worth emphasizing this position by presenting it separately.

In 1958 Roy Macridis pointed to important factors that eventually would cause the PCF to change, even though these same factors could then account for the "immobility of" the PCF's "leadership and ideology."[46] In suggesting why the party might ultimately change, Macridis pointed out that

> by appealing to the many predispositions—even if contradictory—of the French and by trying to bring into the party many groups with many and very often contradictory interests, the party has also reached a common denominator. Its own image of its role has changed. If, according to the early post-war slogan, it is a "party to be counted in the millions," it is slowly becoming a captive of the many and diverse forces whose support it has cultivated. It has reached a dead center of compromise and synthesis beyond which there can be no movement in one direction or another without serious electoral, and perhaps organizational and ideological, dislocations. The party is becoming progressively embedded in the social and ideological structure of France, and as a result is beginning to reflect within itself the very contradictions of the French society.[47]

The conclusion is clear. The leadership of the PCF will have to change the ways—and perhaps the organization—of the party because of the gap it will ultimately encounter and recognize between itself and its followers (more exactly, the electorate) of the party. Waterman goes further in this analysis and includes the new *militants* of the party as another factor in future change.

> The newer generation is more "reformist" though still verbally committed to the waging of class conflict and to the dictatorship of the

proletariat as a means of achieving "socialism." It is more willing to "play the game" than are its elders. Despite its ideology, the PCF has in practice become a revisionist group with a still rather inflexible way of going about its revising, and a screen of revolutionary rhetoric which hides the change.[48]

To Waterman, writing in 1968, the change has begun but promises to be more pronounced and evident in the future, a process that will take some time. This is what Maurice Duverger also believes. Duverger, an authority on comparative political parties, now sees a certain development in the PCF and suggests as another factor in future change the evolution taking place in the Soviet Union. Duverger makes his point with an analogy between the party and the Catholic church.

> Léo Hamon . . . has said that the Catholic church itself could not renounce the idea of eternal life. Of course, but it has been quite a while since it gave up establishing the Kingdom of God on Earth in an expeditious manner. It is even renouncing direct conversion of nonbelievers. It thinks that the Kingdom of God will come at the end of the world. But this is far, very far off. Finally, is not the Communist party evolving toward an analogous vision? Things go fast in that respect, even within Catholic Rome. In this fiftieth anniversary of the October Revolution, one has the impression that the Soviet Union still thinks that it animates the world revolution even though it does not imagine that the world revolution will take place tomorrow.[49]

Michel Winock, writing in *Esprit* of May 1970, after Garaudy's expulsion from the PCF, predicted a drastic change in the future for the party.

> It is probable that, although condemned, Roger Garaudy has opened a debate within the Communist party. The pressure of the facts will not fail to broaden this debate. Therefore, it seems doubtful that the P.C.F. can remain eternally the party of a working class the outline and the future of which no longer correspond to the analysis of Marx. It is doubtful that it can remain a party of the Leninist type when Leninism appears more and more clearly as a theory perfectly maladjusted to the times and the places in which we live, a party adopted to the Soviet regime while this regime is progressively losing its mythological attraction in proportion to the extent it reveals itself in our eyes in its true light.[50]

Finally, two French journalists from *Le Monde*, André Laurens and Thierry Pfister, end the introduction to their book *Les Nouveaux Communistes* with the implication that the new generations entering the party are bound to change it and actually have already done so.

> The new Communists are also and above all unknown people . . . these young men with long hair, lying on the grass next to their girlfriends,

who, at the Fête de l'humanité, listen to the speech of Georges Marchais after a rock concert. . . . All have brought something new to French communism. They have given it its own strategy: they have—somewhat—liberalized its methods, adapted its doctrine, and, perhaps, cut the umbilical cord with Moscow.[51]

The PCF and the Soviet Union

In any discussion of the French Communist party—in any discussion of its evolution—one theme is always present: its relationship with the Soviet Union. The perennial question is whether the party, especially since the death of Stalin and the twentieth congress of the CPSU, is still the "Soviet lobby"[52] in France or whether it has "declared" its independence from Moscow. As always, analysts, scholars, journalists, and politicians differ in their conclusions. The French public is also divided. However, according to a poll in December 1970, an increasing number of Frenchmen believe that the PCF is more independent of Moscow than it was earlier. On this point it is interesting to note that opinions on this question varied from one group of respondents to another. Furthermore, the highest percentage of those who believed that the PCF is more independent of Moscow was made up of executives and professionals.

In its explanation *Sondages* does not specify the reasons for the new trend in French public opinion on this question. It simply concludes that the French public believes more and more that "the Communist party in France is less and less the party 'of Moscow' " and that it is "keeping the USSR at a distance."[53]

The magazine *L'Express* comes to the same conclusion: "The evolution of the party is recent. Today, it is a fact: it does not see the need to equate in every case the strategic interests of the Soviet Union with those of the international working class."[54] *L'Express* presents as one example of this evolution a PCF request to Egypt for clemency for accused Egyptian Communists and the sending of a political protest without prior approval (or so it seemed) from the Soviet Union.[55]

Some French Communists themselves of course make it a point to argue that the PCF is not a tool of Moscow.[56] In an interview with *L'Express*, Louis Aragon, the famous French Communist writer, made this interesting remark: "But I would like to call to your attention that the Soviet Union is a country that is under the jurisdiction of a party which is not mine. Me, I am a French Communist."[57]

One of the latest entries on this side of the debate, Laurens and Pfister's *Les Nouveaux Communistes*, points to two major events (among others) as proof of the great change in relations between the PCF and the Soviet Union. The first was the fall of Khrushchev in 1964, to which the PCF responded by sending a delegation to Moscow to ask for an explanation. As the authors queried: "Can one imagine Maurice Thorez speaking to Stalin in this manner and asking him to account for his actions?"[58] And they conclude their version of the event by saying that "all is well that ends well. Nothing has changed, except the nature of the relations between the PCF and the USSR."[59] The second major event was the public disapproval of the Soviet invasion of Czechoslovakia in 1968 on the part of the PCF. Again, Laurens and Pfister argue that

> one should ... give [the PCF] more credit to have, on this point, disassociated itself from Moscow. A glance into the past, looking back on fifty years of allegiance, shows the incongruity, so to speak, of its conduct. Of the diverse visible evolutions in the recent history of the PCF, the one that shows an emancipation in regard to Moscow is the most spectacular. The Communists are themselves astonished by their audacity. They need to digest their conquest.[60]

The PCF's unprecedented position and action of August 21, 1968, is then considered as a watershed in the relations between the PCF and the Soviet Union. This event has led not only to the conclusion by many that the PCF is now quite independent of Moscow but also to a search for the reasons why such an unexpected eventuality could have taken place. In this endeavor, four main theses have been proposed: (1) changes in the international communist movement since 1960; (2) changes in international relations (the "end" of the cold war); (3) the renewed desire on the part of the PCF for another attempt at taking part in a governmental coalition; and (4) the character and background of the new PCF leaders and membership.

Many observers of the PCF, including the most knowledgeable and assiduous among them, remain unconvinced. Regardless of what happened in 1964 or 1968, for these commentators the dictum that has been attributed to Guy Mollet, "les communistes ne sont pas à gauche mais a l'Est,"[61] still is the basic truth about the PCF.

As far as the writers and editors of *Le Crapouillot* are concerned, the party has always been, still is, and always will be a tool of Moscow: "[The French Communists] drape themselves at times in the French flag. But they remain the party of unconditional fidelity to the USSR. They readily take themselves for the defenders of order. But their order is that which holds sway in Prague or Budapest."[62] Jacques Soustelle, writing in that same magazine, concluded that "whatever the problem posed to the conscience of the militants, it is ultimately Moscow which lays down the law."[63] Kriegel completely concurs with this opinion. In a lecture at the University of Chicago, she spoke about the events surrounding the 1970 PCF congress, at which the question of replacing the incapacitated Waldeck Rochet came up. Unlike Thorez, Waldeck Rochet had not designated his successor and was unable to do so. Kriegel related that at the first meeting of the central committee on the question everyone felt Marchais was the likliest candidate, but no one dared to nominate him. Finally, someone proposed Marchais, who was the representative of the PCF in Moscow and Perhaps vice versa.[64] This anecdote exemplifies perfectly the reasons behind Soustelle's conclusion.

On the question of Marchais's nomination as acting secretary general of the PCF, Louis Couturier, although less specific than Kriegel, supports her anecdote: "The election of Marchais to the top post, in spite of his empty past, [reveals] the mechanism of the rise of the cadres in the PCF and the immense influence that the Soviet *still* possess in their selection."[65] Before his rise to the top, Marchais was secretary for the party's organization, a post considered to be a stepping-stone to that of secretary general.

One can distinguish four hypotheses about the leverage the Soviet Union has over the French Communist party. First, there is the moral suasion that the Soviet Union seems to have over the PCF. This moral suasion is explained by the very strong psychological attachment of the PCF to the "motherland of socialism." Second, there is the financial pressure that the Soviets could eventually apply in case the PCF should cause displeasure in Moscow. This, it is hypothesized, results from the supposedly great reliance of the PCF on Russian funds. Third, perhaps as a result of the first two hypotheses, the leaders of the Soviet Union have acquired the ability to control individual careers within the PCF and are thus able to select and place at the top of the French party the most complaisant people. Finally, perhaps as a consequence of all the above, the Soviet approval ultimately is required for the legitimization of the PCF's leaders, policies, and actions.

If these hypotheses have some validity, it can be argued that they are subject to change, especially should the PCF come to share or to control power in France. Certainly, the financial dependence on Moscow, if it is now crucial, would practically vanish. Soviet control over PCF personnel might continue but might also require, as the case of Czechoslovakia demonstrates, drastic Soviet action. The effectiveness of Soviet leverage would definitely change and probably decrease. It can also be argued that such a development might take place if the PCF seriously attempted to gain power in France through coalition tactics—that is, by following the rules of the game of the present French regime. It could be argued further that Soviet leverage on the PCF might decrease or might have already decreased because of certain changes in the USSR itself, as well as a new presentation of that country in the PCF press.

Some changes have occurred already. One central fact is the unprecedented criticism of the Soviet Union on the morning of the Warsaw Pact invasion of Czechoslovakia in 1968. Therefore, it is appropriate to quote the spectacular PCF editorial on this point.

> Some very grave events are taking place in Czechoslovakia. Soviet, Bulgarian, Polish, Hungarian troops and troops from the Democratic Republic of Germany have entered the entire Czechoslovak territory last night.
>
> The political bureau of the French Communist party, which has positively stated its great satisfaction following the Cierna and Bratislava meetings and their positive conclusions, expresses its surprise and its reprobation following the military intervention in Czechoslovakia.
>
> In the last period, the central committee of the French Communist party has specified that it considered that the problems arising between communist parties had to be examined and resolved by fraternal discussions during bilateral and multilateral meetings, respecting both the sovereignty of each country and the free determination of each party, and conducted in the spirit of proletarian internationalism.
>
> Our party, which had expressed its preoccupation with certain aspects of the Czechoslovak reality, had equally asserted that it behooved the Communist party of Czechoslovakia to act against the antisocialist elements in order to preserve and enlarge the socialist conquests.
>
> The French communist party has never stopped struggling in this sense by making known its opposition to any military intervention coming from the outside. . . .
>
> The political bureau has decided to call an extraordinary session of the central committee.[66]

Considering the past positions of the PCF during the Soviet armed repressions in Berlin in 1953, in Poland, and especially in Hungary in 1956, one must admit that this is a drastic change. The central question here is what led the PCF leaders to write such an editorial and to decide to publish it on the front page of their most widely read publication. We know, and they knew, that whenever they wholeheartedly supported similar Soviet actions, such as in Hungary in 1956, the losses to the party in membership and electoral support were minor and easily recuperated in a matter of weeks or months.[67] The explanation that the PCF was then seeking in earnest to regain an active role in French politics via some sort of agreement with the French Socialists is not very satisfying. The Communists' "ulterior" motives would still be questioned, and they were. So, why this change in attitude? Why take the risk not only of angering the Soviet Union but maybe of alienating a great many members of the party?[68]

Many factors were probably involved in the taking of this decision, not the least of which was the personality of Secretary General Waldeck Rochet. However, a good case can be made to show that one of the major factors for the action of the PCF leaders was their assumption that the party membership in general would accept this stand, if not expect it.[69] For example, five months before the invasion, a PCF cadre confided to *L'Express:* "Even if Dubček, himself outflanked on his right, called upon Soviet tanks, we could not accept it."[70] And a majority of the party membership did not accept the Soviet invasion. Although certain older members disagreed openly with the decision to criticize the USSR, most approved it. Probably many shared the feeling expressed to Denis Lacorne by a Communist municipal official: "Là j'ai été très heureux quand ils ont pris position contre l'intervention. . . . Là j'estime que le parti a fait quelque chose de très bien."[71]

During the 1960s it was on the subject of the Soviet standard of living and the quality of life that *L'Humanité* demonstrated its greatest shift in the depiction of the USSR. In their attempt at presenting the truth, the articles falling into this category paint a most unflattering picture of the motherland of socialism. Since this turnabout, articles dealing with wage increases, for example, go beyond the mere reporting of such news. Here is an example:

> One of the last acts of the Soviet government for the year 1968 was the decision . . . to increase the wages of the construction workers. This increase will be on the average of 25 percent. . . .
> An official communiqué explains that the decision has a goal notably to promote . . . the reduction of delays and . . . the amelioration of construction.[72]

This particular article thus informs the reader that the Soviet Union actually uses wages as incentives (as is done in capitalist countries) and that construction in the USSR is neither all that rapid nor that good. A similar article published in January 1969 dealt with the increase in the average Soviet monthly wage and mentioned that "paid vacation, which was for certain categories twelve days per year, has been increased to fifteen working days."[73] To the French worker, who has been getting a month of paid vacation per year since the late 1950s and who practically lives the rest of the year waiting for his next summer vacation, this development must not have been very impressive. The article also pointed out that many consumer items were still not available in quantity in the Soviet Union.[74]

Perhaps the most interesting article on the Soviet standard of living appeared in two parts in October 1971: "Vivre à Moscou—où en est le bien-être des soviétiques en 1971?"[75] is a model of objectivity compared to previous pieces in the PCF daily, and for this reason it deserves more than a passing remark. The article begins by asking: "Is the standard of living of the Soviets lower than that of the French or the English? If yes, does the first increase faster than the others? Has the standard of living in general reached a threshold in the USSR, or is it progressing more slowly than required?"[76] These questions are interesting, and the fact that they appear in *L'Humanité* at all is in itself an event. The article, however, does not answer them directly—obviously because the answers cannot be favorable, especially if one takes into account the information reported. Thus, much of the report, and especially its second part, is devoted to the difficulties of comparing one standard of living to another. The author, Max Léon, puts it this way: "To evaluate the standard of living of a population is almost as difficult as to weigh a soul."[77] This is again taking the easy way out—an apology. The implication to the French reader, however, is rather clear: he is better off living in France than he would be in the Soviet Union.

Although the article does not present conclusive answers to the questions it initially asks, it does *explicitly* give some astonishing (for *L'Humanité*) information about the USSR: (1) the USSR is not a paradise; (2) some buildings are indeed badly built; (3) many consumer goods are difficult to obtain, causing long lines in stores; (4) there are "criminals" in the USSR—to be sure, only traffickers in dollars or black marketeers or cab drivers cheating their company; (5) boots are expensive (almost half an average monthly salary); and (6) there are islands of poverty in "certain sectors of services and industry." Perhaps the most devastating piece of information in this list is the fact that there is a black market in the USSR. To Frenchmen, a black market recalls life during the last world war. Léon writes:

> For example, theater tickets for certain performances are resold for a very high price. *Idem* for certain cosmetics from Paris or, for a time, for nylon shirts and Italian shoes. The taxicab driver lets himself be tempted—but not always—and charges a second and a third customer, each paying the total of the cost of the drive shown on the meter.[78]

The second part of the article, which is less devastating to the Soviet Union, is devoted mostly to problems of comparison and evaluation of what Léon calls the "tone" of the standard of living. An illustration of what he means by this term is given: a large picture, covering one-fifth of a page, of a Russian couple kissing! The reader might wonder whether this kind of tone is peculiar to the Soviet Union. Actually, the photo and its caption seem to suggest that things are not all that bad in the Soviet Union; people still manage to love each other.

This part of the article also quotes extensively from a Soviet statistical handbook. But, as Léon demonstrates, the Soviets have far to go to reach the standard of living of the French.

> In the great centers especially, the housing shortage remains despite the accelerated construction at the rate of two million apartments a year and of more than a hundred thousand in Moscow. . . . Numerous goods of great consumption and certain foodstuffs are sometimes lacking in the state stores. The number of Soviets who covet a car grows larger. The disposable funds of families rise . . . yet the Volga plants making the Fiat-Jigouli will not operate at full capacity for a year or two (600,000 cars a year). [79]

In view of the fact that this unflattering article on the Soviet Union was published shortly before a state visit to Paris by Brezhnev, one must surmise that the readers of L'Humanité must have been rather perplexed.[80]

As far as individual freedom in the Soviet Union is concerned, L'Humanité on the whole continues to say that it does exist and that it is perhaps greater there than anywhere else. However, the subject is usually discussed only in response to attacks on the USSR by the "bourgeois" press. For example, L'Humanité on August 31, 1965, ran the headline "Are There Any Unemployed in the Soviet Union?" and counterattacked the "discovery" by the Reuters agency that unemployment in the USSR could be estimated at 20%.[81] In this article the PCF daily also emphasized that Soviet workers could move freely from one job to another. And it added: "Ils ne s'en privent pas."[82] However, there are many articles, especially in the late 1960s and early 1970s, that reveal that at least one freedom, that of the press, is rather limited in the Soviet Union. L'Humanité at times is critical.

> The magnificent exploit of the American cosmonauts [Apollo 8] captivates the Soviets more and more. . . .
> The press, however, remains excessively prudent and, aside from the commentaries of the academician Petrov . . . it limits itself more often than not to brief information from the agency Tass. . . .
> In its daily news, television itself reduces the news from Cape Kennedy to brief bulletins.[83]

The PCF daily even went so far as to print a letter from a party member that divulged the fact that during the invasion of Czechoslovakia, L'Humanité was not allowed in the Soviet Union.[84]

In the domain of Soviet morality and justice, sometimes hard to distinguish from the question of individual freedom, during the 1960s and early 1970s L'Humanité several times openly criticized the Soviets. The most notable instances have involved Soviet Jews. After the Kiev publication of an illustrated pamphlet by Tropline Kichko, Judaism Undisguised, the PCF daily took exception: "The presentation, if not the content, of this pamphlet, is susceptible to fueling anti-Semitic hatred. It is, in fact, illustrated with several malevolent caricatures that tend to arouse sentiments of contempt."[85] In December 1970, during the Leningrad trial of Soviet Jews who had attempted to hijack a plane to Israel, the PCF daily regretted the conditions under which the trial was held (behind closed doors) and the severity of the sentences, two of which were capital. When these sentences were commuted by the Soviet Supreme Court, *L'Humanité* informed its readers that the PCF had interceded with Moscow in favor of the defendants.[86] Thus, as Kriegel observed, the PCF and *L'Humanité* were at least in this case repudiating an official institution of the Soviet state—its justice.[87]

In 1968, *L'Humanité* indicated its displeasure with Soviet justice in reporting (to be sure in a very small article) the trial of Yuli Daniel, his wife, and four others for demonstrating against the invasion of Czechoslovakia. The PCF daily reported:

> According to the agency Tass, they are accused of "having attempted to attract the attention of passers-by" and of having "disturbed traffic on Red Square, hindered the tourists visiting the center of the Soviet capital, and made difficult access to the museum located in the old Church of the Blessed Basil." The trial is supposed to last three days. The accused could get a sentence of three years in prison.[88]

Two days later, *L'Humanité* reported, again in a very small article, the result of the trial. The headline stated: "Severe sentences for the five Soviet citizens tried in Moscow," and the article reiterated the accusation of "having disturbed the public peace on Red Square."[89] The sentences ranged from two and one-half to five years of exile ("not in a resort") and three years of prison for one defendant. Nothing was said about Yuli Daniel, and there was no editorial comment. However, the simple publication of this information and the PCF's judgment on the sentences indicated by the words *dures condamnations* ("severe sentences") demonstrated again the PCF's attempt to be more truthful about the Soviet Union and its reluctant disapproval. At any rate, the reader could now at least compare Soviet justice and freedom to French justice and freedom. Again, the conclusion was bound to be unfavorable to the USSR.

These developments in the PCF are recent and have no precedent in the history of the PCF. There is no need here to demonstrate how the PCF and its press, from the birth of the party in 1920 to the 1960s, unfailingly supported in every way Soviet policy, even at the time of the greatest shock of all, the Nazi-Soviet nonaggression pact of 1939. In 1956, the PCF even had great reservations about the policy of de-Stalinization[90] and took a long time to tackle the problem it posed. Moreover, in that same year, during the rebellions of Poland

and Hungary, the party and its press were in full support of Soviet actions. It was, then, only in 1964 that the PCF press demonstrated that the PCF no longer felt bound to support, without question or explanation, all Soviet moves that had possible international repercussions.

On October 14, 1964, Khrushchev was abruptly relieved of his functions in the USSR. The leadership of the PCF, headed by Waldeck Rochet, decided to go to Moscow to ask for and receive an explanation.[91] After the trip, *Les Cahiers du communisme* reported:

> For the French Communist party, which does not allow any outside interference in its own affairs, it was not in any way an intervention in the internal life of the Communist party of the Soviet Union, which, like any other party, regulates itself in full independently. Because if we speak of autonomy of the parties, is it not logical and reasonable that we recognize it in practice for all, including of course for the one that has the heaviest responsibilities?
>
> ... This is why, as Waldeck Rochet has emphasized in front of the press, for us the question cannot be to approve or disapprove the decision of October 14, which belongs to the central committee of the Communist party of the Soviet Union and to it alone.[92]

Although the PCF here attacks any implications which might bring accusations that it is interfering with other communist parties' internal affairs, the impression given to the reader by its explanation is that, nevertheless, the French party would like to know and feels it should be told what is going on in the CPSU—the party with "the heaviest responsibilities"—the party whose moves might have a great influence on the activities and the life of the PCF.

It is perhaps because of this new attitude on the part of the PCF that, barely four years later, it took the unprecedented step of publicly disagreeing with the Soviet Union. The Soviet invasion of Czechoslovakia, unlike the removal of Khrushchev, was probably not a surprise to the PCF leadership since Waldeck Rochet had, prior to it, traveled to Moscow, Warsaw, and Prague, freely giving his advice. The reason for these extensive travels was his fear of another Hungary; it later became clear that his purpose was to help avoid military intervention in Czechoslovakia.

The now famous PCF reprobation of the Soviet Union's action published in *L'Humanité* on August 22, 1968, stunned everybody, especially members and followers of the party, although some have argued that this actually was a mild gesture, as demonstrated by the later position of the PCF on the subject. It is true that the PCF press emphasized that this disagreement did not mean "anti-Sovietism" and kept reminding its readers of the deep-down goodness of the USSR, which had, after all, practically single-handedly liberated Europe from nazism. It is also true that the PCF press showed a certain satisfaction with the "normalization" of the situation in Czechoslovakia in the following months and blamed Garaudy for his continued and "loud" (that is, public) criticism of the Soviet action. However, mildly or not, the PCF had publicly pointed its finger at the Soviet Union; for the first time, it had clearly said on the front page of *L'Humanité* that it "disapproved" of the Soviet Union because it was not behaving according to the norms of interparty relations.

France nouvelle, the PCF central committee weekly, in a sense went even further in censuring the Soviets, accusing the Soviet leaders of lying.

> Let us say right away, so that there may not be any equivocation on this subject, that if the presidium of the Czechoslovak party or the government had considered the situation to be such that they were losing control of Czechoslovakia and if they had called upon the military aid of the brother socialist countries to forestall the counter-revolution, we would not have hesitated one moment to approve an intervention under such conditions. . . .
>
> But we are compelled to observe that neither the leadership of the party nor the government nor any authority democratically elected and responsible to millions of Czechoslovak citizens has admitted either before or after the intervention that the activities of the forces hostile to socialism, whose existence and dangers were nevertheless recognized, constituted an insurmountable counterrevolutionary menace. . . .
>
> Five countries . . . took the initiative to cross the Czechoslovak borders, coming from the outside and without the formal accord of the legal authorities of Czechoslovakia. Today, they are finally forced to recognize that indeed there had not been such an accord.[93]

The PCF has often reiterated the theme of its independence, which figured in an article about Jeannette Vermeersch's resignation from the central committee.

> The party has reaffirmed plainly, at all times, its desire to maintain and to reinforce its friendly relations with the CPSU. This desire that animates us *does not preclude a critical spirit;* it does not mean that *we must approve everything.* This would be, in fact, a form of subordination that does not belong to a real friendship. . . .
>
> In the communist movement, one cannot accept conceptions that would lead to an alignment, to a fictitious unity as dangerous as it would be paralyzing, and that carried to the extreme could lead to the idea that there can be a *party guide.* . . . Independent activity is for each party an . . . essential condition.[94]

In the same issue of *L'Humanité*, the PCF leaders went even further in their description of what should be the relationship or position of their party in regard to the CPSU and its policy. And here, unlike what happened after Khrushchev's dismissal, it made or rather underlined its criticism of the CPSU, which was already rather clear from its reprobation of the invasion of Czechoslovakia.

> Some comrades are of the opinion that any difference with the CPSU is inadmissible and challenges the fundamental solidarity of our parties. This follows an erroneous conception of the relations of friendship between brother parties. *No party is infallible;* no party is, then, safe from an error of method or analysis.[95]

L'Humanité also made an unprecedented direct attack on communist propaganda: "The idea, which some comrades hold, that the intervention was necessary, inevitable, is given support by propaganda material coming from socialist countries."[96] From then on, the readers of *L'Humanité* would be warned not only about the lies of the bourgeois press but also about those coming from the communist world. In light of the history of the PCF, this was a remarkable development.

These remarks about Soviet policies appeared in the PCF press in 1968. Subsequently, of course, things have been much more subdued. Perhaps this is the result of the replacement of Waldeck Rochet by Georges Marchais at the helm of the PCF—Marchais, the man supposedly chosen by Moscow. *L'Humanité*, in other areas of Soviet policy, continued to support the CPSU, especially in its dispute with China. And when Garaudy, under attack, was allowed to publish an article in *L'Humanité* on January 2, 1970, before the nineteenth PCF congress, one paragraph and part of one sentence, particularly critical of the Soviet Union and of its policies in Czechoslovakia, were deleted. *L'Humanité*, however, mentioned that short deletions were made of "certain passages of his article [that] were in contradiction to the norms that govern relations between brother parties."[97] It is now clear that the PCF wants the Czechoslovakian chapter to be closed.

However, *L'Humanité* again took exception to the Soviet Union, which, as it had done in 1965, seemed to interfere with the French presidential elections of 1974. Before the second round of that election, the Soviet ambassador to France visited candidate Giscard d'Estaing (then minister of finance) ostensibly to discuss Franco-Soviet economic relations and trade matters. *L'Humanité* declared the next day that "the initiative of the ambassador from the USSR to France is ill-timed. It is all the more regrettable in that it has created a pretext for political speculation that represents this as being a display of preference for the right-wing candidate." Although this reproach might be considered mild, it nevertheless is still critical. And once more, along with what was written during that "long" period in the second part of 1968, it must have been engraved in the minds of PCF members and supporters.

"Democratization" within the PCF?

It was primarily during the tenure of Waldeck Rochet as secretary general of the PCF that the party developed a new image and first expressed a new attitude toward the Soviet Union. It was also primarily during Rochet's tenure that much was said and written about a "liberalization," a "democratization," of the PCF—a change in its ways and in its internal life.

Rodger Swearingen, in the preface to *Leaders of the Communist World*, remarked:

> The truth seems to be that the man matters; ideology notwithstanding, each Communist Party reflects in its leadership two important features: first, that power retreats into the inner councils of ruling bodies until, in a dictatorship, it finds its natural expression in the supreme concentration of power in one pair of hands: and second, that each leader embodies the traditions and specific gravity of the country it rules.[98]

The shift in the leadership of the PCF in May 1961, when Rochet was made deputy secretary general to take over much of the burden from the aging and ailing Thorez, and developments after the latter's death in 1964 constituted perhaps the most momentous changes within the PCF since 1945. It is not clear why Thorez chose Rochet as his successor. There is no direct evidence bearing on this question. Perhaps it was because of Rochet's "Stalinist" past or because of his unshakable fidelity to the party and its leader. Or perhaps Thorez saw in him the best man to assume the role of a "Pope of transition" between the "Stalinist" period of the PCF and the party's internal "liberalization." The secret seems to be gone with Thorez. At any rate, Thorez chose to pass on his legitimacy to Rochet. And Rochet, as Kriegel has remarked, became or started a "phenomenon" within the party. In either case, it seems "the man mattered."

It is now clear that this supposedly mediocre man, Waldeck Rochet, this strict follower of Moscow's orders, this true Bolshevik, was also, as even Claude Harmel, one of the staunchest critics of the PCF, admits, "the most 'liberal' (if one dares to debase this beautiful word) of the leaders of the PCF."[99] It is also clear that he tried to accomplish a great deal for the PCF during his relatively brief tenure. His accomplishment, his great design, as Kriegel puts it, was to rid the PCF of its "Stalinism,"[100] to change the party, to free it from the old ways. Rochet had a taste for collective work and for confrontation, and according to Laurens and Pfister this led him to introduce a degree of freedom in "discussions and doctrinal research that introduced a new outlook in all the organizations of the party."[101] He wanted to rejuvenate the party and to this end attempted to return to the political bureau the essential role that the secretariat had for so long assumed.[102]

His great design, again according to Kriegel, had three major components: (1) an international component in which the PCF would become a mediating force in the quarrels of the communist world, a "force of political negotiation," taking a position akin to that of the Italian Communist party and thus becoming a new center, a regional pole; (2) a national component in which the party would adopt a new thesis about socialism—that of the plurality of parties under a socialist regime; and (3) a third component tying the two together that would transform the PCF from "objective ally" of Gaullism to its true opponent, united with the rest of the French Left.[103]

Kriegel comes to the conclusion that Rochet did not succeed. But in comparing him to two other reformers of the communist world, Khrushchev and Dubček, she suggests that he went much further than they did. The PCF, then, as did Prague, had its spring.

Since 1964, several important developments have taken place within the party that seem to have had an impact on the internal life of the PCF—leading to what one might call, for want of a better word, a "loosening up" of old ways. One can point to four such developments: (1) the publication of new statutes for the party in 1964; (2) the increase in internal discussion of issues with some perceptible tolerance of a greater amount of dissension than earlier; (3) the "modernization" of the party; and (4) the production of new slogans. Each of these developments will be investigated in turn.

Compared to the 1945 statutes, those of 1964 are more numerous—fifty-eight articles instead of thirty-seven—and are much more specific on certain points such as the principle of democratic centralism and the rights and duties of party members. Much of their content is new. As a matter of fact, the rewriting of the statutes in 1964, as Guy Rossi-Landi has remarked, was "a considerable event" for the new statutes were not a "simple revision of some articles, but entirely new texts."[104]

In these new texts, one can point to three interesting and important changes. First, there is an eight-page preamble that states the composition, functions, goals, and major principles of the party. Therein, the PCF asserts that it *is* the party of the French working class and that it intends to act for the ultimate triumph of socialism, of communism. However, the preamble, although mentioning that the PCF is the heir of the "democratic and revolutionary traditions of the French people," does not clearly say that the PCF is a party dedicated to revolution. Indeed, the word "revolution" is not used at all. The goal of the party is simply stated thus: "The French Communist party has as its fundamental goal the transformation of capitalist society into a collectivist or communist society, a fraternal society without exploiters or exploited."[105] The preamble goes on to explain how this transformation will take place, yet it does not say what will be the prime mover of the process. Actually, the text suggests that the primary goal of the party is reformist in nature. It implies evolution rather than revolution.

> The French Communist party, without ever losing sight of the fundamental goal of its action, acts to defend and enlarge the liberties, the rights, the advantages, even partial, conquered by the people of France during its age-old struggles. It directs the struggle of the working class, of the working peasantry, and of other working strata, in support of their economic, social, and cultural demands, in order to impose any measure, any democratic reform ameliorating their living conditions.[106]

Nowhere is there even a hint that the PCF will act beyond the bounds set by the rules of the present French regime. Quite the contrary, the preamble declares that the party "struggles to establish the most advanced *possible* democratic regime under the conditions of the capitalist system."[107] Thus, the opening section of the statutes makes clear that the PCF now believes firmly in the possibility of a peaceful way to socialism.

The second important aspect of these new statutes consists of the guarantees given by articles 12 and 13 to party members against unjustified sanctions. All sanctions, which range from internal censure to expulsion from the party, must be ratified by the section committee and the federal committee—the intermediary organizations between the cells and the central committee. Article 12 further requires all expulsions to be ratified by the central committee. Article 13 adds that "any organization, any member of the party liable to be penalized must be informed of the charges made against him and must have the opportunity to justify himself. Appeal to the superior bodies, including the central committee, is permitted in all cases."[108] These guarantees did not exist in the 1945 statutes, and they certainly limit arbitrariness within the party. (The Garaudy affair of 1970 demonstrated that this article of the PCF statutes is indeed operative. In his battle within the party over the question of Czechoslovakia, Garaudy was able to justify himself first in *L'Humanité* and then at the nineteenth party congress of February 1970. Of course, this did not prevent his expulsion from the party later that year, but one must admit that the party went to great lengths to show that its decision was not arbitrary. Indeed, for the first time in the PCF's history, a dissenter was allowed to speak from the podium of one of the party's great shows—its congress.)

A third important change has to do with the conduct of elections within the party. To begin with, articles 22, 30, and 35 include the principle that the election of delegates to superior bodies must depend on the number of members in the lower organizations. In other words, the principle of proportional representation was adopted. However, each article mentions that the total number of delegates is fixed by the section committee, the federal committee, or the central committee. Nevertheless, these articles insure more representative assemblies. To be sure, this change does not seem so far to have made a great difference in the internal politics or policies of the party, and it does not prevent the national party congress from having a configuration of delegates whose mean age is deliberately lower than that of the total party membership.[109]

Article 44 institutes for the first time the secret ballot for the election of candidates to the leading organizations at the three levels—that is, the section committees, federal committees, and central committee. This is a novelty for the PCF. However, there is a catch: although article 43 says that all organizations of the party can propose candidates for the superior leading organizations, article 44 states that

> all these candidates are examined by a commission elected for this purpose by the section conference, the federal conference, or the national congress of the party. The commission for candidacies proposes the candidates the most likely to insure good leadership in a number equal to that of members to be elected to the section committee, the federal committee, and the central committee. The commission gives the reasons for this choice to the conference or the congress, which discusses it. The election takes place by secret ballot. All candidates receiving more than half of the votes cast are proclaimed elected.[110]

Asked about this strange procedure, a party *responsable* from Paris answered: "We thought that [the secret ballot] could contribute to the development of democratic life in the party and, in particular, with regard to the election of the leaders."[111] This was, of course, the explanation given by Marchais at the seventeenth congress of the PCF.[112] However, this party *responsable* explained further that after the candidacies are announced by the commission

> it explains the reasons why such a comrade is presented . . . and another is not. Discussions always begin, but since they are discussions about names, about persons, these discussions are always difficult and do not necessarily go very far because one does not dare to say such and such a thing about such and such a comrade. And experience has often shown that certain reservations of some comrades were expressed neither in the discussions nor during the public vote. And, because of this, one had in the leading organizations some comrades who were elected but who were not elected with the full consent of all the section members—it was the same at the levels of the federation and of the central

committee. And thus the desire . . . for the possibility that all reservations be expressed at the elections through the secret ballot.[113]

Although this explanation makes some sense, the change is less
dramatic than it seems at first glance: elections are still not true
contests. One could thus conclude, as Rossi-Landi has, that "the
reform is less considerable, that if, for example, the congress voted
on all candidates . . . there would be then a choice among several
names." Under present "conditions one does not clearly perceive the
practical effect of this change."[114] It is in a sense the institutionali-
zation of Michels's iron law of oligarchy.[115] However, one should
not dismiss completely the novelty of the secret ballot as simply a
superficial sign of democratization given to potential allies of the
PCF in French electoral politics. One can argue that it shows a new
interest on the part of the PCF leadership in what the party members
at large think and desire (this new interest has been demonstrated
also by the public opinion polls the PCF itself sponsored—polls
containing questions about the party).[116]

What has actually happened within the PCF? What has actually
changed in the internal life of the party in the 1960s? A Parisian
responsable interviewed in 1968 stated that to him the most striking
change within the PCF over the preceding ten years was the increase
in discussion. He emphasized that there actually was a stimulating
debate within the party, especially over the question of France's way
to socialism.[117] Laurens and Pfister present a similar assessment:
"There was never so much talk inside the party. Since 1968, discussions have been proceeding unabated in the cells: what to think of
the attitude of the party during May of that year? of Garaudy's
theses? of the military intervention in Czechoslovakia? what to
answer to noncommunists on these delicate subjects?"[118] Unlike the
debate called for by Thorez in his famous series of articles in
L'Humanité during August and September 1931, the purpose of
which was merely to heap discredit upon the Barbé-Célor fraction
within the party,[119] the present debate is genuine, Garaudy's expulsion from the party notwithstanding.[120]

To be sure, debate within a party—even if the debate be genuine—does not necessarily mean resolution of differences on certain
issues. However, if the debate is to continue or continues for any
length of time, it does mean that divergence of views is tolerated. In
other words, a certain amount of dissidence must be tolerated among
the members of a group. And much of the evidence points to the fact
that this has been the case within the PCF since the mid-1960s.

Although it is true that during Waldeck Rochet's relatively short
active tenure as secretary general of the party many members were
expelled, no *grandes affaires* occurred. Indeed, it has been suggested

that if Rochet had remained at the helm, Garaudy might not have been expelled from the party.

It is a fact that since the sixties dissidence within the PCF has been much more widespread than ever before. This dissidence has taken different forms and has had different causes. Accordingly, the leadership of the party has dealt with it in different ways. However, what has been done clearly demonstrates a new tolerance, even if ultimately the dissidents were dealt with severely, like the radical student wing of the party, and finally expelled, like Garaudy.

Four major examples of dissidence have occurred: (1) that of the radical student wing; (2) that of Garaudy; (3) that of Louis Aragon; and (4) that of Jeannette Vermeersch. These examples are widely different as to both cause and resolution but they all give witness to what must be considered a very important change in the party, namely, tolerance of open or thinly veiled disagreement with the decisions and actions of the PCF leadership.

The cautious "liberalization" announced by the 1964 rewriting of the party statutes was put to the test too early by the Soviet invasion of Czechoslovakia. The Garaudy affair was in a sense a symptom of what was going on within the party. There is evidence that many of Garaudy's ideas were shared by some members of the PCF central committee and by other militants and that the party was moving along the lines defined by the dissident.

Garaudy's expulsion did not necessarily signify the end of the new tolerance of dissidence within the PCF. Garaudy went too far—he became too public. Other dissidents, such as Aragon, the prestigious Communist writer and member of the central committee, have retained their positions within the party. The difference between them and Garaudy is that they play the game according to the rules of the party. Although it could be concluded that dissidence that is limited in scope and more private than public is not really dissidence, it is clear from a review of earlier *grandes affaires* of the PCF that even such limited dissidence was not allowed when Thorez was at the helm. It is likely that party members such as Aragon and Roland Leroy, a member of the politburo, believe that by remaining inside the party they can perhaps influence its course.

Aragon contends that the PCF is changing internally for the better and that he therefore has the possibility of influencing this change. In an interview with *L'Express*, he stated that he would have left the PCF had it not reacted as it did to the Soviet invasion of Czechoslovakia.[121] Aragon himself sharply criticized this invasion, but he unlike Garaudy never went so far as to imply the need for clear repudiation of the Soviet leaders by the PCF, which would have meant "a break that would lead to a split within the socialist camp."[122] On that point Aragon remained on the side of the party, although he has continued to dissent on other points: "When people ask me why I have not left my party, I answer them: I have not left it because I believe that some day it will be the future. But I do not want it to happen as it might have happened elsewhere. I think simply that if everybody left, nothing would be done together."[123]

Aragon is a special case, but he does represent what seems to be a growing number of party militants who are not wholly satisfied with the internal life and the policies of the PCF. However, the PCF is "their" party, and they do not want to leave it for many different reasons but perhaps mainly because they think they can change the party. Moreover, some of the older members could not abide even this degree of tolerance.

To the surprise of nearly everyone, on October 22, 1968, *L'Humanité* announced in a communiqué from the PCF central committee that Jeannette Vermeersch (Thorez's widow) had resigned from both the politburo and the central committee. The communiqué explained:

> After the central committee session [of August 22, 1968], comrade Jeannette Thorez-Vermeersch expressed a divergent and contradictory position in the politburo. While declaring that she was against the military intervention, she presented a collection of pretexts tending to justify it and criticisms of the politburo and the central committee, which disapprove of this intervention. On September 23, she made known her intention to resign from the politburo.
>
> Following the party's principles, which imply that each militant has the right to look at a problem in a way he believes just, with the reservation that he must apply the decisions taken democratically, the secretary general of the party, mandated by the politburo, asked Jeannette Thorez-Vermeersch several times not to resign. The central committee was of a similar opinion.
>
> However . . . comrade Jeannette Thorez-Vermeersch, who did not participate in the sessions [of the central committe] of October 21, sent to the secretary general of the party a letter of resignation from the politburo and the central committee.
>
> The central committee rejecting unanimously the point of view of comrade Jeannette Thorez-Vermeersch, takes note of her resignation, which it believes unjustified.[124]

Vermeersch exemplified in 1968 another current of dissidence from the PCF line: that of members who still believed, as she had stated in 1951, that "one does not discuss the requirements of Soviet tactics"[125] and that the position of the politburo on August 21, 1968, would foster anti-Sovietism.[126] The strength of these dissenters is not clear, even though on October 23, 1968, Rochet gave a few statistics that implied that internal opposition to the PCF's stand on Czechoslovakia was rather small.[127] Probably many of these dissenters were old-timers, and their number certainly included those who nevertheless went along with the party.[128]

The case of Vermeersch's resignation—a very special case indeed since it involved the widow of the great PCF leader—raised many points or questions in which the PCF-USSR relationship is included. Charles Tillon, an old PCF member who was expelled in 1970 for supporting Garaudy and his "theses" and who is engaged in a personal vendetta against the present leadership of the party, felt that the party's response was unfair and discriminatory.

> When Jeanne [sic] Thorez-Vermeersch resigned from the politburo because she did not accept the communiqué of Waldeck Rochet condemning the entry of the Russians in Prague, we had here more than an act of insubordination, a public snub of the new leadership by the widow of Maurice Thorez, in connivance with the Soviets. Not only were no sanctions taken, but the politburo suffered humbly the unpublishable expletives with which she gratified it when she left.[129]

Tillon implies that the Soviet Union attempted in this case to bring about a serious split among the top leadership of the PCF. Thus, the party's response, as discriminatory as it may have seemed to Tillon, was judicious.

This point aside, the Vermeersch case is yet another example of the PCF's new tolerance of internal dissidence. No sanctions were taken not simply because Vermeersch is Thorez's widow but because her dissidence remained within the rules of the party: it certainly could not be called anti-Sovietism or public.

The Vermeersch case further demonstrated two other changes within the PCF. First, and this is clearly related to the new tolerance, it gave credence to Dominique Desanti's assertion about another development within the PCF: "Until the 1960s, the PCF did not accept (contrary to the Italian party) the idea that a militant could resign: one left the party only by being expelled."[130] Certainly, this was the first time in the history of the party that a leader willfully left a high post on a matter of policy. Second, it pointed to a new frankness on the part of the PCF leadership about the internal problems of the party.

The PCF and the Socialists

Socialism, as the PCF understands it, will indeed never become a reality unless the majority of Frenchmen accept the idea. To achieve this goal, then, the PCF (or rather Waldeck Rochet) has come up with the slogan *démocratie avancée*. What does this slogan really mean? It refers to the political regime that would come about after the election of a coalition of the PCF and other "democratic" parties—mainly the French Socialist party. This regime would continue, as the present one, to be based on a multiparty system. Under such a regime, many reforms would be made including, to begin with, large-scale nationalization of the key groups of the economy and, subsequently, a transformation of French political institutions along lines that the PCF has demanded for a long time, namely, a parliament based on proportional representation. Under such a regime all fundamental liberties would be guaranteed and even enlarged. Freedom of the press would certainly not be abolished for the PCF leaders say again and again that a multiplicity of parties implies a multiplicity of newspapers and thus freedom of the press. Under such a regime, there would never be a case like that of Solzhenitsyn.

> For us, there is no possible blooming of creation without freedom of creation, no progress in thought without freedom of thought, no freedom of creation and of thought without freedom of their expression and diffusion. I indicated this clearly during a television interview at the beginning of 1973, when the case of *a* Soviet writer was mentioned: with the Communists in the government, this one or any other could perfectly well publish his books as soon as this or that publisher would decide to do so. Of course, we would be free to express afterward our opinion on these works as on any others, even to attack their ideas.[131]

All this is neither very convincing nor appealing to the opponents and critics of the PCF from either the right or the left. On the left, André Barjonet's critique is the most interesting. After pointing out the contradictions in the PCF's definition of *démocratie avancée* he concludes:

> *Démocratie avancée*, as it is now defined by the PCF (a truly democratic Parliament and domination of the monopolies), could correspond only to a historical period marked by extremely grave internal tensions excluding any even relative political or social stability.
>
> In presenting the phase of *démocratie avancée* today not as a period of transition but as an epoch, if not idyllic at least progressive in comparison to the present society, the PCF seems to have much more recourse to electoral slogans and propaganda than to an analysis of reality. . . .
>
> At the level of political strategy, this slogan is likely to achieve less than its authors expect. In fact, by dint of leaving socialist perspectives in the background and of advancing democratic solutions, the PCF fails to contribute to the development of the revolutionary conscience of the masses. [132]

On the right, the question most asked is what the PCF would do if, after the advent of the *démocratie avancée*, it was voted out of office. The PCF's answer is noncommittal. Actually, the party does not accept the question as valid. A Parisian PCF *responsable* put it to me this way:

> This is a difficult question to answer. We think that it will not come up, that it cannot come up if it is true that a democratic policy of socialism, which is ours, is a policy that corresponds to the interest of the majority of the French. The implementation of this policy during a sufficiently long time—a term of the legislature (five years)—cannot bring about a contrary reaction from the French; rather, it should bring about more support.
>
> Actually, what worries us is that in the early period of a government of the Left, the bourgeoisie would try to put an end to the experiment by violent means.[133]

What worries the French bourgeoisie, on the other hand, is that the PCF would dominate an elected leftist coalition and take over all powers, as has been attempted in Chile and in Portugal. Indeed, in 1968 Georges Pompidou accused the PCF of planning such a strategy in mentioning a *petite phrase terrible* ("terrible little sentence") that appeared on February 24, 1968, in a common electoral declaration of the PCF and the now defunct Fedération de la gauche démocratique et socialiste. This "terrible little sentence" stated that "the two bodies were in agreement over examining in common the measures to be taken to defeat attempts of any kind aiming at keeping a government of the Left from implementing its program."[134] Pompidou's warning was and is not without foundation for the PCF itself has reiterated several times that it must play a vanguard role in the new regime. Point 7 of the so-called Champigny Manifesto makes this clear,[135] and thesis 17 of the nineteenth PCF congress proclaims that "the possibility of building and defending socialism is tied to the capacity of the Communist party to play the role of the vanguard of the working class in the socialist society."[136]

Marchais, on the other hand, reassures everyone by seemingly tackling the question directly in subtitling a section of his book *Le Défi* "The Question of 'Alternation' [*alternance*]." He states: "We will respect *in all cases* the verdict expressed by direct, universal, secret, and proportional suffrage, whether it is favorable or unfavorable to us. How, for example, could we think of starting or continuing the construction of a socialist society in France without the support of the French people?"[137] However, note that Marchais puts the word *alternance* in quotation marks, thereby giving the impression that he does not think that such a situation can exist or will exist after the PCF becomes the governing party or even simply part of the government.

The slogans and ideas embraced by *démocratie avancée* indeed indicate evolution of the PCF. But the question remains as to whether this is a genuine "liberal" evolution. Perhaps these slogans are simply part of a Machiavellian scheme on the part of the PCF, speaking about the multiplicity of parties but remembering Bukharin's warning: "In a regime of the dictatorship of the proletariat, there can be two parties. But one is in power and the other in prison."[138] Are these new slogans simply part of an electoral strategy, as Barjonet concludes? If not, then why is the PCF so reluctant to speak about government *alternance* and to accept the idea or even to give the impression that it accepts the idea? These questions are difficult to answer, but one may conjecture that at this point the PCF is content with having, with the help of these slogans and the tactic of unity of the Left, gotten out of the political ghetto to which it was confined in the 1950s and early 1960s and with continuing to play the important role that the Gaullist regime gave it and that the Giscard-D'Estaing administration continues to give it— that of the principal interlocutor of the government in French politics, that of the only French political opposition worth that name.

Whether or not these slogans are logically consistent or present a practical solution to French problems or propose a somewhat original way to socialism for France, they have had at least a practical effect for the party. They have made the party look even more reasonable and democratic (in the Western sense) in the eyes of the French. The slogans have paid off, if we consider the near victory of François Mitterrand, backed by the PCF, in the presidential election of 1974 and the party's majority position in current polls.

The Common Program

The road to the writing of the Common Program of 1972 was a long and rocky one. It started in the early 1960s with the realization on the part of both the PCF and the Socialists that the whole French Left had to be unified if it were to play a significant role under the new French regime of the Fifth Republic. The PCF was the first to call for a common program (as early as 1963). Such calls fell on deaf ears until the rise, during the presidential campaign of 1965, of François Mitterrand as a national leader acceptable to the PCF and well disposed to the idea of making a pact with the party. The PCF supported the candidacy of Mitterrand, who managed to deny a first round victory to De Gaulle. After the election, however, and during 1966 and 1967, Mitterrand was more interested in the unity of the noncommunist Left, consolidated as the Fédération de la gauche démocratique et socialiste (FGDS), than in seriously negotiating with the Communists. Nevertheless, a rapprochement was made with the Communists in 1966 through an electoral pact that realized substantial gains for the whole French Left in the legislative elections of 1967 and that demonstrated the reliability and usefulness of the PCF. After this success, a joint working group of PCF and FGDS members was set up that concluded its work in February 1968 with a common declaration or common platform. This declaration made manifest the agreements and differences between the two groups and came close to a common program of government. However, the events of 1968 broke the momentum toward unity and killed the FGDS. During the presidential election of 1969, the PCF demonstrated its strength relative to the moribund noncommunist Left, no longer under the leadership of Mitterrand. The situation of the French Left was like that in the pre-1965 period.

Learning from their mistakes, members of the defunct FGDS decided to form a new party, the Parti socialiste (PS), that would no longer be just a federation of distinct political groups. The new PS, born in July 1969, soon after entered into yearlong discussions with the PCF. The result of these contacts was the publication in December 1970 of the agreements and disagreements between the two groups. Six months later, in June 1971, Mitterrand reentered the stage and became first-secretary of the new Socialist party. Again, as in the FGDS period, Mitterrand tried to consolidate the noncommunist Left, including the drafting of a specific program. The PCF once more called for a common program and put pressure on the Socialists by publishing its own program in October 1971. This was an unprecedented step for the PCF, and this program demonstrated a softening of the PCF's previous differences with the PS as well as a willingness to compromise. However, the Socialists continued to work on their own program, which they finally published in March 1972. In content, the PS program was not too far from that of the PCF. Thus, negotiations between the PS and the PCF got under way and were rapidly concluded with the publication of the Common Program two months later in June 1972.

The Common Program, a sort of synthesis of the programs of the PCF and the PS, was made possible by numerous concessions on the part of the PCF on such subjects, for example, as governmental alternation. On the other hand, the Socialist program was much more to the left than any program one would have expected from a social democratic party. The Common Program was possible, then, because of the leftward movement of the Socialists and the resolve of a strong leader, Mitterrand, to make a workable alliance with the PCF as much as because of the willingness of the PCF to change its image and its proposals in order to effect the alliance.

The Programme commun de gouvernement du parti communiste et du parti socialiste was indeed what PCF leaders had been advocating for almost a decade and had formalized just nine months earlier in their own program, which ended thus:

> The French Communist party offers this *program for a democratic government of popular union* for debate and approval of French men and women of all professions, of all beliefs, and of all convictions.
>
> It submits it to the other democratic parties and groups with which it wishes to achieve in the near future a program of government elaborated together and applied together.[139]

The Common Program is a legislative program—that is, it is supposed to serve for five years as a basis for action of a unified Left government. But since both parties have agreed that to install socialism in France will take more than five years, the program is to lead France on the road to socialism, in an irreversible way, it is hoped. The Common Program is, then, the introduction to what Waldeck Rochet and the PCF have defined as *démocratie avancée*.

The program is divided into four parts: (1) to live better and to change the conditions of life; (2) to democratize the economy, to develop the public sector, and to plan economic progress; (3) to democratize French institutions and to guarantee and develop freedoms; and (4) to contribute to peace and to foster international cooperation. In other words, the program deals first with social policy, second with economic policy, third with political institutions, and fourth with foreign policy. The first part, which is the longest, was apparently the easiest to draw up, and it takes into account practically all the demands of the trade unions. The second part was probably harder to write since the continuing disagreement between the PS and the PCF over "workers' management" of industries remains thinly veiled. On this point the program states that in the public sector

> when the workers of the enterprise will express the wish and when the structure of the enterprise will indicate the possibility, the intervention of the workers in the management and direction of the enterprise will take new forms—which the Socialist party registers in the perspective of *autogestion* and the French Communist party in the permanent development of democratic management—determined through an agreement among the democratic government, the management of the enterprise concerned, and the trade unions.[140]

On economic policy the PS made some concessions by agreeing to more nationalizations than it had intended in its own program. But the PCF moderated its own demands. The Common Program foresees state control over thirteen industrial groups, whereas the PCF program included twenty-five. On the question of political institutions, the common program shows an evolution of the PCF's position. The mode of election of the president of the Republic will not be changed, but the presidential term of office and powers will be reduced. The PCF seems to accept more clearly the principle of governmental alternation. As Laurens and Pfister have noted:

> The PCF . . . concedes to the Socialists that the National Assembly will not be automatically dissolved at the first governmental crisis. . . . The Communists wished the establishment of a system of automatic dissolution in the case of a governmental crisis because they fear—with reference to the past—a reversal of alliances during the legislature whereby the Socialists would look for new support on their right. As for the latter, they did not want to give the PCF the opportunity to provoke new elections at a date it would choose with a system of automatic dissolution. It is thus that a mechanism of dissolution in two phases was arrived at.[141]

Thus, dissolution of the National Assembly will take place only if the attempt to form a new government does not obtain the approval of the majority of the Assembly.

The Common program intends to bring back something very akin to the system of the Fourth Republic: the major political role would be returned to the Assembly. Furthermore, elections would be conducted under the system of proportional representation. On these critical points, the desires of the PCF were fulfilled.

In terms of foreign policy—perhaps the most touchy subject— much has been conceded to the PCF. On the question of NATO, the program states:

> The government will declare itself for the simultaneous dissolution of the North Atlantic Treaty and the Warsaw Treaty. It will foster all measures that will permit it to reach this goal by stages, which implies the progressive and simultaneous weakening of existing politico-military alliances to arrive at their complete disappearance.[142]

However, its attitude toward NATO is hostile and it competes with the Gaullists in the nationalism of its foreign policy. Only at the last moment did the central committee of the PCF rescind its instruction to press for condemnation of Western imperialism and NATO in the document issued by the major communist parties at Berlin in June 1976.[143] And the program also vies with the extreme Gaullists in its hostility toward what it labels German imperialism.[144] In this respect the PCF is quite different from the PCI, whose secretary, Berlinguer, has firmly maintained PCI commitment to Italy's international alliance, even at the twenty-fifth CPSU congress.

On the question of the Common Market, the Socialists again moderated their European views, and the PCF obtained their support for the rule that requires the EEC council's decisions to be taken only unanimously (a Gaullist position) and not by majority vote. Moreover, the secretary of the PCF, Marchais, opposed Greek and Spanish membership in the EEC because of competition with French farmers.[145]

After long advocating the scrapping of the French atomic bomb—a policy adopted by the united Left and included in the Common Program of 1972—now that there was a prospect that the Left might come to power in the near future, the PCF completely reversed its position. In 1976, the party's leadership declared itself publicly in favor of a French "defense that was genuinely national, that was not integrated in NATO, and that would be employed against any eventual aggressor, whatsoever."[146] Commenting on this statement, Jean Elleinstein, a French Communist writer, expressed the view that such a position really meant "in the short or long run . . . the acceptance of the French nuclear force because one cannot imagine a genuinely national defense based solely on the slingshot or conventional armaments."[147]

On May 11, 1977, Jean Kanapa presented a report to the PCF central committee in favor of the French nuclear force. In this report, Kanapa reaffirmed his earlier statement about a strategy directed against all potential aggressors (*tous azimuts*) as well as an antiforce rather than an anticity strategy. However, the PCF asked that the use of the nuclear force be reserved to a special committee including all the principal political leaders of the country. The Socialists were to meet before the end of 1977 to redefine their military policy, and it seems likely that the stand in the Common Program on the French nuclear force will be changed.[148]

Thus, one can say that the PCF now accepts the French nuclear force as long as it is not integrated under the military command of NATO and as long as the PCF has influence in a decision to use it.

The influence of the Socialist party—specifically, the CERES group—on the Common Program poses some problems to the leadership of the party. Although Mitterrand, at the PS congress of Pau in 1975, was successful in keeping members of its left wing out of the secretariat, CERES has grown in influence and support. This group within the PS accounts for 20% of the electoral support of the party and has become in a sense a party within a party, with its own meetings, its own press, its own members, its own funds, and its own doctrine. During the municipal elections of 1977, CERES took great liberties with the directives of the PS leadership and presented the latter with several faits accomplis in the nomination of candidates. The behavior of this group has been more and more in violation of article 4 of the PS statutes, which forbids the creation of organized *tendances*.[149]

However, at the PS congress of June 17, 1977, in Nantes, CERES renounced its status as an "organized *tendance*" by relinquishing the means to support its own organization. But, at Nantes, the political and ideological differences between CERES and the PS majority remained unresolved and the CERES group increased its support to nearly 30% of the delegates to the congress.150 Thus, Mitterrand faces strong opposition within the Socialist party in his effort to control the Common Program and the PCF. Nor does the alliance with the splinter group of the Radical Socialist party—the Radicaux de gauche—ease his position.151

The Common Program was condemned, sometimes virulently, by the Gaullists, the centrists, the Radical Socialist party, and all those opposed to an alliance with the PCF. However, the most serious and thoughtful critique of the program was made by Raymond Aron in February 1973. His critique, dwelling mostly on the economic side of the program, suggested that this plan for action of the Left would enable the French Communists, with their strong influence in the trade unions, easily to reach their "maximum" objectives and would lead France rapidly to the level of "popular democracy" of Eastern Europe.152

It is not my purpose here to pass judgment on the Common Program. Nevertheless, many during the presidential elections of 1974, while voting for Mitterrand, expressed the opinion that they did not believe that if the Left won the election the program could be applied. Some foresaw a repetition of the failures of 1936 as inevitable if such an attempt were made.153 Whatever the great flaws or merits of the Common Program, we are concerned here with the consequences of this rapprochement between the French Communists and Socialists specifically on the PCF and on the potential development of the relations between the two parties.

The strategy of unity with the French noncommunist Left that the PCF followed under the Fifth Republic had several important results both outside and inside the party.

Outside the party, one can say that the PCF strategy to some extent forced the French Socialists to take certain positions further left than many of them felt and still feel necessary. Indeed, one could say that since the middle 1960s, the rapprochement has been more of a movement on the part of the Socialists toward the Communists than vice versa. Unlike the Social Democratic party of West Germany, which in its Bad Godesberg program of 1959 defined itself as "a party of freedom and thought, constituting a community of men inspired by different ideologies and confessions" and which defined socialism as merely "a permanent task to conquer liberty and justice and to maintain them," the French Socialists have never renounced Marxist ideology.154   Certainly the PS has renounced much of the Marxist revolutionary verbalism in recent years, but its leaders, perhaps because of their seemingly greater credibility in their commitment to apply their program, have in a sense become more Marxist than they ever were.

Although this is this case, the PCF strategy of unity has nevertheless not greatly lessened the distrust of the Communists felt by many Socialist leaders and voters. This was clearly demonstrated by public opinion polls taken before the legislative elections of 1973.

> Public opinion polls showed that given a Socialist-Gaullist run-off, more than 90 percent of communist first round voters would back the Socialist. However, given a communist-Gaullist run-off, only some 50 percent of the socialist electors would vote for the communist, while the remainder would either vote for the Gaullist or abstain.[155]

And Mitterrand himself has stated:

> It was in the resistance that I got used to having exchanges with the Communists. Many friendships, which years have not diminished, date from that time. Among many other acts of kindness that I owe to them, they did me the favor of teaching me not to close my eyes if I wanted to avoid being crushed by their formidable machine. An equilibrium difficult to maintain between vigilance, which does not permit anything, and trust, which permits everything. I am still at this point.[156]

Furthermore, the unity achieved was not a return to the pre-congress of Tours period.[157] The Common Program specifically states that "the French Communist party and the Socialist party naturally will preserve their personalities. They both will follow principles that are the basis of their existence."[158] This was perhaps another indication of distrust on the part of the Socialists more than on the part of the Communists.[159] But quite likely, this requirement was felt necessary by both parties to achieve their joint goal. Some have argued that a true union would probably have put the Communists in a dominant position. Most of those who fear that the PCF would ultimately take over if the united Left came to power in France do not offer a precise scenario but base their predictions on their analysis of the seizure of power by communist parties now in control in other countries. They point out that all these parties followed a policy of a united front, like the PCF today, and that because of the nature of the united front's program and the party's superior organization the communists were able to overtake and overpower their allies and set up their tyranny.

These theorists also point out the already considerable infiltration of Communists into many echelons of the government such as the armed forces, the intelligence service, and the police. They also mention the great influence the party has in the media, education, the professions, and especially the trade unions.[160] This infiltration and influence, they feel, is increasing with the victories of the PCF in the municipal elections of 1977 and will increase if the PS-PCF coalition wins in 1978. On top of all this, much is made of the great commercial and financial empire of the party[161] and of the fact that the Socialist party has moved much more toward the PCF position than vice versa, with, they argue, considerable infiltration by the Communists into the left wing of the PS, CERES. They see all these developments as preparatory steps for an ultimate takeover.

Aron, for example, has often predicted such a development, first in his critique of the Common Program in 1973[162] and more recently in *Le Figaro*.[163] However, the Red Army was present in those Eastern European states in which the communists took control except Czechoslovakia in 1948, in which case the threat of its deployment and the clear noninterventionary policy of the United States were decisive. Also in the latter case, the Communist party was the majority party, controlled the interior ministry, and was in top command positions in the army. Thus, the parallel to France is at least open to question. In any event, Mitterrand and the Socialists rejected a "true union." Instead, a very close alliance was established, and the PCF now could be said to be indeed fully reintegrated in the French political system as an extremely important actor.

To achieve this goal, the PCF has given much. Many of its internal changes seem to have been directed toward that end. The question now is whether this reintegration in the French political system and this union with the noncommunist Left will foster further evolution of the PCF.

Conclusion

What is the French Communist party today? It is certainly a different party from *"le Parti de Maurice Thorez."* The PCF has been "liberalized" and modernized under the pressure and with the help of many factors, both national and international. However, there are not yet any real signs that these factors have brought or will bring about a truly democratic trend in the party's organization and in the mentality of its membership as a whole.

The party has nevertheless managed to change its image in the eyes of the French public. It has become respectable; people are no longer afraid of it; and it is widely considered to be a party "like the others." Furthermore, it has managed to achieve one of its long sought goals—to be an integral part of a united French Left with a common program of government—and is anticipating sharing power in the near future. Thus, the party's policies and tactics of recent years have been highly successful even if the credit for such development cannot be given entirely to the party leadership.

However, as the party has grown in respectability and importance, its electoral support has stagnated around 20%. In these terms, the great beneficiary of the grand alliance of the Left has been the new and vigorous Socialist party, which is now reaching the 30% mark. But, because of the electoral system of the Fifth Republic and the great electoral discipline within the alliance, the PCF realized greater gains in the municipal elections of 1977 than the PS, especially in cities of over 30,000 inhabitants, where the PCF's total of municipal councillors climbed from 1256 to 2306, against a PS total of 2259.

With the great victory (52% of the vote) of the French Left in March 1977, another such victory is predicted for the 1978 legislative elections. It is indeed difficult to see what would or could break the momentum of the Left now that their opponents' coalition is in disarray, with its leaders arguing among themselves, short of renewed (and not entirely unlikely) conflict between the PS and the PCF. It is clear that the French want change and may vote it even though many who will vote for the Left do not really believe in its promises. The quite possible victory of the Left in 1978 may see the PCF regain a significant share of national power after thirty-one years.

The question then will be how long the experiment will last. A victory of the Left may well lead to the constitutional crisis that analysts of the constitution of the Fifth Republic have predicted since the birth of the regime. Beyond the fact that Mitterrand, as leader of the new majority, would become prime minister of a president who was leader of the opposing coalition and who had three years left in office, the contents of the Common Program would be the real cause of the crisis because although its supporters now play according to the rules of the present regime, the program is not compatible with those rules. As Aron has stated: "Either the president will try to compromise by supporting certain points from the program not incompatible with the present regime or, if the newly elected majority refuses its confidence to the government, the president must dissolve the Assembly and seek the arbitration of the country."[164] Most people agree that the second development is more likely. The crisis then could be a repetition of the MacMahon episode of a century ago. President Giscard, his statements to the contrary notwithstanding, could also resign. Either route could mean the end of the Fifth Republic, which then would be replaced, according to the Common Program, by a regime akin to that of the Fourth Republic. The constitutional crisis with the implementation of the Common Program would also precipitate both an economic and a social crisis of perhaps Chilean proportions. In such a case the experiment would be short-lived; the ultimate outcome, uncertain.

Mitterrand, during the elections of March 1977, stated that "the Socialists have neither the intention nor the taste to add a grave political crisis to the economic crisis they will inherit."[165] Although no plans have been drafted to modify the Common Program in any significant way, Mitterrand, aware of the above scenario and looking toward the presidency in 1980, might indeed attempt to avert a constitutional crisis and adopt a "go slow" policy vis-à-vis implementation of the program and to effect some type of accommodation with Giscard. One can infer this from recent discussions between the PS and the PCF on the "actualization" of the Common Program. Indeed, a constitutional crisis accompanied by economic and social crisis is not in the interest of Mitterrand although it may be in the interest of the PCF. The options Mitterrand will dispose of after the elections will to a great extent depend on *who* gets elected in the new majority. The more Mitterrand men elected, the less responsive Mitterrand will be to pressure from the PS left wing and from the PCF. An option to form a center-Left coalition might become available if the victory by Mitterrand were large enough and the center not lost to Gaullist momentum. This is the double cross that the PCF fears and this is why the PCF argues for full and rapid implementation of the Common Program and more nationalizations than the program already proposes.

In fact, the PCF has never had too much confidence in the alliance, as has been made clear by its repeated criticisms since 1972 of the PS and its leader. Marchais warned again in June 1977 that Mitterrand should not hope to have a totally free hand with the coalition and that the PCF would not recognize a dominant role for the PS.[166]

The PCF actually is faced with a sort of dilemma for it knows that the alliance has not worked out to its advantage in its contest with the PS. In case of a victory of the Left in 1978, it knows it cannot really aspire to lay down its law. By the summer of 1977, the PCF was engaged in a war of nerves with the Socialists. If the Left holds together for victory, an intense conflict between the PCF and the PS is likely to occur. If Mitterrand decides to restrict the role of the PCF to the less sensitive ministries—excluding the PCF from interior, foreign, and military posts and hemming it in on the major economic posts—it will have to decide whether to break up the coalition or to bide its time. In either case, a PCF offensive against the Socialists may be the only scenario in which Mitterrand can move to the center, at least in the short run, without breaking up the PS and thus destroying the potential centrist majority that may be his long-run alternative. Alternatively, the tension between the PCF and the PS may produce a victory for Giscard.

Notes

1. Alfred Grosser, "France: Nothing but Opposition," in Robert A. Dahl, ed., *Political Oppositions in Western Democracies* (New Haven: Yale University Press, 1966), p. 291.

2. Mattei Dogan, "Political Cleavage and Social Stratification in France and Italy," in Seymour M. Lipset and Stein Rokkan, eds., *Party Systems and Voter Alignments: Cross-National Perspectives* (New York: Free Press 1967), p. 176.

3. Giovanni Sartori, "European Political Parties: The Case of Polarized Pluralism," in Joseph LaPalombara and Myron Weiner, eds., *Political Parties and Political Development* (Princeton: Princeton University Press, 1966), p. 137.

4. Ibid., pp. 157-158. "An opposition is forced to be responsible if it knows that it may be called to execute what it has promised—to respond. But such motivation is tenuous if the opposition knows that at most it may only share some peripheral governmental responsibility behind the smoke screen of discontinuous and shifting coalitions. And no such motivation exists for the parties which oppose the system."

5. Gabriel Almond, *The Appeals of Communism* (Princeton: Princeton University Press, 1965), p. 386.

6. Suzanne Berger, "The French Political System," in Samuel H. Beer and Adam B. Ulam, eds., *Patterns of Government: The Major Political Systems of Europe* (New York: Random House, 1973), p. 404.

7. Annie Kriegel, *Communismes au miroir français* (Paris: Gallimard, 1974), p. 18.

8. See Annie Kriegel, *Aux origines du communisme français, 1914-1920* (Paris: Mouton, 1964).

9. Grosser, op. cit., p. 300.

10. *L'Humanité*, 3 August 1971, p. 1.

11. Ibid.

12. The result of the French presidential election of May 19, 1974, in which Mitterrand, the Socialist candidate backed by the PCF, got some 49% of the votes seems clearly to demonstrate this fact.

13. "Les Français n'ont plus peur du communisme," *L'Express*, 16 July 1964.

14. *Le Nouvel Observateur*, 23 February 1966.

15. *France nouvelle*, 18 January 1967.

16. Monique Fichelet et al., *Les Français, la politique, et le Parti communiste* (Paris: Editions sociales, 1968).

17. *L'Express*, 25 March 1968. The results of these surveys have been the object of further lengthy analyses by Monique Fichelet and Raymond Fichelet, Guy Michelat, Michel Simon, Alain Lancelot, and Pierre Weill in the Cahiers de la Fondation nationale des sciences politiques *Le Communisme en France* (Paris: Armand Colin, 1969), pp. 255-303.

18. *L'Express*, 2 August 1971.

19. Ibid., 28 October-3 November 1974. *L'Express* commented: "It is the result of Mr. Georges Marchais's strategy" (p. 33).

20. See how a Canadian scholar explains this problem: Denis Lacorne, "Analyse et 'reconstruction' de stéréotypes communistes et socialistes face au 'socialisme soviétique,' " *Revue française de science politique*, XXIII, No. 6 (December 1973): 1171-1201.

21. In the July 1971 poll, after the question "Do you think that the Communist party has changed during the last few years?" people were asked: "More precisely, has it become more or less (a) open to discussion, (b) dynamic, (c) faithful to its principles, etc.?" It was not made clear, however, whether the percentages of the answers were from the total of the poll's respondents or simply from those who felt that the party had changed—that is, 45% of respondents.

22. According to *Sondages*, the French public opinion report, many qualifications must be made about this public image of the PCF. See *Sondages: revue francaise de l'opinion publique*, Nos. 1 and 2 (1971): 67:

> The opinion toward the Communist party at the end of the year 1970 could be summarized as follows:
> An increased acknowledgment and an acceptance of the role of the Communist party in French political life.
> A great skepticism as to the chances of a Communist regime's being installed in France in a relatively short time.
> A great pessimism about the national and personal consequences that such an event would have for the life of the French and for the destiny of the country.
> The feeling that the ties of this group with the USSR are progressively lessening.
> On the whole, there is acceptance of the role of the Communist party as an opposition party, an interest group, in the present political system, but rejection of the idea, and it is not believed, that it could bring about a Communist regime in France.

23. Interview with Annie Kriegel, Chicago, 9 November 1970.

24. Annie Kriegel, lecture given at the University of Chicago, 11 November 1970.

25. Ibid. Kriegel developed this point in the conclusion of her excellent book on the PCF, *Les Communistes français* (Paris: Editions du seuil, 1970, pp. 247 ff.

26. *La Nation*, 14-16 October 1966.

27. François Fejtö, *The French Communist Party and the Crisis of International Communism* (Cambridge: MIT Press, 1967), p. 204.

28. Ibid.

29. Roger Garaudy, *Toute la vérité, mai 1968-fevrier 1970* (Paris: Bernard Grasset, 1970), pp. 8-9. Edgar Faure, in a lecture given at the University

of Chicago in 1969, characterized Roger Garaudy as a Communist and "un original." He suggested that it seemed unlikely that Garaudy could remain both, thus indirectly giving his estimation of the PCF.

30. Charles Tillon, Un *"Procès de Moscou" à Paris* (Paris: Editions du seuil, 1971), p. 61. Tillon was expelled from the party for similar reasons as Garaudy—among others, mainly because of their continuing criticism of Soviet actions in Czechoslovakia. However, Tillon's book is mostly an indictment of the PCF of the 1950s. More than three quarters of the book is devoted to the events of 1950-1952 and not much space is devoted to his expulsion from the party in 1970. However, Tillon makes a good case for his conclusion.

31. Jean-François Revel, *Ni Marx ni Jésus* (Paris: Robert Laffont, 1970), pp. 35-36.

32. Kriegel, *Les Communistes français*, p. 257. One can object to this analysis as not entirely conclusive. After all, Khrushchev was also throughout his career a staunch Stalinist and yet he was the source of quite a few changes in the Soviet Union during his tenure as secretary general of the CPSU. Also, one can point to the case of Waldeck Rochet, who succeeded Maurice Thorez as head of the PCF, and whom Kriegel herself calls "the phenomenon Waldeck Rochet."

33. J.-M. Domenach, "Notre affaire Tillon ou la vitrine de l'appareil," *Esprit*, June 1971, pp. 1246-1254.

34. Harvey Waterman, *Political Change in Contemporary France: The Politics of an Industrial Democracy* (Columbus: C.E. Merrill, 1969), p. 63.

35. François Borella, *Les partis politiques dans la France d'aujourd'hui* (Paris: Editions du seuil, 1973), p. 189. The results of the public opinion polls about the PCF mentioned earlier could be taken as an indication of the correctness of Borella's conclusion.

36. What these writers may have in mind, although it is not very clear, is that the PCF no longer uses or has modified what Nathan Leites has called "the Bolshevik operational code." See Nathan Leites, *A Study of Bolshevism* (New York: Free Press, 1953).

37. For a definition of social democratic (or perhaps more exactly socialist) party see Maurice Duverger, *Political Parties*, trans. Barbara North and Robert North (New York: Wiley, 1963), pp. 1-2. One might say that the difference between a "Bolshevik" or "Stalinist" and a social democratic party is a question of organization and discipline.

38. Domenach, op. cit., p. 1254.

39. Actually, the idea is absurd—a logical impossibility. Either the party will evolve into something that can be precisely called a social democratic party, following a given definition of that term, however difficult such a definition might be to find, or it will not.

40. Kriegel disagrees. She points out in *Les Communistes français* that "we have seen some communist parties crumble and disappear—the German Communist party—some communist parties change strategy, tactics, policy, dimension, language, chiefs, obedience, but we have not yet seen any become a social democratic party" (p. 247).

41. Fejtö, op. cit., p. 204.

42. Georges Lavau, "Le Parti communiste dans le système politique français," in *Le Communisme en France*, p. 9.

43. Revel, op. cit., p. 47, seems to agree with this point: "There cannot be any revolution in France . . . because *in theory* the most powerful opposition party [the PCF] wants to make it and *in practice* it does not want it."

44. Lavau, op. cit., p. 18.

45. Ibid., p. 22.

46. Roy C. Macridis, *Political Parties: Contemporary Trends and Ideas* (New York: Harper Torchbooks, 1967), p. 198.

47. Ibid., pp. 197–198.

48. Waterman, op. cit., p. 63.

49. Maurice Duverger and François Goguel, "Permanence et changement dans le système de partis français," Association française de science politique, *Débat*, No. 8 (June 1968): 39–40.

50. Michel Winock, "La Contradiction du PCF," *Esprit*, May 1970, pp. 896-897.

51. André Laurens and Thierry Pfister, *Les Nouveaux Communistes* (Paris: Stock, 1973), p. 12.

52. According to Jacques Julliard in *Esprit* of March 1972, this is one way to look at the PCF. He enunciated three other ways: (1) a tribune power; (2) the left wing of the opposition; and (3) an organized revolutionary force. See Jacques Julliard, "Le Socialisme à l'ordre du jour," *Esprit*, March 1972, pp. 455 ff.

53. *Sondages*, Nos. 1 and 2 (1971): 68.

54. *L'Express*, 13–19 September 1971, p. 21.

55. Ibid.

56. This is made clear by the detailing of the results of public opinion polls presented by *Sondages*, Nos. 1 and 2 (1971): 75.

57. *L'Express*, 20–26 September 1971, p. 71. Aragon went on to say: "My party, in contrast with other parties, is in favor of the plurality of political parties, which implies the necessity of the plurality of newspapers and, consequently, freedom of the press."

58. Laurens and Pfister, op. cit., p. 114.

59. Ibid., p. 115.

60. Ibid., p. 230.

61. "The Communists are not to the left but to the east." This statement has been attributed wrongly to Guy Mollet. The author of this quip, Edouard Depreux, was national secretary of the PSU from 1960 to 1967. See Raymond Barrillon, *La Gauche française en mouvement* (Paris: Plon, 1967), p. 20, n. 1.

62. *Le Crapouillot*, May–June 1970, p. 4. Note the use of the word "fidelity," which brings us back to the question of the PCF's "love" for the Soviet Union.

63. Jacques Soustelle, "Leur dernière trouvaille," ibid., p. 5.

64. Annie Kriegel, lecture given at the University of Chicago, 9 November 1970.

65. Louis Couturier, *Les "grandes affaires" du parti communiste français* (Paris: François Maspero, 1972), p. 85; italics added. Formerly a PCF Stalinist, Couturier is now a member of the Ligue communiste, a Trotskyite group.

66. *L'Humanité*, 22 August 1968, p. 1. The next day, the central committee approved this editorial and added that it *"disapproved* of the military intervention in Czechoslovakia." See *L'Humanité*, 23 August 1968, p. 1; italics added.

67. See Roy C. Macridis, "The Immobility of the French Communist Party," in *Political Parties*, p. 189:

> In the election of November 2, 1956, the Party's vote increased in absolute terms *though it fell* in relation to the total number of votes cast by less than one per cent. . . . In six cantonal elections held between October 15 and October 30, 1956 (that is, after the Khrushchev Report and the events in Poland and during the Hungarian uprising), the Communists retained and even improved their positions.

68. A case in point was the unprecedented resignation a few weeks later of Jeannette Vermeersch, the widow of Maurice Thorez, from the central committee because of her disagreement over this specific stand of the party.

69. In *Est et ouest*, Branka Lazitch states that during his tenure as secretary general "Waldeck Rochet has been probably the only one to want to take into account the base [of the PCF] in his personal attitude toward the Soviet Union." See Branka Lazitch, "L'Electorat communiste et le socialisme soviétique," *Est et ouest*, 16–31 March 1974, p. 4.

70. *L'Express*, 1–7 April 1968, p. 18.

71. Denis Lacorne, "Analyse et 'reconstruction de stéréotypes communistes et socialistes face au 'socialisme soviétique,'" *Revue Française de Science Politique*, December, 1973, p. 1190. "I was very happy when they took a stand against the intervention. . . . I consider the party did something very good." Lacorne also quotes another Communist municipal official who stated that "60 percent here [in his district, I suppose], a small majority!—were in agreement to condemn [the Soviet Union]" (ibid., p. 1189).

72. *L'Humanité*, 31 December 1968, p. 3.

73. Ibid., 27 January 1969, p. 2.

74. Ibid. During this period, because of such reports or simply because of the new view of the USSR that the PCF leaders now have, articles discussing problems encountered by French workers never make comparisons with how such problems are solved in the USSR.

75. Ibid., 14–15 October, 1971. The article title loosely translates: "To Live in Moscow—What Comforts Do the Soviets Enjoy in 1971?"

76. Ibid., 14 October 1971, p. 2.

77. Ibid.

78. Ibid.

79. Ibid., 15 October 1971, p. 2.

80. *L'Humanité* already had shown some "boldness" on the subject of the Soviet standard of living. In 1967, it mentioned that 52% of the people questioned in a French public opinion poll believed that over the next twenty years the standard of living in the West would still be higher than that in the communist countries. See ibid., 18 January 1967.

81. Ibid., 31 August 1965, p. 1. It must be noted that an earlier era the question would not have been asked (see my examples, especially from the 1930s) and that the word "discovery" in quotation marks (in the subtitle) perhaps suggests the urge to confess a certain skepticism.

82. Ibid. "They do not deprive themselves of the opportunity."

83. Ibid., 25 December 1968, p. 8; italics added.

84. Ibid., 9 January 1970, p. 4. This letter was nevertheless very pro-Soviet.

85. Ibid., 24 March 1964; quoted in Kriegel, *Communismes au miroir français*, p. 190.

86. Laurens and Pfister, op. cit., p. 119.

87. Kriegel, *Communismes au miroir français*, p. 190.

88. *L'Humanité*, 10 October 1968, p. 3. The quote leaves out only the names and professions of the accused. The article was indeed short.

89. Ibid., 12 October 1968, p. 3.

90. For an excellent explanation of this event see Fejtö, op. cit.

91. Fejtö, op. cit., pp. 183-184, suggests that some PCF leaders might have known in advance about what was going to happen in the CPSU.

92. *Les Cahiers du communisme*, December 1964, p. 108.

93. *France nouvelle*, 25 September 1968, pp. 11-12.

94. *L'Humanité*, 23 October 1968, p. 10; italics added.

95. Ibid., p. 5; italics added.

96. Ibid.

97. Ibid., 2 January 1970, p. 4. For the deleted passages see Garaudy, op. cit., pp. 150, 152.

98. Rodger Swearingen, ed., *Leaders of the Communist World* (New York: Free Press, 1971), p. x.

99. *Est et ouest*, 1-15 March 1973, p. 3.

100. See Kriegel, *Les Communistes français*, p. 227. She phrases it "amener son parti à cesser d'être un parti stalinien" in her more recent book *Communismes au miroir français*, p. 239. Like Laurens and Pfister, op. cit., Kriegel suggests that this was perhaps the reason Thorez chose Rochet as his successor.

101. Laurens and Pfister, op. cit., pp. 74-75.

102. Jacques Fauvet, *Histoire du Parti communiste français*, vol. II: *Vingt-cinq ans de drames 1939-1965* (Paris: Fayard, 1965), p. 320.

103. Kriegel, *Les Communistes français*, pp. 228-230.

104. Guy Rossi-Landi, "Le parti communiste français, structures, composition, moyens d'action," in Cahiers de la Fondation Nationale des Sciences

politiques, *Le Communisme en France* (Paris: Armand Colin, 1969), p. 194.

105. *Statuts du Parti communiste français* (Paris: 1964), p. 3.
106. Ibid., p. 5.
107. Ibid., pp. 5–6; italics added.
108. Ibid., p. 21.
109. See Rossi-Landi, op. cit., p. 191.
110. *Statuts*, pp. 37–38.
111. Interview with Claude Quin, secretary of one of the PCF's sections in Paris and a participant in federal conferences, Paris, 26 August 1968. Quin also collaborated in several economic reviews of the PCF and is a former leader of Catholic movements.
112. See Georges Marchais, "Intervention au XVIIe congrès," *Les Cahiers du communisme*, June–July, 1964, pp. 321–324.
113. Interview with Claude Quin, Paris, 26 August 1968. Quin added that names not given by the commission on candidacies can be handwritten on the ballots. But he admitted that he had never seen a case in which an election had to be repeated.
114. Rossi-Landi, op. cit., p. 196.
115. Robert Michels, *Political Parties* (New York: Collier, 1962).
116. See *Les Cahiers du communisme*, December 1967 and January 1968.
117. Interview with Claude Quin, Paris, 26 August 1968.
118. Laurens and Pfister, op. cit., p. 229.
119. These articles were entitled "Pas de mannequins dans le parti!" "Que les bouches s'ouvrent!" "Enfin on va discuter!" and "Jetons la pagaille!" See *Histoire du Parti communiste français (manuel)* (Paris: Editions sociales, 1964), p. 226; see also Couturier, op. cit., p. 11.
120. The beginning of this genuine debate within the party can be dated to before 1964 if we take the rewriting of the statutes as an index. It may have been a cause for the PCF leaders' going to Moscow in October of that year to ask questions about the dismissal of Khrushchev.
121. *L'Express*, 20–26 September 1971, p. 71.
122. Ibid.
123. Ibid., p. 73. Aragon, a member of the PCF central committee, avoided voting for the expulsion of Roger Garaudy in 1970 by asking for "more information." See ibid., 25–31 May 1970, p. 12.
124. *L'Humanité*, 22 October 1968, p. 4.
125. Quoted in Tillon, op. cit., p. 73.
126. *L'Humanité*, 23 October 1968, p. 5. The Communist daily went so far as to state that "none of the members of the leadership of the party could pretend to hold by himself the monopoly of friendship with the USSR."
127. See ibid.
128. For example, the last member of the old guard, Jacques Duclos, although he voted for condemnation of the Soviet invasion, managed to write the

last volume of his memoirs without saying one word about Czechoslova-kia! I wrote to Duclos mentioning this fact to him. He answered me on March 21, 1975, shortly before he died, evading my inquiry, with a cover letter for the party pamphlet *Le Parti communiste français et les evene-ments de Tchechoslovaquie.* The message was thus very clear. But it is noteworthy that he bothered to answer me at all. See Jacques Duclos, *Memoires,* Vol. VI, *Et la lutte continue . . . 1959–1969* (Paris: Fayard, 1972).

129. Tillon, op. cit., p. 184.

130. Dominique Desanti, *L'Internationale communiste* (Paris: Payot, 1970), p. 344. Desanti was a member of the PCF from 1943 to 1956.

131. Georges Marchais, *Le Défi démocratique* (Paris: Bernard Grasset, 1973), pp. 130–131. Note that Marchais does not use Solzhenitsyn's name.

132. André Barjonet, *Le Parti communiste français* (Paris: Les Editions de John Didier, 1969), p. 56.

133. Interview with Claude Quin, Paris, 26 August 1968.

134. Quoted in *Le Monde,* 27 February 1969.

135. See *Les Cahiers du communisme,* January 1969, p. 135.

136. Ibid., February–March 1970, pages not numbered.

137. Marchais, op. cit., pp. 116-117.

138. Quoted in *Le Nouvel Observateur,* 29 March–6 April 1975, p. 67.

139. *Changer de cap,* p. 242.

140. *Programme commun de gouvernement du Parti communiste et du Parti socialiste* (Paris: Editions sociales, 1972), p. 111.

141. Laurens and Pfister, op. cit., pp. 79-80.

142. *Programme commun,* p. 174.

143. *New York Times,* 24 June 1976.

144. *New York Times,* 28 June 1977.

145. *New York Times,* 2 June 1977.

146. Jean Kanapa, *L'Humanité,* 23 June 1976.

147. Jean Elleinstein, *Le P.C.* (Paris: Bernard Grasset, 1976), p. 25.

148. See *Le Point,* 6 June 1977, p. 69.

149. See Maurice Duverger, *Lettre ouverte aux socialistes* (Paris: Albin Michel, 1976), pp. 103–104.

150. See *Le Monde,* 21 June 1977.

151. *Programme commun,* p. 50.

152. See *L'Express,* 19–25 February 1973, pp. 30–34.

153. This is also the opinion of Raymond Aron; see ibid., p. 31.

154. See Borella, op. cit., p. 166.

155. Richard F. Staar, ed., *Yearbook of International Communist Affairs, 1973* (Stanford: Hoover Institution Press, 1974), p. 137.

156. Mitterrand, p. 27.

157. The Socialist congress of Tours in 1920 split the French Left into the SFIO (the then Socialist party) and the PCF.

158. *Programme commun*, pp. 49–50.

159. After all, Communists have always followed the principle that "any agreements between the Party and outside groups must be regarded as aiding the future liquidation of these groups and as a barrier against the liquidation of the Party by them" (Nathan Leites, *The Operational Code of the Politburo*, p. 88).

160. See *Le Crapouillot*, June 1970; James Burnham, "The Protracted Conflict," *National Review*, 22 June 1977, p. 821.

161. See Jean Montaldo, *Les Finances du P.C.F.* (Paris: Albin Michel, 1977).

162. See *L'Express*, 19–25 February 1973, pp. 30–34.

163. See *Le Figaro*, 15 March 1977, p. 1.

164. *L'Express*, 19–25 February 1973, p. 32.

165. *Le Point*, 21 March 1977, p. 62.

166. *Le Monde*, 25 June 1977.

3

Portuguese and Spanish Communism in Comparative Perspective

Eusebio M. Mujal-León

The last few years have seen a revival of interest in the long dormant politics of the Iberian peninsula and, particularly, in the politics of the Spanish and Portuguese Communist parties. For a time after the April 1974 coup, which overthrew Marcello Caetano, it was the seemingly inexorable drive to power by the Portuguese Communist party (PCP) that captured the attention of most foreign observers. More recently, as the Portuguese revolution has given increasing evidence of grinding to a halt and perhaps of succumbing to a Thermidorean reaction, there has been a shift in focus toward Spain and the role the until recently illegal Spanish Communist party (PCE) will play in that country's politics. This chapter will explore and suggest reasons for the differing approaches the Portuguese and Spanish Communist parties have adopted on such matters as political and social alliances, internal organization, and relationship with the international communist movement, in particular, with the Soviet Union.

Impact of Clandestine Period

The PCE and PCP emerged from the long night of clandestine-ness—the Portuguese spent nearly fifty years underground, the Span-

122

ish just under forty—the best organized and most effective political forces in their countries. Beyond that shared experience, however, there is little that joins the two parties. The PCE is a major component of the nascent southern anxis of European communism and was one of the first Western European communist parties to adopt the pluralistic and consensual stance that is increasingly becoming an important part of the ideological baggage of European communism. The contrast with the Portuguese Communists is striking. The PCP, a party characterized by an intransigent Leninism, makes no apology for either its sectarian posture or its all too obvious disdain for bourgeois political parties and institutions.[1]

For the Portuguese Communists, the experience of clandestineness reinforced the view that only a cohesive, unyielding, and well-disciplined organization, which gave life to Lenin's steel fist metaphor, could expect to lead the working class to socialism. Nowhere does this outlook come through more vividly than in a relatively obscure article written by Alvaro Cunhal, PCP secretary general, and published in early 1974.[2] Entitled "The Moral Superiority of Communists," the article makes repeated references to "moral strength" and exhorts its readers to "moral endurance," revealing the almost religious intensity with which Cunhal (and, we may safely presume, his party) view the communists' duty not only to be "the revolutionary political vanguard of the proletariat" but also its "moral vanguard." Even the slightest deviation from the classical Leninist code, Cunhal stressed, would have a "demoralizing" effect on all aspects of the party's work and therefore be an obstacle to the fulfillment of its historical mission.

Such a perception evidently affected the party's relations with other organizations and the types of alliances into which it was willing to enter. As far as the PCP was concerned, the other groups in the opposition had only a very limited and historically transitory role to play in the revolutionary process. Certainly, the Communists were advocates of the broadest possible unity against the Salazar and Caetano dictatorships, but, as they never ceased to point out, theirs was the only organization extant during the 1920s (the Republicans, Anarcho-syndicalists, and Socialists had in effect disappeared as organized groups by the late 1940s) that survived that period, emerging with the nucleus of a party apparatus still intact. Communist advocacy of broad alliances and the leading role the PCP played in the constitution of various antiregime united fronts—first the MUNAF (National Antifascist Unity Movement), created in October 1943, later the MUD (Democratic Union Movement), and, finally, the CDEs (democratic electoral commissions) of the late 1960s—particularly in the later years of the Estado novo, were in fact less concerned with galvanizing a powerful opposition front than with making sure that the ambivalent posture these groups assumed vis-à-vis the regime did not lead to an anticommunist coalition between the moderate opposition and erstwhile reformers within the regime.[3]

One incident in the late 1960s may be cited to show that Communist fears on this score were not unfounded. The situation developed after Caetano, upon becoming prime minister after Salazar suffered a massive and incapacitating stroke in 1968, announced a loosening of internal political restrictions and promised the liberalization of the regime. Caetano's efforts encountered significant opposition within the regime and he was eventually unable to press forward with even his timid reform program, but not before he raised the hopes of some by authorizing the return of two prominent exiles: Antonio Ferreira Gomes, the bishop of the northern city of Oporto and a critic of church-state relations in Portugal under Salazar, and Mario Soares, a prominent Socialist lawyer. The PCP criticized Caetano bitterly for what it termed his *manobra demagogica* and admonished the other opposition forces to beware of the consequences of joining with the regime and trying to isolate the Communists.[4] Their suspicions were confirmed when, shortly after Soares's return from exile, his group, the ASP (Portuguese Socialist Action), issued a manifesto keeping open the possibility of some sort of collaboration with the "liberals" in the regime should the latter give some evidence of internal reform. The document, moreover, prominently reproached the Communists for their advocacy of "totalitarian socialism."[5] These circumstances exacerbated the already thinly veiled hostility between Soares and the Communists and resulted in the former's withdrawal from the umbrella opposition organization known as the CDE.[6] Soares eventually reentered the CDE, but the rivalry between what was to become the nucleus of the Partido socialista português after April 1974 and the PCP would not subside.

An essential element of the broad alliance strategy advocated by the PCP was its insistence that the opposition use all legal and semilegal opportunities such as participation by the opposition in the periodic National Assembly elections and in the regime's "vertically" organized labor movement. But the Portuguese Communists were nevertheless adamant that the Estado novo would have to be overthrown by force.[7] How the party expected the "final, decisive clash against the dictatorship" (in Cunhal's words) to begin never became especially clear and it is quite probable that the party leadership itself had no precise idea as to how the "national armed insurrection" was to come about.[8] The very rejection of the possibility that the regime could be transformed peacefully was highly significant inasmuch as it represented an attack not only on what the PCP termed the "fascist" character of the regime and its institutions but, more important, also on the moderate opposition's capacity for effective political action.

Such an approach, it should be noted, had not always been the official party position. The program adopted at the fifth PCP congress in 1958 had in fact conceived of a change in regime occurring in relatively peaceful fashion via a general political strike coordinated with other opposition groups. That policy, which was remarkably similar to the national reconciliation line enunciated in 1956 by the Spanish Communists and which signaled the beginning of the shift in the PCE's orientation, led to heated intraparty polemics in the PCP with critics charging that abandonment of the scheme for a classic armed uprising also meant abandonment of the party's commitment to revolutionary change. The internal conflict led to the subsequent convocation of a special central committee plenum in March 1961 at which Cunhal, who had escaped from Peniche prison in Portugal the year before, successfully led the struggle against the "anarcho-liberal" deviationists.[9] The change in policy was ultimately unsuccessful in preventing the exodus of disaffected leftist (Maoist, Castroist, etc.) elements from the PCP during the 1960s, but it shows Cunhal and his supporters to have had a rather sympathetic susceptibility to persons critical of the party's program from the Left. The thrust of their efforts then, and also after April 1974, was not simply to preserve the élan of the party's militants but also to undercut actively the claims other organizations might make to the mantle of revolutionary leadership. Thus, it was quite in character for the Communists, when groups like the PRP-BR (Revolutionary party of the Proletarian-Revolutionary Brigade) and the LUAR (Revolutionary Union and Action league) began to sabotage military installations and carry out urban guerrilla type actions, publicly to denigrate the effectiveness of isolated acts of violence and to castigate those organizations for their "petit bourgeois" prejudices,[10] while at the same time launching their own paramilitary organization, the ARA (Armed Revolutionary Action). It would be tempting to see in all this nothing more than window dressing of the sort any self-described radical party might engage in. But, as events after Caetano's overthrow were to demonstrate, the radical and sectarian tendencies the PCP developed during its underground period indelibly affected the party's behavior after it formally entered the Portuguese political arena.

The military revolution of April 1974 confirmed for the PCP the essential correctness of its approach to the question of how to seize political power. During the first phase of the revolutionary process (April–September 1974), the PCP acted primarily as a force for order and moderation. At one level, the party vehemently insisted on the importance of unity with other parties and groups, but its vision of the political process left little doubt that it expected most of them to fall by the wayside in the not too distant future. According to the party's theoretical scheme, a dichotomy between economic and political power existed in Portugal after April 25. "Political power" had passed into the hands of "democratic forces" after that date, but "economic power remained in the hands of the monopolists and latifundists." It was a situation that the PCP believed could not go on much longer. "Either the monopolies and the latifundia take over political power, installing a new dictatorship in Portugal," declared Cunhal at his party's seventh congress in October 1974, "or the democratic forces, in order to construct a new Portugal, must put an end to [their] economic power."[11]

This analysis implicitly presented some rather stark alternatives. There was to be no place for a Western European style parliamentary democracy in Portugal: the country's social structure, with its weak middle class, could not support "monopoly capitalist" economic concentration and broad political democracy at the same time. The monopoly capitalist class that ruled the country economically could not maintain its domination and level of exploitation without resorting to violence and establishing a new "fascist" dictatorship. After Antonio de Spinola's resignation in September 1974 and, even more, after the attempted coup to which he lent his name on March 11, 1975, it became clear that the radicals of the MFA (Armed Forces movement) were ready to fill the vacuum left by the overthrow of the ancien régime by moving in the direction of a rapid advance of the revolutionary process and that the moderate parties of the center and Left, committed to parliamentary politics, seemed unable to block this move. The PCP went with the tide, trying as best it could to make itself indispensable to the MFA. The Communists did not, in any case, have much to lose: the April 1975 Constituent Assembly elections had shown their party to have a markedly regional base of support (focusing almost exclusively in the working class of the Lisbon-Setúbal region and among the agricultural laborers of the Alentejo) and judging by the results they could expect to play little more than a secondary role in the country's politics. The summer of 1975 saw the culmination of a drive to power on the part of the PCP and its allies in the MFA. It was unsuccessful and the dénouement came in two stages. First, there was the removal of Communist sympathizer Vasco Gonçalves[12] from the premiership in August and the appointment of Admiral Pinheiro de Azevedo as his successor in early September 1975. Then, in the aftermath of an abortive leftist coup in November 1975, in which the PCP was partially implicated, there was a government purge of radicals in the armed forces and throughout the state apparatus.[13]

For the Spanish Communists, that sequence of events revealed the inappropriateness of traditional Leninist methods of reaching power in advanced industrial societies. After an initial period of euphoria, during which they confidently expected that events in Portugal presaged the beginning of an offensive by the Left throughout Mediterranean Europe, the Spanish Communists, like the Italians, moved to disassociate themselves from the actions of their Portuguese counterparts.[14] Relations between the two parties had never been particularly close, but the radicalization in Portugal threatened to undermine the long and patient efforts of the PCE to convince others on the Left and all but the party's most irreconcilable enemies on the Right that the PCE intended to abide by the rules of the democratic game.

Whereas Portuguese Communist policies have been predicated on the need for conflict and polarization, those of the Spanish party have emphasized reconciliation and national unity. Certainly, at a surface level, the two parties have coincided in their calls for broad alliances to overthrow the dictatorships in their respective countries. The coalition could have as its base the working class but would pass through the peasants and intellectuals and include broad sectors of the middle class, all of whom were or objectively should be interested in supporting social change directed at the ruling representatives of the "financial oligarchies and latifundist aristocracy."[15] But the PCP's *ouvriériste* orientation and its opinion that the political parties of the bourgeoisie were rapidly becoming obsolete was never far from view. The Spanish Communists, by contrast, espoused extended interclass collaboration.

During the Spanish Civil War, the PCE had been an advocate of moderate policies, ceaselessly and ruthlessly opposing the maximalist postures of the Anarchists and many Socialists and insisting that the war had to be won before a revolution could be begun.[16] These policies obeyed above all the exigencies of Soviet foreign policy; yet it is noteworthy that after the defeat in 1939 the PCE in many ways retained the outlook forged during the Popular Front period and continued to act as if its political space were still preempted on the Left. A deepening of the Spanish Communist orientation in that direction did not come until 1956, when control of the party changed hands and a new generation of leaders grouped around the present secretary general, Santiago Carrillo, assumed a dominant position. Symbolic of the direction in which these men hoped to move the PCE was the call for national reconciliation the party issued in mid-1956 on the twentieth anniversary of the beginning of the Civil War. On a tactical level, the appeal was remarkably prescient, setting the tone for many later antiregime initiatives. More important, it underscored the new leadership's intention to eschew exile politics and to direct the party's energies at the new generations of Spaniards who had neither fought nor lived through the Civil War and for whom the bitter animosities spawned by that conflict (between the "victors" and the "vanquished" and, within the defeated Republican camp, between the Communists and their erstwhile allies, the Anarchists and the Socialists) made little sense.

National reconciliation was to become the touchstone of Spanish Communist policy after 1956. As the PCE saw things, the overthrow of the regime and the establishment of political liberties would be a relatively peaceful process, taking place not through a classic armed assault on the state but through a well-coordinated series of strikes (the *huelga general política* leading to the *huelga nacional*) that would paralyze the country.[17] The opposition alliance would be so broad as to include all who fought against the regime, regardless of social or political background; as a result, the armed forces would not be called upon to play an active role in the undertaking.[18] Carrillo was quite forthright on this point in an interview with *L'Humanité* in 1970: "[The party will join] with any Spanish political group, even with those who fought us in the past and with groups who will undoubtedly fight us in the future."[19]

One concession the Spanish Communist leadership did make to its critics on the Left in the early 1960s was to insist that the downfall of Franco was imminent and would set the structural conditions for the forces of the Left to eliminate what the PCE considered to be the existing system of state monopoly capitalism. The theoretical justification for this assessment need not concern us here. What is important is that, along with this assessment, the PCE argued that if the Left did not succeed in destroying the economic power of the monopolies and in beginning the construction of a *democracia política y social* as an intermediate stage on the road to socialism, a new dictatorship would be imposed on the country. This formulation was very similar to the one made by the Portuguese Communists and both flowed from a reliance on the scheme devised by the Comintern in the 1930s to explain the phenomenon of fascism in less developed countries. We have seen that in the Portuguese case this assessment led ultimately to an argument that saw the alternatives reduced to either fascism or revolution rather quickly. The Spanish were more careful. For them, as for the Italian Communists, *democracia política y social* was to be a lengthy transitional stage lasting for several decades, during which time there would be a plurality of parties and broad freedom of expression, criticism, and assembly.[20] For a variety of reasons, not the least of which was the fact that many of the moderate opposition were bothered by the apparent contradiction between the PCE's moderate approach to the question of how to transform the regime and its socioeconomic vision of what would come thereafter, the Spanish Communists abandoned that formulation in the early 1970s. The party's program manifesto, published in September 1973, explicitly states that once the "fascist" structures are torn down, it will indeed be possible for Spain to follow the "neocapitalist" path taken by other Western European countries after World War II. They still kept open the possibility that the changes after Franco would be of a sufficient magnitude to make Spain the first Western European country to take the road to socialism. But, as time went on and Franco's heirs gave increasing evidence of being able to transform the political system, the Spanish Communists insisted on the latter perspective less and less.

Despite their moderate policies, prior to 1974 the Spanish Communists had had a difficult time forging a broad alliance of groups interested in overthrowing the regime. Perhaps this was in part the result of the unwillingness of the traditional organizations of the Spanish Left to forgive or forget what they considered the Communist betrayal of the Spanish revolution to the exigencies of Soviet foreign policy. Possibly, too, the noncommunist Left was unwilling to come to terms with an organization that was far and away the best organized opposition force. Whatever the answer, it was only in the aftermath of the December 1973 assassination of the Spanish head of state, Admiral Carrero Blanco, that the first real signs of a system-wide crisis became apparent and that the PCE was able to break out of the ghetto into which it had been placed after 1939. In July 1974, the PCE secretary general, Santiago Carrillo, was able to announce at a Paris news conference the formation of a *junta democrática* joining together various opposition parties and personalities, among them Rafael Calvo Serer, a prominent liberal monarchist and member of the secular-religious order known as Opus Dei; the Partido carlista, made up of supporters of the pretender to the throne, Don Javier de Borbón Parma; the Partido socialista popular, a Socialist group led by Enrique Tierno Galván; and the Comisiones obreras. The Communists insisted that the junta was the "democratic alternative" to the regime and would form the nucleus of the provisional government to follow Franco.[21] These claims proved to be rather extreme, but it is clear that the formation of the junta was a political triumph of the first order for the PCE and for its policy of national reconciliation. It was the first opposition front in which the PCE had participated since the resignation in 1947 of the Communist minister from the Republican government in exile. It was almost anticlimactic, in a sense, that the junta and another opposition front, the Plataforma de convergencia, grouping together Socialists, Christian Democrats, and Maoists, formally fused in March 1976.

The PCE remained firm in its insistence well into 1976 that the Franco regime could not be reformed and that Francoist institutions such as the Cortes would prove incapable of paving the way for parliamentary democracy. This affirmation (which, it might be noted, was shared by a good many less radical opponents of the regime) has been proven incorrect. King Juan Carlos and Premier Adolfo Suárez successfully engineered a political reform program through the Francoist Cortes in November 1976 and sponsored elections to the new Chamber of Deputies and Senate in June 1977. The Communists had broken out of clandestineness little more than a year after the Caudillo's death. Carrillo publicly surfaced at a well-attended Madrid news conference in December and, although subsequently arrested, he was quickly released and permitted to engage in political activity. Formal legalization of the PCE did not come about until April 1977, roughly a month after Carrillo and his party had been hosts to a "Eurocommunist" summit in Madrid attended by Georges Marchais of the PCF and Enrico Berlinguer of the PCI. Communist candidates participated openly in the June elections, and during the campaign the PCE aired most of its verbal blasts at the neo-Francoist Alianza popular and hardly criticized the incumbent Suárez. It is unclear whether this stance helped the party's own performance in the election but it undoubtedly contributed to the Alianza's poor showing. The Communists received 9.2% of the national vote and secured 20 seats in the 350-member Congress of Deputies and 3 in the Senate. Despite their relatively low percentage of the vote—representing, nonetheless, over 1.5 million voters—the Communists emerged as the third largest political force in post-Franco Spain, trailing only the centrist coalition of eleven parties headed by Suárez (34% of the vote: 168 seats in the Congress and 105 in the Senate) and the Partido socialista obrero español (Spanish Socialist Workers party) (29% of the vote: 118 seats in the Congress and 47 in the Senate). They are certain to play an important role in the country's politics over the next decade.

Relations of PCP and PCE to the Church and the Labor Movement

Our discussion of the domestic policies of the PCE and PCP has focused so far on the more narrowly political strategies of the two parties. With that as our background, we now examine the stance the two parties adopted vis-à-vis two fundamentally important sectors of Spanish and Portuguese society: the Catholic church and subculture and the labor movement.

THE CHURCH

The Catholic church in Spain and Portugal, as in the rest of Latin Europe, consistently has functioned as a bulwark of conservative reaction and as an opponent of social change. Both the Spanish and Portuguese churches officially supported the establishment of the authoritarian Franco and Salazar regimes and benefited over the years from a symbiotic relationship with them. Guided by Cardinal Cerejeira in Lisbon and his counterparts Gomá, Herrera, and Pla y Daniel in Madrid, the two churches came to assume privileged institutional roles in both regimes.[22] Beginning in the 1960s, however, the Spanish church began an evolution away from that role and has taken an increasingly neutral stance with respect to the government. The dissociation of the Spanish hierarchy from Franco reached its climax in February 1974, when the government ordered the arrest of, and sought to deport, the bishop of Bilbao for demanding greater civil rights for Basques. Important though this event was, it was in some respects but a faint echo of the changes affecting the lower levels of the church in Spain, where anticapitalist and antiregime positions became the order of the day. This was particularly the case in worker neighborhoods and in strongholds of Basque and Catalan nationalism, harshly repressed by Madrid.

This evolution did not take place in the Portuguese church. The hierarchy there never moved away from either Salazar or Caetano and the influence of the *aggiornamento* produced elsewhere by the Second Vatican Council in 1964 was minimal. The April 1974 coup surprised the hierarchy and, for the first year or so of the revolution, the church remained discreetly in the background.[23] By 1975, however, when the Socialists and the less radical members of the MFA were leading a coincident attack on Gonçalves and the Communists, the most conservative sectors of the church shed their caution and came out openly against the Left. Particularly in the north of the country, where parish priests enjoyed enormous authority, the church lent the struggle overtones of a crusade. In the city of Braga, to cite but one prominent example, a mob burned and sacked PCP headquarters after hearing an inflammatory speech by the archbishop.

Although the ultraconservative stance of the church in Portugal [24] could not have helped but convince an already sectarian PCP that Catholicism is a feudal bastion to be stormed by the revolutionary forces,[25] the PCE, thanks in part to the fact that it faced a less stolid church, adopted a less frontal and more subtle response to the Catholic subculture in Spain. Although many other organizations of the Spanish Left found it difficult to shed their traditional anticlericalism, the PCE encouraged its militants to enter into dialogue with

Catholics at all levels. Catholic-Communist interaction became a reality in the early 1960s because of the activities in the labor movement of apostolic labor organizations such as the Hermandades obreras de acción católica (HOAC) and the Juventud obrera católica (JOC). According to the terms of the August 1953 concordat signed by Madrid and the Vatican, the HOAC and the JOC had the right to organize among the working class and to function independently of the official vertical syndical structure, the Organización sindical. (Catholic Action never really got off the ground in Portugal despite the efforts of some socially conscious clergy.) The failure of the regime sponsored structures to respond to the demands of an expanding working class in the late 1950s and early 1960s gave the apostolic labor organizations an opportunity to fill the organizational vacuum. Not surprisingly, HOAC and JOC militants, their radicalization fueled by a sense of shame about the church's relationship with the regime, played in many cases a decisive role in fostering the growth of the parallel, opposition labor movement known as the Comisiones obreras; their radicalization was likewise fueled by the sense of shame many of them felt about the church's support for a repressive regime.

THE LABOR MOVEMENT

The Franco and Salazar regimes, products of successful conservative reaction to the demands of an emerging working class, presented their "corporatist" structures as an original and altogether felicitous way of disposing of the problem of class conflict in Spain and Portugal, respectively. The process of economic growth begun by both Spain and Portugal in the late 1950s, albeit of significantly different dimensions, helped disprove that assiduously cultivated myth by setting the structural conditions for new sources of working class dissent.

Having instructed their militants from early on to combine legal and illegal activity in the regime sponsored *sindicatos*, the Portuguese and Spanish Communists were in a position to take advantage of those developments. It was PCP labor activists, already holding important posts in the official textile, metallurgical, and construction unions, who created in October 1970 the opposition labor front known as InterSindical. The organization grew vigorously but had to face the harsh repression the regime directed at its activists. When the MFA overthrew Caetano in April 1974, InterSindical numbered several dozen unions and functioned as *the* syndical alternative to the vertical syndicates. The Portuguese Communists wasted little time after the coup in consolidating their control and transforming the old

Ministerio de corporaçoes. They were aided in their efforts by the fact that the labor minister of the first provisional government, Bento Gonçalves, was a party member long active in the banking employees union and, although he resigned in July 1974 as a result of a cabinet reshuffle, his successor, Captain Costa Martins of the MFA, was very close to the PCP and permitted the party to continue to expand its influence. Indeed, it was Costa Martins who helped draft the law, approved in principle by the MFA in January 1975, that made InterSindical the national labor confederation. By mid-1975 of the most important unions in the country only that of the chemical workers was not under the control of the PCP or its sympathizers. Beginning in the summer of 1975 an unstable alliance between Socialists and extreme leftists from the MRPP (Reorganizing Movement of the Party of the Proletariat) and AOC (Worker-Peasant Alliance) won a few notable victories against the lists presented by the Communists in some unions like those of journalists and banking employees in the north, but this mesalliance disintegrated in the fall of 1975 once the PS (Socialist party) took on major responsibility in the government and had to shoulder responsibility for price and wage control measures. Subsequent efforts to dislodge the PCP from its control of labor have all floundered and the party retains in the trade unions a potent weapon against the present Socialist government's efforts to isolate the Communists and bring the economy under control.

Like the Portuguese Communists, the Spanish ably exploited the foothold they gained in the regime's vertical syndical structures. As far back as 1948, when the PCE abandoned a guerrilla struggle against Franco, it had advised its militants to work within the *sindicatos*. The revisions of the collective bargaining system undertaken by the government in 1958 in order to help spur a stagnating economy made this a particularly prescient decision.[26] But, whereas the PCP had virtually no competition from other groups in the labor field (Catholic Action never developed into a real contestant in Portugal and the Socialist party had its audience among the liberal professions), the Spanish Communists had to cope with various groups. Of traditional working class organizations like the Anarchist CNT (National Labor confederation) and the Socialist UGT (General Union of Workers), the former had virtually disappeared and the latter retained influence only in some areas of the country; yet the PCE nonetheless had to deal with Catholic activists from the HOAC and the JOC, who in the early 1960s played a much greater role than the Communists in fomenting strikes and labor unrest and who later helped spawn many radical groups. The Communists' greater organizational and ideological cohesion eventually carried the day and the party came to assume a preponderant role in the Comisiones obreras.

But it was constrained in its efforts to achieve hegemony. All through the 1960s, the PCE had insisted that the Comisiones were the vehicle to take over the Organización sindical and would become the axis upon which the united labor confederation would be built. The Portuguese Communists had used similar tactics prior to and after April 1974, and although the Spanish Communists criticized the PCP for riding roughshod over others and imposing labor unity, it is highly probable that had they been able to capture a similar position their party would have proceeded in much the same style. They might have phrased the effort more delicately, insisting on the nonpartisan nature of the Comisiones, rejecting the traditional Leninist "transmission belt" concept of party-trade union relations—and perhaps even meaning it.[27] However, the short-term result would probably have been the same. We have already emphasized the numerous groups in the Spanish labor movement as a factor that worked against the PCE. Another is that the Spanish working class finds itself dispersed in several major industrial centers. Coordinated action has been made difficult by distance and further complicated by the existence in Spain of a serious nationalities problem, focusing in the Basque country, Catalonia, and Galicia. Portugal, on the contrary, is largely homogeneous, has about one-fourth the population of its neighbor, and finds its working class concentrated in the Lisbon-Setúbal region and in the Alentejo.

Party Organization and Practice

So far we have been concerned with analyzing the political and social alliance strategies of the PCE and PCP. There is also an organizational dimension of Portuguese and Spanish communism that merits consideration. That both parties survived a lengthy clandestine experience and emerged as the most effective opposition organizations should not surprise us. Communist parties traditionally have been able to adapt to clandestineness much more easily than other political forces: their democratic centralist structures and their militants' willingness to give great demonstrations of heroism permit them to bear the weight of the repression unleashed by the most authoritarian of regimes. (The Portuguese Communist twenty-two-man central committee, elected at the party's seventh congress in October 1974, had collectively served over 300 years in prison.)[28] The PCP, for example, entered the Portuguese political arena in April 1974 with nearly 3000 members and the PCE, operating under perhaps less brutal conditions, had perhaps 10,000 members in Spain in the early 1970s. These figures, reflective of those of *partidos de cuadros* and certainly not of mass organizations, nevertheless compare very favorably with other groups.

Both the Spanish and Portuguese parties have functioned as highly centralized organizations whose leaderships tolerated little dissent and in which selection of *dirigentes* took place through cooptation into the leading bodies. One notable demonstration of this aspect of party life came, in the case of the PCE, in September 1970, at a time when Secretary General Carrillo was under challenge from a pro-Soviet faction led by Enrique Líster. On his own initiative and to make sure matters did not get out of hand, Carrillo coopted twenty-nine new members into the central committee. As of mid-1977 the PCE central committee, one of the largest in the world, has over 120 members, its executive committee 34. Although there have been sporadic reports of opposition to Carrillo's leadership, particularly among middle level cadres, all indications are that he has matters firmly under control and will step aside when he is ready. Nonetheless, it is important to remember that he is sixty-two years old: and in the not too distant future the party will have to find a replacement for him and others of his generation (who fill about half of the executive committee). The Portuguese Communist party, until recently, has had a much smaller leadership group: only in November 1976 did the PCP, a party with over 150,000 members, expand its central committee from 36 to 90 persons.[29] Alvaro Cunhal has played in the internal affairs of the Portuguese party a role very similar to that of Santiago Carrillo in the Spanish. Ironically, both men have availed themselves of democratic centralism to achieve opposite results—Carrillo, to overcome opposition to his efforts to direct the PCE along a more accommodating and moderate path; Cunhal, to retain for his party its Leninist ideological and political orientation.

Because the organizational dimension is in some senses the touchstone of an evolution in Western European communism and the PCE appears to be in the vanguard of that process, it may be well to discuss this feature in the Spanish party at greater length. In 1960, the PCE abandoned the idea of being a cadre party in the future, and at the party's sixth congress that year the delegates modified the statutes so as to permit membership in the party without participation in cell activity.[30] These were the first timid steps by the PCE to prepare itself to become a mass based party. More recently, at a July 1976 central committee plenum in Rome, the Spanish party abandoned the use of the cell structure altogether and ordered the creation of *agrupaciones* similar in organization and in concept to those used by the PCI (Italian Communist party): these bodies are to be based on neighborhood and work areas, which would hold public meetings to which militants and sympathizers alike would be invited.[31] The central committee session also set a target figure of 300,000 members to be reached by the end of 1977, a number that would make the PCE the third largest communist party in Western Europe. Unabashed users of democratic centralism during their party's clandestine existence, the Spanish Communist leadership repeatedly insisted that once the PCE became legal, differences of opinion would be not only tolerated but even encouraged so long as they did not crystallize into outright factions. One has the sense that there is a great deal of sometimes heated discussion within the PCE at this time, although it is perhaps true that internal liberalization was adopted more out of tactical expedience (how else could one manage a mass party?) than commitment to liberal democratic values. The essential ambiguity of its behavior should not, however, obscure the fact that the PCE as an organization is not simply in the world but of it and that at some future date the party could become something less than Leninist in its organizational approach as well.

A final comment about the social composition of the two parties. As befits the *ouvriériste* orientation of the PCP, 60% of its members come from the industrial working class or agricultural proletariat and another 18% are tertiary sector employees.[32] The party finds its electoral base in the industrial belt around Lisbon-Setúbal and in the Alentejo. In the north of Portugal, where small and medium size landholding and traditionalist values predominate, the Communist battle cry of agrarian reform and "The land to who tills it" connotes expropriation, which is anathema to small rural proprietors; as a result, the party has scant support in that part of the country.

Detailed information on the social composition of the PCE is as yet unavailable; thus, remarks about the Spanish party have to be more speculative. Outside the working class Spanish Communist influence is strong among professionals such as doctors, lawyers, and engineers and in the universities. Indeed, it is reflective of a larger trend in the party's orientation that over 40% of the incumbent central committee may be classified as intellectuals or professionals.

The International Dimension

We have explored so far in some detail the similarities and the contrasts in the alliance strategies and organizational approaches of the Portuguese and Spanish Communist parties. We can now turn our attention to the international dimension of Iberian communism, an area in which the differences in outlook between the two parties are perhaps most striking and in which they have given rise to the most comment.

Explanations of the behavior of communist parties have generally emphasized the primacy of international relationships and ties to the Soviet Union in the determination of communist policy. For many years, students of revolutionary politics studied communist parties from a perspective that stressed that they were essentially alien forces, national only in a very formal and narrow sense, and tenaciously resisting integration into their respective societies.[33] With the growth of mass based communist parties in Western Europe and the manifest splintering of the international communist movement in the late 1950s and early 1960s, the utility of the "combat party" model lessened. Research on the French and Italian Communist parties suggested that in the years after World War II the influence of the international dimension had been overstressed and that the national context in which these parties operate has had and will continue to have a profound impact on their behavior.[34] The analytic framework proposed by Donald Blackmer for the study of the PCI, to cite one example, argued that the maintenance of links with the international communist movement and with the Soviet Union in particular was but one of three basic interests the party pursued and among which it sought to effect a reasonable working balance.[35] More recently, Ronald Tiersky posited the primacy of the domestic context in which the PCF operates as the key to understanding French Communist policy.[36] Finally, in an essay comparing the postwar strategies of the Italian and French parties and dealing with the nexus between domestic and international policies, Peter Lange stressed "contextual factors" and went so far as to declare that "the influence of the USSR has been to sanction, or in rare cases to attempt to impede, developments in party strategy that were stimulated by structural conditions in the parties' environments."[37]

The focus of "revisionist" studies of this kind has been the communist parties of the major industrialized countries of Western Europe. By contrast, little attention has been paid to the politics of Iberian communism and the degree to which the Soviet Union has played a determining role in the formulation of Spanish and Portuguese Communist policies. One reason for this neglect[38] was that the acquisition of materials, their evaluation, and the objective analysis of the activities of the PCE and the PCP were extremely difficult. But perhaps the most important reason for the lack of attention was the prevalence of the notion that a wide analytical gulf separated legal mass parties like the PCF (French Communist party) and PCI from their clandestine, and perforce more restricted, counterparts like the PCE and PCP. The radically different situations in which legal and illegal parties operate, it cannot be denied, affect their mode of operation, but the image of a clandestine party as a party primarily, or almost exclusively, responsive to the wishes and policy needs of the Soviet Union is a distortion by caricature.

It is certainly an inappropriate description of the PCE. In the 1960s and particularly after the invasion of Czechoslovakia in August 1968, the Spanish Communists assumed an independent and highly critical stance toward the Communist party of the Soviet Union (CPSU).[39] The PCE condemned the Czech invasion and in subsequent years moved to the brink of a rupture with Moscow. There is no need to explore the deterioration in relations in any great detail: suffice it to point out that the Soviets and many of their Eastern European allies made little effort to conceal their sympathy for and give organizational and financial assistance to the splinter groups headed by a former PCE organizational secretary, Eduardo García, and a Civil War veteran, Enrique Líster. These efforts failed largely through Carrillo's adroit handling of the situation and the financial and moral support he and his associates received from the Italian, Rumanian, and Yugoslav parties.

Since 1968, the PCE has moved beyond simple assertions in favor of organizational independence vis-à-vis Moscow to broader critiques of Soviet domestic and foreign policies. The party singled out the Soviet Union's European policy for particular criticism, asserting that the Kremlin was more interested in assuring its control over Eastern Europe than with assisting the Western European communists in their efforts to bring about profound structural transformations in the societies of the West.[40] Certainly, this idea had been implicit in some of the formulations made by other parties, notably the PCI, but no other party was as explicit in its criticism of the Soviet Union on this score as the PCE. A corollary to this argument was the Spanish Communist insistence that the Western European communists help forge a united front of the European Left and build a European socialist community that, taking advantage of the superpower confrontation, would have its own specific, independent weight in the international arena. The idea was anathema to the Soviets, and in February 1974 the CPSU central committee journal, Partiinaia zhizn, published a vitriolic and unprecedented personal attack on Manuel Azcárate, the principal PCE ideologist. There were several counts in the indictment against the Spanish Communist leader; yet clearly the most important criticism directed at him concerned his efforts in various articles to justify the growth of an autonomous Western European communist movement. The journal accused Azcárate of "having sided with the declared enemies of the Socialist community" and his ideas of "reeking with nationalism."[41] Subsequently, and perhaps due to the mediation of the PCI, both sides stepped back from a rupture of all relations. The two parties issued a joint communiqué in October 1974, but the formula used to describe the talks—there had been a "frank and comradely exchange of views"—indicated that the PCE had not backed down from its positions and that the two sides had simply agreed to disagree.[42] A new low point in PCE-CPSU relations came with the publication in June 1977 of an article in the Soviet journal *New Times* attacking Carrillo for the highly critical remarks he had directed at the Soviet Union in his book *Eurocommunism and the State.*[43] It is unlikely, at least while Santiago Carrillo remains at the helm of the Spanish party, that the breach will close. In any case, many in the PCE have concluded that the Soviet Union and the Warsaw Pact present as significant an obstacle to the fulfillment of Spanish Communist domestic and regional objectives as the United States and NATO.

Apparently the PCP is a better example of the traditional view that the policies of parties that are clandestine, or have only recently been legalized, are subservient to the Soviet Union. We have already examined in some detail the sectarian domestic policies the Portuguese Communists pursued before and after April 1974. Internationally, at a time when most other European communist parties are trying strenuously to mark their distance from Moscow (even if they have not gone as far as the PCE), the Portuguese have seemed to relish the spotlight of orthodoxy. They have stubbornly backed the CPSU against the Chinese since the early 1960s and gave wholehearted approval to the invasion of Czechoslovakia and to the subsequent "normalization" there.[44] More recently, the PCP has sided with the CPSU and its principal allies (particularly the East Germans and the Bulgarians) during the lengthy procedural negotiations leading to the Berlin communist summit in the summer of 1976. For the PCP, and to quote Secretary General Cunhal upon his return from the twenty-fifth CPSU congress in February 1976, the Soviet Union is "the principal fortress of the workers and of the forces of peace and progress throughout the world" and its existence is like "the sunlight on the earth."

At a time when unconditional supporters of the CPSU are few and far between, Portuguese Communist solidarity is no doubt especially appreciated. The model of socialism advocated by the PCP is similar in its essential respects to the Soviet and Eastern European one: the party supports broad front tactics but its view of democracy is an instrumental one with the vanguard and privileged position belonging to the PCP. Echoing the Soviet stance, Cunhal has emphasized the existence of "fundamental, general, and universal features of the socialist revolution," and in his speech to the Berlin communist meeting in June 1976 he rejected the idea advanced by the Spanish, Italian, and other parties that there could be "a common

recipe or common obligatory road for all Western European countries taking the road to socialism."[45] The PCP has continued to
oppose Portuguese entry into the European Economic Community
(the Spanish party changed its stance in 1972 and now supports
Spanish entry into the EEC once democracy is established in the
country),[46] arguing instead for replacing "the power of the monopolies" in the member countries.[47] This is in line with the Portuguese
Communist view that the EEC is an instrument for North American
and European monopolies to insure their economic domination. The
PCP's attitude toward NATO has been more ambiguous. Prior to
1974, the party demanded the outright withdrawal of Portugal from
the Atlantic alliance, but after Caetano's overthrow the PCP argued
that withdrawal should be put off and effected in the context of
more general East-West force reduction talks.[48]

There can be little doubt about the obdurately pro-Soviet position of the PCP and the less than cordial relations it maintains
with the other major parties in Western Europe, with the significant exception of the PCF. It is one thing to stress the pro-Soviet
attitude of the PCP and quite another to insist that this dimension
has been the determining factor in the policies pursued by the
Portuguese Communists since the April 1974 coup and particularly
in the summer and fall of 1975. Such an interpretation is incorrect
on both factual and interpretative grounds. Not only did the Soviet
Union never develop a cohesive policy toward Portugal, but events
in that country sparked lengthy and complex debates within the
Soviet foreign policy establishment that could only have constrained whatever efforts the Soviets might have wanted to make
to influence the Portuguese Communists.[49] More important, from
our point of view, seeing the PCP as essentially a tool of the
Kremlin ignores the fact that unswerving fidelity to the Soviet
Union was a consequence of, and not a condition for, the shaping
of the tough, sectarian outlook on politics that the PCP developed
during the clandestine period. After April 1974, the Portuguese
Communists found themselves in a situation that lent itself to
Leninist politics. That the PCP eventually failed in its thrust for
power is largely irrelevant in this context for the fact remains that
its strategy was not at all unreasonable in a situation that saw a
radicalized MFA increasingly willing to dispense with traditional
electoral politics. In the end, it was not that the PCP failed to
penetrate the state apparatus or to win the battle of street demonstrations—the Communists did do both—but that the radicals in the
MFA did not have the cohesion to marshal the popular support to
carry through their schemes.

Past, Present, and Future

Our discussion of the Portuguese and Spanish Communist parties has explored the similarities and differences in the perceptions of domestic political realities, organizational needs, and international relationships the two parties have developed over the last two decades. At first glance, their shared background of long clandestine experience would suggest that the PCE and PCP have much in common. As we have seen upon closer inspection, this is not the case. It is the differences between the two parties that predominate. An explanation of these differences must take into account dissimilarities in the histories of the two parties and in the environments in which they operate. It should also stress the roles played in the development of these parties by their leaderships. Clandestine, exile parties are highly centralistic organizations in which strong leaders can play inordinately important roles. We have noted the ascetic, almost religious intensity with which Alvaro Cunhal and his associates approach political affairs. That vision of the political struggle was forged through four decades spent underground, in jail, or in Eastern European exile, and it found ready acceptance in a party at work in an underdeveloped (by European standards) and extremely hostile environment. In some ways, even in exile or underground, the Spanish Communists faced a less harsh climate, particularly after the mid-1960s, but what was most important in determining the course of the PCE was the moderate and accommodating style developed by the Spanish leaders. Changes in 1956 helped spur their evolution from Stalinism as did the personal antagonism Santiago Carrillo and others developed toward the Soviet leaders after the Czech invasion. But, in some ways, the gradualist ideas they now espouse have their origins in the Civil War experience and, specifically, in Spanish Communist participation during those years in a genuinely popular struggle against Franco. The Portuguese Communists, by contrast, never had the experience of leading a mass movement and always intuitively felt that political problems could be resolved by an elite.

After April 1974, the Portuguese Communists gambled on seizing power along with various radical groupings in the MFA. They lost and although the party retains the allegiance of a majority of the Portuguese working class and about 15% of the electorate, they can look forward to an essentially marginal role in the political process of the parliamentary democracy Mario Soares seems to be constructing. Now that blunt Leninism has apparently failed in the Iberian peninsula, it is the turn of the Spanish Communists. Their policies are highly ambiguous and are certainly much more difficult to assess than the straightforward approach of a hard-line party like the PCP. The results of the June 1977 parliamentary elections, in which the PCE did not attain as high a relative proportion of the vote as its Portuguese counterpart did a year before, would seem to suggest that the prospects for Spanish communism are not all that good in the short and medium term. This would be too hasty a judgment for although the PCE did not do as well as its leadership might have supposed or hoped, given the pivotal role the party played in Spanish opposition politics after 1973, the political situation in Spain is still quite fluid. For one thing, there is the fissiparous state of the Unión de centro democrático (Union of the Democratic Center), which Premier Suárez helped put together and which won a relative majority in the election. Moreover, the Spanish Socialists have yet to prove they deserve the hegemony on the Left that the 1977 election results apparently have conceded them. The PCE may well be able to take advantage of a deteriorating economic situation to increase its political leverage substantially over the next few years. Nonetheless, the question of whether the Spanish Communists will come to play as important a role in their political system as their counterparts in Italy and France must be left unanswered as must final judgment be suspended on their democratic intentions and on that elusive union of socialism and democracy they pursue.

Notes

1. Those interested in more detailed analyses of Spanish or Portuguese Communist policies and actions should consult the following. For the PCE: Guy Hermet, *Los comunistas en España* (Paris: Ruedo ibérico, 1972); Paul Preston, "The Dilemma of Credibility: The Spanish Communist Party, the Franco Regime, and After," *Government and Opposition*, XI (Winter 1976): 69–72; and Eusebio M. Mujal-León, "Spain and the PCE," in Rudolf L. Tokes, ed., *European Communism and the Age of Détente* (New York: New York University Press, 1978). For the PCP: George W. Grayson, "Portugal and the Armed Forces Movement," *Orbis*, Summer 1975, pp. 335–378; Arnold Hottinger, "The Rise of Portugal's Communists, *Problems of Communism*, July–August 1975, pp. 1–17; Kenneth Maxwell, "The Thorns of the Portuguese Revolution," *Foreign Affairs*, January 1976, pp. 250–270; and Eusebio M. Mujal-León, "The PCP and the Portuguese Revolution," *Problems of Communism*, January–February 1977, pp. 21–41.

2. *World Marxist Review*, January 1974, pp. 25–35. The English version carried the more neutral title of "Communist Ethics."

3. For a general overview of the period since 1945 see the last few chapters of A. H. de Oliveira Marques, *History of Portugal* (New York: Columbia University Press, 1972), Vol. 2.

4. Alvaro Cunhal, *O radicalismo pequeno-burguês de fachada socialista* (Lisbon: Ediçoes avante, 1971), p. 31.

5. Mario Soares, *Portugal, amordazado* (Barcelona: Dopesa, 1974).

6. Soares founded a rival organization, the CEUD, to run in the 1970 National Assembly elections. The election results, as expected, showed the official Uniao nacional party with over 88% of vote as the overwhelming victor, but the CDE made an entirely credible showing under adverse conditions to gain 10% of the vote. More important, in two highly politicized areas, Lisbon and Setúbal, the CDE received 18.5% and 34% of the vote, respectively. For its part, Soares's CEUD did not do very well, receiving less than 2% of the total.

7. See *Programa do Partido comunista português* (sixth congress in 1965) (Lisbon: Ediçoes avante, 1974), pp. 71-77.

8. Alvaro Cunhal, *Rumo à Vitória: as tarefas do Partido na revoluçao democrática e nacional* (Oporto: Editorial a opiniao, 1974), p. 29.

9. See the interview with PCP secretariat member Joaquim Gomes in *Avante*, 18 October 1974.

10. Cunhal, *O radicalismo*, p. 197.

11. See Cunhal's address to the PCP congress in *VII Congreso (extraordinário) do PCP* (Lisbon: Ediçoes avante, 1974), pp. 21-48.

12. The issue of whether Vasco Gonçalves was or is a formal member of the PCP is unclear. See Hottinger, op. cit., p. 8.

13. See the *Relatorio preliminar da Comissão de inquerito aos acontecimentos do 25 de novembro* (Lisbon, 1976). For the PCP reaction: *Avante*, 22 January 1976.

14. *Mundo obrero*, the PCE weekly, in the first week of July 1974 carried extracts from an interview Santiago Carrillo gave to *Le Nouvel Observateur*.

15. Santiago Carrillo, *Después de Franco, qué?* (Paris: Editions sociales, 1967). See also the PCE's program manifesto, which was published in draft form in September 1973 and approved in final form at the second conference in September 1975. The Portuguese analysis is contained in the program approved in 1965 as well as in the one presented after the seventh congress in October 1974.

16. Santiago Carrillo, *Demain l'Espagne* (Paris: Editions du seuil, 1974), pp. 107-108.

17. See Carrillo's speech to the eighth PCE congress in *Hacia la libertad* (Paris: Editions sociales, 1972), pp. 48-52.

18. *VIII Congreso del PCE* (Bucharest, 1972), p. 234.

19. *L'Humanité*, 3 December 1970.

20. *VIII Congreso*, pp. 338-339.

21. *Mundo obrero*, 31 July 1974.

22. For the Portuguese church see Silas Cerqueira, "L'Eglise catholique et la dictature corporatiste portugaise," *Revue française de science politique*, XXIII (June 1973): 473-513. For the Spanish, Alfonso Alvarez Bolado, *El experimento del nacional-catolicismo* (Madrid: Editorial cuadernos para el

diálogo, 1976), and José Chao Rego, *La iglesia en el franquismo* (Madrid: Ediciones Felmar, 1976).

23. See "Os bispos Falam do 25 de abril da democracia e dos partidos," issued by the Portuguese episcopal conference in July 1974.

24. To be sure, as early as 1947, Alvaro Cunhal had called on his party's militants "to unite with and attract nonfascist Catholics" and the PCP declared that membership in the PCP was open even to priests. His gesture came nearly ten years before Dolores Ibárruri shocked many in the Spanish Communist old guard and made a similar gesture toward the Spanish clergy.

25. The quote in note 24 above is from "Unidade, garantia da victória," a report to the central committee delivered in June 1947.

26. The evolution of the collective bargaining system is thoroughly and insightfully discussed in Jon Amsden, *Collective Bargaining and Class Struggle in Spain* (London: Weidenfeld & Nicolson, 1972).

27. See Nicolas Sartorius, *El resurgir del movimiento obrero* (Barcelona: Editorial Laia, 1975), pp. 55–56.

28. *VII Congreso*, p. 271.

29. *Avante*, 18 November 1976.

30. Hermet, op. cit., p. 60.

31. See Santiago Carrillo, *De la clandestinidad a la legalidad* (n.p., n.d.), pp. 64–66. This was the report Carrillo presented to the central committee meeting.

32. *O militante*, June 1975, p. 11. This is the organizational bulletin of the PCP.

33. This model is in some ways the counterpart of the "totalitarian" model developed for the study of Soviet politics by Carl Friedrich and Zbigniew Brzezinski in *Totalitarian Dictatorship and Autocracy* (Cambridge: Harvard University Press, 1956). For the application to communist parties see Maurice Duverger, *Political Parties* (New York: Wiley, 1954), pp. 116–124, and Philip Selznick, *The Organizational Weapon* (New York: McGraw-Hill, 1952), pp. 1–73.

34. This point is made by many of the contributors in the volume edited by Donald L. M. Blackmer and Sidney Tarrow, *Communism in France and Italy* (Princeton: Princeton University Press, 1976).

35. Donald L. M. Blackmer, "Continuity and Change in Postwar Italian Communism," in ibid., pp. 22–23.

36. Ronald Tiersky, "French Communism in 1976," *Problems of Communism*, January–February 1976, pp. 20–47.

37. Peter Lange, "The French and Italian Communist Parties: Postwar Strategy and Domestic Society" (mimeographed), p. 16.

38. The one exception is Hermet, op. cit. He argues that the PCE, even at the height of clandestineness, performed a partly constructive role in the political process and could by no means be considered a pure opposition type.

39. See Eusebio M. Mujal-León, "The Foreign Policy of the PCE" (paper presented at a U.S. State Department conference held at Airlie House, Warrenton, Virginia, May 1977).

40. Manuel Azcárate, "Sobre algunos problemas de la política internacional del Partido," in *VIII Congreso*, pp. 183-206.

41. For the version broadcast by Radio Moscow see *Foreign Broadcast Information Service* (Soviet Union), 16 February 1974, pp. A1-10. For valuable discussions of the Soviet article see Kevin Devlin, "Soviet Attack on Spanish CP," *Radio Free Europe, Russia*, No. 2008, 27 February 1974, and "Spanish CP Stands Firm against Soviet Attack," ibid., No. 2046, 10 April 1974. The ostensible target of the Soviet article can be found in the PCE theoretical journal *Nuestra bandera*, No. 72 (1973): 15-30.

42. *Pravda*, 16 October 1974.

43. See Santiago Carrillo, *Eurocomunismo y el estado* (Barcelona: Editorial Grijalbo, 1977), and the attack in *New Times* (Moscow), No. 26 (June 1977): 9-13.

44. See the communiqué issued August 23, 1968, and broadcast over Radio Free Portugal on September 25, 1968, *Foreign Broadcast Information Service* (Western Europe), pp. X1-X2.

45. *Avante*, 8 July 1976.

46. Juan Gómez, "Sobre el Mercado comun europeo," in *VIII Congreso*, pp. 207-216.

47. See Cunhal's speech to the January 1974 conference of Western European communist parties. *Avante*, March 1974.

48. Compare the party program approved at the seventh congress in October 1974 with that of the sixth one in 1965.

49. On this point see the insightful and provocative piece written by Joan Barth Urban, "Contemporary Soviet Perspectives on Revolution in the West," *Orbis*, Winter 1976, pp. 1359-1402.

4

The Soviet Legitimacy
Crisis and its
International Implications

Mikhail Agursky

Introduction

Our present task is to elucidate the connection between Soviet
foreign policy and Soviet ideology. Is foreign policy independent
from ideology or is it influenced by it in one way or another?
Indeed, the problem is evidently more complicated: Soviet foreign
policy is influenced by different ideological and nonideological factors in mixed and even controversial ways. There are many approaches to this problem.

Over the last decade many discussions took place that touched
on the ideological state of Soviet society. One of them turned around
Zbigniew Brzezinski's report on the Soviet political system (5*);
Andrew Ezergailis (18) examined whether communism is monolithic
or crumbling. The central point of Brzezinski's report was his statement on the degeneration of the Soviet political system. On the one
hand he claimed that the number of political alternatives in the
USSR had substantially diminished. But on the other hand, he saw in
Soviet society several groups that "certainly can lobby and, in turn,

*Refers to fifth entry in references list for this chapter, pp. 188–93.—ED.

146

be courted by ambitious and opportunistic oligarchs. . . . Taken together, they represent a wide spectrum of opinions, and in the setting of oligarchical rule there is bound to be some correspondence between their respective stances and those of the top leaders" (p. 10).

This view leads to the question of whether these groups have ideological differences as well or whether their "spectrum of opinions" is limited by some organizational or economic dimension. There is some internal contradiction between Brzezinski's statement about the decline in the number of political alternatives and the acknowledged fact that certain influential groups have emerged relatively recently in the Soviet Union.

The emergence of these groups has caused one commentator (1) to argue that there are some fundamental contradictions in Soviet society that one should not underestimate. Isaac Don Levine (15), for instance, forecasts dramatic changes in Soviet society. Such a development is not excluded by Frederick Barghoorn (4) although he is much more cautious in his predictions.

A second controversy (21, 43, 49, 60, 64, 69) gives us more material from which to judge the diversity of opinion over the ideological state of the Soviet Union since Ezergailis presented this problem in a very sharp and controversial way. He considered two extreme approaches. According to one of them, communism is still monolithic and is the exclusive and unifying ideology of all countries and parties calling themselves communist. According to the second approach, communist ideology has ceased to be central to Soviet decisions, especially in matters of foreign affairs.

Ezergailis has acknowledged the fact that there were doubts about Soviet motivations even immediately after the revolution. But he treats this problem in the spirit of dialectics claiming that unity and divergence are two ways of dialectically strengthening the communist movement. It is highly disputable whether the apparatus of dialectics is a successful scientific tool in resolving such matters. Moreover, Ezergailis makes another entirely unscientific statement: he claims that the "communist faith" can exist only in one of two states. Thus, he argues that "it is psychologically impossible to be 'a little bit' Communist. . . . For the true Communist, faith in the ideology, or the loss of it, must be total" (p. 7). This assertion totally ignores all the empirical evidence. And Ezergailis has been severely criticized. As Tibor Szamuely (64) points out: "Not only is it possible to be 'a little bit Communist,' or to embrace some parts of the faith while rejecting others, but this has today become an extremely widespread phenomenon" (p. 6). Alec Nove (49) goes much further:

There is a complex problem of changes in objectives or priorities within a party which nominally retains the same ideology and the same formal aims. History has known not a few examples of such changes but when they occur they cannot be proved by doctrinal quotations, since value and legitimacy attach to the principles of continuity and orthodoxy. In other words a tightly controlled and nominally monolithic political system may devote itself to the pursuit of nationalist great-power causes, while continuing to adhere to "Marxism-Leninism" (p. 19).

This phenomenon was noticed long ago by a number of scholars who stressed the growing retreat of the Soviet elite from monolithic communism toward nationalism. Richard Lowenthal, for instance, wrote (40):

It is becoming increasingly difficult to maintain the hold of the Communist ideology over both the Soviet elites and the Soviet masses at the present stage. . . . The disintegration of the Communist faith that first became visible in the emergence of different national versions has begun to affect developments within the original citadel itself (p. xv).

Thomas Bird (84) recently emphasized the disintegration of the communist faith among the Soviet masses. According to Bird, "the sterile dogmatic materialism of Marxist-Leninist orthodoxy ceased to be very satisfying to large segments of the multimillion population of the Soviet Union" (p. 17).

In another discussion Daniel Bell (81) insisted on the fact that in the USSR "the discrepancy between ideology and reality becomes a continuing source of strain" (p. 597). Thus, he contends that "an ideology to be effective must be 'congruent' with reality" (p. 596). According to Bell, "Marxism-Leninism as a unified doctrine is becoming disjointed and losing its élan" (p. 599). He also claims that "the different segments of the elite must maintain an allegiance to the creed with some degree of intensity. Clearly the different social strata within the elite display variable sensitivities to the vicissitudes of ideology" (p. 597).

So there is considerable evidence that Marxism-Leninism is at least challenged in the USSR. But this is evidently an understatement since there are signs that this challenge provokes critical or at least dramatic situations. Judson Mitchell (47) in his important analysis of the USSR said that the recent "major ideological campaigns reflect a 'crisis of legitimacy' in the system" (p. 137).

The so-called Soviet ideology consists of at least two conflicting ideologies that are partly subjects of pragmatic manipulation and partly sources of inspiration for some groups in the Soviet leadership. The official façade of Marxism-Leninism does not reflect the complexity of ideological phenomena in the Soviet Union.

The conflicting ideologies result from the unsuccessful adaptation of the original Communist attack on Russian society since the existing reality was not receptive to a communist utopia. These ideologies have a complex interrelationship and the priority of each of them differs in every case.

The crucial objective of every ideology of a ruling group is the legitimacy of the existing order. Bell (81) aptly has remarked that "even the most coercive of societies has to establish some justification of coercion. It has to transform 'macht' into legitimacy in order to govern without turning an entire society into a concentration camp" (p. 594).

The ideology that might be called Marxism-Leninism in a first approximation is still able to legitimate policy in some cases, especially in foreign affairs, because its consumers are still ready to accept the myth of the USSR as a socialist country based exclusively on the theory of Marxism-Leninism. This ideology is now much less effective in providing legitimacy to solutions of domestic national problems. Nevertheless, Hugh Seton-Watson (59) assumes that Marxism-Leninism provides a new form of legitimacy for multinational countries (p. 27). It does not, however, provide sufficient legitimacy for many Soviet nationalities or, what is even more important, for the dominant part of the Soviet population, the Russians themselves. The legitimacy of the Soviet system as a whole can no longer be based entirely on this ideology, and it certainly is not.

An alternative ideology (mentioned in the quotation from Nove) is a variant of nationalism that can be called national bolshevism, a term used for the first time in 1921 in an attempt to combine the dogmas of Marxism-Leninism with Russian chauvinism. National bolshevism is now in a state of growing conflict with Marxism-Leninism. Some scholars have pointed out that the USSR is basically a nationalist oriented state. Barghoorn, for instance, argued in his extremely valuable book (3) that "the 'internationalist' and 'socialist' Soviet Union is a much more nationalistic state with far more ethnocentric attitudes, than was imperial Russia" (p. 177). Nicholas Timasheff and Walter Kolarz were so impressed by Soviet military success during the Second World War that they proclaimed the general and final retreat of the USSR from Marxism (36, 67). (Indeed, Timasheff entitled his book *The Great Retreat.*) According to Timasheff, Stalin's policy "in the course of a few years transformed Russia into a country with much more fervent nationalism than ever . . . before" (p. 166). Seven years later he (68) had to recant, blaming Marxism-Leninism for Soviet expansionism.

Can the Soviet system as such base its legitimacy only on national bolshevism? This is extremely doubtful in spite of the fact that it is, as Jerry Hough (26) has said, "a major basis" of its legitimacy.

It is very difficult and even impossible to present any persuasive concept of the interrelationship between Marxist-Leninist and national bolshevik components of Soviet ideology without exposing the historical background of national bolshevism. Moreover, only such a historical background can provide the basis for understanding Soviet foreign policy in the past and in the present. Thus, Ezergailis (18) has argued correctly that

> it is of little use to show that the Communism of today has become pragmatic, nationalistic and Machiavellian, unless it can also be shown in what way these qualities influence present Soviet policy differently from the way they influenced Soviet policy in the past (p. 6).

We can formulate our model more exactly starting with the survey of existing models made by Hough (27). He classified all the existing models into three groups: (1) "directed society"; (2) "oligarchic petrification"; and (3) "institutional pluralism." No one of these models fits the concept of this chapter although the first model can be rejected at once. Our model of the Soviet system has many features in common with the second and third models, but one might call it a "conflict model." A basic characteristic of the latter model is the deep contradiction between Marxism-Leninism and national bolshevism. This contradiction is in turn a consequence of a deeper conflict in Soviet society: the conflict between the radical right nature of the Soviet system and its radical left legitimacy. Indeed, national bolshevism is only one feature of this radical right orientation. Another feature is the social and economic oppression of the majority of the population by the relatively small "new class" (105), whose makeup and mode of operation were brilliantly exposed by Milovan Djilas (85).

I do not have space to analyze in full all the aspects of the Soviet system. I will concentrate only on the origin, emergence, and development of national bolshevism as the alternative source of legitimacy for the Soviet system. The phenomenon of national bolshevism is a very important aspect of the Soviet system that, as Reddaway (54) has noted, "has been little explored" (p. 64).

We must also take into consideration the fact that radical left legitimacy is still a "superstructure" of the Soviet society that contradicts its "base." Nonetheless, this superstructure is very influential, as all superstructures have been in Soviet history (106). That is why it would be a serious mistake to consider the official Communist legitimacy as only a fiction. There is an interdependence between superstructure and base.

However, this model does not pretend in any way to serve as a general model of Soviet society. Soviet society and Soviet foreign policy are much more complicated. They are the product of diverse factors many of which have been investigated by scholars and political analysts. My intention in the following pages is to introduce a crucial dimension that is usually neglected because of the overestimation of the so-called monolithic character of the Soviet state. At least for the last ten years the Soviet political system has not been monolithic, a state of affairs that has had a big impact on Soviet foreign policy.

The Historical Background of National Bolshevism

Acknowledgment of the traditional component of the Soviet system is now a commonplace in Soviet studies. One of the best generalizations on this subject is that of Alex Inkeles (29), who said: "It appears that despite the massive destruction of the main formal elements of the old social structure and the extensive elaboration of new social forms, a large number of basic attitudes, values, and sentiments as well as traditional modes of orientation, expression, and reaction markedly persisted" (p. 14).

Some scholars have tried to distinguish specific traditional influences. Boris Nicolaevsky (48), for instance, singled out Ivan Aksakov, Nikolai Danilevskii, Nikolai Strakhov, and Konstantin Leontiev as roots of what he called "Soviet imperialism." He quoted a letter from 1890 by Leontiev in which the latter proposed support of the Western socialist movement by the Russian monarch. This theory never formed a basis for any Russian policy before or after the revolution, but it manifests a Machiavellian mentality ripe for bolshevism. This is, however, only one of Leontiev's ideas relevant to the Soviet Union. He praised violence as an excellent social and political tool and detested Western liberal democracy although he was not a Russian nationalist. Leontiev was also sure of the eventual victory of socialism in Russia and claimed that it would be the single way for Russia to overcome its growing internal weakness.

Later we will see that the main proponent of national bolshevism, Nikolai Ustrialov, who first articulated this concept in 1921, was under the exclusive influence of Leontiev and Danilevskii. This particular circumstance was neglected by Boris Nicolaevsky and by others though Nicolaevsky distinguished the source of the traditional influence absolutely correctly. Robert MacMaster (96) asserted in his monograph on Danilevskii that his ideas were the genuine precursor of Soviet totalitarianism. If we connect Danilevskii with Ustrialov and with another movement—the so-called Eurasians—we see that MacMaster is basically right. Nikolai Danilevskii introduced the concept of Slavic civilization as absolutely distinct from European civilization. In contradiction to early Slavophiles he categorically rejected any morality in politics and urged a total, merciless war between the

Slavs and Europe. Danilevskii based his conclusions on his theory of cultural-historical types, thus anticipating Spengler and Toynbee. Unfortunately, Barghoorn (3), who also investigated the problem of the continuity of tradition in the Soviet system, did not see any similarity between Soviet ideology and the ideas of Danilevskii except for the "excited emotionally charged tone" (p. 235) common to both of them.

Another important source of traditional influence in the Soviet system was the militant Russian radical Right. Nicolaevsky has noted only the earliest representative of this trend, Ivan Aksakov (94). There is a very interesting feature in Aksakov's outlook that might be called "Russian anti-capitalist nationalism." Aksakov basically defended the idea of local self-government (the so-called *zemstvo*) under the absolute moral authority of a monarchy that protects the people's democracy from usurpation by the bureaucracy and by capitalists. In his articles he tried to persuade the Russian government that socialism as such was not dangerous for Russia. He described socialism as a system in which idealistically oriented youths tried to find social truth. Aksakov was strongly anti-Semitic and was inclined to use violence as a political method. One must take into consideration also that Aksakov was very popular in his time.

Explicit anticapitalist motivations and moods can be found among the later Russian radical Right—the Black Hundreds during and after the 1905 Revolution. Some leaders of this movement, for example, Nikolai Markov II, underlined this feature especially after the Bolshevik Revolution. The deputy chairman of the Union of the Russian People, Apollon Maikov, published a booklet in 1906 (95) with an appeal to revolutionaries. He wrote that the teaching of the Black Hundreds "has the same objective" as that of the revolutionaries, "namely, the improvement of conditions of life, and has much in common with the teaching of Social-Anarchists in the explanation of the peculiar burden of our life but contradicts it completely by its outlook and by the means with which it hopes to improve the fate of suffering humanity" (p. 22).

There are many signs that a considerable number of radical Right activists joined the Bolshevik side during and after the October Revolution but there are no reliable data about the level and character of their infiltration.

The Formation of National Bolshevism

There is a common shortcoming in Soviet studies: neglect of the emigrant dimension of Soviet history. Without this dimension it is impossible to understand significant transformations of the Soviet system, including its ideology. Emigration was an extremely important source of ideological development. It presented important political alternatives to the Soviet Union that did not require changes in its leadership or in its long-range political objectives.

The end of the civil war put the Bolsheviks in a very difficult position. According to Boris Souvarine (62), "Si les bolchéviks sont vainqueurs, l'essentiel du bolchévisme traditionnel a vécu. Il n'en subsiste en 1920 que la conception militaire d'organisation des révolutionnaires professionnels" (p. 239).

The introduction of the New Economic Policy (NEP) seemed for many Bolsheviks to be "the end of ideology." Lenin was very much afraid of such a development and started a large-scale ideological war and even something like a cultural revolution (70, 107). He wanted to preserve Marxism-Leninism as the ruling ideology in conditions of economic freedom, but he could not. A political alternative was already waiting at the door of Soviet Russia.

Early in 1920 a former chairman of the eastern section of the Constitutional-Democratic party, a young professor named Nikolai Ustrialov, who also had been the propaganda boss of the short-lived Kolchak government in Siberia, published a booklet (in Harbin) that influenced Soviet history (73). He claimed that the armed struggle against the Bolsheviks must be ended as soon as possible. According to Ustrialov, the "anti-Bolshevik movement has connected itself because of the force of circumstance with foreign elements and has given the Bolsheviks a certain national halo" (p. 5). He even asserted that Soviet power was a "national factor in modern Russian life." Ustrialov forecast that

> the interests of Soviet power will coincide fatally with Russian state interests. . . . This logical development will lead the Bolsheviks from Jacobinism to Napoleonism (p. 13). . . . Only the power of revolution is able to restore Great Russian power and international Russian prestige (p. 57).

He also asserted that "bolshevism with its international influence and omnipresent connection is turning into an excellent tool of Russian foreign policy" (p. 59). According to Ustrialov, there was now a revolutionary liquidation of the revolution and there would be no such thing as a world revolution. According to Ustrialov Lenin was a great political opportunist. Ustrialov also said that the defeat of the Bolsheviks would be a great tragedy for Russia.

Ustrialov's book immediately led to a new political movement among radical Right emigrés, and in 1921 a collection of articles entitled *Smena vekh* (*The Change of Milestones*) was published in Prague by a group of influential right-wing emigrants (33, 41, 52, 65,

73). Among them were Yurii Kliuchnikov (33), former foreign minister of the Kolchak government; Alexander Bobrishchev-Pushkin, a vice-chairman of the important Russian right-wing party the Octobrists; and Sergei Lukianov (41). All of them expressed their enthusiasm over the military successes of the Bolsheviks and claimed that all the Whites must go to "Canossa" (65) and actively collaborate with the Bolsheviks, the true Russian national leaders. They all expressed the hope that Soviet Russia would develop into a strong national state that rejected internationalist ideology. They maintained that the spirit of bolshevism was Russian despite the fact that the majority of new Soviet leaders were non-Russian. The latter fact was explained by the attraction of non-Russian Bolsheviks to the Russian national spirit. The *"Smenovekhovtsi"* explicitly stated that they expected a further development of the Bolshevik leadership despite its Communist phraseology (which they regarded as a guise); but they evidently preferred restoration of a private sector, though with some limitations. Thus, they favored the NEP system, including a strong Bolshevik leadership, with Comintern policy as a tool of Russian foreign policy.

As I have said, the term "national bolshevism" was proposed by Ustrialov in September 1921. He said that to mix bolshevism and communism was a great mistake. Bolshevism was a genuine Russian phenomenon whereas communism was a foreign influence alien to the Russian spirit. In October 1921, Ustrialov presented his program in a more elaborate way: (1) liquidation of communism; (2) economic relations with foreign countries and the attraction of foreign investment; (3) dictatorship; and (4) the denial of restoration. This program was essentially radical rightist. In November 1922 Ustrialov (75) claimed that in Soviet Russia only "terminology and the dream of the world revolution are left from communist ideology" (p. 141).

Lenin had an ambivalent attitude toward smenovekhism. On the one hand, he was afraid of this movement because he saw it as the ideology of "bourgeois restorers." Lenin was not able to understand their genuine readiness to accept Soviet reality. He immediately warned the Communist party about the danger of Smenovekhist "degeneration." But at the same time Lenin was aware of the political benefit of smenovekhism (70). He even recommended inviting Yurii Kliuchnikov as an expert to the Soviet delegation in Genova, which was conducting very important diplomatic negotiations there. Smenovekhism was a very important topic during the eleventh congress of the Communist party in 1922. Many speakers, including Lenin, Skrypnik, Antonov-Ovseenko, and Yakovlev, warned about the Smenovekhist danger. One can see from all these facts that Smenovekhist ideology was very well known both to the leadership and to the rank and file party members in Soviet Russia.

Stalin made his first statement on the smenovekhism issue in a report to the twelfth congress of the Communist party in April 1923. He (63) said that

> as a consequence of NEP Great Russian nationalism is growing, intensifying. The idea of smenovekhism was born. The wish to do peacefully what was not achieved by Denikin is common, namely, to create the so-called one and indivisible. [This was a slogan of White nationalists during the civil war. "One and indivisible" refers to the Russian empire as a territorial entity as it was before the revolution.] Thus, in connection with NEP a new force is appearing in our internal life—Great Russian chauvinism, which nests in our offices, penetrating not only into Soviet but also into party institutions (pp. 238–239).

So Stalin was very well informed about this trend although at that time he seemed to have a negative attitude toward it. The *Smena vekh* issue was again in the forefront during this congress. It was touched upon also by Grigori Zinoviev and Nikolai Bukharin. Bukharin found in smenovekhism a nonidentified party trend. Zinoviev begged in an ironic way to be protected from Smenovekhist compliments. Bukharin even claimed that "when a Smenovekhist is loyal he is even more dangerous." It is interesting that Ustrialov, commenting on this congress, praised mainly Leonid Krasin, who was then foreign trade minister, for his moderate economic program; later, however, he expressed his sympathy mainly for Stalin.

By the end of 1923, smenovekhism caused even more polemics among influential Bolsheviks. Mikhail Pokrovskii, Andrei Bubnov, and others blamed smenovekhism for different sins. Taking issue with Pokrovskii, who blamed Ustrialov for a lack of dialectics, Ustrialov (75) wrote that on the contrary, according to dialectics the idea of internationalism reaches the level of antithesis: "If communism in Russia only provokes a proprietary reaction, an excessive passion for internationalist maximalism will lead only to the morbid hypertrophy of the inevitable coming nationalism" (p. 174). According to Ustrialov "Communist" Russia was objectively the least socialist state in modern, "bourgeois" Europe (p. 175).

All this was written at the very end of 1923. But at the end of 1924 Stalin for the first time proclaimed his famous idea about the possibility of building socialism in one country. It was the first productive national bolshevik idea from a party official. The eventual dependence of this idea on Ustrialov is beyond doubt. Yet Stalin was the person officially responsible for national policy and could better anticipate national development in Soviet Russia.

There was already a strong Russian national reaction because of the policy of internationalism and because of drastic demographic changes resulting from the revolution. The policy of internationalism turned out to be directed against Russian traditional values (consider, for instance, Trotsky's campaign against Russian customs in 1922-1923). Moreover, the revolution brought to the cities and to central Russia a very large Jewish population, which, together with other minorities, temporarily constituted a new Soviet middle class and also a highly influential part of the Soviet leadership (108, 109, 110).

Erwin Oberländer (97) also binds together the emergence of national bolshevism (which he calls *Sowiet-patriotismus*) with the idea of building socialism in one country: "Politisch gesehen hängt die Propagierung des Sowiet-patriotismus aufs engste mit dem Aufbau des Sozialismus in einem Land zusammen" (p. 20). The slogan of building socialism in one country appeased Russian nationals. Meanwhile, the polemics between Stalin and Trotsky were perceived by many people as the beginning of a struggle against the Jewish presence.

Ustrialov's influence on Stalin (and Bukharin) was so evident that many oppositionists accused Stalin of holding such views. Arthur Rosenberg (55), once a prominent German Communist, has described this situation well:

> Stalin and Bukharin are going to restore the bourgeois national state in Russia despite their formal socialism. . . . In these years Ustrialov has become downright famous as the ideological leader of the bourgeois adherents of Stalin. The friendship of this group is for the Soviet regime over the party . . . (pp. 201-203).

Ustrialov (75) did not conceal his support of Stalin. In October 1926 he wrote: "We are now not only 'contre Zinoviev' but we are definitely 'pro Stalin'" (p. 239). If in January 1926 he stated openly that "the party is going more and more forward from Lenin's epoch" (p. 231); a month later he went further claiming, "One cannot help rejoicing in seeing how [the Communist party] is now being led on a confident iron march by the great Russian Revolution to the national pantheon prepared for it by history" (p. 232). At the end of 1926, Ustrialov wrote: "The twilight of the old Lenin guard is coming" and "good people" from the opposition are much worse than "bad ones" from the majority (p. 236).

(At this time Ustrialov was a kind of spokesman for Stalin among the emigrés.) Ustrialov's proclaimed continuity with Konstantin Leontiev is especially characteristic: "Leontiev's slogan, which dozed until now—'It is necessary to rule impudently!'—is wandering free on the boundless Russian plains" (p. 185).

The majority of scholars did not pay much attention to Ustrialov's personality and his influence on the Soviet system. One can mention as a rare example an apologetic reference made by Walter Kolarz (36), who, inspired by his wartime enthusiasm (exactly as was

Nicholas Timasheff), wrote that Ustrialov anticipated the "patriotic" development of Soviet Russia (Kolarz probably did not know about Ustrialov's execution two years after his return to the USSR in 1935). However, Michael Heller (91) has noted that in the old polemics between Westernizers and Slavophiles, after the temporary success of Marxism, the Westernizers were defeated. After a fifty-year interval, according to Heller, Smenovekhist ideas, the ideas of national bolshevism, had returned to the USSR (pp. 334–335). One can only reply that these ideas had returned to Russia immediately after the revolution, though in a distorted form. Another substantial contribution to the problem of smenovekhism is the survey made by Oberländer (111).

Smenovekhism was not at that time the only trend in the 1920s among Russian radical Right emigrants who saw in the new Soviet reality a national phenomenon. Another important movement was the so-called Eurasianism (16, 17). It emerged simultaneously with smenovekhism in 1920–1921 and was presented by a brilliant group of Russian intellectuals, including Prince Nikolai Trubetskoi, the philosopher Lev Karsavin, and a former minister of the provisional government, Anton Kartashev. Its main thesis was the concept of Eurasia as an entirely distinct civilization that because of its historical destiny and historical features must differ greatly from the European. Basically, Eurasianism also was a Russian nationalist ideology influenced by Nikolai Danilevskii. The Eurasians criticized the Smenovekhovtsi for their neglect of ideology. They noted, for example, the acknowledgment in smenovekhism that, under the surface of the Communist folly, a genuine national Russian ideology was developing (16, p. 6), but argued that this insight had not been developed.

Prince Dmitrii Mirskii (Sviatopolk-Mirskii), who later joined the Communist party and returned to the USSR (to be executed in 1937), expressed the Eurasian outlook in the following way (112):

> Russia was not part of Europe; the European civilization was alien to Russia . . . the revolution, though in its conscious will it was a particularly vigorous affirmation of a European-made ideal, [supported] the Russian masses against the domination of a Europeanized and renegade upper class (p. 318).

"The Russian people," Eurasians claimed in their program (16), "made the Bolshevik-Communists carry out many extremely important things contrary to their intentions" (p. 6). Eurasians blamed Europe for its abstract universalism and considered Genghis Khan's invasion the Eurasian birthday. They were very critical of tsarist Russia as is seen in the passage from Mirskii. The Eurasian program underlines this view: "The death of the old Russia is better defined as the alienation of the ruling elite from the people and its self-destruction" (p. 46).

One can see among Eurasians (16) the same basic claim made by the Smenovekhovtsi that the "International is an unconscious tool of a weakened Russia" (p. 50). They also asserted, together with the Smenovekhovtsi: "Communist ideology undoubtedly . . . is dying" (ibid). There was, however, one substantial difference between the two positions. The Eurasian accent on religion in its Orthodox Christian form made the Eurasian ideology completely unacceptable to the Soviet regime, at least for public discussion. There was no religious aspect to the Smenovekhist movement. Nevertheless, in their radical economic program the Eurasians (17) were more receptive than the Smenovekhovtsi to a centralized economy and they maintained that the "social system must be put in the service of the interests of toilers" (p. 9).

Although the Eurasian influence was not as significant as smenovekhism in the USSR, its ideology was a subject of careful examination by the Soviet government. The Eurasian movement was infiltrated by a Soviet provocateur organization, the so-called Trust, until 1927. The Trust organized a "secret" Eurasian congress inside Russia, almost all the delegates to which were emigrants. They left Russia unmolested (104). Geoffrey Bailey (80) has remarked that from the acceptance of the Eurasian ideology

> to the acceptance of Soviet rule and then even its active promotion, there was but a step—which the Soviet leadership early realized. Starting in 1924, therefore, the OGPU proceeded to infiltrate the "Eurasian" movement and by 1926, it had already done so well, that the Chekist Langovoy . . . had become persona grata in émigré "Eurasian" circles . . . and it had become generally difficult to determine where genuine philosophy ended and Communist propaganda began (pp. 276–277).

In 1924–1925 Stalin started more or less openly using anti-Semitism as a tool of his policy to appease the strengthening national reaction, which he considered to be a much more solid base for his personal power than dying internationalism. But of course he used this tool very cautiously: he was afraid of a strong reaction from the still internationalist party elite. According to Trotsky (71), Stalin

> and his henchmen even stooped to fish in the muddied waters of anti-Semitism. . . . Stalin's attitude toward this growing anti-Semitism was one of friendly neutrality. But matters went so far that he was forced to come out with a published statement which declared: "We are fighting Trotsky, Zinoviev and Kamenev not because they are Jews, but because they are Oppositionists" and the like. It was absolutely clear to everyone who thought politically that his deliberately equivocal declaration was aimed merely at the "excesses" of anti-Semitism, while at the

same time broadcasting throughout the entire Soviet press the very pregnant reminder "Don't forget that the leaders of the Opposition are Jews." Such a statement gave carte blanche to anti-Semitism (pp. 399–400).

This was also noticed by some shrewd anti-Semitic emigrants such as Vasilii Shulgin (58). The Smenovekhovtsi and Eurasians, however, were not explicitly anti-Semitic. Another emigrant anti-Semitic writer, D. Petrovsky (51), in no way sympathetic to Stalin, also recognized this fact in describing Stalin's struggle with the opposition.

> Stalin made clear that the party was divided in two currents: one of which turned to the workers and peasants, to nationalism, and the other, the extreme left, toward a world revolution. . . . Stalin chose the first current (p. 315). . . . The opposition consisted only of Jews and . . . the faction led by Djugashvili (Stalin) engendered anti-Semitism among the workers and the peasants (p. 316). . . . The expulsion of Bronstein [Trotzky] and Rosenfeld [Kamenev] was opposed by the Jews and persuaded the government to continue its anti-Semitic position (p. 319).

According to Petrovsky, the *Chicago Tribune* "certifiait énergiquement que le Parti communiste était devenu un parti antisemite" (p. 327).

Many modern scholars also have recognized a nationalist component to the party polemics. William Korey (113), for instance, maintains that "a deepening Russian nationalism . . . was a dominant characteristic of the struggle against the 'internationalism' of the 'old guard' " (p. 122).

There are of course serious doubts about whether Stalin's anti-Semitism was only a political choice. Many facts, especially from his later activity, point at the possibility that it was much more than a political decision. Adam Ulam (72) is quite right in saying that "Stalin's anti-Semitism was not simply a matter of political choice, but toward the end of his life became a veritable obsession" (p. 585).

There was another methodological influence that was noticed in a very shrewd way by Souvarine (62).

> Stalin evidently had not read Machiavelli, even less the astonishing *Dialogue in Hell between Machiavelli and Montesquieu*, the anonymous book of a proscribed republican, Maurice Joly, that was published in exile. But he adopted instinctively the line of conduct recommended in this ironic manual of knavery and duplicity, the precepts of which can be given literally but briefly in a few examples: to separate morality from politics, to substitute force for right and wisdom, to paralyze the spirit of the individual, to deceive the people with appearances, to suppress liberty under the weight of terror, to appeal to national prejudices, to keep the country ignorant of world affairs and the capital

ignorant of what happens in the countryside, to kill and to exile
without remorse, to require approval of the government's actions, to
write its own history, . . . to create a cult or religion of the regime, . . .
to create apathy in the public, . . . to encourage vices in society, always
to say the opposite of what one thinks, to corrupt the meaning of
language. . . . All this seemed to be written expressly for Stalin (p. 533).

Souvarine is too cautious. Indeed, experts know that Maurice
Joly's book is a main source of the compilation of the notorious
fraud "The Protocols of the Elders of Zion," with which Stalin was
familiar. Stalin, therefore, assimilated Joly's maxims from the infa-
mous "Protocols." Anti-Semites (including Hitler) often referred to
the similarity between Joly and Stalin, and Souvarine repeated it
only in a more sophisticated way.

Stalin might well have followed Joly's recommendations, as
embodied in the "Protocols," in his unlimited thirst of power.
Later he might have developed a very ambivalent attitude to this
book. If he experienced success from applying its principles, he
could even start believing, as did Hitler, in its authenticity. The
Machiavellian and Jolian aspects in Stalin's thought were reinforced
by Leninism, which advocated the concealment of real objectives
behind false slogans. In his use of the Machiavellian art Stalin was
a real genius. And he well might have projected his own plot to
obtain power upon the Jews.

The idea of a Jewish plot could also have made a strong impression on Stalin even if taken as fiction. The possibility of pursuing
power but under the guise of quashing a Jewish plot was an interesting option for Stalin. If one takes into consideration how many
state leaders in prerevolutionary Russia and outside it after the
revolution believed in the authenticity of the worldwide Jewish-
Masonic plot, it is no surprise if someone would try to use this belief.

Stalin's turn to national bolshevism found new supporters among
the emigrants. There were signs of a reevaluation even among the
radical Right; for example, in 1926 a small radical Right group
proclaimed itself the National Maximalists. The leading proponent of
this view was Prince Yurii Shirinski-Shikhmatiev (2, 61), who earlier
had made a report on national bolshevism. In comparison with
Ustrialov, Shirinski-Shikmatiev was explicitly anti-Semitic and he
was willing to support Soviet power as long as it was national and
anti-Semitic. (Shirinski-Shikhmatiev later turned from his anti-
Semitism and it cost him his life.) For this group the crucial question
was a national one. For them "revolution was the unconscious
straightening of the national-historical trend." National maximalism
once again underlined the basic difference between bolshevism and
communism. Bolshevism was for them Sten'ka Razin (the leader of a
popular uprising in the seventeenth century) and communism was a

Jew, Karl Marx. "Now," said Shirinski-Shikhmatiev (61), "Communist messianism is being overcome, but its world scope still exists. A supranational messianism is coming instead." He proposed the slogan "Not to struggle with the revolution but to seize it." The main hope of national maximalism was the Komsomol, which this group called a "source of peculiar fascism." It was a radical turn from smenovkhism or Eurasianism toward a deeper identification with the USSR as such.

It is very interesting that the Trust tried to take advantage of Shirinski-Shikhmatiev but he rejected its proposal (104, pp. 143-157). Later, during the war with Germany, he was deported by the Nazis and vanished in a concentration camp.

These trends in the emigration were evidently noticed by Stalin, who had to follow emigration life and literature very closely since the emigration was still a political problem for the USSR. The GPU regularly presented the politburo with full reports on the situation of the emigrants. Moreover, Stalin seemed to be involved in an ambiguous game that the GPU played with radical right emigrants through the Trust. His participation in this provocateur activity was very important if not decisive. The "secret" visit to the USSR of an active radical anti-Bolshevik leader (57, 104), Vasilii Shulgin (before the revolution Shulgin was a Russian nationalist leader) was the culmination of this activity. Thus, the GPU, although it did so primarily as a provocation, could skillfully articulate radical rightist programs. This visit obviously had to be approved by Stalin, at least for pragmatic purposes.

In his book *1920* Shulgin prophetically anticipated the appearance of a future dictator who would destroy all his old party comrades and restore Great Russia. Possibly Shulgin's prophecy later served as a model for Stalin during the Great Terror. In any event, *1920* was reprinted in the Soviet Union in full, including his forecast of a future party gravedigger. Shulgin explicitly said that neither Lenin nor Trotsky would play such a role. All of Shulgin's anti-Semitic remarks were also included in the Soviet reprint, which was exceptional in the USSR at that time. The publication seemed to be a kind of national mobilization by Stalin, but nobody in the old guard seemed to understand its covert message.

At approximately the same time as *1920* was published in the USSR, Shulgin made his "secret" journey. He was allowed freely to leave the Soviet Union and only later did it become known that he had played some mysterious role. A day or two before his departure a meeting took place in a train with a GPU man who presented himself as "a representative of some national forces" in the establishment and who made an extremely interesting statement. He begged Shulgin to deliver his message to the emigrés.

Shulgin's book about this journey (57) was commented on by the Soviet press and was read by Stalin. So even if one supposes that the GPU was preparing a provocation, it was articulated so well that in this form it could have an influence on Stalin. In spite of the exposure of the Trust in 1927 and consequently of the circumstances of Shulgin's trip, his book influenced the right-wing emigrés.

The time came when smenovekhism suddenly lost all its credentials because the end of the NEP in 1928 ruined the economic illusions of Ustrialov, who had connected his national and political program too closely with his preference for free market economics. Ustrialov, like almost everybody (including the left-wing opposition) in the Soviet Union itself, inaccurately accepted the turn away from the NEP as a radical step to socialism. Instead, it was an eventual radical Right social and economic transformation of Soviet society. Crushing all the remnants of free market economics, Stalin did not give industry to the collective ownership of workers but subordinated it to the party elite, which was quickly transformed into a new ruling class. As concerns the peasantry, under the mask of collectivization, it was forced into a "plantation" system that employed "slave labor" (82). So Ustrialov did not deserve his humiliation as a false prophet since he had forecast correctly the movement of the USSR from the left to the right.

In spite of the fact that Ustrialov himself was executed in 1938 after his return to the USSR, some former Smenovekhovtsi not only survived but also played a very important ideological role in the USSR. The Soviet historical encyclopedia (56) lists as former Smenovekhovtsi a prominent Soviet historian, Evgeni Tarle (about his influence on Stalin see Avtorkhanov [79, pp. 549-553]); a leading Soviet writer, Count Alexei Tolstoi, who contributed a lot to Stalin's cult; and an influential author, Marietta Shaginian. Another Smenovekhist (not mentioned by Figurovskaia), Lezhnev, turned out to be an extremely influential personality in the party establishment: in 1926 he was expelled from the USSR for his Smenovekhist activity but at the end of the twenties he returned, joined the Communist party, and was appointed by Stalin as head of the literature department of *Pravda*. From that position Lezhnev had a strong impact on Soviet literature. Thus, he had a key role in the almost complete destruction of the Left vanguard of early Soviet literature and promoted so-called socialist realism. Lezhnev's own literary works, not surprisingly, consisted of an appreciation of the works of Mikhail Sholokhov, an advocate of national bolshevism himself.

Among the emigrés in Paris a new radical rightist, pro-monarchy party—the *Mladorossi* (Young Russians)—emerged in 1928. They were profoundly influenced by smenovekhism, Eurasianism, and national maximalism. It differed from the latter on two points: the lack of explicit anti-Semitism and the emphasis on personal rule. (In the beginning—at least in 1928—the Mladorossi made several anti-Semitic statements but later dropped this position.) The Mladorossi formed a passionately Russian, radical Right movement that waxed enthusiastic over Soviet military, economic, and state development and that ignored both the mass persecution of peasants during collectivization and the persecution of religion (even though the party claimed to be strictly Russian Orthodox). The Mladorossi imitated the Communist party's organizational patterns. They had a strong leadership and a membership with no fewer than two thousand committed members and numerous sympathizers. The leader of the party was a young nobleman from a distinguished family of Persian origin, Aleksandr Kazem-Bek. Kazem-Bek published many articles and speeches (30, 31, 32) that are extremely important in the analysis of the genesis of national bolshevism. These writings show a very shrewd insight, quite different from that of most foreign observers, who were often hypnotized by official Communist slogans.

Kazem-Bek and his party were opposed to Stalin, but they saw in his policy an acceptable adaptation to Russian reality. In this way, their conclusions coincided with those of Barghoorn, who said more than twenty years later (3) that "political realities forced Stalin to exploit Russian nationalism" (p. 29).

In 1931 Kazem-Bek (30) said that Stalin was trying

> to provoke the hatred of the West for a successful struggle with the West. He is simply forced to provoke this energy and this hatred. He has no choice. Meanwhile, all this kindles a stormy nationalism among youth. . . . Moreover, it is necessary to take into consideration that this nationalism is still anonymous. . . . This nationalism could not help emerging as a result of the revolution. When it was appearing it coincided with the needs of communism and Communists tried and are still trying to use it. Two typical Bolshevik slogans—"Forsake Europe!" and "Overtake America!"—used expressions of a primitive, crude, imperial but powerful nationalism, from the outside still Soviet but already become Russian. We know that it is the root of our national renascence. . . . The adjective Russian would already have filled up the chasm that had been dug between yesterday's Reds and yesterday's Whites (pp. 24-25). . . . Communism, so-called communism—that is, the power that accepts the Communist phraseology—is successful only when it goes along with the Russian mood. . . . There is no organic link between words and deeds. . . . We are together with those in Russia who even under the Communist banner are serving the national cause (pp. 26–27).

It is remarkable that Kazem-Bek's conclusions coincided with opinions of certain Western experts. The same year J. Carlton Hayes (24) wrote:

One may also note the development of the Bolshevists in Russia who beginning as economic and social reformers, with loud protestations against militarism, imperialism and nationalism, soon discovered ... that the world is not equally prepared for their messianic altruism, and have ended by exalting a peculiarly integral nationalism in the USSR— living for themselves alone, serving their own interests, brandishing a sword, destroying democracy and liberty, and worshipping at the shrines of their dictators that are now their national heroes. ... The extreme nationalism of the Russian Bolshevists is likely to be remembered, when the details of their economic experiments shall have been forgotten (pp. 166–167).

In a more laconic way Merle Fainsod (19) said much later that "as the appeal of its revolutionary ideology has dimmed, it has placed greater reliance on the cementing force of nationalism. ... The Soviet regime has been able to draw strong support from identification with a native fund of patriotic sentiment" (p. 22).

It is interesting to note that this strange acceptance by radical Right monarchists of Soviet reality was substantially foreshadowed by a part of the Russian tsarist family that had been in the West since 1923. Grand Duke Kirill Vladimirovich (14) condemned at Christmas 1925 any foreign intervention since "under the slogan of the struggle against bolshevism such leaders will bring to our motherland a new enslavement of her originality, will bring the plunder of her natural resources." Several years later the Grand Duke Dmitrii Pavlovich, who earlier had participated in Rasputin's murder, joined the Mladorossi and was appointed honorable chairman of that party (14).

In the period 1930–1932 Stalin's appeal to the radical Right emigrants was strongest. These were the years of the so-called Dmitrievskii affair. In 1930 Sergei Dmitrievskii, a secretary at the Soviet embassy in Stockholm, asked for political asylum in Sweden. He subsequently published three books (11–13) that contained surprising praise of Stalin as a hero of the struggle for national Russia. Indeed, this praise increased from book to book. Dmitrievskii hailed Stalin as leader of the strong, purely Russian group that had a very difficult and dangerous fight against the Jewish internationalist clique of which Trotsky was leader. Dmitrievskii said that Molotov, Andreev, Voroshilov, and other Russian leaders were also inspired by this national struggle.

Dmitrievskii, as had Ustrialov, claimed that Lenin himself was not only a revolutionary but also a national leader. Lenin was an ardent Russian patriot. He loved Russia strongly. Dmitrievskii was especially sharp in his criticism of Trotsky, Zinoviev, Litvinov, Radek, Yaroslavski (Gubelman), and Lunacharskii (who was not a Jew) and blamed them for pursuing their own Jewish interests. He further maintained that the entire country, and even the majority of the party, was anticommunist. The Soviet Union was filled by the spirit of growing nationalism. Especially nationalistic, although unconsciously so, was the Komsomol. Dmitrievskii claimed that a Great Russian national revolution was needed and that some of the present Soviet leaders would be in the ranks of this revolution and even among its leaders.

A striking feature of Dmitrievskii's writing is its resemblance to recent Soviet nationalist and anti-Semitic literature published officially in the USSR. The same language, the same argumentation, and nearly the same set of political ideas occur. If Dmitrievskii preferred to call Soviet leaders of Jewish origin internationalist, non-Russian, and even non-Asian (*vide* Eurasianism), present Soviet authors use a more straightforward approach and call them "Zionist," which is an accepted substitute for "Jewish" in the Soviet political vocabulary. On the other hand, his position fit the Mladorossy outlook so well that Dmitrievskii was greeted by that party loudly and was often given the opportunity to express his views in Mladorossy publications.

The question arises immediately as to why Dmitrievskii asked for political asylum if he liked Stalin's leadership so well. Was he perhaps the bearer of a message to the emigrants, whom Stalin saw as potential support in a critical situation? As a good politician Stalin would not have overestimated the force of the emigrés but he did not need that group as a force. He could use it also as a kind of ideological laboratory that could provide him with valuable information, for instance, on how to mobilize social and national forces to make his personal power more stable.

The idea of a possible special function for Dmitrievskii was suggested by a senior Nazi official, Reinhard Heydrich, in 1940 (44). Heydrich wrote a secret report about a new Dmitrievskii appeal to Germany not to take any steps against the USSR since that country was steadily going along the road to national socialism. This information about the "silent" Dmitrievskii diplomacy was found by Meir Michaelis in Nazi archives. (In 1933 Dmitrievskii had appealed to Hitler to help create a large Russian national socialist party since Russia was ripe for this trend, as Michaelis [45] reports. It is also of note that in 1934 Dmitrievskii published a book on Hitler—in Swedish only.)

It is, however, also possible that Dmitrievskii was not an agent of Stalin's (Heydrich did not claim this categorically), in which case he is even more important since then he really represented a nationalist trend among the Soviet elite.

The existence of such a trend is also confirmed by Joseph Berger, the former secretary general of the Palestinian Communist party. In

1935 Berger met, in prison, a Russian poet and senior party official named Parfienov, who claimed that he belonged to such a movement (116).

Some scholars date the official resurgence of Great Russian nationalism in the Soviet Union to 1934 (97). Nevertheless, this development was long in the making. Timasheff (67) rightly has pointed out that "after 1928, the internationalism of the Russian Communists was no longer as it had been; perhaps it could be termed 'ambivalent' " (p. 156).

One can think that the reason for this change toward nationalism was the Nazi danger and the necessity of reliance in large measure on patriotic sentiments. But the Nazi danger was merely a pretext for Stalin's implementation of a nationalistic policy. There was some resistance to this policy—for instance, the last Bukharin opposition: on March 30, 1934, he published an article severely attacking Russian nationalism that prompted official condemnation of Bukharin in the press. Hans Kohn (34) is nevertheless right in seeing a German influence in the new wave of Russian nationalism: "The new Stalinist nationalism with its chauvinistic fixation on Russian originality and priority and its antiplutocratic and anti-Western appeal to the masses probably owed much to the triumph of Hitler" (p. 223). Of course, this trend was determined much earlier and Trotsky (71), in his rare insights into the origins of Stalinism, was very close to the truth: "Had the Bolsheviks not seized power, the world would have had a Russian name for Fascism five years before the march on Rome. . . . Russia could not isolate itself from the profound reaction that swept over post-war Europe in the early twenties" (p. 412).

Ustrialov (75) almost fifteen years earlier had made a more successful generalization than Trotsky. Answering Bukharin's accusation of fascism in 1926, he wrote ironically, "Why do we need fascism when we have . . . bolshevism? Obviously it is unnecessary to plight one's betrothed. . . . It is not chance . . . it is destiny. . . . Certainly, Russian bolshevism and Italian fascism are phenomena of a new epoque. They hate each other with the hatred of brothers" (p. 409).

The proximity of bolshevism and fascism was also underlined by Dmitrii Mirskii (112) from a Eurasian point of view.

> Here again Communism and Fascism have to be regarded as rough approximations to a perfect ideocratic state. The insufficiency of Fascism lies in the essential jejuneness of its ruling idea which has little content apart from the mere will to organize. The insufficiency of Communism lies in the only too obvious contradiction between a policy that is ideocratic in practice, and the materialist philosophy it is based on, which denies the reality of ideas, and reduces all history to processes of necessity (p. 318).

It is necessary to put national bolshevism into the context of the radical rightist movement in Europe in the twenties and thirties (99). There was a general radical right reaction to the Bolshevik Revolution and to attempts by Western communism to seize power in some countries. There was also a psychological mainspring, "an imperceptible transformation" of radical leftist Marxism-Leninism into radical national bolshevism. Eugene Weber (99) labeled this mainspring a reconciliation that

> proves possible between radicals of Right and Left. . . . The former can join in a politique du pire to bring the existing order down; and many a rapprochement between Nationalists and Syndicalists; between Fascists and Communists can be explained only by the temporary conjunction of their hatreds. . . . The fact is that, whatever their ultimate intention, activists of any ilk find themselves involved in similar campaigns, similar organizational and didactive problems, so that the sociopolitical dynamism of their enterprise is stronger than the verbal differences between them. Thus, the ideological options they may choose make little difference to the behavior of their agents as long as they remain in the realm of action. Hence the coincidences between extreme Right and Left (Introduction).

So for Stalin, on one hand, and for Shirinski-Shikhmatiev and the Mladorossi, on the other, it was not difficult to switch from one radical trend to another.

The year 1934 was crucial in Soviet history. The radical right transformation of Soviet society was completed. It was announced in the main slogan of the seventeenth congress of the Communist party that "socialism had won a victory in the USSR." But until the beginning of 1934 Marxism-Leninism was the single legitimating facet of the Soviet system. National bolshevism was only Stalin's personal ideology and possibly that of a very small group of new Soviet leaders around Stalin such as Andrei Zhdanov and Aleksandr Shcherbakov. Starting in 1934, however, national bolshevism had use of the mass media for its propagation, a use that has been constantly increasing since that time. Stalin could persuade his elite and many others in 1934 that the new national Russian accent was only a tactical step used many times by Bolsheviks and by Lenin personally. Unfortunately, some scientists repeated Stalin's argument, for instance, Waldemar Gurian (22), who asserted that "the turn to Soviet nationalism was only an application of the general scheme to concrete situations. Stalinism does not differ in its foundation from Leninism" (p. 7). Such a mistake is no surprise if we take into consideration that many scholars now consider Soviet society to be Marxist or Marxist inspired.

In 1934 Stalin apparently fully realized that a radical leftist Communist party did not fit the new Soviet system. Thus, in many respects, he destroyed the old radical Left elite in the party and created a new radical rightist organization that was ready to accept the new message. This was an essential part of the background of Stalin's great purge, which took millions of human lives, and it helps explain the carefully calculated and cool annihilation not only of the small part of the party that was more or less hostile to Stalin in the past but also of its vast majority, including many sincere and devoted Stalinists. Stalin mercilessly executed almost all his collaborators who had a sense of continuity with the radical Left revolutionary past. Stalin could draw support from them for almost any step, but it was impossible to expect them to accept national bolshevism as a concept or anti-Semitism as a concept rather than a tactical step, as Stephen Dunn (87) still accepts it. These people did not fit the new reality. They were doomed to destruction.

There was a real counterrevolution whose significance and importance is still misunderstood by people who try to see in it only a reflection of mental illness in Stalin (117). It would be a great mistake also to think that the counterrevolution was a triumph of the Russian spirit, as Nicholas Timasheff and Walter Kolarz (36) naively thought because of their wartime enthusiasm. Timasheff (67) wrote that "in turning nationalist once more, Russia proved that in the very depths of her national soul she never had abandoned her historical way, which on the surface seemed lost in 1917" (p. 191). Barghoorn (3) justly has criticized this point (118).

> The Russian supremacy theme is used to support Kremlin policies which do not necessarily have the enthusiastic support of the Great Russian element within the Soviet Union. It is important to make this point strongly because it might be easy to conclude . . . that Soviet Russification is a mere continuation of pre-revolutionary Czarist policy, or at least that it is a Russian nationalist policy. There is of course an element of continuity with the Czarist regime, and there is also at least some reflection of Russian popular sentiment in the policy of the regime (p. 60).

Indeed, the Mladorossi group was furious after the great purge. Kazem-Bek (32) accused Stalin of Bonapartism. Yes, it was a counterrevolution but not of the sort of which he dreamed. The Mladorossi could not imagine that their counterrevolution could be usurped in such a way. This party imagined the national revolution as something that would restore Russian traditional values, even install a new Russian monarch, and bring its members back to Russia to participate in a new society. But Stalin did not need the Mladorossi at all. He saw in their views only a confirmation of his decision to make use of Russian national sentiments, to take advantage of widespread anti-Semitism, and to make his power absolute. It is possible that Stalin already identified himself at that time as an anti-Zionist fighter, a role that was rather openly avowed in his last years.

The Mladorossi group was no longer of use to Stalin. Kazem-Bek for a while turned to Mussolini and even visited Nazi Germany. But during the war he and his comrades started supporting Stalin again. In 1956 Kazem-Bek returned to the USSR and was "thanked" in a peculiar way. He was forced to publish an article in the Soviet press with a statement that he had been an agent of "imperialist circles" and had broken with them. Nobody wanted to acknowledge his contribution to national bolshevism. Nevertheless, Kazem-Bek was given an official post in the Department of External Relations of the Russian Orthodox church and was for many years the best contributor to the official magazine of this church. (He died in March 1977.)

The Mladorossi influence seemed to be the last emigrant influence on Stalin. The new legitimacy was achieved and had to be applied. The way seemed clear.

The Marriage of the Radical Left and the Radical Right

But the situation was more complicated. Stalin could not simply use national bolshevism as a new legitimacy for the Soviet system. He was a prisoner of his own Machiavellian policy. First of all he did not want to eliminate the international appeal of the original communist ideology. A very important feature of his policy was the utilization of this appeal for Russian national objectives. Moreover, Stalin had to claim continuity with the October Revolution in spite of the fact that in reality this continuity was broken. The extent of the discontinuity is still under discussion. Cohen (115) defends the idea of complete discontinuity in the Soviet historical process because of Stalinism.

Stalin was afraid of completely abandoning Communist phraseology, at least at this particular moment. So even the new elite, which had replaced the old, was not yet ripe for national bolshevism. Therefore, elements of the old doctrine had to be retained. As a result, a very ambiguous situation emerged. According to Brzezinski (7),

> Stalin consummated the marriage of Marxism-Leninism and Soviet (particularly Russian) nationalism. The increasing stress on Great Russia's state traditions, on frontiers, on national aspirations and on a civilizing mission vis-à-vis the non-Russian Soviet nations, went hand in hand with the physical transformation of the CPSU from one dominated by a rather mixed lot of cosmopolitan and internationally-oriented intellectuals of Russian, Jewish, Polish, Baltic and Caucasian origin, into a party dominated primarily by Russian (and, to some

extent, Ukrainian) peasants turned into party apparatchiki. The new Soviet elites have tended, accordingly, to be both conservative and nationalist even while professing the universal elements of their ideology. They could thus act in a manner which was essentially dictated by their own interests, and simultaneously believe themselves to be truly internationalists. . . . The cumulative effect has been a mixed pattern of motivation and behavior. . . . The principle of internationalism, even if often violated in practice, did restrain, if only by facing more covert behavior, the inclination towards Great Russian nationalist self-assertion (p. 7).

But simultaneously Brzezinski (7) maintains that Stalinism softened some aggressive features of Russian nationalism: "The historical function of Stalinist Communism may have been to pacify and re-define the phase of the intense nationalistic—even imperialistic— awakening of the Russian people" (p. 8).

Brzezinski is probably right but only for a very limited historical period since at that time the Russians as a nation still had a very powerful demographic base that has been constantly declining since the thirties. Conversely, Barghoorn (3) has argued that to a certain extent Russian nationalism moderated the aggressiveness inherent in ruling Marxist ideology.

There is an intriguing element of paradox in the relationship between militarism and nationalism in Soviet Russia. War contributes to the development of totalitarianism by stimulating centralism, chauvinism, and anti-foreignism. But at the same time, the revival of Great Russian nationalism in the Soviet Union, must to a certain extent at least, be regarded as an *anti-totalitarian* development. We should not, of course, exaggerate the contradiction between these two elements in Soviet ideology. The Kremlin has, to a considerable degree, succeeded in synthesizing them. And yet it is not impossible that the concessions made by the Kremlin to Great Russian nationalism may have introduced modifications in Soviet ideology which contain a promise of easier Soviet-Western relations in the long-term future (p. 264).

But almost all scholars underestimate the conscious element in the emergence of the new ideology. Kohn (35), for instance, thinks that the "marriage of Marxism-Leninism and Russian nationalism," using Brzezinski's expression, was contracted in the interest of communism.

It was not a turning back to Czarist times but a difficult and precarious attempt to balance in the interest of Soviet communism, and as it was then seen of communism in general, Soviet nationalism and proletarian internationalism, Soviet supranationalism and the reawakened vigor of Russian nationalism as the decisive support of Soviet communism in times of unprecedented danger. The balancing act led inevitably to many ambiguities: only an authoritarian regime could attempt it with some degree of credibility and success. The Soviet Union paid its respect to the rising tide of nationalism all over the globe (p. 57).

Barghoorn (3) considers the situation a result of the rationalization of political development toward the style of the radical Right. He argues that "the new Soviet nationalism is an often bewildering combination of traditional Great Russian nationalism, elements of Western universalist Marxism, and, most important of all, a system of rationalization of the political order" (p. vii). He gives an even more precise definition: "This new kind of integral nationalism is the 'justifying ideology' of a new type of politico-economic structure, that of Soviet 'state monopoly capitalism' " (p. 4). Barghoorn even has proposed a model of such rationalization, which according to him was basically an unconscious process.

> A leadership group, however, which on the conscious level may be highly rationalistic and manipulative, may at the same time unconsciously cling to historically determined attitudes of which they are not fully aware. Eventually their formal doctrine can relapse into a pattern of rationalization for actions determined by factors not consistent with their ideology (p. 151).

Indeed, there was rationalization. But one must distinguish the elements of this process. Social and economic components of the new system were definitely rationalized since it is not clear that Stalin himself understood what the radical rightist transformation might be. But national bolshevism as an ideological concept was pursued by him consciously. The Machiavellian policy adopted by Stalin did not allow him to expose his genuine objectives. However, the conscious will of the growing group around Stalin to reinforce national bolshevism in the Soviet Union was the core of the process.

A paradoxical situation arose in the USSR. If radical right national bolshevism was an almost inevitable reaction to the utopian attempts at the socialist transformation of Russia by the original Bolsheviks, the national bolshevism of the thirties had to contend with the new political reality, namely, a big, multinational country that was not amenable to naked Russian nationalism, a population (at least the youth) indoctrinated in Marxism-Leninism, and an international arena in which the Communist appeal was a very valuable tool of Soviet foreign policy.

So the Machiavellian policy had its natural limits. Nevertheless, one can see the growth of national bolshevism since the great purge. One of the main indicators of this process was the spread of anti-Semitism. William Korey (113) makes more or less the same observation: "Official anti-Semitism must clearly be seen as a function of national developments during the late thirties and early forties" (p. 122). And Peter Viereck (77) insists that some very important

features of the Soviet system can be "understood in the West [only]
when one realizes the importance of anti-Semitism (disguised as
anti-cosmopolitanism) in National-Bolshevik propaganda." Viereck
claims that national bolshevism was "a cousin to German National-
Socialism" (p. 27). Nonetheless, one comes across strange counter-
views such as those of Dunn (87), who assumed that "the Soviet
government policy is not, properly speaking, anti-Semitic. Rather,
the regime had found itself forced for historical, cultural, and political reasons, to adopt certain measures which from an American
perspective look anti-Semitic" (p. 75).

Another aspect of the new ideological change was shown by
Nazi-Soviet relations. Almost all that is known about these relations
suggests that the policy was not simply opportunistic. The USSR not
only stopped all anti-Nazi propaganda (including the prohibition and
removal of all anti-Fascist and anti-Nazi propaganda literature from
Soviet libraries) but even praised the Nazis in a way that was not at
all necessary for appearance and for diplomacy. Thus, there was
Molotov's notorious statement blaming the Western countries for the
struggle against Nazi ideology. This cannot be explained merely as
political opportunism. Nevertheless, the Nazi-Soviet rapprochement
was shaky from the very beginning because of the aggressive nature
of both totalitarian states. The proximity of systems is not a guarantee against conflict.

Basic Conflicts in Soviet Society

During the war the quest for a new national Bolshevik legitimacy
accelerated greatly under the pressure of political reality. The first
wartime requirement was to carry out a Russian national mobilization against Germany. Wartime needs also accelerated the "concordat" with religion and especially with the Russian Orthodox church,
which had been in progress since 1939 (89). The rate of this development was no slower after the war, and militant and open anti-
Semitism along lines common to all radical right movements was one
of the principal indicators of the process.

If the original and even the wartime national bolshevism were
more or less within the framework of political reality, postwar
national bolshevism started exposing its inherent irrational features.
The original anti-Semitism could find its legitimacy partly as a
reaction against the big demographic change in Russia or as a reaction to the disproportionate Jewish participation in the Soviet system. The postwar, militant anti-Semitism could not be justified in
such a way. Jews had been excluded from high ranking political

positions after the great purge and the last Jewish "show" figures were purged from the leadership on the eve of the war. Besides, the Jewish population of the USSR was almost halved by the Germans during the war.

After the war Jewish political participation did not exist except for some token figures. The internal political situation in the country seemed to be stable and no longer needed additional anti-Semitic actions for instrumental reasons.

The so-called doctors plot and preparations for the final solution to the Jewish question at the end of Stalin's rule were the culmination of this irrational development and the best illustration of the new ideology. Earlier I quoted Ulam's remark about Stalin's anti-Semitic obsession at the end of his life. But, properly speaking, his anti-Semitic attitude was no more obsessive than the anti-Semitism of those radical right movements outside the USSR that professed anti-Semitism (99). Consider, for example, Stalin's remark to his daughter (78) about the Zionist indoctrination of all the old generation after the revolution (the subject of the conversation was Svetlana's broken first marriage to a Jew). "Zionists," said Stalin in 1948, "had given you your first husband." And, sharply answering his daughter's timid objections, he categorically replied: "All the old generation is infected by Zionism and they are teaching youth" (p. 182).

This remark only confirms my hypothesis that Stalin already identified himself as an anti-Zionist fighter on a global scale. Moreover, it may disclose one of his great purge motivations. If Zionist activity was so dangerous and if all the old generation was infected by Zionism (which must be understood not as the movement toward a Jewish national state but only in the framework of the "Protocols"), the old generation had to be eliminated.

One might argue in reply perhaps that anti-Zionism was only a rationalization of the great purge, but this does not make that big a difference. An obsessive, irrational, anti-Semitism was so open among the Soviet leadership that a senior Soviet official, Lesakov, not only did not conceal this attitude from Milovan Djilas and his delegation at the beginning of 1948 but even boasted of it. Lesakov (86) told Djilas that "Comrade Zhdanov has cleaned up all the Jews from the Central Committee!" He explained the reason for the dismissal of the deputy chief of staff, General Antonov, by saying with indignation, "Can you imagine, it was disclosed that he had Jewish origins" (p. 160). One can fancy what kind of discussions took place among the Soviet leaders when they were alone.

In 1952 Stalin seemed to have decided to solve the basic conflict of Soviet society—that between the radical right nature of this society and the continued legitimacy of Marxism-Leninism. He was eager to solve this conflict by a new great purge, an irrational plan but one no more irrational than any other policy of radical right movements in the twentieth century.

Stalin prepared a new, enlarged presidium of the central committee in which his old politburo was only a minority. After this they easily could be replaced by young competitors who had very limited continuity with the past. This attempt was not successful and Stalin's death permitted a temporary victory of the vestiges of communism over national bolshevism. This victory, however, was and could not be decisive and did not solve the basic conflict of Soviet society.

As a whole, Khrushchev's rule was an adventurous attempt at a radical left restoration in a radical right society. He tried inconsistently to restore some features of an earlier Soviet communism. But that ideology was not an organic part of the society. Therefore it could not win out but it was too necessary for legitimacy to be eliminated. Khrushchev tried to discredit the great purge and Stalin's rule as a substantial deviation from original communism. He tried to restore the continuity with the radical leftist past by the rehabilitation of the elite eliminated by the great purge. And he once again proclaimed a war against religion, which after the war had peacefully coexisted with national bolshevism. He also softened the militant, irrational anti-Semitism of Stalin. Naturally, Khrushchev failed.

The Crisis of Legitimacy

The conflict was not resolved and provoked what Judson Mitchell (47) has called "the crisis of legitimacy" (p. 6). According to Mitchell, "recent Soviet political history has been marked by a resurgence of emphasis on Marxist-Leninist ideology" (p. 137). He identifies the beginning of this crisis as 1968, but it seems to date from 1965. It is connected most notably with the name of Alexander Shelepin, who challenged the leadership directly in terms of national bolshevism (25, p. 18).

There is little information about Shelepin's attempt to take power and it is not clear when exactly national bolshevism was chosen by him as his political platform. Probably in the beginning his program was only a vague concept of terrorist rule that gave insufficient attention to the legitimacy of the system. But when Shelepin failed in his direct challenge (in the beginning of 1966), he advanced the cause of national bolshevism to justify his attack on the leadership, who in the interests of their own legitimacy had to rely on Communist party ideology. The Six-Day War in 1967 gradually opened the door for the legitimacy crisis of the Soviet system, but the real outbreak occurred during the Polish and Czechoslovakian unrest.

The main battlefields on which the clash between the two legitimacies took place were anti-Zionist propaganda literature and fiction and literary criticism. Anti-Zionist propaganda represented only a slightly covert national Bolshevik offensive and it flooded the Soviet book market. Anti-Zionism was not only a password but the very essence of the movement as well. "Zionism," "communism," and "Soviet" were code words that were very well known to Soviet readers. Such retrogressive symbolism (in principle not specifically related to anti-Semitism) was noticed long ago, for example, by Barghoorn (3), who said that "the Soviet themes and symbols in Soviet ideology mask 'covert' or 'latent' Russian attitudes" (p. 12). In this code "Zionism" means "Jews," "communism" means "our" and "Soviet" means "Russian." So the message of books like *Caution, Zionism* by Yurii Ivanov (first published in 1969) was absolutely clear to almost everybody in the USSR (108).

Another battlefield was fiction and literary criticism. Anti-Zionist themes were prominent in the works of passionate anti-Semitic writers such as Ivan Shevtzov, a navy officer (100, 101), and Yurii Kolesnikov (93). Both books by Shevtzov were published in 1970 and Kolesnikov's novel was first published in a magazine in 1972. One can find in these writings the comprehensive historiosophy of national bolshevism. It is highly revealing that (according to a confidential source) permission to publish Shevtzov's *Ljubov i nenavist* (*Love and Hatred*) was given personally to the director of the publishing house by a politburo member named Dmitrii Polyansky (119). Since the fact of the publication provoked a considerable scandal abroad, it was condemned by the politburo. And Polyansky (according to the same source) received a reprimand. (Polyansky usually is associated with Shelepin in the Soviet leadership.)

There is much information about national bolshevism in Soviet fiction and literary criticism. Several years ago several pieces were published (84, 90, 92) on this topic. Jack Haney (90) has presented a very interesting account of the Russian nationalist trend in the Soviet magazine *Molodaia gvardiia* (*Young Guard*) and of the polemics over this issue in the Soviet press. Haney characterizes the position of the magazine as one "that sought to cultivate a Great Russian patriotism at the expense of 'proletarian internationalism' and 'Soviet patriotism'" (p. 8). This formulation, if taken in the framework of our model, shows clearly the legitimacy crisis that openly emerged in fields such as fiction that were marginal to the leadership. Without doubt, the magazine had substantial support. Thomas Bird (84) has tried to identify the source of this support and has pointed cautiously at the armed forces, which "have fostered the cult to strengthen their own position vis-à-vis party officialdom" (p. 18).

We will consider this problem later. George Kline (92) also assumes that *Molodaia gvardiia* "seems to be trying to use Russian chauvinism to fill the ideological void left . . . by the collapse of traditional Marxism-Leninism" (p. 33). One must recall that this new literary trend emerged at the end of the 1960s.

But the open challenge to Marxism-Leninism was made by the opposition Russian nationalists, allegedly not without unofficial support from Shelepin, Polyansky, and others. In 1971 this movement started publishing a nonofficial manuscript magazine *Veche* (popular assemblies in ancient Russia were called by this name) (93, 103). This movement was not as a whole national bolshevik but it included some outspoken representatives of national bolshevism such as Mikhail Antonov, an architect who published an open national bolshevik statement in *Veche* in 1971. A national bolshevik group in the Soviet leadership probably tried, though very cautiously, to take advantage of this trend to mobilize additional support in the struggle for power from outside of the party.

More evidence of the legitimacy crisis in 1971–1972 surfaced with the Jewish problem, namely, the problem of Jewish emigration from the USSR (120). Although some observers believe that Soviet policy on Jewish emigration has been consistent, it seems rather to have been the result of a consensus between two groups at least until the beginning of 1975. There is some reason to believe that Jewish emigration was favored by the national Bolshevik group, which used it to provoke the legitimacy crisis. Indeed, any substantial Jewish emigration would be a challenge to communist ideology, which appears helpless and invalid in this crucial case. If the communist oriented group in the Soviet leadership allowed a large-scale Jewish emigration from the USSR, it would reveal to its competitors in the leadership that party ideology is ineffective as regards the solution of the problem of Soviet Jews and, therefore, ineffective vis-à-vis other national problems. On this point, Russian national bolsheviks could draw support also from republican national group leaders such as Petr Shelest or Vasilii Mzhavanadze. But it was vital to the interests of the communist oriented group in the Soviet leadership not to allow a large-scale Jewish emigration, which is why Brezhnev arranged one of the strangest shows in Soviet history—a Jewish press conference by prominent Soviet Jews whose Jewish origin previously had been carefully concealed. This press conference was aimed at demonstrating that the Jewish problem was basically solved and that the majority of Soviet Jews had a reliable Soviet identity. This conference took place in 1971 at the height of the legitimacy crisis.

Mysterious fluctuations in Jewish emigration from the USSR in 1971–1974 seem to be explained better by the conflict between communist and national bolshevist trends than by any other hypothesis. They were finished by the beginning of 1975. Indeed, Aleksandr Shelepin was ousted from the politburo in April 1975, when Jewish emigration was almost blocked. Another apparent supporter of this position, Dmitrii Polyansky, was expelled from the politburo a year later. So Soviet policy toward Jewish emigration probably gives us a good timing for the internal conflict in the leadership.

Another interesting development took place at the end of the period of the legitimacy crisis. This was the beginning of the persecution of *Veche*. Until 1974 this magazine was silently tolerated by the authorities. In the middle of that year, however, a judicial procedure was started against *Veche*. In November 1974, its editor, Vladimir Osipov, was arrested. A short time before Polyansky's dismissal, Osipov received an extraordinarily long prison term in comparison with other opposition figures—eight years. The severity of Osipov's sentence indicates that the *Veche* case was used against Shelepin and Polyansky to discredit them.

But Brezhnev's victory does not mean that national bolshevism is defeated in the USSR. Mitchell (47) has noticed that along with the emphasis on Marxism-Leninism "there has been a marked revival of nationalist themes in Soviet ideological pronouncements, including a coupling of 'Soviet patriotism' and 'Socialist internationalism' that is reminiscent of the Stalin era." The basic conflict in Soviet society is still not solved though there are some efforts being made to solve it. First of all, Brezhnev is by no means a pure Marxist. As Mitchell indicated (47), official Soviet Marxism is deviating more and more from original Marxism. For instance, it now recognizes a division of labor under communism. This means that Soviet Marxist theoreticians are eager to make communism increasingly resemble present Soviet reality. But even though Brezhnev needs to retain a Communist platform, he is not necessarily fully committed to communism. William Griffith (21) underlines this point very well.

> Brezhnev and Mao are certainly not just Great Russian and Han chauvinists. But if only because the capacity of the human mind for rationalization and self-delusion is unlimited, ideology rarely, if ever, contradicts national self-interest in the minds of rulers of states (p. 2).

Meanwhile, the picture of the mentality of Soviet leaders given by Thomas Hammond (23) is rather unjustified.

> To say that the members of the Politbureau give top priority to Soviet national interests is not to say that they are indifferent to the spread of Communism or that they are cynical about Marxism-Leninism. . . . They have all been thoroughly indoctrinated in Marxism-Leninism and

they probably get a visceral feeling of pleasure at the prospect of Communism winning out in yet another part of the globe. The spread of Communism helps to reinforce their beliefs, provides evidence that Communism is the wave of the future, and helps to justify their careers, their policies and their continued rule in Russia (p. 55).

The Soviet leaders' communism is now strictly functional. It depends mainly on their group positions. Naturally, they are attached to national bolshevism, and the type of Soviet official Nove (49) describes is highly characteristic. Nove depicts the typical provincial secretary as "nationalistic, anti-intellectual, anti-Semitic and above all wholeheartedly devoted to his own position" (p. 19).

Soviet officials become committed communists primarily and perhaps only when they are members of such institutional groups as the ideological apparatus or when they are responsible for international communist relations. These groups are still necessary in the framework of the system. That is why they have to generate a pattern of Communist ideology though substantially modified and rationalized. So communist ideology is in a defensive position in the USSR; yet, it is still very far from defeat. It can survive only if its proponents give some proof of its efficiency. The foreign policy benefits are one of the main arguments for Communist ideology in the USSR.

The presence of at least two competing trends does not mean that all the members of the Soviet leadership have a polar identity. There is also a growing indifference toward ideology as a whole, as many observers have noted (26). But the decisive political role always belongs to people with an active identity.

Push-Pull Expansion because of the Legitimacy Crisis

Soviet foreign policy is influenced by many political, economic, and social factors. The USSR must guarantee its survival in the complicated international system. It has many enemies, actual as well as potential. Their relative importance depends both on the overall international situation and on the power of the Soviet Union. The multinational structure of the USSR and the multistate character of the Soviet bloc make the Soviet Union very sensitive to any attempt to change the status quo in the Soviet sphere of influence. Nonetheless, Soviet policy never has been static. Since 1917 the USSR has been constantly expanding. Moreover, although a superpower, the USSR is not the only superpower in the world. It has powerful rivals in the United States and China. China seems to be a very vocal rival of the USSR, using every opportunity to weaken Soviet influence.

My objective here is to single out how Soviet expansion is influenced by its ideology and more precisely by its legitimacy crisis since the latter is essentially a new factor in Soviet life. Ideology is certainly not the only factor that influences Soviet expansion. Soviet expansion also can be explained as an attempt to strengthen Soviet strategic positions vis-à-vis other superpowers. But this latter explanation never has been sufficient.

Some scholars consider Soviet expansionism explicitly as a striving for world revolution. But this position is very problematic. It is a consequence primarily of terminological ambiguity and substitution. Thomas Hammond (23), for example, claims that "many in the West mistakenly interpreted the Stalin-Trotsky debate to mean that Trotsky was for revolution while Stalin was against it. Actually, Stalin was probably just as much in favor of revolution as Trotsky was, but differed with him over timing and methods" (p. 50). This conclusion, however, is valid solely if we equate the terms "revolution" and "expansion." For Trotsky the revolution was an end in itself; for Stalin, it was a means to eventual domination and expansion. It is impossible to believe that revolution, or world revolution, was an end in itself for Stalin. So this terminological confusion is inadmissible. Even if Soviet occupation policies "communized" local social systems, the purpose was to increase Soviet control not to create a revolution. Moreover, all the social transformations in Soviet satellites had a radical rightist character; thus, the term "revolution" is especially inadequate.

In December 1952 Notre Dame University arranged a symposium entitled "Who Is the Enemy: Russian Imperialism or Soviet Communism?" (22). Waldemar Gurian insisted on the exclusive responsibility of communist ideology because of its universality. For him national bolshevism is only tactical. An especially firm stand on blaming communism for the expansion was taken by Nicholas Timasheff (68), who seven years earlier had claimed that there was a great retreat from communism in Russia under the reliable hand of Stalin (67). But he placed some blame on Hitler, too, for Soviet expansion: "Historical instances are there to show that successful defense against an aggressor may induce a tendency to develop unlimited imperialism" (p. 36).

At almost the same time, however, Hans Kohn (34) condemned only traditional elements for the Soviet policy of expansion: "Russian nationalism did not confine itself to a defensive patriotism, the chauvinism of which might be explained by the military catastrophe facing the country. It immediately asserted itself in an aggressive way" (p. 227).

Essentially the same point was repeated three years later by Frederick Barghoorn (3), who argued that "like all extreme forms of nationalism, that of the Soviet Union is imperialistic. It is expansionist and its horizon of ambition is bounded only by the realities of geography and counterbalancing power" (p. 4). William Griffith (21) holds more or less the same opinion. The danger according to him emanates "not from 'communism' but rather from imperialist, expansionist powers whose national interests are contrary to ours in many respects, specifically the Soviet Union and the Chinese People's republic. Their Communist ideological orientation perhaps makes them more expansionist; but the Russian and Chinese empires also were expansionist" (p. 3). But Hugh Seton-Watson (60) thinks that neither communist ideology itself nor Russian imperialism but the totalitarian features of the Soviet system are responsible for the expansion: "What has long threatened the United States and world peace—is not Marxist doctrine or the infectious example of a nonexistent Communist paradise, but the implacable hostility of men organized into a well-disciplined apparatus of political power and possessing immense military and industrial resources" (p. 11).

Thus, the spectrum of opinions is quite broad. But all of these views reflect some part of the reality of different periods in Soviet history. The first Soviet expansion during the civil war can be explained almost exclusively by communist ideology and by the striving for world revolution. Stalin's actions against Poland, the Baltic states, Finland, and Rumania on the eve of the Second World War were caused mainly by the imperialist motivation of national bolshevism. The same relates to Soviet expansion after the war. Later, however, the situation changed and there was a "push-pull" interrelationship between communist ideology and national bolshevism. One cannot consider this problem only ideologically. It is necessary also to take into consideration other factors influencing the Soviet expansionist policy, all of which factors admittedly are bound up with ideology.

Alan Besançon, in his brilliant essay (82), considers the Communist expansionist drive as a kind of élan vital for the Soviet system. He consistently unfolds this view and presents the USSR as a monolithic state. However, the USSR is not at all monolithic from any point of view, including the ideological one. There is in the Soviet Union a diminishing ideological élan vital but it acts together with certain other forces. These forces can sometimes counterbalance the ideological drive, but they also can figure in a very dangerous push-pull interrelationship. Barghoorn (3) realistically assesses this possibility: "The question arises whether in spite of the imperialist surge still contained in Soviet nationalism, the Kremlin's will to power is not balanced somewhat by counter forces operating within Soviet society" (p. 275).

Now, instead of this counterbalance one can see a dangerous instability because of the legitimacy crisis. Because it is in a state of defense, communist ideology needs some proof of its vitality and necessity. It is the legitimacy of the communist component of the Soviet system that is at issue. There are some institutional groups in the leadership whose legitimacy rests either in communist ideology or in a substitute for it. First of all there is the huge and powerful ideological party apparatus that embraces both the professional staff in ideological branches of the party and a big army of professional Marxism-Leninism teachers, writers, and instructors (in Daniel Bell's terms they are hierophants). This is still a highly influential party group. Another group consists of all the people involved in direct relations with foreign communist parties, at least with nonruling ones. Then the party leader himself is legitimized by communist ideology.

The former groups face rival institutional groups whose dependence on communist ideology is much weaker or even nonexistent. Of course, the organizational, administrative, industrial, and local party groups need something for their legitimacy. But national bolshevism can suit them, and their dependence on Soviet foreign policy is not significant. Above all, the national republican apparatus is unlikely to need communist ideology for its legitimacy.

On the other hand, one can distinguish certain powerful groups that can be either actively or passively opposed to foreign expansion. Paradoxically, the Soviet military can serve such a function, at least the ground forces, which are the most politically influential army group. The army (ground forces) does not need expansion for its legitimacy. Moreover, any expansion is a substantial risk to the army (including the high command). The navy is in a different position since it does need foreign expansion, at least in the sense of bases, for its own expansion—but only within limits that would not involve it in the risk of a major confrontation with the United States.

Malcolm Mackintosh (42) has introduced a similar division in analyzing military influence on Soviet foreign policy. He points out that the military establishment in the USSR likely would be very firm about keeping the present Soviet empire intact but very cautious about further Soviet expansion. At the same time, one must take into consideration that the Soviet military establishment seems to be the most receptive medium for national bolshevism. The basic nationalist orientation of armies in general is well known. Roman Kolkowicz (37) enumerates the following natural military traits: elitism, professional autonomy, nationalism, detachment from society, and heroic symbolism (pp. 20-28). Likewise, Mackintosh (42) suggests that "basically, the present Soviet military leaders want to serve—as well as have some influence over—a strong and nationalistic party and government with some sense of political mission" (p. 12). This was said by Barghoorn (3), too: "[The] Soviet army is probably the most thoroughly and traditionally 'Russian' agency of the whole system" (p. 136). Thomas Bird's assumption that the armed forces supported the Russian nationalist trend expressed by *Molodaia gvardiia* was quoted earlier. Thus, it is not by chance that the books written by Ivan Shevtzov were published by the military publishing house.

An indicator of a deep distrust in the party of the military establishment was the recent appointment of civilian party leader Dmitrii Ustinov as defense minister. Indeed, the Soviet army, as Colton (9) emphasizes, is "an integral part of an established political order" (pp. 160–163), but this order is already less monolithic than it once was. One can find also an opposite opinion that there is no specific nationalism in the army since the army is an agency that integrates the Soviet nationalities (50), but this view neglects the fact that such integration in fact constitutes a policy of Russification.

The Soviet government can take some risky foreign steps even without direct military participation. Possibly one of the reasons for sending Cuban forces to Angola (121) was to avoid any need for approval from the Soviet military establishment.

There is a lack of reliable information about the military influence on Soviet foreign policy though there are many reasons to believe that the Soviet military establishment would not wish to embark on any adventures outside the Soviet bloc. A distrust of Soviet soldiers who likely would have to be forced to fight for objectives they do not understand is one cogent reason (122). Another is a result of the general ideological erosion of Soviet society. Communism as an ideology is very weak in the USSR and cannot be a sufficient motivation for risking one's life. As for national bolshevism, it is more a defensive ideology than an offensive one. The reason for this lies in the big demographic changes in the USSR and the consequent decline in the Russian portion of the Soviet population. The Russians as a nation have suffered greatly from Soviet rule. They are now the main source of manpower in almost all industrial and mining jobs throughout the country. Russians also are the majority of those who engage in physical labor in almost all Soviet republics. The indigenous populations prefer agriculture or public service. The birthrate among Russians has declined greatly in comparison with that of the other nations. George Kline (92) insightfully argues that one of the reasons behind the Russian nationalist trend is the "demographic trauma" experienced by many Russians after the last census (123). According to J. A. Newth (123), "The Russians are losing their dominant position in the Soviet population." The most interesting information one can find is an unpublished report by

Lubomir Hajda (124), which states that over the last decade there
was an 8% drop in Russians for the age group birth- ten years. There
is evidence that the census was falsified to increase artificially the
number of Russians. Let us also quote Besançon (82) on this subject.

> The Russians . . . now are worn out, demographically stagnant, and
> aging. Furthermore, the Russian weight diminishes in the other repub-
> lics despite the intensity of Russification. This is producing discontent
> among the great Russians who see their imperial role menaced. They
> would consent to any regime no matter how ruinous if only it assured
> them domination over the other republics. . . . The alliance of national-
> ism and Leninism, which has been so decisive in the bolshevik world
> advance, is not perhaps as solidly established in Russia as was hereto-
> fore the case (p. 41).

Many Russian nationalists realize that additional expansion
would not be in the interests of the Russians as such. The Russians
are still the most politically reliable group of the population for the
leadership. To control any distant areas outside the Soviet bloc by
non-Russians is impossible. So further expansion would demand an
additional dispersion of Russians. A serious confrontation would
endanger the very existence of the Russians as a nation, as Aleksandr
Solzhenitsyn forecast (102). One must take into consideration that
the Russians in the USSR are aware of the hostility of other national
Soviet groups and further Russian dispersion outside the country
would only reinforce local nationalism. On the other hand, other
nationalities cannot be substituted for Russians in many crucial kinds
of state service.

Much has been written about local nationalism in the USSR.
Teresa Rakowska-Harmstone (53) summarized it not as something
accidental but as "an outgrowth" of the social development of the
Soviet system (pp. 1- 22). Three factors are responsible for local
nationalism: (1) the formation of indigenous elites throughout the
USSR; (2) the Soviet federal system; and (3) the Great Russian
political, economic, and cultural hegemony.

It would be a mistake to think that this hegemony needs to be
oppressive to create hostility toward the Russians. Even good features of the Russian national program produce the same effect. This
was noticed by Seton-Watson (59), who wrote: "It is a common
fallacy to assume that cultural benefits win the gratitude of colonial
peoples, or that colonial nationalism is mainly created by oppression.
On the contrary, it is often the best things that colonial governments
do that bring them most hatred" (p. 64).

Brzezinski (8) refers to "the imperial genius of the Russian
people" (p. 79) and assumes that this is a very important historical
reality. This "genius" cannot work, however, without the appropriate demographic base, which is apparently disappearing.

The growing internal criticism of Soviet expansionism dialectically leads to the further encouragement of expansion by ideologically
committed groups since their legitimacy is at stake. Adam Ulam (72)
has made a very interesting remark about Russian prerevolutionary
foreign policy: "In fact, a strong fatalism appears to have enveloped
the internal-external policy nexus of the empire. An aggressive foreign policy was believed to be a remedy for the internal ills" (p. 9).
The same analysis can be applied to Soviet foreign policy today. Its
push-pull expansion is caused by the basic internal conflicts in Soviet
society, including that between ideology and nationalism, which
contradict and yet reinforce each other. The situation is worsened by
the "oligarchical petrification" of the Soviet establishment, in
Hough's terms (27). This is shown by the establishment's "abstention
from imposing any major policy change" (p. 32), which only sharpens the general fatalism of the system.

One of the best examples of an irrational and even fatal push-pull
expansion in Soviet policy is the Soviet attitude toward the possible
victory of the communist parties in Western Europe.

Eurocommunism

Stalin never tried to promote "revolution." This goal was completely alien to the new Soviet system. His real objective was to
establish Soviet domination with the help of communist claims.
Stalin never tried to encourage a decisive communist victory in any
area not controlled by Soviet troops. Moreover, he needed assistance
from local, indigenous communist movements only in a short transitory period after victory, which usually ended in a local great purge.
Prior to 1941, he had managed such purges in the western Ukraine
and western Byelorussia and Bessarabia. Only in the Baltic states was
the pattern breached because of the lack of collaborators there.

After 1949 Stalin carried out repeated purges in almost all the
satellites to destroy local, indigenous communist elites that were
indoctrinated in internationalism and Marxism-Leninism and to
break continuity with their past and to get rid of the Jewish component. This policy precisely fit the doctrine of national bolshevism,
though with some differences. The objective now was to make each
satellite country more receptive to Soviet hegemony.

Stalin decisively opposed the bid of the French Communists to
take power in 1944–1945. Ulam (72) supposes that "Stalin knew
that it would be a direct and intolerable challenge to the Anglo-
Americans to make this bid" (p. 457). But it is not clear what kind
of reaction the Western allies would have been able to manifest in

this situation because the French Communists were extremely influential in their country. Stalin, however, was afraid of a possible communist competitor in a great industrial country. He well remembered Lenin's (39) words: "After the victory of the proletarian revolution in at least one of the advanced nations, a sharp change will probably come about. Russia will cease to be the model country and will once again become (in the 'Soviet' and the socialist sense) a backward country" (p. 6).

Stalin's behavior toward China was especially characteristic. He and Molotov tried to persuade foreign diplomats that the Chinese Communists were not communists at all. Molotov (72) even said that "the so-called Chinese Communists were related to Communism in no way at all. It was merely a way of expressing dissatisfaction with their economic condition" (p. 474). Stalin's policy in China after the war was a strange mixture of fear of an independent communist country and of an opposite fear of losing possible loot.

Djilas (86) provides interesting information on how Stalin was eager to wind up the Communist uprising in Greece. Stalin was clearly afraid that a Communist Greece would escape his control and, together with Yugoslavia and possibly Albania, create a strong and independent communist bloc.

Cuba turned out to be an exception because Khrushchev was in the midst of attempting a restoration of communist ideology. After the risky official proclamation of Cuba as a Communist country, the USSR had to defend it from a change of status quo; but the cost to the Soviet leadership was high. Cuba is an unreliable ally.

One can easily imagine what kind of problems the USSR would have in the case of a Communist victory in France or in Italy. There is a big controversy in the Soviet Union over its policy toward Eurocommunism. The victory of communists in big industrial countries is highly undesirable from the standpoint of Soviet national interests. On the other hand, the Soviet ideological establishment is tuned to help external communist movements. As a result, there is a Soviet consensus to assist Western communists to the verge of victory but no further. In this way the Soviet ideological establishment can reconcile its position with Russian national interests, and the rest of the leadership can maintain the fiction of its ideological fidelity. This, however, is a situation that tends to defy control.

Hammond (23) showed profound insight into Soviet policy toward possible communist takeovers in mentioning "the conflict between Soviet national interests and Communist ideology." He is absolutely right in assuming that "a Communist takeover is not necessarily a gain for the Soviet Union" (p. 61). According to Hammond, "Russia probably is opposed to any more states becoming Communist unless they are under strong control and the only sure way to ensure such control is to occupy the country with Soviet troops. Such a step seems unlikely in the case of Italy or Spain" (p. 62). Hammond also mentions such important factors as the influence of internal policy and the requirements of extending military or economic support. At the same time, he mistakenly considers the Soviet leaders to be committed communists. Even such distinguished scholars as Carl Friedrich (20) have claimed relatively recently that Stalin proved his commitment to Marxism! These writers demonstrate only that they do not understand the radical right character of the Soviet regime.

To speak of the communist indoctrination of Soviet leadership leads to many mistakes. Another error is overestimation of the level of rationality in Soviet politics. Alex Inkeles (29) more than twenty years ago made a very keen remark about the inherent mysticism of Soviet policy when he asserted that one of the most dangerous elements in totalitarian policy is the pursuit of irrational objectives by a seemingly rational route. This is true of Soviet policy today.

Indeed, weakening from inside, the USSR is able to control its empire only by increasing effort and cost. The Russian demographic base, which was the background of Soviet domination, is now declining. Even if we suppose that the USSR is able to crush the West European defense line (without nuclear confrontation), what then? How would it control all the new areas? With the help of local communist parties? This is highly disputable. The growing strength of Western communist parties makes them more and more independent of the USSR. Ronald Tierski (66) notes that

> "the French road to socialism" today implies (1) increasingly solid resistance to the Soviet experience as blueprint and to reliance on Soviet (or any external) conditions to guide the action of the French Communists in France; and (2) a broader and longer-term basis for political and social alliances with non-Communists. In sum, a "nationalization" of French Communism continues in the realm of domestic strategy and objectives (p. 44). . . . [in spite of the fact that there is] . . . the steadily decreasing likelihood of a situation which would force the party leaders to choose openly between . . . Soviet interests and a permanent opposition role in French society on the one hand and the power and program interests of the PCF itself on the other (p. 21).

Western European communists seem to use the Soviet factor on one hand to frighten their political opponents and on the other to take advantage of the Soviet myth to influence voters. They possess more or less independent organizations that would be even more independent if Western communists were in power. Possibly, competition between Eurocommunism and the USSR would assume the character of a struggle between the radical Left and the radical Right.

Otherwise, the struggle could take the form of the dreadful Orwellian dystopia with several totalitarian superpowers in deadly conflict.

It is the fate of the USSR to produce its enemies one by one. Thus, it is difficult to understand what made Klaus Mehnert (43) think that competition and hostility among communist parties will diminish in the future. This is one of the reasons for the growing resistance of national bolshevism to Eurocommunism for it foresees the baneful impact of Eurocommunism on Soviet foreign policy. The desire to avoid these consequences might unleash an ideological revival of communism in the USSR, which would then attempt to forestall a conflict with Eurocommunism by irrational expansion. Such a situation could have very dangerous consequences for world peace.

Conclusion

Some experts do take into consideration the national bolshevik political alternative in the USSR (82). The most eloquent exponent of this prospect seems to be Isaac Don Levine (15).

> In the light of the emergence during the last three decades of an essentially nationalist Russia from the cocoon of Messianic internationalism, it is more than likely that the next phase in the transformation of the leadership will be a classical coup d'etat by a coterie of iconoclastic arch-nationalists inside the Kremlin. Such a group would discard some more of the relics of the Communist ideology and attempt to find a way out of the economic blind alley and the foreign relations impasse in which the Soviet state is now trapped (p. 46).

Brzezinski (6) also does not exclude such a development. He speaks about the possibility of a "more assertive ideological-nationalist reaction, resting on a coalition of secret police, the military, and the heavy industrial-ideological complex" (p. 45) though he evidently still sees the USSR as a country with a Western type of Marxism (7). However, this view is not realistic since it is as difficult to expect in a radical right (but a "left-wing," brainwashed country) a social democratic or liberal reaction as it was to expect a conservative reaction in Spain or Portugal after the long rule of right-wing dictatorships (99).

Another question concerns the kind of consequences national bolshevism would have. Frederick Barghoorn, who accepts the moderating influence of national bolshevism on Soviet foreign policy, is pessimistic about its full victory (3): "If spontaneous Russian nationalism were allowed free reign within the Soviet Union, or, to speculate for a moment, after the disappearance of Soviet power, its excesses might in some ways be as difficult to deal with as those of the Bolshevik regime" (p. 60). Barghoorn made this remark when the Russian demographic base was still strong. Now the situation has changed. Excesses of national bolshevism likely would have mostly internal consequences. However, a sharpening of internal national conflicts in the USSR might produce international consequences. On the other hand, national bolshevism could be opposed not only by Marxism-Leninism but also by other trends including anticommunist Russian nationalism (46).

The problem of Eurocommunism is explosive. It could have repercussions similar to those of the Sarajevo assassination in 1914. On one hand, it could ruin the balance of power in the world. On the other hand, it would create for the USSR an, unbearable challenge to its exclusive leadership in the communist bloc. Thus, a national bolshevik reaction in the USSR against this development might not be the worst political alternative. Karl Deutsch (10) reminds us, however, that after the Bolshevik Revolution anticommunists "entertained the theory that nationalism should be promoted as an antidote to Communism" (p. 55). This antidote proved no better than the original illness. Thus, we observe the Russian dilemma but refrain from recommendations.

References

1. BANDYOPADHYAYA, J. "The Changes Ahead." *Problems of Communism*, Vol. XVI, No. 2, 1967.

2. *Partiinoe stroitel'stvo*, No. 6, June 1934.

3. BARGHOORN, F. *Soviet Russian Nationalism.* New York: 1956.

4. BARGHOORN, F. "Changes in Russia: The Need for Perspectives." *Problems of Communism*, Vol. XV, No. 3, 1966.

5. BRZEZINSKI, Z. "The Soviet Political System." *Problems of Communism*, Vol. XV, No. 1, 1966.

6. BRZEZINSKI, Z. "Reflections on the Soviet System." *Problems of Communism*, Vol. XVII, No. 3, 1968.

7. BRZEZINSKI, Z. "The Soviet Past and Future." *Encounter*, March 1970.

8. BRZEZINSKI, Z. "Political Implications of Soviet Nationality Problems." *Soviet Nationality Problems.* Edited by E. Allworth. New York: 1971.

9. COLTON, J. "Civil-Military Relations in Soviet Politics." *Current History*, October 1974.

10. DEUTSCH, K. *Nationalism and Its Alternatives.* New York: 1969.

11. DMITRIEVSKII, S. *Sud'ba rossii.* Berlin: 1930.

12. DMITRIEVSKII, S. *Stalin.* Berlin: 1931.

13. DMITRIEVSKII, S. *Sovjetskie portrety.* Berlin: 1932.
14. PAVLOVICH, D. *Rechi.* Paris: 1936.
15. LEVINE, I. D. "The Crisis Ahead." *Problems of Communism,* Vol. XVI, No. 1, 1967.
16. *Evraziistvo.* Paris: 1926.
17. *Evraziistvo.* Prague: 1932.
18. EZERGAILIS, A. " 'Monolithic' vs. 'Crumbling' Communism." *Problems of Communism,* Vol. XIX, No. 1, 1970.
19. FAINSOD, M. "Roads to the Future." *Problems of Communism,* Vol. XVI, No. 4, 1967.
20. FRIEDRICH, C. "Totalitarianism: Recent Trends." *Problems of Communism,* Vol. XVII, No. 3, 1968.
21. GRIFFITH, W. "Ideological Cobwebs." *Problems of Communism,* Vol. XIX, No. 2, 1970.
22. GURIAN, W. *Soviet Imperialism.* Notre Dame: 1953.
23. HAMMOND, T. "Moscow and Communist Takeovers." *Problems of Communism,* Vol. XXV, No. 1, 1976.
24. HAYES, J. C. *The Historical Evolution of Modern Nationalism.* New York: 1931.
25. HODNETT, G. "Succession Contingency in the Soviet Union." *Problems of Communism,* Vol. XXIV, No. 2, 1975.
26. HOUGH, J. "The Soviet Elite." *Problems of Communism,* Vol. XVI, Nos. 1, 2, 1967.
27. HOUGH, J. "The Soviet System: Petrification or Pluralism?" *Problems of Communism,* Vol. XXI, No. 2, 1972.
28. INKELES, A. "The Totalitarian Mystique." *Totalitarianism.* Edited by Z. Brzezinski and C. Friedrich. Cambridge: 1954.
29. INKELES, A. *Social Change in Soviet Russia.* Cambridge: 1968.
30. KAZEM-BEK, A., and SHTENGER, M. *K Sovietskoi Evrope ili k molodoi Rossii.* Paris: 1931.
31. KAZEM-BEK, A. *Rossiia, mladorossy, i emigratsiia.* Paris: 1936.
32. KAZEM-BEK, A. *Pered faktom Bonapartizma.* Paris: 1938.
33. KLIUCHNIKOV, Y. "Smena vekh." *Smena vekh.* Prague: 1921.
34. KOHN, H. *Pan-Slavism.* Notre Dame: 1953.
35. KOHN, H. "Soviet Communism and Nationalism." *Soviet Nationality Problems.* Edited by E. Allworth. New York: 1971.
36. KOLARZ, W. *Stalin and Eternal Russia.* London: 1944.
37. KOLKOWICZ, R. *The Soviet Military and the Communist Party.* Princeton: 1967.
38. KOREY, W. *The Soviet Cage.* New York: 1973.
39. LENIN, V. *Left-wing Communism: An Infantile Disorder.* Moscow: 1970.
40. LOWENTHAL, R. *World Communism. The Disintegration of a Secular Faith.* New York: 1964.
41. LUKIANOV, S. "Revoliutsiia i vlast." *Smena vekh.* Prague: 1921.

42. MACKINTOSH, M. "The Soviet Military Influence on Foreign Policy." *Problems of Communism*, Vol. XXII, No. 5, 1973.

43. MEHNERT, K. " 'Polydoxy' vs. 'Monodoxy.' " *Problems of Communism*, Vol. XIX, No. 1, 1970.

44. MICHAELIS, M. "Rosenberg's Foreign Policy Office and 'Jewish Influence' in the Soviet Union." *Soviet Jewish Affairs*, No. 1, 1974.

45. MICHAELIS, M. "The Third Reich and Russian 'National Socialism.' " *Soviet Jewish Affairs*, No. 1, 1975.

46. Interview with M. Agursky, *Die Welt* (Hamburg), 20 September 1975.

47. MITCHELL, R. J. "Continuity and Change in Soviet Ideology." *Current History*, October 1975.

48. NIKOLAEVSKII, B. "O korniakh sovetskogo imperializma." *Sotsialisticheskii vestnik*, No. 2, 1954.

49. NOVE, A. "The Way the Cookie Crumbles." *Problems of Communism*, Vol. XIX, No. 1, 1970.

50. ODOM, W. "Soviet Military: The Party Connection." *Problems of Communism*, Vol. XXII, No. 5, 1973.

51. PETROVSKY, D. *La Russie sous les juifs*. Paris: 1931.

52. POTEKHIN, Y. "Fizika i metafizika Russkoi revoliutsii." *Smena vekh*. Prague: 1921.

53. RAKOWSKA-HARMSTONE, T. "The Dialectics of Nationalism in the USSR." *Problems of Communism*, Vol. XXIII, No. 3, 1974.

54. REDDAWAY, P. "Politics and Policies in the USSR." *Problems of Communism*, Vol. XVII, No. 2, 1968.

55. ROSENBERG, A. *Geschichte des Bolschevismus*. Berlin: 1933.

56. FIGUROVSKAIA, N. "Smenovekhovstro." *Bolshaia sovietskaia entsiklopediia*. Vol. 13, pp. 73–75. Moscow: 1971.

57. SHULGIN, V. *Tri stolitsy*. Berlin: 1927.

58. SHULGIN, V. *Chto nam v nikh ne nravitsa*. Paris: 1929.

59. SETON-WATSON, H. *Nationalism and Communism*. London: 1964.

60. SETON-WATSON, H. "Decline and Durability." *Problems of Communism*, Vol. XIX, No. 1, 1970.

61. *Soiuz russkikh natsional-maksimalistov*. Paris: 1927.

62. SOUVARINE, B. *Staline*. Paris: 1935.

63. STALIN, I. "Doklad o natsional'nikh momentakh v partiinom i gosudarstvennom stroitelstve." *Sobranije sotchinenii*, Vol. 5, 1953.

64. SZAMUELY, T. "A Problem of Semantics." *Problems of Communism*, Vol. XIX, No. 2, 1970.

65. TCHAKHOTIN, S. "V Kanossu." *Smena vekh*. Prague: 1921.

66. TIERSKY, R. "French Communism." *Problems of Communism*, Vol. XXV, No. 1, 1976.

67. TIMASHEFF, N. *The Great Retreat*. New York: 1946.

68. TIMASHEFF, N. "Russian Imperialism or Communist Aggression." *Soviet Imperialism*. Edited by W. Gurian. Notre Dame: 1953.

69. TREADGOLD, D. "Faiths Eroded." *Problems of Communism*, Vol. XIX, No. 1, 1970.

70. TRIFONOV, I. *Lenin i bor'ba s burzhuaznoi ideologiei v natchale NEPa.* Moscow: 1969.

71. TROTSKY, L. *Stalin.* London: 1967.

72. ULAM, A. *Expansion and Coexistence.* New York: 1974.

73. USTRIALOV, N. "Patriotica." *Smena vekh.* Prague: 1921.

74. USTRIALOV, N. *V bor'be za Rossiiu.* Harbin: 1920.

75. USTRIALOV, N. *Pod znamenem revoliutsii.* Harbin: 1927.

76. USTRIALOV, N. *Na novom etape.* Harbin: 1930.

77. VIERECK, P. "The Mob within the Heart." *Soviet Policy Making.* Edited by P. Juviler and H. Morton. New York: 1967.

78. ALLILUYEVA, S. *Twenty Letters.* New York: 1967.

79. AVTORKHANOV, A. *Tekhnologia vlasti.* Frankfurt: 1976.

80. BAILEY, G. *The Conspirators.* New York: 1960.

81. BELL, D. "Ideology and Soviet Politics." *Slavic Review*, Vol. XXIV, No. 4, 1965.

82. BESANÇON, A. *Court traité de sovietologie.* Paris: 1975.

83. BIEHAHN, W. Marxismus und Nationale Idee in Russland. *Osteuropa*, Vol. 9, 1933–1934.

84. BIRD, T. "New Interest in Old Russian Things." *Slavic Review*, Vol. XXXII, No. 1, 1973.

85. DJILAS, M. *The New Class.* New York: 1958.

86. DJILAS, M. *Razgovory so Stalinym.* Frankfurt: 1970.

87. DUNN, S. "A Turning Point in the Discussion of Soviet Jewish Policy." *Slavic Review*, Vol. XXIV, No. 4, 1965.

88. EVSEEV, E. *Fashizm pod goluboi zvezdoi.* Moscow: 1971.

89. FIRESIDE, H. *Icon and Swastika.* Cambridge: 1971.

90. HANEY, J. "The Revival of Interest in the Russian Past in the Soviet Union." *Slavic Review*, Vol. XXXII, No. 1, 1973.

91. HELLER, M. *Kontsentratsionnyi mir i sovietskaia literatura.* London: 1974.

92. KLINE, G. "Religion, National Character, and the 'Discovery of Russian Roots.' " *Slavic Review*, Vol. XXXII, No. 1, 1973.

93. KOLESNIKOV, Y. *Zemliia obetovannaia.* Moscow: 1974.

94. LUKASHEVICH, S. *Ivan Aksakov.* Cambridge: 1965.

95. MAIKOV, A. Revoliutsionery i chernosotentsy. St. Petersburg: 1907.

96. MACMASTER, R. *Nikolai Danilevski.* London: 1967.

97. OBERLÄNDER, E. *Sowietpatriotismus und Geschichte: Dokumentation.* Cologne: 1967.

98. POSPIELOWSKI, D. "The Revival of Russian Nationalism in Samizdat." *Survey*, No. 86, 1973.

99. ROGGER, H., and WEBER, E., eds. *The European Right.* New York: 1966.

100. SHEVTZOV, I. *Vo imia ottsa i syna.* Moscow: 1970.

101. SHEVTZOV, I. *Liubov' i nenavist'.* Moscow: 1970.

102. SOLZHENITSYN, A. *Letter to the Leaders.* New York: 1974.

103. "Veche." *Volnoje slovo,* No. 17-18, 1975.

104. WOYCIECHOWSKI, S. *Trest.* 1974.

105. AGURSKY, M. "Modern Social-Economic Systems and Their Prospects." *From under the Rubble.* Edited by A. Solzhenitsyn. Boston: 1977.

106. LEWIN, M. "The Social Background of Stalinism." *Stalinism: Essays in Historical Interpretation.* Edited by R. Tucker. New York: 1977.

107. AGURSKY, M. "Der misslungene Versuch zur Vernichtung der Russische Orthodoxen Kirche in der Jahren 1922-1923 und die Niederlage des linken Kommunismus." *Ostkirchliche Studien,* 1973.

108. AGURSKY, M. "Selling Anti-Semitism in Moscow." *New York Review of Books,* 16 November 1972.

109. AGURSKY, M. "Russian Neo-Nazism a Growing Threat." *Midstream,* No. 2, 1976.

110. AGURSKY, M. "Russian Nationalism and the Jewish Question." *World Jewry and the State of Israel.* Edited by M. Davis. New York: 1977.

111. OBERLÄNDER, E. "Nationalbolschewistische Tendenzen in der Russischen Intelligenz." *Berichte des Bundesinstituts für Ostwissenschaftliche und Internationale Studien,* No. 4, 1968.

112. MIRSKII, D. "The Eurasian Movement." *Slavonic Review,* Vol. 6, 1927-1928.

113. KOREY, W. "The Origins and Development of Soviet Anti-Semitism." *Slavic Review,* Vol. XXXI, No. 1, March 1972.

114. TUCKER, R. "Stalinism as Revolution from Above." *Stalinism: Essays in Historical Interpretation.* Edited by R. Tucker. New York: 1977.

115. COHEN, S. "Bolshevism and Stalinism." *Stalinism: Essays in Historical Interpretation.* Edited by R. Tucker. New York: 1977.

116. BERGER, J. *Krushenige pokoleniya.* Florence: 1973.

117. TUCKER, R., ed. *Stalinism: Essays in Historical Interpretation.* New York: 1977.

118. AGURSKY, M. "Natzionalni vopros v SSSR." *Kontinent,* No. 10, 1977.

119. AGURSKY, M. "Politbureau Axe Falls on Polyansky." *Jerusalem Post,* 14 March 1976.

120. AGURSKY, M. "The Kremlin and the Jews." *Jerusalem Post,* 26 May 1976.

121. AGURSKY, M. "The Kremlin's Angola Connection." *Jerusalem Post,* 25 January 1975.

122. AGURSKY, M. "Ivan non è cosi terribile." *Il Giornale* (Milan), 28 April 1976.

123. *The Soviet Union since the Fall of Khrushchev.* Edited by A. Brown and M. Kaser. London: 1975.

124. HAJDA, L. "Nationality, Age, and Social Processes in the USSR." Paper presented at the 1977 Annual Meeting of the New England Slavic Association.

5

Eastern European
Communism
in the Seventies

Teresa Rakowska-Harmstone

The Environment

The internal environment usually acts as one of the major determinants of a country's political and social change, whereas the external
environment intrudes only occasionally. But in Eastern Europe[1]
since the end of World War II the relative impact on change of
internal and external variables has been reversed. The very establishment of communist political systems there, the basic policies of East
European communist parties, and the parameters of internally generated change have all been the function of Soviet policies. The Soviet
Union's hegemony in the region was established by force of arms
after the 1945 collapse of Nazi Germany, triggered by a long-
standing Soviet perception that Eastern Europe is of primary strategic importance for Soviet security and for opening up a gateway to
Western Europe.[2] The hegemony is enforceable—and has repeatedly
proven to be so—because of the basic asymmetry of power between

In the preparation of this chapter I am deeply indebted to my colleagues
Andrew Gyorgy and Richard V. Burks for their constructive comments and
criticisms. Needless to say, the responsibility for the final product is entirely
mine. The section on U.S. policy alternatives was written in collaboration with
Andrew Gyorgy, George Washington University.

the East European states and the Soviet Union and because of the low priority consistently assigned to the region in Western strategic considerations. Consequently, although changes in the nature of East European communism are generated by specific conditions prevalent in each country, their outcomes and outer limits are directly dependent on, and circumscribed by, changes in the nature of Soviet communism. Any spontaneity in East European developments is always subject to the current judgment of the Communist party of the Soviet Union (CPSU), which determines the limits of permissible deviation.

EXTERNAL VARIABLES

One expert has characterized Soviet policy toward Eastern Europe as alternating between the aims of "cohesion" and "viability,"[3] the first attempting a complete adherence to the Soviet model, the latter allowing a degree of differentiation, dictated by specific conditions. The first period of "cohesion" began in 1948, after three years of consolidating Soviet power in the region, and ended with Stalin's death in 1953. In that period Eastern Europe underwent a process of coercive *gleichschaltung* that resulted in the establishment of identical, mini-Stalinist systems tied to the Soviet Union by bilateral and all-pervading ties and run by Soviet "advisers" placed in strategic positions in the party, the police, and the military establishments of the captive countries.

Political patterns began to change after 1953 with a relaxation in Soviet domestic policies related to the struggle for power among Stalin's successors; the impact diffused throughout Eastern Europe on a timetable determined largely by the domestic situation in each country. The changes involved a gradual shift in the CPSU's modus operandi from coercion to persuasion and its new willingness to allow greater autonomy to East European parties; most of the advisers were withdrawn and a system of direct supervision was largely replaced by consultations. The new autonomy offered opportunities to deal with specific domestic problems: the shock of de-Stalinization and the doubts it has awakened not only in the correctness of the late dictator's policies but also by extension in the validity of the crucial dogma of the infallibility of the CPSU suddenly made the search for novel solutions acceptable.

Clearly the situation had changed, but the new rules of the game were extremely fluid. The 1956 eruption of national forces in Poland and Hungary swept away the two countries' Stalinist regimes with apparent impunity. But the final outcome of the Hungarian revolution was the Soviet military intervention, leaving little doubt that the

CPSU would not tolerate either a threat to its hegemony in the region or any basic changes in the nature of the Soviet type political systems. Nevertheless, Khrushchev's subsequent policies left sufficient leeway to East European parties to allow them to seek individual solutions to specific domestic problems and to attempt to validate their political authority in the support of their national constituencies. Hopes for greater autonomy were also encouraged by examples of successful defiance of Soviet authority in Yugoslavia, China, and Albania, by the growth of polycentrism in the world communist movement, and by an apparent willingness of the CPSU to make some concessions to meet the demands of other parties—as in the case of the 1955 Belgrade compromise.[4] All of the East European parties embarked on more or less cautious attempts at innovations, still uncertain but testing the limits of Soviet tolerance. The differentiation found today in Eastern Europe is the result of this 1956–1968 relaxation ("viability") phase in Soviet policy.

It was the Czechoslovak experiment, which had been terminated by the 1968 Warsaw Pact military intervention, that brought this phase to a close and once again made Eastern Europe feel the heavy hand of Soviet imperial presence. The momentum of the Czechoslovak developments and the impact they had not only within the bloc—as seen in the Polish ferment, in the barely disguised Hungarian approval, and in the open Rumanian support—but also on the national aspirations of the restive Soviet Ukraine[5] brought home to the Soviet leaders the danger that East European "spontaneity" represents to the political status quo. The use of force once again was felt to be imperative both because of the threat that forces of pluralism present to the monopoly of power exercised by the communist parties within the political system and because of the specter of ethnic nationalism that haunts the bloc as much as it does the multiethnic Soviet empire.

The 1968 intervention marked a return to the cohesion that has been the hallmark of Soviet East European policies in the seventies. Less crude and infinitely more difficult to implement than in the Stalinist period because of changes in the domestic, the regional, and the international situation, the policy of cohesion is nevertheless designed in the long run to integrate Eastern Europe into the Soviet body politic.[6]

The nature of East European sovereignty was spelled out in the so-called Brezhnev Doctrine and a policy of comprehensive integration of the "socialist commonwealth" was introduced, spearheaded by "fraternal cooperation" among parties led by the CPSU. Pursued vigorously since 1971 within the institutional Warsaw Treaty Organization–Council for Mutual Economic Assistance (WTO-CMEA) framework, this integration policy has already forced a partial retreat on the more innovative East European parties, ushering in a return to the emphasis on bilateral patterns of relations. In the international arena this policy has been complemented by the long sought provisions of the 1975 Helsinki conference on security and cooperation in Europe (CSCE), which gave an international imprimatur to the postwar boundary arrangements and to the westward shift of the Soviet sphere of influence. A successful conclusion to the second round of this policy of cohesion may, however, prove more difficult than in the days of Stalin. A period of relative autonomy has given some East European parties stronger roots and their populations a renewed vigor to defend the gains that have been realized. Also, the birth of Eurocommunism and Soviet efforts to restore a semblance of unity to the world communist movement even at the price of tactical concessions to individual parties' autonomy have given East European parties new allies and new ammunition in resisting the push toward complete subjugation. As part of the broader picture of détente, the eagerly sought and growing economic ties of East Europeans with the West also contribute to their greater viability and differentiation. In addition, the new international support for human rights—the other side of the Helsinki coin—encourages popular appeals to Western public opinion.

INTERNAL VARIABLES

The ubiquitous Soviet shadow apart, several variables have been decisive in shaping East European communism and in determining the dynamics of interaction between the ruling parties and their populations. Their character differs from country to country.

Nationalism might have been invented in Eastern Europe. Its strength has not diminished since World War II: if anything, it has grown because of the "conquest" of the area by the Soviets. The turbulent history of the region since 1945 testifies to the fact that communist party leaders are not immune to the disease, whatever their professed loyalty to "proletarian internationalism" may be. A historical legacy of hatred for the Russians is part and parcel of nationalism in Poland, Hungary, and Rumania and spills over into popular attitudes toward the Communist systems brought in "on the tips of Red Army bayonets." This attitude deeply undermines the efforts of the area's communist leaders to build genuine political authority. A long national memory in some states, notably Poland and Rumania, nurtures a sense of territorial loss to the Soviet Union, notwithstanding gains elsewhere. Rumanian nationalism is also enhanced by the leaders' efforts to assimilate national minorities. The two Russophile states, Bulgaria and Czechoslovakia, have had historic friendships with the Russians based on common Slavdom and past patronage. These factors found their reflection in Bulgarian and Czech attitudes and in their perception of the Soviet role. In Czechoslovakia these attitudes were present in wartime negotiations and in the expectations of the "Prague spring," but the illusion of a friendly and reasonable neighbor, already badly shaken by 1948, was transformed into hatred in 1968. Czechoslovakia also has the problem of Slovak nationalism, the pressures of which contributed to the events of 1968. Pro-Soviet sentiments continue strong in Bulgaria.

The East German position on the nationalism spectrum is both different and ambiguous. The Prussian traditions left an image of Russia as a sometime enemy, sometime ally, with alliances usually built on a division of East European lands between the two powers. But World War II, the four years of direct Soviet occupation, and the continuous presence of Soviet troops in the German Democratic Republic (GDR) have all reinforced the enemy side of the image in the popular mind. The ally image, on the other hand, is consciously used by the ruling Socialist Unity party (SED) in its effort to create a new East German nationalism as an integral component of the bloc's "proletarian internationalism," mindful not only of the fact that the GDR's very existence depends on Soviet support but also of the need to reinforce the *Abgrenzung* and to neutralize the ever present pull of West Germany.[7] The linkage of the new nationalism with proletarian internationalism may well prove to be self-defeating, however, as the latter concept enshrines Soviet predominance in bloc affairs and thus undercuts the one source of support for the new nationalism, that of loyalty to a strong future socialist Germany of which the GDR is but the nucleus. This may be more true as the SED hopes for a "special relationship" with the CPSU within the bloc have faded with the exit of Walter Ulbricht from the German political scene. At any rate, there is little evidence of East German nationalism in the popular mind, with the lure of West Germany still all but irresistible.[8]

In at least half of the cases, then, nationalism in Eastern Europe has been significantly dysfunctional to the establishment of communist regime legitimacy during the first period, that of cohesion; in the viability period, on the contrary, it has been highly functional vis-à-vis the pursuit of autonomy although it has also carried an inherent conflict potential in relation to the Soviet Union. In the current integration period nationalism is obviously the key factor undermining bloc unity except in Bulgaria and possibly the GDR.

Each country's political culture has been a vital factor in explaining the relative success and/or failure of communist authority and in the nature of the pressures generated in response to communist policies. The political system exported by the Soviet Union is a product of the Russian heritage and reflects its failure to develop any subsystem autonomy or significant restraints on the exercise of power. In Eastern Europe only Rumania and Bulgaria share the Byzantine heritage of the Russians, though each has developed variations of its own. Bulgaria's peasants have some traditions of self-government; Rumania's past rulers have had to contend with powerful vested interests in the three historical principalities. All other East Europeans have been on the Western side of the culture line that runs across the region, have participated in Western European culture and in the traditions of the Roman Catholic church, the Renaissance, and Reformation, and have developed strong traditional social structures and market elements[9] that do not fit well into the system of a monopoly of power exercised by a vanguard party. Western type democratic pluralism has developed only in Czechoslovakia, but the so-called authoritarian political culture of the other East European states, a favorite cliché of Western analysts, covers a multitude of sins. The term does apply to the GDR, with its dominant Prussian traditions reinforced during the Nazi period, but the aristocratic cultures of Poland and Hungary feature highly individualistic patterns of political behavior and a defiance of authority as well as strong subsystem autonomy, periods of strong rule alternating with veritable anarchy. Particularly in Poland,[10] these patterns have survived.

SYSTEMIC CONSTRAINTS

The basic weakness of communist regimes imposed by an alien power on largely inimical political cultures has been compounded by the absence of strong communist traditions in East-Central Europe. Communist parties existed in all of the East European states, but only in Germany (including what is now the GDR) and in Czechoslovakia did they enjoy significant support among the working class. Even in these countries most workers gave allegiance to the Social Democrats, as was the case in Poland and Hungary notwithstanding the ambiguous (in the national sense) legacy of "internationalist" socialist movements in the latter two countries: the Polish splinter SDKPL (Social Democracy of the Kingdom of Poland and Lithuania) and the short-lived Hungarian Communist republic of Béla Kun (November 1919- March 1920).[11] Bulgaria and Rumania were predominantly peasant countries and lacked the base for the development of a communist movement. Communist parties were proscribed throughout most of Eastern Europe; they were generally tools of the

Comintern and their leadership was decimated in the Stalinist purges of the thirties. The survivors formed a hard core of leadership in each country after the war.

The constraints on change imposed by the political system itself fall on the border line between external and internal environment. Imposed from the outside, each Marxist-Leninist system has acquired a different style in the thirty years of its existence. Nevertheless, they have all retained the basic features of the Soviet model, which so far has imposed immovable limits to change, thus depriving the indigenous system of the capacity for adaptation[12] and directing all of its energies toward maintenance.

The preoccupation with system maintenance (in the sense of the preservation of existing patterns of relationships) stands as the major obstacle to system persistence, i.e., its ability to adapt to changing circumstances.[13] Although the preservation of the systemic status quo in Eastern Europe is the object of tireless Soviet vigilance, the pursuit is also clearly self-generated and reflects the ruling elite's ideological hang-ups and their perception of the need for self-preservation. Even in Czechoslovakia the 1968 reformers stopped short—or tried to—of violating the key systemic principle, that of the "leading role of the party," i.e., its monopoly of power.[14] The leading role of the party as the vanguard of the working class is ideologically legitimated by the claim that it possesses the only true science of history, a role that is essential in order to direct spontaneous forces toward mankind's ultimate and perfect destiny: socialism.

The theory and practice of the leading role of the party—the latter based on the operational principle of democratic centralism—have proved highly functional to the mobilization stage of the system. But the leading role is a liability in the postmobilization stage, when forces stimulated by changes already achieved in the social system demand complementary political changes. The leading role imposes limits on the system's capacity to innovate, as well as on its capacity to allow genuine representation of social interests. It also bars the flow of information and the influence of market forces necessary for an efficient performance in public administration and in the economy. In short, while allowing room for administrative tinkering and routine adaptations through bureaucratic channels, the leading role prevents fundamental changes.

The problem thus created is present in all communist systems but becomes more acute with higher levels of social and economic development. Most East European states have reached the postmobilization stage and their leaders are caught by the lack of congruence between their political systems and their social, economic, and cultural base.[15] Significantly, the pressures have been less acute in the two countries that are least advanced economically and that have political cultures least inimical to the system, namely, Rumania and Bulgaria.

The system, in the words of Polish philosopher Leszek Kolakowski, imposes a tyranny of a "single alternative"; [16] it is caught in outdated Leninist myths; and, most important, *it does not have a mechanism for substantive change.* The potential for internal conflict is maximized because of the absence of institutional mechanisms for change in three key areas: leadership, bureaucratic politics, and interest articulation.

An absence of routine procedures for a change in political leadership almost always precipitates a crisis and a factional struggle when a leader dies or is retired, except in those rare cases in which an heir apparent is sufficiently well entrenched to forestall potential rivals (Nicolae Ceausescu's takeover at the death of Gheorghiu Dej is one such example) or in which a Soviet preference for a more pliable leader speeds up the retirement of a venerable but independent-minded comrade (as in the case of Ulbricht's replacement by Erich Honecker). Normally, a leader removed must also be discredited so that his "wrong" policies do not undermine the systemic myth: the infallibility of the party. Party bureaucracy also suffers from the primacy of the political principle that recruitment and placement based in the practice of *nomenklatura* are governed by political reliability and patron-client ties; ability is only a secondary consideration. Attempts to institutionalize cadres' tenure and turnover as well as leadership incumbency have so far been abortive.[17] As a result, the communist bureaucracies reflect mediocrity rather than talent, and in the absence of mechanisms to regulate conflicts, factionalism is rife and Byzantine type politics prevail.

The party's monopoly on policy initiation reduces other political forces to the role of supporting actors. This situation breeds not only political and social conflict but also administrative and managerial inefficiency. Party bureaucrats view with deep suspicion any attempts at subsystem autonomy or interest articulation outside traditional (i.e., party-state bureaucratic) channels. Responsiveness to social pressure is seen as weakness, the result of either "an ebbing strength of the political system" or a "growing power of destructive forces."[18]

Throughout Eastern Europe the provision of some channels for interest representation has been the most urgent, controversial, and—because of external constraints—the most dangerous area of reform. Recognition of the importance of the problem is widespread and has constituted the keynote of revisionism in its search for new alternatives once de-Stalinization has shaken the myth of the infallible party that Stalin built.[19] But with the exception of the Czech reformers, the ruling regimes have approached the question gingerly.

For all the rhetoric invoking "popular participation," no attempts were made (except in János Kadár's Hungary) to allow social organizations to abandon their orthodox role of transmission belts in favor of genuine interest articulation. The one significant innovation by these regimes, designed to improve the efficiency of systemic performance, has been the cooptation of technical and professional elites into party ranks. Rather than violate, this practice enhances the leading party role.[20] Moreover, the more pragmatic approach to policymaking and the need for efficiency, better data collection, and communications essential for success has caused the parties to support scientific research. Not only have cybernetics and computer research become fashionable, but the social sciences (particularly sociology) have elicited increased attention. Even so, social science research (developed most widely in Poland, Czechoslovakia even now,[21] and Hungary) is a "closed" science. Findings unfavorable to the regime are not published, and in exchange for privileges some social scientists have become vociferous apologists for the system.

Fear of the snowball effects produced by the Czech events stimulated renewed emphasis on the principle of "the leading role of the party"[22] in programmatic pronouncements, agitprop work, and practice. The desire further to streamline the control apparatus has caused two parties, the Polish United Workers party (PUWP) and the Rumanian Communist party (RCP), to move beyond traditional Soviet practice. Abandoning the CPSU principle of a party-state operational dichotomy (the party to guide and control; the state to implement), the PUWP and the RCP both have fused the key party and state positions at the level of local administration so that there is one incumbent.[23] This development is also reflected at the top in Rumania but not in Poland, where Edward Gierek's power consolidation is more apparent than real.

On the whole there are variations in the fusion of top party and state posts in Eastern Europe reflecting, presumably, either the degree of personal ascendency of the leader within the respective politburo (following the Soviet pattern),[24] as in the case of Ceausescu, or Soviet support, as in the case of Gustav Husák. An absence of a fusion in Hungary may be an indicator of Kádár's personal style rather than of his personal authority, which by all accounts is unquestionable (see Table 1).

Major socioeconomic pressures for change and the incipient political demands thereby generated have been felt throughout the bloc (inclusive of the Soviet Union) under the impact of the basically similar, ideologically stimulated policies pursued by the communist regimes. But the character, strength, and intensity of these pressures have been shaped by the particular conditions prevailing in each country and have been influenced by specific patterns of political

TABLE 1.   East European party leadership; fusion of party-state functions, 1977.

COUNTRY	HEAD OF THE PARTY	HEAD OF STATE	HEAD OF DEFENSE
GDR	Honecker	Honecker	Honecker
Poland	Gierek	Jablonski	Jaruzelski
Czechoslovakia	Husák	Husák	Husák
Hungary	Kádár	Losonczy	Czinege
Rumania	Ceausescu	Ceausescu	Ceausescu
Bulgaria	Zhivkov	Zhivkov	Zhivkov

culture. It has been the tragedy of Eastern Europe that while endemic economic problems and rising social tensions are more pressing there than in the Soviet Union, their accommodation depends not only on the instinct for survival of the ruling elites but also on the Soviet perception of the actual need for change.[25] The latent political instability of Eastern Europe that results is further aggravated by the frustration of aspirations to independent statehood. The communists of Eastern Europe might be more responsive to domestic pressures in the interests of their own survival but find themselves trapped within the rapidly shrinking limits of their relative autonomy. At the same time they also face the ever present danger of a landslide effect of reformist changes, which although they may be tolerable in one state might not be so in another. Because they are unable to respond, East European parties are forced into greater dependence on Soviet support; this, in turn, heightens the possibility of explosion.

Carl Linden's assessment of this paradox in the Soviet system throughout the second half of the twentieth century applies even more forcefully to Eastern Europe.

> If the system's rulership were to begin to permit a spontaneous growth of a public life and culture, it would at the same time start to destroy itself. If on the other hand, it seeks to stabilize the party-state in immobility and stifle the cultural energies of the society it rules it could slowly suffocate itself. This may not express a new truth about the Soviet ideocratic system, but it is a truth which presses more forcefully on that system with the passage of time.[26]

The contemporary political systems of Eastern Europe lack organic roots in the region's political cultures, making the process of change and adaptation extremely difficult and they cannot engage in a genuine interplay with internally generated forces because of the presence, the power, and the policies of the Soviet Union.

Patterns of Policy and Performance

LEADERSHIP

The attitude of the CPSU toward an East European party and its leadership—related to the nature of the national political culture as much as to the personality of the leader—sets the basic parameters of action in any given East European country. The degree of leeway left to individual parties is on the whole directly proportionate to their placement along the trust-suspicion continuum in relation to the Soviet Union. The "satellite spectrum parameters" (see Figure 1) range all the way from the close affinity and correspondingly high degree of trust enjoyed by the Bulgarian Communist party (BCP) to the complete distrust of the Czechoslovak party (KSC). Under Soviet military occupation since 1968, Czechoslovakia has had almost no autonomy in decisionmaking and thus for all practical purposes defies the principal typologies and classifications that follow. Czechs as well as Slovaks are seen as totally untrustworthy; moreover, the "federal" balance between the two nations established in 1968 and nominally retained after the invasion is not working, and Slovak nationalism is again on the rise. Since 1956 the PUWP has ranked notoriously low on the trust spectrum. At present, however, its dependence on the Soviet Union has been increasing, primarily because of economic reasons and because of the potential for explosion growing in the country at least since 1975. Like the Poles, the Hungarians have seldom been considered trustworthy, but the Hungarian Socialist Workers party's (HSWP) policies since 1957 have been extremely careful to take into account all the basic Soviet desiderata. Consequently, the party now stands reasonably high on the spectrum. East German's SED depends heavily on Soviet support

Figure 1. Satellite Spectrum Parameters for 1977

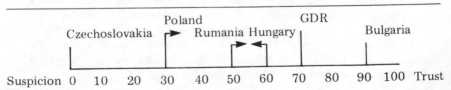

Values here are arbitrarily assigned for the purpose of illustration. In the historical context the placement has varied in response to particular events and the personalities of communist party leaders. Arrows indicate the probable direction the East European countries may be moving on the spectrum.

and enjoys a relatively high degree of trust, especially since the replacement of Ulbricht by Honecker in May 1971. But the temptations offered by the country's westernmost position and its special German "connection" are factors that always lurk in the background. In Melvin Croan's phrase, there is "the growth of a degree of mixed motivation on the part of the GDR towards the FRG [Federal Republic of Germany] and therefore in part also toward the Soviet Union."[27] Rumania is an interesting case—constant exceptions to most generalizations are the despair of analysts of the East European political scene. Consequently, on our scale in Figure 1 Rumania might logically serve as a benchmark at the halfway point on the spectrum. Under the leadership of Ceausescu it is fully trustworthy in is essentially Stalinist domestic politics but highly unreliable in foreign policy. Recently there have been signs that Rumania has been giving in to Eastern pressures and moving somewhat closer to the Soviet Union in foreign, economic, and military policies.

The classification of East European parties as either ideological or pragmatic presents a serious problem because of an inevitable confusion between true ideological fervor and a variety of crude Soviet pressures. For purposes of this discussion it is assumed that an "ideological" label, as applied to a given party includes its leadership's perceived need for a "safety valve" vis-à-vis actual or potential Soviet threat. It also includes the need for the ideological crutch in the absence of genuine legitimacy as well as ideological convictions on how best to motivate the country's population. The degree and sincerity of the latter two, and the overall mix in any given case, are impossible to determine with certainty. The "pragmatic" label is a leadership's preoccupation with "making things work" at home and reordering national priorities in light of the people's steadily rising expectations. Directed toward the building up and strengthening of the leading elite's political authority, this tendency also reflects a growing embourgeoisement, a rediscovery of the primacy of bour-

Figure 2. East European Communist Parties in 1977: From Pragmatism to Ideology

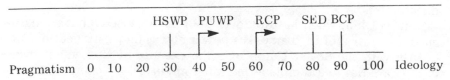

On the assignment of values see the Figure 1 legend. The KSC, as a special case because of Czechoslovakia's military occupation, is not included in this figure.

geois economic and political values. In foreign policy it has implied the pursuit of national interests within the new parameters of dé- tente and to the extent allowed by the general lines of bloc foreign policy (see Figure 2).

The HSWP has been the most pragmatic among the East Euro- pean parties. The image of the PUWP under Gierek has also been one of pragmatic conservatism, but Gierek's mounting internal problems have brought about a greater emphasis on ideological conformity. Although the SED and BCP are both highly ideological, their policies have also been characterized by a considerable degree of pragmatism. The RCP here again defies classification; it is highly ideological in domestic policies but pragmatic in the extreme in its foreign policies to the point that, unlike any of the other East European communist parties, it has generally pursued an independent line in violation of bloc constraints.

It would be meaningless to include the KSC in this classification as it is now directly controlled and managed by the CPSU. On the whole, the sixties showed a general trend among the East European parties toward a degree of deideologization and a strong trend toward pragmatism. Although these forces may currently have been checked, and possibly reversed by the Soviet intervention of 1968, a reversal of this kind cannot be viewed as permanent. On the con- trary, suppression of these tendencies in the long run may well contribute to the intensification rather than the lessening of such truly endemic pressures.

Croan offers a classification of stability for the GDR: intraparty stability; consolidation of the party's rule in society; stability of the unique socioeconomic political structure; and the formation of a distinct national identity.[28] Except for the final point, which is applicable only to the GDR (where the rating is low), the classifica- tion is valid also for the other East European countries.

Intraparty stability and factionalism vary from party to party. In the SED factionalism traditionally has been shaped by infighting for the support of Moscow, but the changeover from Ulbricht to Hon- ecker preserved the appearance of party stability. There is the usual hard-line group, composed of functionaries in charge of security, defense, and ideology, but no factions in foreign policy are discernible.[29]

Since 1965, when he took over the RCP, Ceausescu has strength- ened his control of the party. His power now is unquestioned, but his quarrel with the Soviet Union over the exercise of Rumanian sover- eignty gave rise to attempts at factionalism; in 1972 General Ion Serb and the RCP secretary, Vasile Partilinet, were purged, presumably for pro-Soviet factionalism.[30] The president's ascendancy has also been reflected in some nepotism; in the three leadership reshuffles in early

1977, Ceausescu's wife and son were placed in important positions, concentrating the power even further in the hands of the family.[31]

The Hungarian party also has shown remarkable stability under Kádár's able and cautious leadership. Kádár managed to accommodate the economic reform faction without unduly alarming Moscow and hence leaving no opening to his own hard-liners. Moscow's increasing emphasis on bloc integration, however, has forced a retreat in the Hungarian economic reform and has resulted in important changes in the politburo at the March 19-20, 1974, plenum of the HSWP central committee. Rezsö Nyers, the architect of the New Economic Mechanism (NEM), and György Aczél, the advocate of cultural tolerance, lost their politburo membership and were replaced by members of the antireform faction and proponents of economic integration within the CMEA, Károly Németh as the politburo member and Imre Györi as the central committee secretary.[32] Premier Jenö Fock, another supporter of reform, resigned in May 1975 even though he remains in the politburo. His replacement, György Lázár, is considered a supporter of CMEA integration. Taking into account Kádár's excellent record in mediating past differences of view, and his high credibility among the Hungarians, his continued leadership does not seem in danger.

In Poland the party has had a record of extreme instability and factionalism: twice, in 1956 and in 1970, the party leadership was changed in consequence of popular upheavals. Since coming to power, and owing largely to Moscow's support, Gierek has been able to fend off a challenge by the right-wing nationalist Natolin faction led by Mieczyslaw Moczar in 1971 and by security police head Franciszek Szlachcic, an advocate of greater national autonomy, in 1975.[33] Although outwardly fully in command, Gierek is far from secure in his office. His number two man, Piotr Jarószewicz, politburo member and prime minister, is popularly regarded as "a Moscow man"; Gierek's dependence on Soviet support is considerable; and he again faces popular unrest, which may lead to another explosion.

In contrast, the Bulgarian party leadership under Todor Zhivkov (in power now for 22 years) has shown a remarkable degree of stability if not a lack of factional challenge, as witnessed by the long struggle with the Chervenkov group, finally removed in November 1962, the abortive military "conspiracy" in April 1965, and the purge of Mitko Grigrov in 1966.[34] Factional struggles in the Bulgarian leadership apparently continue, however. In April 1976 some members of the politburo were removed[35] and in May 1977 the number two man, Boris Velchev, widely regarded as a likely successor to Zhivkov, was ousted from all his party and state posts (including membership in the politburo and the central committee) "on considerations of expediency."[36] The high degree of trust that Zhivkov enjoys among the Soviet leadership has undoubtedly been an important factor in his ability to maintain himself in power.

The past record of instability in the KSC is at present irrelevant. As reconstituted after the 1968 invasion the party lacks potential for change in leadership, except change generated by Moscow. Husák is the captive of the CPSU, his obedience reinforced by the hard-line, Moscow oriented faction of Alois Indra, Drahomir Kolder, Oldrich Svestka, Vasil Bilak, and Lubomir Strougal.

Internal party stability or instability is generally matched by the degree of political authority enjoyed by the party. Such authority appears to be high in the GDR, where it is supported by an effective socioeconomic structure, and relatively high in Hungary and Bulgaria: in Rumania it also appears high, primarily because of the national sovereignty emphasis of the Ceausescu regime, but this generalization may not apply to members of the two important minorities, the Hungarians and the Germans. In Poland, on the other hand, the credibility and authority of the party and the government appear to be reaching a zero point, and party authority is virtually nonexistent in postinvasion Czechoslovakia.

The quality of individual leaders and their ability to assess the situation realistically seems to have meant the difference between success and failure. A vital condition in realistic assessment has been the ability to maintain open channels of communication both to the populace and to Moscow. Here, the patterns differ, ranging from the apparent success of Rumania's Ceausescu, Hungary's Kádár, and Bulgaria's Zhivkov to the failure of Poland's Gomulka and Czechoslovakia's Dubček. If any general rule can be drawn, the key to effective system maintenance (or at least to the survival of party leaders) has been the ability to respond to some of the country's basic popular demands while staying within the limits of Soviet tolerance—the correct perception of which is one of the most difficult aspects of the relationship between the CPSU and the East European parties—and maintaining good *personal* contacts with the leaders in Moscow. This task has appeared next to impossible in some countries (such as Poland) and relatively easier in some others (such as Bulgaria and Rumania). Leaning too far either in the direction of responding to the domestic environment (Dubček) or in that of conforming to the Soviet model (Gomulka) inevitably results in the leader's failure and removal; respectively, either in a Soviet intervention or in a popular explosion. The stability of the East European communist regimes has been easier to maintain in countries in which political culture patterns are not markedly dysfunctional to the communist political system and in which nationalism can become a source of support rather than a disruptive force. In this context it is surely not accidental that the countries least culturally and socially compatible with the Soviet Union have also proved to be the most volatile.

POLICY AREAS: PROBLEMS OF CHANGE AND STABILITY

In the search for greater viability, for a genuine political authority, as well as better performance, the East European parties have singled out three policy areas for innovation: in the political and social area—to minimize popular alienation and the potential for conflict; in the economy—to deal with the endemic inability of the system to move from an extensive to an intensive growth pattern; in foreign policy—to increase national autonomy. None of the parties has attempted reform in all three areas; the timing of the reform impetus has been different in each of the countries involved; and, except for the economic reform measures integrated under the CMEA for 1976–1980 plans, none of the attempts has been synchronized across parties. This lack of synchronization alone is an important indicator of the Soviet failure to promote real integration with, as well as within, the region and a testimony to the survival of traditional enmities among the East European states. Despite an impressive formal common framework and ceaseless rhetoric on the subject of fraternal cooperation, the pattern of relations within the bloc is still determined largely by each country's asymmetrical dependence on the Soviet Union. East European publications comparing the level of integration of Eastern and Western Europe explicitly acknowledge that their achievements in this field rank far below those of Western Europe.

Because of the dangers involved, there have been few experimenters in political devolution: in 1956–1957 Gomulka had to respond to popular pressures with concessions most of which were later rescinded and in the period leading up to 1968 Dubček and his group made an attempt at a genuine reform. The Kádár regime in the sixties and seventies has achieved a degree of political decompression without outwardly invoking the inevitable threat to the leading party role. Others have been content with the elite cooptation techniques as well as with the more traditional use of socialization.

The problem of economic reform has preoccupied all of the Eastern European parties. In this sphere two distinct alternative approaches have been pursued: indicative planning combined with the socialist market—a major innovation introduced only in Hungary (and in Dubček's Czechoslovakia)[37]—and decentralization of management within the command planning system. The latter model, initiated by the GDR, was eventually followed by all the other members of the bloc, the Soviet Union included. In foreign policy,

Rumania has been the only innovator, if one discounts the ill-fated Hungarian attempt in the last stages of the 1956 revolution. All of the Eastern European parties, however, avidly took advantage of the openings to the West provided by détente.

POLITICAL AND SOCIAL CHANGE

The key question of how to deal with interest articulation pressures in political, social, and cultural life has preoccupied party elites as well as "revisionists." Zvi Gitelman has proposed a fivefold classification of East European attempts to resolve the problem from Marxist-Leninist positions: neo-Stalinism; the "reactionary Left" (aiming to overcome the "new class" degeneration of the system by a reenactment of the proletarian revolution); Marxist humanism (a moral stance rather than a political program); socialist pluralism; and "efficient authoritarianism."[38]

Hard-liners in Czechoslovakia, Poland (the old Natolin faction), and all other East European parties generally adhere to neo-Stalinism. Jacek Kuron and Karol Modzelewski, the Polish dissidents, are the current advocates of the reenactment of the revolution.[39] Marxists humanists, strong in Poland and Czechoslovakia, are to be found also in Hungary and Rumania, and socialist pluralism was the theme of the Czech reformers. Humanism is also advocated by Hungary's ex-premier and current dissident Andras Hegedus. The efficient authoritarianism school, which maximizes material outputs combined with nationalistic appeals, seems to be most attractive to leaders such as Ceausescu, and the majority of the East European parties now hover close to this solution, with more or less determination and efficiency and mixed results.

From the outset communism was ill-adapted to the upward transmission of social demands in the more developed East European countries. Accelerated policies of industrialization and modernization that followed communist seizures of power resulted, throughout the region, in major social shifts and increasingly complex social structures. But no appropriate changes were made in the political structures to accommodate the demands, and pressures have mounted. This is true particularly in the countries of the more developed northern tier and in Hungary. Under existing constraints some easing of tensions was achieved through a technique of cooptation of professional, especially technical, elites into the party. This policy has been effective in the GDR. In Hungary, under the NEM other groups also were able to establish better communication patterns with the party because of the higher degree of political tolerance made possible under Kádár's famous slogan "Who is not against us is with us." The Czechoslovak experiment traveled far on the road to pluralism, but it was cut short, and its promise remains unfulfilled.

On the whole, the parties' major problem has been that of communication. The existing bureaucratic structures inclusive of "transmission belts"[40] provide the form, but not the substance, for social communication and interest articulation of groups they nominally represent. Vestigial political parties, wherever they survive, are organized into a national front directed by the respective communist party. Such vestigial parties also function as socializers rather than representatives of their political constituencies. National fronts still exist in Poland, Czechoslovakia, Bulgaria, and the GDR. In Poland alone, the Catholic church survives as an independent social institution because of its identification, over the ages, with the Polish nation and the Poles' fierce loyalty to it. In its uneasy relationship with the Communist government, the church has managed, with great difficulty, to retain an independent voice. In times of political stress the church has been a moderating force but has always taken a firm stand on its right to independent existence and in support of basic human and civil liberties. Its very existence is a standing challenge to the PUWP. The PUWP has been powerless to destroy the church and, as in the case of the 1957 decollectivization, has been unable to restructure the society fully on the Soviet model because of the fear of popular resistance and of its effects on the rest of the bloc. This powerlessness has been particularly evident in the events of the summer of 1976 and their aftermath.

In the absence of institutionalized channels for interest articulation, social group demands in Eastern Europe line up along the traditional social spectrum: creative intelligentsia; youth; and workers and peasants. The only way these groups can express their demands is dissent, violent action, or abstention from approved activities.

The creative intelligentsia traditionally has played a major political role in East European societies and the influence of this sector remains important even though only a minority actively engage in political action. Intellectuals played a key role in the 1956 events in Hungary, in the 1968 crisis in Poland, and in the development of the Prague spring; their sometimes lonely voices are heard also in Rumania, the GDR, and Bulgaria. In the current upsurge of demands for human rights in Poland and Czechoslovakia, which invoke the so-called basket three provisions of the CSCE final act, intellectuals are in the forefront once again. This is the activist minority. There are also numerous members of the creative intelligentsia who have been "tamed," serving as party mouthpieces in exchange for privileges. Most members of the group are alienated because of the constraints on freedom of expression imposed by the system.

Deep political alienation also exists among East European youth, as validated by the few available opinion surveys[41] and as suggested by repeated official exhortations. A new emphasis on the political socialization of youth and on the politicization of the educational system has been visible in all of the countries that rank high on the ideological spectrum. By all accounts, the majority of the young people are concerned only with immediate material gains and personal advantage and abstain from any political activity. Few want to join the party. But some among them turn to revisionism and have sparked political ferment and dissent along with the intellectuals.

If the official propaganda is to be believed, the workers are the ruling social strata. In fact, their only access to the ruling group is through the party led trade unions. The idea of workers councils, government *by* rather than *over* the workers, surfaces every time there is a popular upheaval only to disappear when order is restored. None of the East European trade unions has the right to strike or the right to make decisions affecting the interests of workers. Only in Hungary under the NEM did the 1967 labor code give the unions important rights of consent, decision, control, veto, and consultation, some of which have been used by labor leaders to good advantage.[42] Worker alienation throughout the bloc is indicated by the fact that labor productivity is a key economic problem, and neither exhortation nor higher wages seem to have done much to overcome it, suggesting that psychological incentives and liberalization are at least as important in motivating workers as are material incentives. In fact, it has been particularly irksome to the Polish party that the leaders of labor unrest in 1970 and 1976 were skilled workers, members of the "labor aristocracy," one of the most highly paid groups in the country.

In defense of their rights, German workers took to the streets in 1953; Polish workers, in 1956, 1970, and 1976. It is of great significance that twice—in both 1956 and 1970—labor riots resulted in change of the Polish party leadership. This gave the Polish workers a taste of power and has not passed unnoticed in the rest of the bloc. The signals could not have been clearer and yet no modification in the role of the trade unions in Poland has been forthcoming despite solemn promises, repeated once again in the wake of the June 1976 riots. The Czech workers, once active participants in the workers councils of 1968, are now quiescent and again alienated, as seems to be the case to a lesser or greater degree elsewhere in Eastern Europe.

Throughout, the peasants are the least politically active class, their numbers thinning out through exodus to the cities. Paradoxically, collectivization seems to have worked well after initial upheavals, with productivity increasing and earnings adequate or even high.

Especially in Hungary, the "bourgeois" instincts of the peasants have found a new outlet under the NEM, and their earnings are higher than those of the workers, a major worker grievance. By contrast, in Poland, where the peasants were decollectivized, agricultural productivity is a perennial problem. The key to poor agricultural performance has been the small size of farms and the peasants' uncertainty concerning the future, i.e., the threat of resocialization—a subject of constant official discussion.[43] The peasants are further discouraged by preferential treatment given to the socialized sector in matters of taxation, machinery, machinery parts, fertilizer, and other supplies. The spurt of increased productivity that followed Gierek's post-1970 concessions has now subsided, and depopulation of the Polish countryside is proceeding at a rapid rate, with young people leaving en masse for the cities.[44]

The degree of dissatisfaction felt by different social groups varies, and sometimes the grievances work at cross-purposes, thus making easier the party's task of social control. It is rare that an alliance between social groups appears. The 1956 alliance of Polish workers and intellectuals was not repeated in 1968, when ferment was limited to intellectuals and students, nor in 1970, when the workers' revolt caught other classes unawares. Since 1975, however, and particularly in the wake of the June 1976 riots, an alliance appears to have taken shape among workers, intellectuals, and students, with the church also coming in to support civil rights demands. This situation, in which a spark may cause a conflagration, has resulted in the regime's precipitous withdrawal of price increases, the proverbial straw that broke the camel's back. The Poles appear to be quite ready, as in the past, to take to the streets, and the PUWP leaders have been treading a narrow path between half-hearted concessions and repressions. In contrast, the parallel demands for civil rights being made in Czechoslovakia (Charter 77 and others) are the intellectuals' weapon for shaking world public opinion and for keeping the case of Czechoslovakia alive, depending on outside support and intervention rather than on direct action. Even when one considers the lessons of the recent Czech experience, the contrast underscores the difference between the Polish and the Czech political culture.

Throughout Eastern Europe the picture is that of mass alienation combined with individual efforts to carve out the best possible personal life. Absenteeism, corruption, poor work habits, indifference, and drunkenness, as well as an inward turn to one's own family, social group, and religion, appear, from East European press accounts, to be widespread if not endemic. One is reminded of Robert C. Tucker's "dual Russia," a dichotomy between "official" and "unofficial" Russia based on the total alienation of Soviet society from its government.[45] Whatever the East Europeans' pre-communist civic vices, such alienation was not one of them. Under the Soviet shaped and Soviet imposed systems, Soviet "values" and behavior patterns seem to be seeping through into Eastern Europe, a frightening, long-range prospect.

ECONOMIC CHANGE

The nature of the problem of economic change[46] is analogous to that of political change. The command planning system of economic management cannot accommodate the needs of market forces and efficient management as these have developed under the impact of technological change in the world at large and the industrialization and development policies of the communists. But the parties' emphasis on the primacy of politics and their own leading role makes central planning a must.[47] At the same time, a shift to an intensive growth pattern and the need to maximize efficiency of economic performance are also a must in view of the imperatives of economic development and the necessity of continuing improvement of unsatisfactory living standards.

The two basic reform alternatives, as referred to earlier, are the GDR's New Economic System (NES), a decentralized command planning model, and the Hungarian NEM, an indicative planning— socialist market model.[48] The advantage of the first model, which has now been adopted throughout the bloc with the exception, still, of Hungary, is that it safeguards the priority of central planning (i.e., the primacy of the party). It replaces administrative controls by economic "levers"—macroeconomic instruments designed to provide market orientation—inclusive of a heavy dependence on computerization.[49] As it is promoted now, however, the NES model is a considerably recentralized version of the original. The NEM model retains central planning of an indicative character and decentralizes economic decisionmaking down to the enterprise level, the better to respond to market demands without, however, fully decontrolling prices; nevertheless, there also some of the centralization mechanisms have been restored.[50] While basically only "tinkering" with the system, the NES model has served to improve the efficiency of economic performance in East Germany. It is questionable, however, whether its recentralized version will bring comparable benefits to less developed and considerably less disciplined East European countries, which also lack the special economic relationship with West Germany that had been partly responsible for the GDR's *wirtschaftswunder*.

The NEM has greatly improved Hungarian living standards and by allowing more freedom to the interplay of social forces has contributed to political relaxation in that country. But according to the experts,[51] neither model has been developed to its full capacity. The disproportions and dislocations among their various elements have combined with the built-in resistance of economic bureaucrats, who favor the "safe," old system, to produce a trend toward recentralization. In the seventies, with the impact of the economic integration policies of the CMEA, a "reformed Soviet model" became more or less obligatory throughout the bloc. This sine qua non of bloc economic development was openly expressed by an East German economist: "In all the deliberations designed to bring the system of planning and incentives of the various Comecon countries closer to each other, there exists only one basic point of departure, i.e., the basic orientation must be towards the system being developed in the USSR."[52] If present trends continue, it is unlikely that the NEM model, now an anomaly in the integrating economic system of the bloc, will be allowed to survive even in a scaled down version, despite its undeniable success. The risk of political pluralism inherent in the socialist market model (as demonstrated in Yugoslavia and in the Czech experiment) outweighs, for the CPSU, the model's probable economic benefits. Nevertheless, some aspects of the Hungarian experience, notably the innovations in agricultural management, have elicited considerable interest in the Soviet Union and other bloc countries and may eventually be incorporated into the "reformed Soviet model."

In summary, however, the new "acceptable" patterns of economic reform do not promise to alleviate outstanding economic problems: intensive growth and greater efficiency are still necessities. The key to the future apart from decentralization in economic decisionmaking and technology transfer from the West is improved labor productivity and qualitative innovations. These depend not only on economic incentives but also primarily on social attitudes that the communists have been unable to generate except in a more liberal political climate.

FOREIGN POLICY

In foreign policy there is only one deviationist in the bloc: Rumania. The question as to how Ceausescu has been able to get away with this heterodoxy is usually answered by pointing to his highly orthodox domestic policies and to Rumania's geographic position deep within the bloc, which precludes effective withdrawal from the Soviet sphere of influence.[53] Rumania's independent policy is defined strictly in terms of national interest and has manifested itself in relations with the U.S. and other Western countries (as in the continued recognition of Israel); in relations with the deviant Communist states China and Yugoslavia; and in Rumania's insistence on its sovereign rights in the CMEA and the WTO.

The other East European countries have faithfully followed the Soviet Union in foreign policy, either because of recognition of complementarity to their own national interests, as in the case of the GDR, Poland (vis-à-vis the "German problem"), and Bulgaria, or because of prudence, as in the case of Dubček's Czechoslovakia or Kádár's Hungary, or because of Soviet military occupation, as in Husák's case.

The Soviet Union strongly enforces this conformity, as seen in the insertion of appropriate clauses into East European constitutions of which the last and most controversial was the Polish one in 1975 and in the establishment of a consultative foreign policy agency under WTO (at the 1976 Bucharest meeting). Nevertheless, given a choice, the East European regimes, except the GDR and Bulgaria, would just as likely pursue their own foreign policies, à la Rumania.

The GDR, as seen previously, is a special case although even there a policy of new options toward the Federal Republic of Germany is not necessarily excluded.[54] Poland, Czechoslovakia, and Hungary traditionally have had a pro-Western foreign policy orientation, and even now Poland is cultivating its own "special connection" with France.

Most of Eastern Europe's prewar trade was with the West. This relationship was rapidly reversed after 1945. Now Eastern Europe heavily depends on imports of fuel and raw material from the Soviet Union, largely as the result of disastrous autarchic economic policies followed under Soviet dictation in the Stalinist period.[55] This dependence on the Soviet Union is rapidly increasing. At the same time, the economic interests of the "western four," and particularly of Hungary, desperately require development of trade with the West, and all the regimes need Western technology as a matter of vital necessity rather than free choice.

The policy of comprehensive bloc integration initiated in 1969–1970 has been theoretically justified by the formation of the new "socialist world system," a new stage in the development of relations among the socialist countries based on the principle of "socialist internationalism." The system "spearheads" the world "progressive forces" of peace and antiimperialism on the road to socialism in Europe and in the Third World.[56]

A companion to the policy of détente, the policy serves, in Pierre Hassner's words, "to immunize the socialist countries against a double pluralist virus"—whether from within or without the bloc—against the consequences of Western contacts.[57] The phrase applies equally well to the dangers represented by Eurocommunism, with its emphasis not only on the national sovereignty of each party but also on accommodation to political pluralism (that is, with its implied threat to the leading role of the party). Marshal Tito of Yugoslavia has long been a hero, if not openly acknowledged, to most East European leaders and the attraction of Eurocommunism is highly infectious. Western communist parties, particularly the Italian, strongly supported the Dubček experiment. In 1976-1977 their support, which came enthusiastically from the Spaniards and the Italians, grudgingly if at all from the French, was of great importance to the human rights movements in Poland and Czechoslovakia. Since the 1977 conference of the French, Spanish, and Italian parties in Madrid, however, such support has been considerably toned down, probably as a quid pro quo for the softer Soviet line on their independence.[58] Official East European attitudes toward Eurocommunism predictably reflect the Soviet ties and domestic situation of the regimes, ranging from Kádár's "today . . . there are varying 'roads to socialism' and the Western parties know their own conditions best"[59] to the Bulgarian central committee's warning against the infiltration of nationalist elements, using Eurocommunism as disguise.[60]

Eurocommunism poses a dilemma for the Soviet Union. To paraphrase Hassner, the Soviet Union places top priority on the consolidation of its own sphere, but at the same time it pursues a dynamic policy seeking influence in Western Europe and in the Third World. For this it needs a vast coalition of "antiimperialist" forces of "peace," including the Western communist parties regardless of their heresies. But is this compatible with the consolidation of the USSR's socialist empire?[61]

The concessions made to Eurocommunism at the East Berlin conference of European parties in June 1976, however tactical and nonapplicable in the Soviet view to Eastern Europe they might have been, gave the bloc parties a new leverage and a new respectability in their resistance to integration.

The question of an "organic" union between the Soviet Union and Eastern Europe is less a matter of either force or enticement and more a matter of relentless pressure and the operation of "objective" factors. The latter are (1) geographic position; (2) Soviet military presence; and (3) communist political systems. Within this framework there are other strong forces pushing East European parties toward integration: their growing economic dependence on the Soviet Union; their need for support in controlling their own populations; and past Western policies, including the final recognition at Helsinki of Soviet hegemony of the region.

There are also strong contrary forces: nationalism; the impact of Eurocommunism; and popular pressures. In this context, a Western as well as a Chinese future policy that recognizes the long-range impact of these forces may be important. The East European lineup on the integration question is strongly influenced by all these factors. Two members of the bloc see considerable advantage to themselves in joining in; thus, Bulgaria and the GDR strongly support the policy. Indeed, Bulgaria was reported to favor joining the Soviet Union as another republic.[62] And the GDR's security is considerably enhanced by its membership in the bloc. None of the others, on the basis of past record, favors such integration. Poland was fairly lukewarm to begin with, except in foreign policy, but has now switched to fervent support, undoubtedly reflecting Gierek's domestic problems. Czechoslovakia speaks with the Soviet voice. Hungary is markedly hesitant and Kádár has taken advantage of the East Berlin conference's new formulas to emphasize each party's autonomy. Rumania is violently opposed, but both Rumania and Hungary have been seen to backtrack, since the Berlin conference, under strong Soviet pressures.

PROSPECTS FOR CHANGE

In a summary of overall prospects for change the initial statement has to be repeated: any change in the bloc is governed by the Soviet Union and is subject to systemic constraints. Although East European political systems no longer are or never have been congruous with their societies, the record suggests that within existing constraints three alternative models have developed: the efficient authoritarianism model, the NEM model, and the Prague spring model. The efficient authoritarianism model is unable to accommodate rising social pressures but attempts to deal with their manifestations by way of administrative tinkering. This is the model that is now prevalent in Eastern Europe.

The NEM model, if developed, promises a degree of genuine adaptation. At the same time, it preserves, in milder form, the systemic imperatives. None of the innovations developed under the NEM, however, has been adopted by the Soviet Union, a fact that bodes ill for its preservation and further development, let alone its acceptance by other bloc countries. On the contrary, there are signs that regression has already set in.

The Prague spring model was not allowed to realize its possibilities. It revealed a strong momentum toward pluralism, and we shall never know whether or not this would have overcome the basic principle of the leading role of the party. In this respect, perhaps, Yugoslavia's example is instructive. In Yugoslavia, even though strong pluralist forces were allowed to develop, there has been a revival of the emphasis on the party role since the Croatian crisis of 1971. The comparison may not be apt, however, because the two countries' political cultures are in some respects dissimilar.

If the efficient authoritarianism model survives or is replaced by neo-Stalinism (which cannot be totally excluded), the familiar explosion-repression cycle will undoubtedly begin again. One is tempted to look at the situation from the point of view of Crane Brinton's analysis of conditions prevalent in the prerevolutionary stage. In the East European countries, where the record of instability has been high, as in the case of Poland, many such prerevolutionary conditions exist: a government deeply in economic trouble; a highly inefficient bureaucracy repeatedly tinkering with reform; a "desertion of the intellectuals"; and class antagonisms.[63] In Eastern Europe one may also add acute national antagonisms.

These conditions do exist throughout the area even if their level of intensity varies. But, if one accepts the validity of Brinton's analysis, the conclusion is inescapable that prerevolutionary conditions are ripening throughout the Soviet bloc. This generalization also includes the Soviet Union.

U.S. Policy Alternatives

For the past thirty-two years U.S. policy toward Eastern Europe has been caught on the horns of a political dilemma. On the one hand, millions of hyphenated—or "ethnic"—Americans (7.5 million Poles and 3.5 million Hungarians, among others) have demanded that their government show a concern for the countries of their origin and thus have managed to keep Eastern Europe in the American limelight. Compared to the vital national interest of the Soviet Union in this essential sphere of influence region, however, U.S. goals and objectives have been distinctly peripheral. Although American diplomatic moves toward Eastern Europe have tended to fluctuate historically, swinging from limited intervention to truly marginal policy steps (from demands for "rollback," "containment," "liberation," and massive "bridge building" all the way to various forms of benign or malign neglect), generally and by necessity there has been a tacit admission that East Europe is indeed an "organic" Soviet security zone. Almost inadvertently the West has drifted into a "hands off Eastern Europe" policy, into a mood of total diplomatic uncertainty and a sense of ambiguity that thus indirectly and informally acknowledges Soviet geopolitical primacy in a formerly buffer, but currently "satellite," zone. The so-called status quo policy in the area has reflected the fluctuations. The most flagrant illustration of the

U.S. pattern of marginality was the lack of reaction to the Warsaw Pact invasion of Czechoslovakia in 1968.

In the early and mid-1970s several important developments occurred that have tended to change the earlier picture of election conditioned and status quo minded U.S. interest in the region. Within the framework of détente the new East-West initiatives have signaled increased Soviet interest in Western Europe and in the Third World and rekindled the hitherto dormant American and Western European concerns in East-Central Europe and in the Balkans. Prospects of new Eastern markets also intrigue Western businessmen.

Six operational developments (the choice is necessarily based on personal judgment) have recently influenced the pattern of American diplomacy in Eastern Europe: the German Federal Republic's *Ostpolitik;* the development of the EEC; the Helsinki conference; the Mutual Force Reduction (MFR) talks in Vienna; SALT I and SALT II; and the momentous growth of the nonaligned nations movement.

The success of the *Ostpolitik* and of the EEC and the resulting plethora of bilateral and multilateral commercial, technological, and cultural contacts with Eastern Europe not only diverted a large share of the bloc's trade to the West but also infected its populations with this decade's "revolution of rising expectations."

After two and a half years of preparatory negotiations the CSCE finally produced, in Helsinki, its "final act." The impact of this development on Eastern Europe is twofold. On the one hand, it gives the old status quo policy the stamp of international recognition and approval: Eastern Europe was assigned permanently to Soviet tutelage. On the other hand, in the provisions on human rights, it already has become an internal issue in Eastern Europe and is shaping up as one of the milestones between the détente and the postdétente era. The Carter administration's emphasis on the issue has endowed appeals to basket three provisions with new international respectability. But the value of the human rights campaign as the lever to force internal liberalization in the Soviet bloc will depend as much on future American handling of the issue as on Soviet reaction to it.

The Mutual Force Reduction talks are of direct interest to Eastern Europe. Any reduction of Soviet forces stationed in that area is functional to the countries' greater autonomy. The SALT negotiations, although conducted on a bilateral basis, are of vital interest to the nations of East-Central Europe, as elsewhere. In the renewed vigor of the nonalignment movement, Tito's Yugoslavia plays an important role, and the Soviet Union—in its peace and antiimperialism appeal—has been gaining increasing credibility and influence. Rumania's Ceausescu has attempted to become a member of this club but has succeeded only in gaining observer status.

The multiple impact of these events has been to bring Eastern Europe out of its years of isolation, to restore some of its old Western contacts, and to reopen it to Western influence. Every time the Soviet Union agrees to enter a new type of East-West exchange, East European states are seen in the vanguard of utilizing the new window to the West. The results, however, have not been an unmixed blessing from the point of view of maximization of East European autonomy. Because of intrabloc arrangements (the relationship between the center and the periphery and the "socialist division of labor") and because of Soviet insistence on making Eastern Europe secure as a corollary to détente, one of the by-products has been to push Eastern Europe deeper into the bloc.

The period has marked a new expansionism and dynamism in Soviet policy. In the eyes of East Europeans the overall impact of détente has been an upward curve in the Soviet Union's power and influence and a downward trend in U.S. strength, a shift in the balance of global power in favor of the USSR. The perception is shared by the Soviet Union, as seen in numerous authoritative policy statements; for example, in the resolution on the sixtieth anniversary of the October Revolution adopted by the CPSU central committee on January 31, 1977.[64]

The effect of all these developments is that in the global and European context Eastern Europe is now less peripheral to U.S. policy concerns. It is now more germane to efforts to check Soviet expansion. The human rights issue in Eastern Europe also has acquired new dimensions because of the Carter administration's revival, in diplomacy, of traditional American moral values.

In the new context, U.S. interests in Eastern Europe are *neither* critical *nor* totally expendable, which allows for considerable latitude in policy moves by the U.S. government. The key concern is not to precipitate an upheaval that could not be militarily supported by the United States and might well result in a general conflagration (in the case, for instance, of a Polish revolution spilling into East Germany) but to pursue policies that would allow East Europeans maximum latitude and would contribute to the preservation of their distinct international personalities.

All the following suggestions have policy relevance for the United States in the late seventies and in the eighties. Of the six tactical approaches mentioned, three are of a "positive" character and three are of "negative" importance.

1. Although bridge building as a *political* policy does not seem to work (the late Eduard Benes tried it in the 1930s and 1940s with disastrous consequences), as an economic policy, in terms of invigorated East-West trade it is a must both for the industrial West and for the EEC in particular, as well as for the Eastern communist countries

themselves. Stepped-up trade and technological transfer are indeed the essential American contributions to the future welfare of the East European nations, often with important political consequences. Certain caveats should be observed, however, lest Western trade contribute unnecessarily to WTO military strength or to the credit spree of an ambitious East European leader, the effect of which would only be to push him deeper into the Soviet orbit, as recently happened to Poland's Gierek. The enlargement of commercial exchanges also has undesirable side effects for integration, as pointed out previously.

2. The United States must safeguard and promote the future success of West Germany's *Ostpolitik*. In its broadest terms, this policy is a great deal more than the export of West German products and tourists; it is building up a major foothold for all Westerners behind the once monolithic iron curtain of European communism. Its impact on East Germany alone has already opened up some options to SED leadership.

3. The inviolability of European boundaries in general has been effectively changed from de facto to de jure after thirty years of factual existence, especially as a result of the Helsinki negotiations and the formalized final act. The West, including the United States, might as well recognize the long-term stability of post-World War II boundaries—upsetting them by force would create an immediate casus belli between East and West. At the same time, it is important that the preservation of these boundaries not be construed as the continuation of a spheres of influence policy. In view of the changing global picture it is important for the United States to get out of the old Yalta-bound frame of mind.

4. Cultural relations and human rights are already in the forefront of Soviet-American disagreements. Here basket three is bound to have momentous consequences in terms of the championing of human rights, increasing the importance and the role of dissidents. Despite Soviet protests, Americans must vigorously pursue the so-called third basket course of protest and action. The support of human rights *on a global scale* is not intervention in domestic affairs but a vital part of implementing international law, both private and public, as well as the U.N. Charter in its most basic provisions. This gives U.S. policy, long cast in a reactive mold, the advantage in taking the initiative in the area in which the Soviet Union is exceptionally vulnerable and sensitive. In Eastern Europe it is important, however, not to awaken false hopes and not to allow rhetoric to run away from the realities of the situation.

5. One of the major and long-range tactical gambits of American policy must be the promotion of what one can describe only as "irritational inroads" into the Soviet sphere of influence. Our means

are manyfold and can be most imaginative. We must develop *individualized* policies for each East European country that rest on the *particularized* encouragement of broadly based cultural and political contacts and cooperation in order to encourage greater autonomy for them and thus to lessen the burden of economic and political dependence on the USSR. The irritational value of such U.S. policies could be greatly enhanced by taking advantage of the growing Chinese presence in most of these countries. Indeed, nothing would more upset the USSR than a more or less visible process of quiet cooperation in Eastern Europe between the Americans and the Chinese. The next few years may present multiple such opportunities of this kind for U.S. policy, particularly in Rumania and to a lesser extent Poland and Hungary.

6. Finally, the Sonnenfeldt Doctrine notwithstanding, we must make every effort to deny the Soviets' permanent and organic claims to the entire geopolitical region of East-Central Europe. Cleverly tailored and individualized policies, together with stepped-up cultural and economic activities, are bound to provide signals for the subject peoples that we *do* care, that no colonial superpower has organic claims or control over them.

In short, a long-range goal should be to help East Europeans *to maintain their own national and cultural identity and economic viability* under a massive assault not only of Soviet power but also of Soviet "values."

Notes

1. For the purpose of this analysis Eastern Europe includes the German Democratic Republic, Czechoslovakia, Poland, Hungary, Rumania, and Bulgaria. Yugoslavia and Albania are excluded. The inclusion of East Germany illustrates the westward shift of geopolitical boundaries of the region, analyzed by Hugh Seton-Watson in "Is There an East Central Europe?" in *Eastern Europe in the 1970's*, ed. S. Sinanian, I. Deak, and P. C. Ludz (New York: 1972), pp. 5-12.

2. The perception of the primary strategic importance of Eastern Europe has strong historical roots in the policies of imperial Russia. In the Soviet period, the ideological imperative has been added, that of the need to consolidate revolution and to extend it. For this factor in the Bolshevik policy toward Poland in 1920 see Roman Zambrowski, "Uwagi o wojnie polsko-radzieckiej 1920 roku" *Zeszyty historyozne*, No. 38, "Biblioteka kultury," Vol. 268 (Paris: 1976), pp. 3-30.

3. J. F. Brown, "The Interaction between Party and Society in Hungary and Bulgaria," in *Authoritarian Politics in Communist Europe*, ed. A. C. Janos (Berkeley: 1976), pp. 109-114.

4. See Richard Lowenthal, *World Communism: The Disintegration of a Secular Faith* (New York: 1964).

5. Grey Hodnett and Peter Potichnyj, *Ukraine and the Czechoslovak Crisis* (Canberra: 1970).

6. For a discussion of the Soviet theoretical justification of the policy of integration and early efforts at its implementation see T. Rakowska-Harmstone, " 'Socialist Internationalism' and Eastern Europe: A New Stage," *Survey*, Winter 1976, pp. 38–54; and idem, "Socialist Internationalism: Part II," ibid., Spring 1976, pp. 81–86.

7. See Melvin Croan, *East Germany: The Soviet Connection*, The Washington Papers, vol. IV, No. 36 (Washington, D.C.: 1976), pp. 35, 41–43.

8. See Michael Getler, "More East Germans Trying to Get Out," *Manchester Guardian Weekly*, 12 September 1976.

9. T. H. Rigby, "Politics in the Mono-organizational Society," in Janos, op. cit, pp. 64–66.

10. The notorious *liberum veto* of the Polish gentry prevented the development of royal absolutism and contributed to the disintegration of the Polish-Lithuanian kingdom. An old Polish proverb states that "a gentleman on his homestead is equal to a *wojewoda*" ("royal senator").

11. See R. V. Burks, *The Dynamics of Communism in Eastern Europe* (Princeton: 1961).

12. Demonstrating an apparent inability to progress to the stage of a successful "adaptation" envisaged by Samuel P. Huntington in "Social and Institutional Dynamics of One-Party Systems," in *Authoritarian Politics in Modern Societies*, ed. S. P. Huntington and C. H. Moore (New York: 1970).

13. For the application of the concept to Eastern Europe see Zvi Gitelman, *Beyond Leninism: Political Development in Eastern Europe* (Pittsburgh: 1971), pp. 1–2.

14. In *Politics in Czechoslovakia* (San Francisco: 1974), Otto Ulč writes: "The KSC reformers of 1968 found it difficult to accept the prospect of losing the monopoly on political initiative. They abhorred opposition, or any loss of party control over the political process ... many ... appeared to be prisoners of their own Weltanschauung, distrustful of compromise and fearful of dissent" (p. 60). Radoslav Selucky relates that in the discussion among party reformers of how best to preserve the leading party role in a pluralist setting, proposals were made to institutionalize it within a special upper chamber of an otherwise representative assembly (conversations at Carleton University, 1972–1973).

15. For a broad theoretical discussion of problems of change and adaptation in communist societies passing from the mobilization to the postmobilization stage see Chalmers Johnson (ed.), *Change in Communist Systems* (Stanford: 1970), especially pp. 1–116; see also Richard Lowenthal, "The Ruling Party in a Mature Society," in *Social Consequences of Modernization in Communist Societies*, ed. Mark G. Field (Baltimore: 1976), pp. 81–118; and Gitelman, op. cit.

16. Leszek Kolakowski, "Responsibility and History," in *Toward a Marxist Humanism: Essays on the Left Today* (New York: 1968), pp. 96–98.

17. As in the provisions of the 1961 (Khrushchev's) CPSU statutes (revoked by the twenty-third CPSU congress); also in the 1968 statutes of the Czechoslovak Communist party.

18. Ulč, op. cit., pp. 60 ff.

19. See T. Rakowska-Harmstone, "Patterns of Political Change," in *The Communist States in Disarray*, ed. A. Bromke and T. Rakowska-Harmstone (Minneapolis: 1972), pp. 324-333.

20. For an extensive discussion of the practice of "cooptation" see Zygmunt Bauman, "The Party in the System-Management Phase: Change and Continuity," in Janos, op. cit., pp. 81-108; for the GDR see Thomas A. Baylis, *The Technical Intelligentsia and the East German Elite* (Berkeley: 1974). The practice is not always as successful as these studies seem to indicate because it does not necessarily result in the inclusion into the political elite of the most able professionals. Many of those coopted are mediocrities, careerists, and other opportunists.

21. Ulč, op. cit., p. 69. Ulč reports the establishment in 1968 of a new central committee department (retained in 1969), the unit of political and professional sources, which is charged with analysis of a whole range of objective data for the information of the party's policymakers. Research institutes providing the party with objective data analysis exist throughout the bloc.

22. Explicit references to their communist party and its leading role are included in all the East European constitutions.

23. In Rumania, the president of the local people's county (*judet*) council is *always* the local party chairman. See Daniel N. Nelson, "Change vs. Continuity in the Sub-national Political Elite of Romania" (Unpublished paper). In Poland, the practice began in 1973 and it was continued in the whole-scale reorganization of the territorial-administrative apparatus in 1975: the fourteen *województwa* (provinces) were restructured into forty-nine, with the simultaneous abolition of the *powiat* (district) intermediate level. Every *wojewoda* (province chief) is also the local party first-secretary.

24. In the Soviet Union the posts combined at the top have been the CPSU's first-secretary and the chairman of the council of ministers (by Stalin and Khrushchev). At his seventieth birthday, Secretary General Brezhnev assumed the title of a marshall and the commander in chief and in June 1977 he was named chairman of the presidium of the Supreme Soviet.

25. See Gitelman, op. cit.

26. Carl Linden, "Marxism-Leninism, Systemic Legitimacy, and Political Culture," in *The Limits to Change in Communist Societies: Soviet Union and Eastern Europe*, ed. T. Rakowska-Harmstone (Boulder: Westview, 1978), p. 28.

27. Croan, *East Germany*, p. 63.

28. Melvin Croan, in Sinanian et al., op. cit., p. 241.

29. Ibid., p. 242.

30. Trond Gilberg, "Ceausescu's Romania," *Problems of Communism*, July-August 1974, p. 42.

31. Hella Pick, *Manchester Guardian Weekly*, 13 March 1977.

32. Charles Gati, "The Kádár Mystique," *Problems of Communism*, May-June 1974, pp. 23-25.

33. Adam Bromke, "A New Juncture in Poland," *Problems of Communism*, September-October 1976, pp. 6-8.

34. F. Stephen Larrabee, "Bulgaria's Politics of Conformity," *Problems of Communism*, July-August 1972, pp. 43-51.

35. RFE (Radio Free Europe) Research, Bulgaria, No. 11, 5 April 1976.

36. As reported in the *Washington Post*, 13 May 1977.

37. Also, of course, in Yugoslavia. The Yugoslav reforms provided a model and an inspiration for the rest of Eastern Europe.

38. Gitelman, op. cit., pp. 23-28.

39. Jacek Kuron, active in the 1976-1977 intellectual ferment in Poland, was arrested in May 1977 (*Washington Post*, 18 May 1977). [Kuron is now one of the sponsors of a "floating" free university that is only lightly harassed by the regime.—M.A.K.]

40. A more appropriate term, "pre-emptive organizations," is used by Johnson, op. cit., p. 19.

41. See Stefan Nowak, "Like Father, Like Son?" *Polish Perspectives*, No. 7-8 (1976): 10-20; Jaroslav Piekalkiewicz, *Public Opinion in Czechoslovakia, 1968-69* (New York: 1972).

42. Brown, op. cit., p. 118.

43. Discussions of agricultural problems in Polish sources always deny that there will be a return to collectivization; instead, great emphasis is placed on the need to increase the socialized sector by the development of state farms and various kinds of cooperatives.

44. The exodus leaves much of the land fallow and recent government legislation provides for the state's takeover of land that is not properly cultivated, thus serving to enlarge the socialist sector.

45. See Robert C. Tucker, *The Soviet Political Mind*, rev. ed. (New York: 1971), pp. 121-142.

46. Only the most important political aspects of economic reform are considered here. For a comprehensive review of the subject see Hans-Hermann Hohmann, Michael Kaser, and Karl C. Thalheim (eds.), *The New Economic Systems of Eastern Europe* (Berkeley: 1975).

47. For the best discussion of the primacy of politics in economic planning see Radoslav Selucky, *Economic Reforms in Eastern Europe* (New York: 1972).

48. The socialist market model, which has been developed in Yugoslavia and was also introduced in the Czech experiment, has been the subject of heated discussions, pro and con, among East European economists.

49. Even computerization, however, cannot resolve the problem of complex economic relations under a command planning system. Ota Sik, leading Czech reformer stated: "I am convinced that even with the most complex computer system no optimal solution can be found at the center for the individual branches and enterprises, for a computer system of this kind can

only work on the basis of the information and details that are put into the system by the enterprises" (quoted in Hohmann et al., op. cit., p. 555).

50. See Gabor Revesz, "Hungary," in ibid., pp. 155-170.

51. See Karl C. Thalheim, "Balance Sheet," in ibid., pp. 529-568.

52. Quoted in ibid., p. 561.

53. Some analysts even put forth a suggestion that the whole thing is a "hoax," synchronized with the Soviet Union, to serve best the bloc's interests. See Vladimir Socor, "The Limits of National Independence in the Soviet Bloc: Rumania's Foreign Policy Reconsidered," *Orbis*, Fall 1976, pp. 701-732.

54. Croan, *East Germany*, pp. 59-64.

55. Istban Dobozi, "Problems of Raw Materials in CMEA" (unpublished English summary of four of the author's publications in Hungarian).

56. See Rakowska-Harmstone, "Socialist Internationalism: A New Stage."

57. Pierre Hassner, "L'Avenir des alliances en l'Europe" (Paper presented at the International Political Science Association congress, Edinburgh, 16-21 August 1976), p. 17.

58. See, for example, the editorial "Ideinoe oruzhie kommunistov," *Kommunist* (Moscow), No. 18 (1976): 38-46, which praises the PCI, makes a bow to Antonio Gramsci, and discusses "international solidarity."

59. Quoted by Eric Bourne in the *Christian Science Monitor*, 14 February 1977.

60. Quoted by Paul Wohl in ibid., 21 February 1977.

61. Hassner, op. cit., p. 17.

62. Western news services reported in early spring 1976 that Bulgaria was considering becoming the sixteenth republic of the Soviet Union.

63. Crane Brinton, *The Anatomy of Revolution* (New York: 1959), pp. 28-69.

64. See *Kommunist*, No. 2 (1977): 9-13.

6

Eastern Europe, Eurocommunism, and the Problems of Détente

Pavel Machala

The Dialectics of Détente

Détente may well be a failure—for both superpowers—but not for the reasons that we hear so often. According to its critics, détente is a one-way street that benefits only the Soviet Union; according to its advocates, détente diminishes the possibility of a nuclear confrontation and, furthermore, encourages the gradual liberation of Eastern Europe—by which I mean the Soviet bloc countries, East Germany, Poland, Czechoslovakia, Hungary, Bulgaria, and Rumania—and the transformation of the political systems in these countries and in the Soviet Union. However, neither group perceives détente as containing the seeds of its own destruction. The flaw in the détente relationship does not lie in its being a one-way street, as some would have it, but in the fact that at least for the superpowers it is a maze rather than a street. The dialectics of détente may produce the very opposite effect from that which has been intended. In the long run, it may lead not to resolution of the tensions between the superpowers but to destabilization of the U.S.-USSR relationship; thus it may bring these two countries to the brink of a new cold war confrontation over Europe.

It is generally agreed that the issue that started the cold war, that gave it momentum, and that shaped its early course was Eastern Europe. This region has been and still is essential to Soviet security objectives. It was the Soviets' perception of a threat to their *cordon sanitaire* in this region, coupled with the Western refusal to recognize Eastern Europe as a legitimate Soviet sphere of interest, that precluded any resolution of either the global superpower confrontation or the normalization of relations between countries in the European subsystem.

Given this historical context, an analysis of the extent to which the current détente relationship affects the long-standing bipolarity of the European system is in order. Has détente consolidated or jeopardized the control of the Soviet Union and the authority of communism in Eastern Europe? Conversely, has détente supported or endangered the essential American objectives in Western Europe? Finally, to what extent has détente stimulated the possibility of evolution toward an integrated and independent Europe?

Although the strategic confrontation between the superpowers has led to nuclear détente without reducing their competition in non-European parts of the world, Europe has become a showplace for superpower cooperation in the easing of tensions. Despite frequent denials by both superpowers, the reduction of tension has been based on mutual recognition of the status quo in Europe, a matter that had been a point of contention for twenty-five years. Even in the 1960s, peaceful coexistence notwithstanding, the Soviet Union and the United States desired to promote the "peaceful disintegration" of the other side's sphere of influence in Europe. The West tried to detach Eastern Europe through a series of diplomatic and economic "bridges," and the Soviet Union in the same spirit cultivated France's reservations about the Atlantic alliance. However, the Western decision to ignore the Soviet invasion of Czechoslovakia in 1968 and Moscow's decision to disregard the escalation of American involvement in Southeast Asia in 1970 signified that strategic détente had become of paramount importance to both superpowers. It also served to convince the Soviets that the West would never challenge the European status quo. Thus, the link—if not linkage per se—between strategic détente and European détente (which I will henceforth call "Eurodétente") was established. Eurodétente has since become associated with the series of treaties between West Germany and both the Soviet Union and the countries of Eastern Europe that culminated in the Helsinki conference on security and cooperation. The conference was widely interpreted as a multilateral recognition of "the consequences of the Second World War"—i.e., the partition of Germany as well as the primacy of the Soviet Union and the legitimacy of the Soviet allied regimes in Eastern Europe.

These agreements represented an important departure from past policies; the Berlin agreement in particular required concessions from both superpowers and from those European states that were involved. Acceptance of "immobility" in Europe, it should be emphasized, constitutes a central feature of Eurodétente. This means not merely Western recognition of post-World War II boundaries in Central and Eastern Europe but also formal Western acknowledgment of the "legitimate security interests of the Soviet Union" in this region.[1]

Although the strategic confrontation between the superpowers has led essentially to a stable deterrent relationship, and while intra-European conflicts are being normalized, it is the domestic and transnational processes in Europe that are the real sources of instability in the European system. The relative stability enjoyed by both Western and Eastern European societies since the late 1940s was caused primarily by the existence of the cold war. Therefore, it should not surprise us that post-cold war Europe is once again faced with problems similar to those that beset its societies at the outset of the cold war. As in 1947-1948, the Europe of 1977-1978 is, and in all likelihood will continue to be, divided. Similarly, as in the former period, European societies are internally unstable. Social polarization in many Western countries, revivals of nationalistic fervor in Yugoslavia, Spain, and Britain, and social pressures in East Germany and Poland are real and growing phenomena. However, there is one crucial difference from the early postwar years: that difference is the existence of strategic and European détente. Today, the European territorial and political status quo is a generally accepted fact.[2] Neither the events in Portugal and Spain nor those in Poland have been exploited by the adversary superpower. These examples epitomize the new European reality by demonstrating the contrast between the new internal instability of European societies and the stability of the European system as a whole. In the long run, however, it is extremely unlikely that in the absence of a superpower confrontation social and economic crises in these societies can be kept in check or have purely localized political consequences with no significant spillover effects.

Social and political instabilities are characteristic of all societies in transition. They are at present manifested in many different parts of the world. What is unique about social conflicts in Western and Eastern Europe, however, is that they are externalized. Besides its "demonstration effect" on other countries within the European subsystem, ferment in any European country is more likely than not to strain the relations between that country and one of the superpowers. The externalization of social conflicts in turn provides a dialectical link between internal developments in these countries and the process of Eurodétente. This link is a dangerous one: whereas the relaxation of international tension is conducive to continued social instability in Eastern and Western Europe, unrest in these areas is detrimental, and could even prove to be fatal, to European détente.

The European détente relationship, in sum, is characterized by dynamism and instability. The threat to this relationship, however, does not lie in the renewal of a direct confrontation between the superpowers but in the social unrest that may occur in Western and Eastern European societies. These internal developments in one European sphere, in turn, may influence stability in the other European sphere, thus forcing the superpowers to act in order to defend their own interests in Europe.

It would be artificial to equate social instabilities that exist in Western European countries with those that exist in the East. Contrary to the views of certain wishful thinkers, Eurodétente has not significantly destabilized Eastern European regimes but has actually brought them a degree of domestic and international legitimacy. Nor has it undermined Soviet preeminence within the bloc, though it has slightly broadened the limits within which the domestic and foreign policy choices of these regimes can be made. In fact, besides the formal recognition of the legitimacy of the status quo, Eurodétente has generally promoted a feeling of normalcy and a realization on the part of both the governments and the populations of Eastern Europe that any improvement of their domestic and international position is possible only within a communist and Soviet approved framework.

So far, the only casualty of Eurodétente in Eastern Europe has been Walter Ulbricht, who could not adjust to the change in the international climate. Except for Bulgaria, the country thus far least affected by the relaxation of tension in Europe, the Eastern European regimes have benefited from Eurodétente. The East German leadership has remained sensitive to any quick relaxation of tension in Europe. However, in its present form, Eurodétente has enabled it to resolve the "German question" by creating an atmosphere that has permitted East Germany to be diplomatically recognized by most members of the international community and thus, has upgraded the legitimacy of East Germany, both domestically and internationally (the two reinforcing each other). In addition, the two German states participated on an equal basis in the European security conference in Helsinki. Therefore, as far as the East German leaders are concerned, Eurodétente has secured their position by closing off the option of German unification once and for all—a situation they believe is a prerequisite for the social and political stability of their regime. For the Czechs and the Poles, Eurodétente effectively brings to a close previously unresolved border and territorial issues with West Germany. It allows the Rumanians and the Yugoslavs to maintain the independence that their countries have gained vis-à-vis the Soviet Union by diminishing the likelihood of Soviet military action against them (or so their leaders hope). For the Hungarian leaders, Eurodétente makes it easier to carry out certain internal political and economic reforms without risking negative Soviet reaction.

Given the fact that the Soviet Union continues to view Eastern Europe as indispensable for its security, Moscow defines Eurodétente essentially as an environment that guarantees against a renewed Western bridge building policy. The Polish, Hungarian, and Rumanian regimes, on the other hand, see that their security against the Brezhnev Doctrine consists in inducing graduate changes in Moscow's perception of its security needs. For all Eastern European countries, détente has in fact served to help realize the programs of "consumer communism." To this end, it has accelerated their activities in seeking out Western financial and technological assistance. Therefore, the general Eastern European advocacy of this policy must clearly be seen as something more than a dutiful seconding of the Kremlin's current position on Europe.[3] Detente in Europe promises not only to give these regimes access to important Western markets, credit, and technology but also to insure their countries' domestic and international security.

This is not to deny that Eurodétente has also had a certain destabilizing impact on Eastern Europe. However, the political importance of this impact has been relatively small. Yes, it has caused an increase in the number and intensity of dissident activities among the intellectuals and the younger generation whose expectations regarding greater civil rights and expanded international contacts have been encouraged by the so-called third basket of the 1975 Helsinki conference. Yes, "civil rights" protests in the fall of 1976 and in the winter of 1977 in Czechoslovakia, East Germany, Poland, and Rumania were specifically timed to coincide with the June 1977 conference in Belgrade whose purpose was to review the workings of Eurodétente.[4] *But* as long as the dissidents are willing to emigrate, the political significance of these dissident activities as far as the Eastern European regimes are concerned can be only marginal, and thus "manageable."

Even in East Germany, where the Helsinki induced pledge of the government to facilitate the reunion of families has brought about several thousand applications from all social strata for emigration to West Germany, the authorities have regained full control of the situation. As a result of a variety of governmental restrictions, the number of people seeking to emigrate had dropped by the middle of 1977.[5] In other words, Eurodétente per se has not significantly endangered Eastern European regimes. On the contrary, all available evidence suggests that it promotes an automatic "defense" response on the part of these regimes. If their relatively mild reaction to current dissident activities indicates anything, it is the existence of disagreement within the top leadership in these countries over how the dissident problem ought to be handled. This disagreement seems to be the result primarily of their awareness of being watched by Western European communists and *not* of criticism from Western governments.

Similarly, although one cannot deny that Eurodétente has weakened the Soviet claim to hegemony in Eastern Europe and the implementation of the Brezhnev Doctrine, the effect has not been all negative for the Soviet Union. It is true that Eurodétente has to a large extent eliminated the belief that West Germany is Eastern Europe's major enemy, a fear that in the 1960s moved Czechoslovakia and Poland especially to seek protection from the Soviet Union. In addition, Eurodétente has diminished the likelihood of a military operation by Moscow against the Eastern European countries. Consequently, it is not unlikely that some of these countries could try to exploit European détente to win more elbow room from the Soviet Union. Poland, for example, with its Western borders secure and recognized, could seek to play the role of a "middle power" in Europe.

However, although the Eastern European states have become participants, rather than pawns, in the decisionmaking process of bloc policies, in general it should not be assumed that bloc stability has suffered as a result of a relaxed international atmosphere. Besides the existence of the Warsaw Treaty Organization (WTO) and Comecon, the Soviet Union can rely not only on bilateral political and military agreements to maintain regional cohesion but also on willing agents within the highest party and state circles of the majority of the Eastern European countries.[6] For example, in October 1975 (only two months after the Helsinki conference) the Soviet Union signed a treaty with East Germany that clearly affirmed the doctrine of "limited sovereignty."[7] Furthermore, Rumania has considerably muted its defiance of the Soviet Union. In 1973, in fact, for the first time in a decade, Rumania allowed the Warsaw Pact exercises to be held on its own soil and has become more a cooperative member of Comecon. Regardless of a certain divergence between Soviet and Eastern European views concerning the desirable extent of Soviet power in the area, the ruling elites in Eastern European countries realize that in the end their political security is closely bound up with Moscow. It is fair to say that none of these regimes, with the possible exception of Rumania, would like to see an immediate and complete disengagement of the Soviet Union from Eastern Europe, even if this were remotely likely. As far as the extension of Western credit to Eastern Europe is concerned, this is not only acceptable but quite desirable from the Kremlin's point of view because it contributes to higher living standards in the area and consequently reinforces the stability of local communist regimes.

Reduced to its essentials, Eurodétente by itself neither undermines the stability of Eastern European communist regimes nor encourages them to seek independence for their countries. Those Western writers who argue that Eurodétente—or the resulting network of contacts in the economic sphere that has developed in Europe—will liberalize Eastern European societies or Soviet foreign policy in this region are clearly mistaken. Although disincentives for rigidity have become greater in the post-Helsinki era, both the internal policies of Eastern European regimes and Soviet policies in that region prove their determination to protect communist orthodoxy and the hegemonial position of the Soviet Union, even at the risk of slowing down the movement toward superpower accommodation in Europe. Thus, it is unrealistic to expect transformation of the internal systems of Eastern European countries or transformation of Soviet behavior in Eastern Europe as a result of détente or Eurodétente. Nor have recent U.S. administrations been seriously interested in exploiting any such instability to these ends for they well know that interference with Soviet interests in this area would renew the cold war.

With varying degrees of success, the Soviet and Eastern European regimes manage to deal with détente induced unrest in Eastern Europe by institutionalizing the limits beyond which unrest will not be tolerated. Moreover, it is implicit in the Eurodétente relationship that the Soviet Union be allowed to continue controlling developments in Eastern Europe, although admittedly at a lower profile.

Instabilities in Western Europe, on the other hand, are not easily checked; they are, in fact, encouraged by the very existence of détente. Leftist forces in several of these countries are nearer the threshold of power than they have been since the early postwar era, and the possibility that these forces—specifically the communist parties—will enter the government as important partners is very real. In Italy, the Communist party (PCI) emerged from the 1976 election as clearly the foremost party of the left, a close second to the Christian Democrats. The possibility of the PCI's sharing control of the government with the Socialists and even with the left-wing Christian Democrats is not at all unthinkable. In France, a coalition of Socialists and Communists came within two percentage points of winning the presidency in March 1974 and was victorious in the March 1977 municipal elections. Although success at the local level does not assure a leftist triumph at the national level, it does demonstrate the electorate's dissatisfaction with the center-Right government and increases the possibility of a leftist victory in the 1978 parliamentary elections.

This growing legitimization of Western European communist parties is the result not only of changes in the political, economic, and social environment in Western Europe but also of the relaxation of ideological tension in the West that has come with strategic and European détente. At the same time, centrifugal forces set in motion by the process of de-Stalinization and accelerated by the Sino-Soviet conflict have worked toward promoting the independence of these parties vis-à-vis Moscow. Together these two trends—détente and the gradual fragmentation of a once unified international communist movement—have created the phenomenon of Eurocommunism: the existence of communist parties in Western Europe that might not only participate in the government but that would presumably do so as independent and democratic actors. It is difficult to imagine any cataclysm that would be severe enough to prevent or even slow this trend. Nothing short of the total abandonment of détente by either superpower is likely to prevent the inevitable: the "specter of Euro-socialism" haunting Western Europe. This distorted echo of the famous opening sentence of the *Communist Manifesto* sums up the process of change that exists in Western Europe.

Although the communist parties of Western Europe once looked to Moscow for direction in both domestic and foreign matters, they have now developed sufficient individual identity to be able to formulate their own policies either independently or in cooperation with each other. As shown by the PCI and PCF's (French Communist party) declaration, the independent stance of the Italian, Spanish, and French parties at the twenty-fifth CPSU congress, the events of the 1976 European conference of European communist parties, and the separate regular consultations of Western and Eastern European communist parties, polycentrism has become a reality in the European communist "system."[8] The time is long since passed when Soviet interests could dictate domestic and foreign policies to the Western parties. Among the twenty-two Western European communist parties, only seven have remained uncritically pro-Soviet—those of Portugal, Cyprus, Austria, Luxembourg, Turkey, West Germany, and West Berlin. The vast majority offer a broad spectrum of varying degrees of disagreement with Moscow's policies. This, however, does not mean that these parties have reached the point of severing their ties with the world communist environment. On the contrary, they claim their membership in the world communist movement is (to borrow an expression from *L'Unità*) "not the point at issue—it is beyond dispute."[9]

There is, however, little reason for the Soviet Union to be less wary of this dedication to internationalism of the Western European communists than of their public determination to select only a democratic and pluralistic model of socialism as appropriate for their societies. Taken together, these trends pose a double threat to stability in the Eastern bloc countries and to Soviet hegemony in this region. Specifically, although the determination of the Eurocommunists to preserve the independence of each communist party and to observe the democratic process obviously cannot but stimulate the emergence of destabilizing social and political forces in Eastern Europe, their recognition of their place in the world communist community ironically provides the Eurocommunists with a forum within which to criticize certain Soviet and Eastern European policies and practices.[10] For example, the Italian Communist party has on numerous occasions condemned Soviet and Eastern European handling of internal dissidence.[11] Similarly, the French Communist party has expressed its "most unequivocal disapproval" of Soviet labor camps and psychiatric clinics.[12] At the twelfth party congress, PCF general secretary, Georges Marchais, explicitly criticized Soviet repression by declaring: "We cannot agree to the communist ideal's being stained by unjust and unjustifiable acts. Such acts are in no way a necessary consequence of socialism. . . . This is why we express our disagreement when violations of human rights occur in a country that had its socialist revolution fifty-eight years ago."[13] Similarly, the Communist parties of Spain, Britain, Sweden, Denmark, Holland, Greece, and Belgium have recently become increasingly critical of the restrictive measures prevalent in Eastern Europe and in the Soviet Union. These and similar confrontations are likely to go on and to multiply, especially if any of these parties continues to achieve spectacular electoral successes in their own countries.

Moscow's aloof response to these Eurocommunist assertions reflects its indecision over how to cope with the autonomy of liberalized Western European communist parties. Although Soviet leaders still hope to command their loyalties in any East-West confrontation, they find Eurocommunism to be a double-edged sword that threatens their own détente policy. Superficially, the prospect of communists' gaining a share of power in Western Europe and disrupting the Atlantic alliance should appear to be an attractive development for the Soviets, but such is not the case. First of all, the leaders in Moscow understand the fact that any change in the European status quo could put a definite end to their détente with Washington. Second, given their rather satisfactory relations with the noncommunist governments in Western Europe, Soviet leaders are not looking forward to the prospect of Eurocommunism's disruption of the Western alliance.

But most important, what increasingly concerns Soviet leaders is the realization that Eurocommunism is not merely a regional variant of communist strategy but a radically different model of socialism. As such it could represent an ideological alternative to the authoritarian Soviet model in world communism, particularly in Eastern Europe. Specifically, they are aware that by declaring their independence from Moscow, and by insisting on respecting basic democratic freedoms, the Western European communist parties not only challenge Moscow's claim to leadership in the "world communist movement" but also—especially if successful in their own countries—undermine the ideological and political basis on which Soviet leaders justify their continued preeminence and orthodoxy both at home and in Eastern Europe. Even if the commitment of the Western European communist parties to respect democracy is mostly a tactical ploy designed to win electoral support, and not a change in substance, Eurocommunism could create problems not only for the West but for Moscow as well, perhaps even more so for the latter. It is not at all unthinkable that the structural changes that have occurred in the international relations of the communist movement (from one characterized by monocentrism to one characterized by polycentrism) could result in the creation of a multipolar communist international system in which Western Europe would be both the ideological center and the political and military pole.

At this point, three crucial questions must be raised. (1) How likely is it that Eurocommunism will have a positive influence on the Eastern European political elites in promoting the democratization of their societies and increasing their independence from the Soviet Union? (2) If the Eurocommunists do not influence the Eastern European elites to effect such a change, how likely is it that they will nonetheless influence domestic social forces in this direction? (3) What is the likelihood that Moscow will permit the erosion of orthodox communism and/or the emergence of independent states in Eastern Europe? In addition, what impact will the Europeanization of communism have on international relations, particularly on the conduct of Soviet foreign policy?

Eastern Europe in the Seventies

Let us turn now to the situation in Eastern Europe. In order to assess the impact of Eurocommunism on Eastern Europe, it will be useful to differentiate between intrabloc instability and instability within the individual countries. Since the degree of stability in this region varies from country to country, it is necessary to analyze the key factors in each country's political, social, and economic environment. Specifically, I will evaluate the impact of Eurocommunism on internal and intrabloc instability by inquiring into the source and degree of domestic legitimacy of each regime, the extent of homogeneity of its top leadership, the character of its economic policies, and the types and degrees of social pressures in each of these countries.

Many Western analysts argue that as a result of the process of modernization, the increased visibility of socioeconomic elites in Eastern Europe may create political instability that could eventually lead to liberalization and democratization within these countries and to their increased autonomy vis-à-vis the Soviet Union. It is my estimate, however, that any tension between the technical and political elites can at most result in a change of internal party power relations because, curiously, today's technocrats constitute a barrier to major political change. Their role in society, by and large, has not led them to adopt liberal political values; they are "liberal" only in an economic sense. In fact, there is apparently an inverse relationship between the technocrats' demands and liberal values. Technocrats are interested in efficient production and in a disproportionate share of personal consumption. It must be realized that the most efficient means to these ends are frequently in opposition to the forces of liberalization, for efficiency in Eastern Europe, where the population does not have a democratic tradition, does *not* necessarily mean extension of liberal political reforms. In fact, the technocrats' tacit support of the regime as the guarantor of their economic benefits makes them unwilling to oppose the existing political system. Consequently, their inclination is to cling to the status quo. From this it follows that not only do they not support Eurocommunism but rather they are, in fact, indifferent or antagonistic to it.

If the political support of socioeconomic elites depends on the regimes' capacity to insure their material satisfaction, the same can be said about the working class in Eastern European countries. The workers regard security of employment and steady improvement in their standard of living as far more important than a whole array of civil liberties. Even as far as certain liberal provisions of economic reforms are concerned, the workers have strong conservative attitudes that they are not reluctant to articulate. By insisting, for example, on wage equalization, they are hostile to any reforms that would correlate the distribution of income with performance.

It follows from such an analysis that the Eastern European regimes can maintain their political stability as long as they are successful in bringing about economic growth and in satisfying the demands of both the middle class and the workers for consumer goods—the Eastern Europeans love the welfare state with a vengeance. East German and Hungarian leaders recognized this fact in the mid-1960s. Similarly, by diagnosing their major problem as essentially "market difficulties," the Czechoslovak leaders after Alexandr Dubček have made economic growth and a rising standard of living the basic ingredients of their "normalization" policy. The events in Poland of 1970 served to reinforce this general Eastern European trend to incorporate consumerism into the foundations of domestic policies. Since 1971, the policy of the Polish regime has in fact been to promote rapid economic growth and to raise living standards on the assumption that this would stabilize the situation. Finally, since approximately 1972, the leaders in both Bulgaria and Rumania have become concerned with raising wage levels and increasing the variety of consumer goods available in their countries.

These recently defined concerns were, in turn, manifested in very tangible ways. In the 1970s, the living standard in East Germany, already the highest in Eastern Europe, has risen faster than ever before. Even though the 1976 price increases tend to cloud the picture, in Hungary since 1968 personal income has risen at an average annual rate of nearly 6%. In Czechoslovakia, wages have increased consistently between 6% and 8% annually, whereas retail prices have virtually stood still since 1970. In Poland, the crash program to raise the living standard has resulted in an 8% annual rise in wages since 1972—in contrast to the period from 1961-1970, when individual income on the average increased by only 1.8% annually. Rumania and Bulgaria, although still far behind the other Eastern European countries, have nonetheless increased per capita income by similar percentages.[14] In sum, these developments show that the present Eastern European political elites believe that good living conditions will at one and the same time appease workers, blunt the force of demands for institutional innovations on the part of the middle class, and isolate intellectual dissent.

To a great extent, this has, in fact, been the case. With the exception of Hungary, whose New Economic Mechanism (NEM) represents a radical departure from the Soviet type of economic management, the present economic growth and rising standard of living in Eastern Europe were accomplished without any significant economic reforms. On the contrary, all of these regimes have retreated from the economic decentralization of the 1960s and moved back in the direction of an administrative economy.[15] This decision was influenced by the lessons of the "Prague spring." In Czechoslovakia, the economic reforms of the mid-1960s precipitated the demand for a "modern pluralistic democratic system."[16] In light of the Czechoslovak experience, it is hardly surprising that the Eastern European leaders have been determined not to carry economic reforms to the point where they might open the door to political pluralism and thus threaten the "leading role of the party."

Events in Poland in 1970 and again in 1976 were steered in such a way as not to produce a political outcome of the Czechoslovak variety. The core of the Polish economy has remained centrally planned, with emphasis placed on a crash program of economic development aimed at rapidly expanding the national economic base to raise living standards. Although there has been some decentralization of authority, this decentralization has not extended to individual factories but to large-scale economic units, whose responsibility with regard to decisions on investment, wages, etc., has been greatly increased. Similar relationships of production exist in the Czechoslovak and East German economies as well.

If the short-term success of the 1970–1975 "consumer communism" in Eastern European countries has been indisputable, it has not been unqualified. A rising standard of living has been achieved in East Germany as a result of rising productivity; in Czechoslovakia, through expanded imports and a large trade deficit with other Eastern European countries; in Poland and Rumania, through huge credits from the West; and in Bulgaria, through Soviet financial aid. At the same time, the policies of high investment and rapid wage increases have created severe inflationary pressures in these countries, on the one hand, and rising consumer expectations, on the other. The situation in Poland has been especially serious. Although the crash economic program raised wages by an impressive 40% over a five-year period, it has dried up consumer supplies: drastic shortages have been the counterpart in the "controlled" economy of the raging inflation that would have ensued in a "free market" economy. In an effort to counter these shortages, the Polish government sharply increased the prices of many essential consumer goods in July 1976 and thus provoked strikes and riots by the workers. Even in Hungary, where the NEM has by and large been successful in producing consumer goods, some negative consequences that could potentially threaten the stability of the regime are in evidence. Epitomized by economic decentralization and a reliance on the market mechanism, the NEM has led not only to purely economic problems, such as investment "overheating" and inflation (e.g., 10% in 1976), but also to significant income inequalities between the workers and the middle class. Since 1972, the regime has tried to appease the workers by claiming that as the economy grows there will be commensurate increases in their living standard.[17]

Other Eastern European regimes have faced similar problems. All available data indicate that their economies, which performed rather well in the period 1970–1975, have recently shown signs of a permanent slowdown. The severe drought of 1976 led to a large decline in agricultural production in Poland, East Germany, and Czechoslovakia. Furthermore, except for Czechoslovakia, which after the events of 1968 had difficulty borrowing money from the West, by 1977 the Eastern European countries had accumulated staggering debts to Western financial institutions—Bulgaria and Rumania, $2.8 billion each; Hungary, $3.3 billion; East Germany, $6 billion; Poland, $10.8 billion—and these debts are still growing. For example, Poland's debt is expected to reach $11-12 billion by the end of 1978.[18] At the present time, these countries are faced with pressures to repay these loans, but they have difficulty marketing their goods in the West and therefore cannot easily repay. The reason for this difficulty lies in part in the recession in the West and in part in the obsolescence of goods manufactured in Eastern Europe. Many of their industries have remained old and inefficient, and if their manufactured products (both consumer goods and machine tools) are to become competitive in the West, they must be improved. This would necessitate a further infusion of Western credit and technology, which in turn would depend not only on political relations with the West but also on the creditworthiness of the Eastern European countries.

However, a much more serious problem for the Eastern European economies has been the worldwide inflation and the oil crisis. Initially, Eastern European countries had to pay higher prices only for their imports from the West and from the Third World. Intrabloc prices had been determined every five years by the average world price over the previous five years. Thus, the price of oil for the 1971-1975 period was fixed at the average world price that existed between 1966 and 1970. However, in January 1975, the Soviets hiked the price of their oil to Eastern European consumers by some 150%. From that date the price was to be revised annually to correlate with the "adjusted" world price. Although the Soviet Union still charges only about 70% of the going world price for oil sold to Eastern Europe, this price will rise annually through 1978 as prices from the preembargo years are eliminated from the calculation; thus, eventually these countries will have to pay the full OPEC price.[19] The Eastern European countries have faced a somewhat similar problem with their grain imports, a commodity for which the Soviet Union has also become a less reliable supplier.

This drastic rise in the cost of oil and other critical raw materials, along with uncertainty as to their future price and availability, poses extremely serious problems and dilemmas for the Eastern European regimes. For example, at its eleventh party congress in March 1975, Hungary's political leadership acknowledged that its once vaunted economy had encountered serious problems. As a result, the GNP, which had risen an average of 5.5% annually since 1968, has been calculated to grow only 3-3.5% annually for the 1976-1980 period. Janos Kádár, the party's first-secretary, diagnosed the problem as being caused by the increased price of "energy fuels and raw materials."[20] Similarly, the East German government has acknowledged that the country is having trouble coping with price increases on imports of "raw materials from socialist countries."[21] The new pricing is estimated to have siphoned approximately $1.5 billion worth of Eastern European resources into the Soviet Union yearly since 1975. It has also been reflected in the substantial trade deficit of the Eastern European countries in relation to the Soviet Union. Although these countries have raised the prices of their exports to the Soviet Union as well, these increases cover only two-thirds of the higher cost of Soviet raw materials. To make up the difference, the 1976-1980 economic plans prescribe a faster expansion of the production of commodities for export.[22] However, such an objective can be accomplished only by reducing the growth rate of the populations' general standard of living. Fortunately for the regimes, these targets have not so far been met: if successful, they would most likely provoke labor dissatisfaction. Specifically, since the stability of the regimes depends on the at least tacit support of the workers, the decision to call a temporary halt to consumer communism and to replace it with a policy that offers the prospect of only minimum material improvement would be potentially dangerous. Nonetheless, this decision is vital for the maintenance of the long-term economic performance on which, in the end, popular support is based; hence, the dilemma.

There are in fact indications that the top political leaders in the Eastern European countries are undecided as to how to cope with this economic situation and its social repercussions. Both the December 1970 and the July 1976 explosions of "proletarian consciousness" in Poland are certainly fresh in their minds. By such unrest, industrial workers have served notice that if the criteria of productivity and abstract budget balancing entail decisions made at their expense, then such policies are unacceptable to them.[23] The regimes' anxiety over the very real possibility of widespread popular discontent—especially in Czechoslovakia, East Germany, and Poland—is matched only by their fear of an eventual alliance between workers and dissident intellectuals. Historically, such an alliance has been difficult, if not impossible, to achieve in part because of the extremely repressive measures invoked by Eastern European regimes to combat any opposition. More important, however, the interests of these groups simply did not overlap: whereas the opposition of the intellectuals often emanated from an anti-Marxist viewpoint and centered solely on issues such as "liberty," the demands of dissatisfied workers mainly involved their personal material welfare. Furthermore, both groups viewed emigration as a logical solution to their discontent.

Today, however, "old-fashioned" repression is far harder to impose. In addition, although thus far prospects for an immediate "popular front" exist only in Poland (where the rudiments of a genuine labor movement that came into being during the December 1970 upheaval have established links with both middle-class critics of the regime and the Catholic church),[24] opposition to the regimes today is much more sophisticated. In East Germany and Rumania the main dissident problem still involves demands to emigrate;[25] elsewhere, however, dissidents are in a different position. Instead of demanding the right to leave, they are now generally demanding the right to stay and criticize the regime. These critics do not challenge Marxist philosophy despite official attacks that charge that their aim is the "overturning of the socialist system." Indeed, the majority of them remain committed communists. Rather, they want only to spur a "constructive dialogue with the political authorities" and demand rights guaranteed under the constitutions of their respective countries. The legalistic focus of these protests presents special problems to the authorities since it all but excludes the possibility of bringing direct criminal charges against the critics.[26]

This is a new phenomenon on the Eastern European scene, a development that has been further accelerated by the liberal stand of Western European communist parties. Eurocommunism creates a link between intellectual dissent and worker discontent—precisely the situation that the communist governments dread most. It provides a common ideological platform on which both workers and intellectuals can formulate their opposition to the government. By demanding such civil rights as the rights of expression, information, and religion and such social rights as the representation of workers and the autonomy of trade unions, they claim ideological kinship with the Communist parties in Italy, France, and Spain.

Besides the pressures of dissatisfied workers, of restive intellectuals, and, to a lesser extent, of other social groups (e.g., the Catholic and Protestant churches) on the regimes in Eastern Europe, the potential for domestic and bloc instability exists in intraelite infighting as well. However, given the secretiveness of communist regimes in publicizing their internal matters, it is difficult to assess properly the precise dimension of such internal cleavages. What can be said is that, although originally placed and kept in power by Moscow, different political elites have developed their own power base in their societies. With the exception of Rumania and to a degree of Hungary, the Eastern European regimes are by no means homogeneous but are divided into factions. Only the personal preeminence of their top leaders has so far been able to impose a working unity on these factions and to forestall a power struggle among them. Although it is beyond the scope of this chapter to provide a detailed analysis of these factions, it is necessary to deal with one pivotal (and politically, the most interesting) question: to what extent do the present top Eastern European leaders have enough influence and power to retain their dominant position and to what extent do they depend on Moscow?

The Hungarian leadership, although more or less homogeneous and in harmony, is made up of Kádár's reformers, moderate conservatives, and spokesmen for the workers' material interests. Whereas the first group remains committed to the NEM, with its market oriented economy, and is willing to accept its essentially nonegalitarian features, members of the second group, fearing the destabilizing consequences of the NEM, have been trying to slow down the course of the reforms. Significant opposition to the NEM has also developed within the third group not because of the destabilizing consequences of economic decentralization but because of what are perceived to be excessive income inequalities.[27]

Although at the present time neither their spokesmen nor the workers themselves are insisting on political changes, as contrasted with greater material equity, to a certain extent their opposition can nonetheless become a seedbed for political instability. The shift and consequent diffusion of authority from the party and government bureaucracy to the enterprise has been accomplished by an increase in trade union jurisdiction, a change that provides a forum within which the workers can articulate their grievances. In addition, although the regime encourages "passive participation" by such slogans as "He who is not against us is with us," this type of participation could change in the future; indeed, the channels for active participation already exist. There is industrial pluralism, and the entire electoral system has been reformed to give a greater sense of participation to the population at the local level by providing for multicandidate elections in which nonofficial candidates may be nominated and elected.[28]

Because of its often controversial domestic departures from the Soviet model, the Kádár leadership has been extremely careful not to challenge or even to embarrass the Soviet Union internationally. Indeed, it has never deviated from the general direction of Soviet foreign policy, "not even," as Kádár rather succinctly noted, "in the most difficult times."[29] On the issue of Eurocommunism, however, Kádár seems recently to have taken a more independent stand, one that shows that he sympathizes with this movement. At a December 1976 news conference, for example, in reply to a question about an article by Todor Zhivkov, the Bulgarian leader who denounced the "revisionistic tendencies" of the Western European communist parties, Kádár declared that he "did not share this view."[30] New speculation that the Hungarian regime wants to cultivate discreet relations with the Eurocommunists arose during Kádár's June 1977 Italian trip. Although he was ostensibly the guest of the Italian government, his trip implied a cautious gesture of sympathy and support for the Italian Communist party.

This attitude toward Eurocommunism may of course be in part a tactical ploy, reflecting the growing economic strains between the Soviet Union and Hungary. Since 1973, when Moscow started to stress the socialist integration of the Eastern European bloc, Hungary had to cut its domestic investment and begin to pay attention to Moscow's insistence that it commit its capital resources to extracting industries in the Soviet Union. Moreover, since 1975 Moscow has displayed reluctance in granting Hungary its requested long-term guarantees of vital raw materials, guarantees necessary for that country's continued prosperity. Given the fact that in the final analysis, domestic stability depends on continued prosperity, it should not be surprising to see that economic differences between the Soviet leaders and the Kádár regime can lead to political frictions as well. On the other hand, there is a strong indication that Hungary's flirtation with Eurocommunism reflects the latter's ideological appeal, especially as far as its stand on the autonomy of all communist parties is concerned. Hungary thus may hope to gain an important ally against Soviet pressures so that it is able to continue the pursuit of domestic reforms.

Unlike the Hungarian regime, the Czechoslovak leadership is a very loose coalition of at least three groups: hard-liners, moderate conservatives, and those who take their cue from Moscow. Thus, Western analysts have often suspected behind-the-scenes instability within the top leadership. There was much speculation that the hard-liners and the pro-Soviet faction might seek to oust Gustav Husák, a moderate conservative. Such theorizing, however, was laid to rest in May 1975, when Husák, then chief of the party, became president of the Republic (with Moscow's backing). This event would appear to suggest that the moderate conservatives have gained additional influence at the expense of the other factions. The importance of this development lies in the fact that unlike the other factions that advocate a firm stand against those involved in the events of 1968, Husák feels that a measure of reconciliation is an essential prerequisite for the achievement of any long-term economic and thus political success in his regime. He has given an indication of leaning toward some kind of limited economic reforms and of coming to terms with the larger part of the political and professional elite that has been in internal "exile" since 1969.[31]

It is unlikely that the rank and file of the Czechoslovak Communist party would take an initiative toward a liberalization process. The present membership, though restored approximately to pre-1968 levels, consists primarily of people who regard their party affiliation purely as a means of improving their social and economic position.[32] Their reaction to political events is to cling to the status quo. Therefore, the impact of the Western European communist parties on the party in Czechoslovakia could be minimal or even negative, depending on how well Husák manages to deal with recent challenges from prominent intellectuals. Judging by the relatively mild government action taken against the dissidents, some observers have concluded that the party moderates have won the second round over the hard-liners in what may well be a long fight.[33] According to these observers, the dissident issue has given the moderate conservatives an advantage in party squabbles since they can argue that any harsh measures would only increase the vehemence of the protests and hostility from the Western European communist parties. This, however, should not be interpreted to mean that this faction holds any sympathy for Eurocommunism, the ideology of which bears too dangerous a resemblance to that of the Prague spring, the revival of which would be fatal for the entire leadership.

A similar situation exists in East Germany. Although Moscow remains the ultimate guarantor of the preservation of the ruling elite there, the preservation of domestic stability falls to the Honecker regime. It must maintain the passive loyalty of the population by maintaining the rate of improvement in the living standard—not an easy accomplishment in the light of present economic difficulties.

That there have long been tensions and rivalries within the top party leadership concerning the critical problems facing East Germany is well known. These rivalries did not dissipate with Walter Ulbricht's fall and the rise of Erich Honecker to the office of first-secretary in May 1971. On the contrary, the absence of Ulbricht, with his prestige and authority in the party, has only complicated the situation. Until the fall of 1976, it seemed that Honecker's ability to place a number of his supporters in key positions was an indication of his growing strength within the party and government bureaucracies. Honecker's ally, Horst Sindermann, became prime minister and his rival, Willi Stoph, was relegated to the post of head of the state Council, which by virtue of the 1975 revisions of the constitution lost a great deal of its power.[34] However, since then, potentially important changes have taken place within the top hierarchy: Stoph regained his position of prime minister and another politburo rival of Honecker's, Günter Mittag, who led the faction of technocrats responsible for economic reforms in the 1960s, was moved from a government position to the post of secretary of the party's central committee.[35]

What all this means for Honecker personally is far from clear. At the time of these changes, he added to his then current positions as first-secretary of the party and head of the National Defense Council the purely titular post of chief of the state Council. His loyal subordinate, Werner Krolikowski, was appointed as one of the two first deputy prime ministers. At the very least, it seems that although he is in no immediate danger of losing the top job, Honecker is not in a stable position and that a succession crisis still exists within the leadership. What inhibits dissension is the fear that any internal conflict could trigger reactions in the society at large that would imperil the party itself. For the same reason, all factions seem to be unconditionally loyal to the Soviet Union.

This problem explains, in varying degrees, one of the main features of East German foreign policy—an increasingly close and dependent relationship with the Soviet Union. East German leaders are firm supporters of Soviet views on all issues ranging from China to détente; thus, they once again are fitting their own rapprochement with the West into the Soviet timetable. In addition, the Soviet- East German treaty of "friendship, cooperation, and mutual assistance" signed on October 7, 1975, which went further than any similar treaty with other bloc countries, extended East Germany's military obligations to the Soviet Union to include the defense of Soviet borders in Asia.[36] Within the European communist movement, East Germany has continued to be a meticulous supporter of all Soviet positions and the most enthusiastic proponent of Soviet domination of the international communist movement. However, it is not inconceivable that given the impact of certain external events on the East German sociopolitical system, the East German political elites could find it necessary to return to the Ulbricht policy of sabotaging Soviet détente policies. This could be done successfully only by claiming a certain independence from Moscow at either the party or the state level by fostering East Germany's nationalism as a deliberate policy.

In Poland, since he became first-secretary of the Polish United Workers party in December 1970, Edward Gierek, in a series of swift political moves disposed of most of his rivals one by one. The purge of Wladyslaw Gomulka's supporters and the right-wing Moczar group from top party and government positions was completed at the seventh party congress in December 1975.[37] From the top, the purge gradually descended to the provinces and resulted in the replacement of twelve out of the eighteen provincial party secretaries. The vacancies were filled with Gierek's own supporters, mostly younger men from his power base in Silesia, thus establishing him as senior leader in the top echelon of the party. In addition to Gierek, five of the nineteen members of the politburo and the secretariat are Silesians; together with him, they have come to constitute the "inner circle" of the new top leadership. However, in addition to Gierek's moderate "Silesian group," there still exists an influential conservative faction led by Prime Minister Piotr Jaroszeqicz.

Although the regime had achieved a degree of general popularity in its first five years, it has since come under growing criticism both from inside and outside the party for not introducing any comprehensive changes. The 1971-1975 economic policies have not resolved Poland's economic difficulties. Severe shortages of consumer goods persist, and it was the government's effort to counter these shortages with sharp price increases in June 1976 that provoked strikes and riots by the workers. Although, so far no significant split has occurred within the leadership, there are many rank and file Communists who openly demand some immediate political liberalization, without which, they are convinced, the economy will never work well.[38] This is strong resistance, however, especially in the middle echelons of the party and government bureaucracy, to political reform. These bureaucrats are pressuring Gierek to resist any call for reforms and instead recommend more repressive policies under which popular economic measures could be imposed without fear of political crisis.

Although the Gierek team realizes that it has exhausted all conventional means of boosting production and that some economic liberalization is necessary, it is apprehensive on two counts: first, that Moscow might oppose such measures and, second, that if such measures are instituted, the population might make still greater demands for further reforms. The Soviet leaders, however, seem to be aware that given the situation that exists in Poland the regime really has little choice but to proceed with some internal changes. Moreover, the existence of Eurocommunism has potentially enlarged the scope of Gierek's domestic maneuvers. How far he will be disposed to exploit this situation to expand the perimeters of internal and external political freedom is impossible to determine with any certainty. On the one hand, the social profile of the present leadership differs radically from that of the Gomulka group. Besides their relative youth, the Gierek men are products of industrialization; they are not professional revolutionaries, but administrators, and as such they are less ideological and more pragmatic than their predecessors. On the other hand, they represent only the first "postrevolutionary" generation; whereas it requires at least three generations for any ruling elite to develop a moderate political culture.[39] Thus, with regard to the possibility of economic as well as political liberalization, it is more likely that the present regime will continue to give priority to economic over political reforms and that it will make concessions in the political sphere only insofar as they are deemed necessary in order not to impede economic progress.

At the December 1976 central committee meeting, the Polish leadership made a series of important economic decisions that it believes can restore the country's political stability.[40] The most important were the decisions to promote private business and to halt the program of all-out economic growth and inflationary wages that had been in effect since 1971. Instead, it was decided to put more funds into subsidizing the low prices of agricultural produce and into the production of consumer goods in general. This type of situation, however, cannot continue indefinitely for the subsidies that keep consumer prices down cost something like 12% of Poland's GNP. If maintained for any prolonged period, they would dry out future industrial investments.

There is a certain interesting similarity between the situation in Italy and that developing in Poland. As in the case in Italy, sometime during the next few years, a decision will have to be made by the Polish government as to how and when to cut consumer subsidies. Again, as in Italy, where the ruling Christian Democrats have to come to terms with the Communist party, in Poland, the Communist party establishment may have to come to terms with a coalition of discontented workers, restive intellectuals, and rebellious churchmen, who together amount to a center of power outside the governing party. If either government wants to be successful in imposing the necessary austerity measures, it may have no alternative but to consult with the opposition. In Poland, as in Italy, these negotiations could be informal at the beginning in order not to provoke dangerous internal instability or external opposition. Given this similarity between them, it can be argued that Italy's political development may become an inspiration to the Polish regime. Furthermore, if the domestic opposition is supported by the Italian Communists in demanding a "historic compromise" in Poland as well, mere inspiration will have become political pressure.[41]

Turning to the Bulgarian regime, one can see that it has the oldest politburo in Eastern Europe. A cursory survey of the country's top leadership shows that in the near future, the regime will face the problem of succession.[42] Furthermore, although Todor Zhivkov, first-secretary of the party, has been in this job since 1954 and has been prime minister since 1962, he has never really managed to establish his authority either within the party or in the government bureaucracy. How serious a challenge Zhivkov faces today is difficult to establish for since 1965 his position has been strengthened.[43] However, the potential for the emergence of intraparty opposition to his leadership exists, especially from the younger members of the central committee, who seem to be uncomfortable with Zhivkov's orthodoxy. The most recent evidence of an internal feud or a power struggle was the abrupt dismissal of Boris Velchev from both the politburo and the party's central committee in May 1977.[44] Significantly enough, before his dismissal Velebov supervised the Bulgarian party's relations with foreign communist parties. He was replaced by Dmitri Stanishev, the editor in chief of the party newspaper, which had strongly criticized Eurocommunism. This could indicate that in part the backstage conflict was over fundamental policies or ideologies.

If Eurocommunism remains unacceptable to the present Bulgarian regime, it is certainly not to the Rumanian one—despite the fact that both regimes are equally orthodox in their domestic policies. Rumania is a one-man system and, as such, has the strengths and weaknesses associated with any personal dictatorship.[45] Nicolae Ceausescu, general secretary of the Rumanian Communist party and president of the state Council, has not only steadily tightened his grip over the most important political positions in the party and government hierarchies but has also made himself the object of an all-embracing personality cult. Taking over in 1965, he gradually got rid of his old colleagues and, in a manner reminiscent of Khrushchev's, replaced them with younger personal followers. This major shakeup was not confined to the top echelons but was extended through the lower levels of the pyramid as well. In addition, Ceausescu's emphasis on symbolic political participation and on having personal contact with the rank and file members of the party has further strengthened his power position by bypassing bureaucratic channels and structures in obtaining information and by giving him the image of a leader who shows concern for the average citizen.

Although at present there is no identifiable opposition to his leadership, it is safe to say that there must be some apprehension in the party over Ceausescu's growing power. There have been signs of discontent with Ceausescu even in the top ranks of the party and the state bureaucracy. This is the most convincing single explanation for the large number of important personnel changes since 1972 at both high and intermediate levels in the government. In general, Ceausescu's present position depends on both his domestic and foreign policy successes. Although he has encouraged the limited involvement of the masses in Rumanian politics, he has simultaneously reduced the power of the socioeconomic elites. This course, it should be stressed, holds potential dangers for the regime's stability. Although the general population undoubtedly welcomes its new political role, it is probable that its demand for a higher living standard is greater than its desire for the symbolic right of limited political participation. Improved living conditions, in turn, depend on rapid economic development. To deliver such a program, Ceausescu must have the cooperation of the socioeconomic elites. Internally, then, Ceausescu seems to have reached the limits of his independence despite the fact that it can be said that his policy of independence and stress on national tradition has been well received by both the masses and the socioeconomic elites and thus has become one of his regime's chief sources of stability.

Given the link between foreign policy and domestic support, it is not surprising that the Ceausescu leadership views the independent Western European communist parties as welcome allies. To understand the nature of this alliance, we must understand the nature of Rumanian communism. Communism in Rumania is a mix of orthodox Marxism-Leninism, nationalism and populism: the emphasis on the supremacy of the party and democratic centralism is intertwined with the concept of the "national road." According to the latter notion, each communist party must apply the general elements of Marxism-Leninism within the national context—i.e., within the parameters of existing socioeconomic and cultural traditions in each country. Ceausescu has repeatedly rejected any application of a supranational "model" of socialism. According to him, there is a Rumanian way, a Soviet way, a Eurocommunist way, and so on. Thus, for example, when the Western European communists rejected the concept of dictatorship of the proletariat, the Rumanian regime was quick to declare that this concept remained valid for its own society. It is, therefore, in its insistence on independence vis-à-vis Moscow and not on democracy that a convergence of attitudes between the Ceausescu leadership and the Eurocommunists occurs.

Although both the Sino-Soviet conflict and the Soviet-American rapprochement enabled Rumania to carve out its autonomous niche, they have also provided definite limits to its independence. Since the West's acceptance of the status quo Eurodétente, Rumania's independence and overtures toward the West have lost their novelty and much of their attractiveness. On the other hand, Sino-Soviet relations have deteriorated to the point that each country now regards the other as its principal enemy. The conflict, thus, has lost its usefulness for Rumania, which could exploit it only so long as there was a possibility for reconciliation. This being so, any broadening of Rumania's independence in Ceausescu's view can come only through his country's cooperation with those Western European communist parties that demand not only that the leading role of the CPSU be minimized but that it be abolished. Such cooperation—if not an overt alliance—was most visible at the conference of the European communist parties in Berlin in June, where the Rumanian delegation, together with the Yugoslav, sided with the Eurocommunist parties.[46]

Although in assessing the situation in Eastern Europe we have found that both the internal stability and the impact of Eurocommunism on this region varies from country to country, the following general conclusion seems to be appropriate. All in all, Eurocommunism exercises an influence on both internal and bloc relations. By their very existence, the Eurocommunist parties tend not only to encourage the dissident movements in these countries but also to legitimize their demands. Furthermore, by actively supporting domestic opposition in the Eastern European countries either by providing "existential asylum" to prominent Eastern European intellectuals or by publishing their works, the Eurocommunist parties stimulate disagreements within the top Eastern European leaderships.[47] Those disagreements that deal with Eurocommunist bridge building have the capacity to develop into disputes over fundamental social and economic (if not immediately political) issues. Of these, the most important focus on the issues of economic growth and an improved standard of living. The economic difficulties that the Eastern European countries have been experiencing since at least 1974 in part signal the exhaustion of the administrative economic model and thus threaten their internal stability.

It is here that the Eurocommunists' ideological innovations strategically intersect with ongoing crises in Eastern Europe.[48] By recognizing at least in theory the need for genuine democratic participation and political compromise as conditions for solving the economic crisis in the West, Eurocommunism affirms the indispensable contribution to economic efficiency of a broadly based and more open political process. In the search for a solution that would stabilize the domestic situation in their own countries, the Eastern European political elites cannot totally disregard the Eurocommunist model. This is because unlike some other models of socialism (e.g., Maoism and Castroism) Eurocommunism is a phenomenon too close to home to be discounted as distant and primitive and therefore inapplicable to Eastern Europe. Some Eastern European leaders may well decide that the only way to improve their own economies lies in a historic compromise like the Italian, in the gradual opening up of their own political systems. So far, however, there are signs that only the Hungarians and to a certain extent the Poles have taken a positive view of the need for domestic reforms. The Rumanians, though domestically committed to a more or less doctrinaire Marxism-Leninism, are "Eurocommunist" in their foreign policy. As of now, the other Eastern European regimes exhibit varying degrees of hostility toward and fear of democratization. In the immediate future, their tendency will be to suppress domestic opposition and to seek political and ideological support from Moscow.

Consequently, there is every reason to expect that for the next five to ten years, the situation in Eastern Europe will be unstable. On the one hand, in those countries in which the political elites find it impossible to modernize their political system, the dynamics of economic decline will breed social unrest, along with the inevitable repercussions in external relations that come with it. Such a course of events is most likely in Czechoslovakia and East Germany. On the other hand, it is not at all inconceivable that countries like Hungary and Poland will try to protect their domestic reforms against Soviet interference. In addition to forming an ideological alliance with the Eurocommunist parties, they may also attempt to form a subregional union with each other.[49] Finally, for all Eastern European political leaders, Eurocommunism is potentially an important ally against Soviet hegemony. How much autonomy a given regime demands will depend more on its domestic security than on whether it clings to Marxist-Leninist orthodoxy. Like the Sino-Soviet rift, the dispute between the Eurocommunist parties and the Soviet Union can encourage the nationalistic tendencies of otherwise highly authoritarian regimes. That conservative leaders tend to be nationalistic is proven not only by the positions of Enver Hoxha and Ceausescu but also by those of Ulbricht and Moczar.

Soviet Options

Given this general situation, what options are open to the Soviet Union in dealing with Eastern Europe? This question can be dealt with here only in broad terms. Hypothetically, Moscow has four options open to it: (1) a kind of Marshall Plan; (2) socialist integration; (3) Finlandization; and (4) military intervention. The first option would entail providing lavish material aid to the Eastern European regimes in order to help them overcome their economic difficulties. The second option would force an increase in the economic integration of the bloc. The third option would involve allowing the individual countries to follow their own independent domestic political development. Finally, with the fourth option, the Soviet Union could prevent whatever it perceived as threatening its own interests in Eastern Europe through military intervention there.

Of these four options, the first is clearly out of the question. The Soviet Union is obviously in no position to give permanent economic aid to the Eastern European regimes and can give help solely on an emergency basis.[50] Furthermore, with its $16 billion debt to the West, and the need for more Western credit in the future, the Soviet Union must earn hard currency by pushing its exports to the West and not to Eastern Europe.[51]

Recent experience suggests that the Soviet strategy of maintaining control over Eastern Europe falls back on the old formula of more "socialist integration."[52] The *negative* strategic aim of such integration is to prevent forces at either the domestic or the national level in these countries from assuming disruptive dimensions for the Soviet Union. On the *positive* side, the integration of Eastern European economies serves as a means of strengthening Moscow's control over their dealings with the West and over their own domestic affairs. Hence, the expected long-term consequence of this option would be to block not only "different political roads" to socialism but different "economic roads" as well. Whereas in the 1960s Soviet leaders sought integration through the creation of a supranational planning body and failed, in the 1970s they sought integration "from the bottom up": through a systematic interlocking of basic elements of the Eastern European economies with each other and primarily with the Soviet Union, they attempted to create what they hoped would be "irreversible facts." Such was the conception of the "Complex Program for the Further Deepening and Improvement of Cooperation and Development of Socialist Economic Integration of the Member Countries of Comecon," passed in 1971.[53] Rather than the pursuit of economic integration on a market or a monetary basis, its aim was integration of the production process. Although the dream of a "unified common plan" was not given up, the program expressly declared that "socialist integration is not accomplished by the establishment of supranational organs." In addition to an interlocking network of economic interdependence, Soviet leaders put stress on political, military, and ideological integration, too, by setting up the "permanent operational mechanism" for the Warsaw Pact and a foreign ministers' council that would coordinate bloc policies under Moscow's guidance.

Until 1973, the Soviet Union had been largely unsuccessful in uniting all of its Eastern European allies behind these plans. On the one hand, East Germany and Bulgaria advocated increased coordination and specialization among the bloc economies. In fact, these countries had always been eager to build close economic ties with the Soviet Union for the Soviet Union was their most important market, and in the case of Bulgaria a source of financial aid as well. By contrast, Rumania was extremely reluctant to support any Comecon integration efforts. Other Eastern European countries, in one way or another, were also averse to excessive integration, fearing that it would restrict their vital trade with the West. The Hungarian leaders, furthermore, worried that bloc integration would conflict with their domestic economic reforms.[54]

Since 1973, however, the critical world economic situation characterized by Western recession and high oil prices has been conducive to promoting the Soviet Union's Eastern European plans. For their part, the Eastern European members of Comecon, faced with the shrinking possibility of exporting goods to the West as a result of the Western recession, had very little choice but to readjust the structure of their export production toward increased trade with the Soviet Union. The fact that all these countries are poor in most mineral resources and, with the exception of Rumania, have virtually no oil of their own, serves only to compound their problems. Because of their shortages of convertible currencies, they can acquire these commodities in necessary quantities only from the Soviet Union. Thus, the extent of their dependence on the Soviet Union for critical raw materials is still further increased. Table 1 indicates the degree of dependence of the Eastern European economies on Soviet raw materials as a portion of their total import needs.[55]

Economic pressures since 1973 have forced even Rumania to diminish opposition to Comecon. Although its economic cooperation with the Soviet Union remains selective—the Soviet Union still accounts for only 16% of Rumania's foreign trade—its growing balance of payments deficit with the West and the need for raw materials have led it to strengthen its economic ties with the Soviet Union, a move that includes participation in Soviet extracting industries.[56]

In sum, Moscow retains a unique advantage over the Eastern European economies. It is not only the biggest steady customer for their products but also their chief source of oil and other critical raw materials. Realizing these facts, it tried to utilize the world energy crisis to force the Eastern European regimes to accept both joint investment projects and supranational planning. In 1974, these regimes formally agreed to the idea of integrating their own five-year plans with each other and with the Soviet Union, a move that can be regarded as the embryo of some future supranational planning body. When seen in this light, then, a major motivation behind Moscow's 1975 price increases of oil and other raw materials to the Eastern European economies can be interpreted as an additional pressure on their regimes to accept the comprehensive integration of Eastern Europe. By utilizing the energy crisis further to stress Eastern Europe's dependence on the Soviet economy, it hopes to control events there.

T A B L E 1.   **Eastern European dependence on Soviet raw materials.**

	CRUDE OIL AND OIL PRODUCTS	COKING COAL	IRON ORE
Bulgaria	100%	95%	85%
Czechoslovakia	92	20	75
East Germany	89	60	80
Hungary	88	50	77
Poland	90	0	60
Rumania	0	60	60

This strategy of economic hegemony is very risky since it assumes that the Eastern European regimes are not only willing but able to agree to these integrative measures. Given the need of the political elites in each of these countries to secure a rising standard of living for their population—a program that depends on the availability of financial resources and cheap raw materials—it is very unlikely that they could agree to such Soviet demands. Furthermore, the continuation of Soviet economic pressures would only cause the deterioration of the Eastern European economies and thus undermine the stability of the present regimes or force them to assert their independence from Moscow.

The extent to which Moscow will continue to exercise this strategy of economic hegemony is open to question. Forcing the Eastern European countries to increase their participation in long-range development projects in the Soviet Union beyond a certain point may generate tension between the Eastern European regimes and Moscow. It has been reported that the high Soviet prices for oil have sparked intense debate within Comecon. Although the Eastern European leaders are willing to concede that some price increases were necessary, they are apparently balking at the magnitude of the increases demanded by the Soviets. This tension could be further exacerbated by the economics of détente. Domestic interests motivate Soviet leaders to increase their trade with the West. But since it is unlikely that they can pay for Western imports through the sale of their manufactured goods, they will have to divert their exports of raw materials from Eastern Europe in order to do so. A policy of this sort will necessarily generate considerable intrabloc frictions and further intensify the centrifugal forces we earlier saw at work. Specifically, the search of the Eastern European regimes for non-Soviet raw materials may not only further separate their own foreign policy interests from those of the Soviet Union but may also necessitate important domestic reforms in order to meet their new foreign trade obligations. In other words, the strategy of economic hegemony, if combined with the economics of détente, may get Moscow into a situation that it has always tried to avoid: trouble in or with several Eastern European countries at the same time.

Although Moscow has clearly been more willing to tolerate some independent domestic developments in Eastern Europe in return for "solidarity" on international issues, it has always done so within carefully defined limits. Allowing the Finlandization of Eastern Europe (the third option), however, is an altogether different matter. Given the close connection between ideological and military security, Finlandization would not insure Soviet interests in this region since Eastern Europe is not only the Soviet Union's military buffer zone against the West but its ideological shield as well. The Soviet leaders are determined to avoid any democratic changes in Eastern Europe for they fear these changes would appeal to many social forces in the Soviet Union itself. Such an appeal would pose a direct threat to its own internal security. This being the case, the Soviet Union could not allow the individual countries to follow their own independent internal development: sooner or later, their domestic reforms would challenge Soviet ideological preeminence.

This problem was underlined by Moscow's opposition to the Prague spring of 1968. Although it is futile to search for the limits of Soviet tolerance to developments in Eastern Europe, its intervention in Czechoslovakia and its nonintervention in Hungary and Rumania in the same period suggest that *moderate* economic reforms or *relatively* independent foreign policies may be acceptable to the Soviet Union. The modified Czechoslovak political system that had provoked Soviet intervention, entailing as it did freedom of the press and the prospect of institutionalized competition for power, had simply overstepped these limits.[57] However, given the general situation in the bloc countries and the ideological bridge building that is taking place on the part of the Eurocommunist parties toward Eastern Europe, the Prague spring must still be viewed as neither a unique nor an outdated phenomenon in that area. From the preceding background, we must conclude that as long as the Soviets perceive their security in Eastern Europe in both strategic and ideological terms, military intervention will be the only realistic option they have left in coping with Eastern Europe.

The Future of Détente

At the beginning of this chapter, I argued that the structure of both the détente and the Eurodétente relationship was built on the preservation of the status quo in Europe. In the course of this survey, it has become clear that this status quo is currently being challenged by forces in the West as well as the East. The seemingly irreversible growth of the communist parties has seriously undermined the internal and external cohesion of several Western European countries. The dissident movement in many Eastern European countries and the yearning for greater independence by some of their leaders have created similar problems in the Eastern bloc. However, although the instabilities in the East are kept in check by the continuing determination of the Soviet Union to retain control over this region, there is no such "stabilizing" factor in Western Europe. Indeed, the erosion of NATO's military strength and the simultaneous increase of the

Soviet military presence in Eastern Europe have further exacerbated the situation. In the face of these developments the future of both détente and Eurodétente is in doubt.

Perhaps the best way to sort out the prospects for stable U.S.-Soviet relations in Europe is to visualize what each superpower must try to avoid in this region. From this angle it should then be possible to make a more definite diagnosis of the future of détente. From Washington's point of view, the worst thing would be to see Western Europe fall under Soviet political and/or ideological influence. From Moscow's point of view, the worst thing would be to witness some form of unification of Western Europe by leftist forces, these forces treating the Soviet system as ideologically obsolete. In doing so, the Western Europeans would undermine the legitimacy of Soviet preeminence in Eastern Europe and thus the very basis of détente in Europe. Although the U.S. could decide to ignore the breakdown of Eurodétente and continue its détente with the Soviet Union, the chances are that it would be drawn into the conflict since inaction on the part of the United States could well lead not merely to the Finlandization of Western Europe but to its sovietization as well.

These, then, are the foreign policy nightmares that both these powers will try to avoid. What is common to their nightmares is the crucial role that the future of Western Europe plays in them. From this it follows that both powers have an interest in preventing socialism in Western Europe. However, as far as the present situation there is concerned, they both have very few options open. Nothing short of total abandonment of their détente relationship is likely to prevent the eventual radicalization of Western European societies. Meanwhile, however, Western Europe faces the steady buildup of Soviet military power. Given the extreme reluctance of the many lame duck governments to increase their own defense spending, along with the popular perception of the absence of a Soviet threat to that region, Western Europe may well face a state of affairs in which its governments no longer feel strong enough, politically and militarily, to oppose the Soviet Union on major European issues.

What should the long-range American policy objectives in Europe be? All that the United States can do is steer a difficult course between Scylla and Charybdis—that is to say, try to prevent both the deterioration of the European military balance, on the one hand, and the Sovietization of Western European countries, on the other. In order not to get caught in a "no-win" situation in Europe, the United States must realize not only the *limits* and *extent* of its influence over events there but also the *nature* of the challenge. The permanent goal of U.S. interest in Europe has been to prevent the expansion of Soviet power and to encourage its contraction wherever possible. Because of its equation of the international communist movement with the Soviet Union, the United States has historically opposed the Western European communist parties as well. Today, however, the growing autonomy of the Western European communist parties, together with their apparent commitment to civil liberties, seems to detract from the force of the arguments behind U.S. opposition to communism in Western Europe. The U.S. must therefore reaccess its policy toward the Eurocommunists despite the risks involved.

Although the autonomy of the Eurocommunist parties vis-à-vis the Soviet Union is indisputable, their commitment to democracy and their absolute independence from the Soviet Union are not as yet established. Although there is little the United States can do to test the sincerity of their commitment to democracy before they actually come to power, what it can do to insure their independence is to encourage their open split with Moscow. Moreover, any attempts at excluding Eurocommunist participation from Western European governments plays into the hands of the Soviets, for whom these parties remain useful only so long as they remain the opposition. Only in this outsider's position do they remain a dependable source of pressure in their own countries against high military spending and other related defense issues. Only in this position can they serve as bargaining chips in Moscow's European diplomacy.

As noted earlier, a look at the background of the relations between the Soviet Union and the Western European communist parties suggests that the frictions and differences that divide them are significant. Whether for domestic or foreign policy reasons the Eurocommunists are gradually drawing a sharp line between their policies and those followed in the Eastern bloc. They differ not only over the means of the transition from capitalism to socialism but also over the place of Moscow in the international communist movement and (most important) over the true nature of socialist society. Recently, the Eurocommunists have even shown independence on several important foreign policy issues. The line of the Italian and the Spanish parties on NATO and the Common Market is now strikingly divergent from that of Moscow. Although Moscow would welcome the reduction of American troops in Europe, the Eurocommunists publicly oppose any "unilateral change" in the East-West power relationship. In sum, the Eurocommunists are progressively creating an ideology and pursuing basic interests that are unrelated to those of the Soviet Union.

By their very logic, these differences should translate into an open rupture between the two. With increasing frequency, both Eurocommunist parties and the Eastern bloc communist leaders are meeting on a regional basis, thus creating the preconditions for the eventual regional division of pan-European communism. Whether the Eurocommunists are willing to go so far is beside the point. Sooner or later, they will be forced into severing their relations with the Soviet Union over an important international issue: the future of Eastern Europe.

Specifically, they could not but oppose the Soviets' insistence on preserving their ideological sphere of influence if it took the form of military intervention in that region; this would precipitate the final split between them. Here, of course, lies the danger to European détente. The Soviet leaders can complain that the U.S. call for the freer exchange of ideas was actually intended to "disarm" socialism ideologically. However, the Eurocommunists' insistence on the free flow of ideas could not be dismissed so easily. Neither could their proposal calling for the eventual dissolution of the Common Market and its replacement with the concept of a "greater Europe," which would include the Eastern European countries as well.

The Soviet-Eurocommunist rupture could bring old historical conflicts to the surface, conflicts that would be intensified by the ideological competition for the leadership of the world communist movement. According to many Western experts, the Soviet leaders cannot give up this leadership mainly because of imperatives within the Soviet system. Their own domestic legitimacy, and indeed the legitimacy of the political apparatus of the Soviet state, rests in part on their claim that the Soviet Union is the recognized leader of a historical movement that transcends national and regional boundaries. Although Soviet supremacy in the communist world has been challenged by both Yugoslavia and China, a Western European challenge would be much more difficult to contend with because it would represent the first time that the Soviet Union had been challenged by a society superior to its own. As a result, the rupture would simultaneously threaten the ideological-political base of both the Soviet Union's domestic system and its foreign policy objectives, making any realistic East-West compromise very difficult to achieve. Thus, although the détente atmosphere may be compatible with the "struggle of ideas" between states that maintain adherence to *different* ideologies, it may ironically not survive the ideological tension between states that claim devotion to the *same* ideals.

The growing irrelevance of communist ideology for the problems of international relations is shown not only by the gradual fragmentation of the communist movement but by its polarization as well. In this context, then, it may even be argued that the split between Moscow and the Eurocommunists could lead to the gradual "deideologization" of Soviet foreign policy and thus create prospects for a genuine détente between the superpowers. The Soviet leaders could recognize that the benefits connected with the withdrawal from communist universalism far outweigh the losses. They may redefine their foreign policy objectives in terms of the traditional great power game, thus putting emphasis not on ideology but on economic and military power. Indeed, there are already some indications that Moscow is thinking along these lines. As we have seen in their relations with the Eastern Europeans, for example, the Soviets have been stressing economic hegemony. Consequently, Eurocommunism could be credited with one colossal achievement: an early "decoupling" of Soviet foreign policy interests from communist ideology.

Notes

1. See, for example, President Nixon's February 1970 message to Congress, cited in Bennett Kovrig, *The Myth of Liberation: East-Central Europe in U.S. Diplomacy and Politics since 1941* (Baltimore: Johns Hopkins Press, 1973), p. 293. Contrary to what most other people say, Richard Davy ("The CSCE Summit," *The World Today*, September 1975, pp. 349-353) cleverly argues that the main reason behind Western insistence on the "basket three" of the Helsinki declaration was the preservation of the status quo in Eastern Europe:

   > The main threat to security since the end of the Second World War has been the discontent in Eastern Europe caused by the suppression of human rights as well by economic deprivation. Bring to Eastern Europe a basket full of human rights, human contacts, and economic benefits, it was argued, and the governments of the area would become more popular, more secure, and less dependent on the presence of Soviet troops. Tension would then be lowered and security increased.

2. Curiously enough, the remaining territorial disputes exist only within the respective blocs: Transylvania, Macedonia, Bessarabia, Cyprus, and South Tyrol.

3. Although not always in full accord, the basic security interests of the Eastern bloc regimes, with the exception of Rumania, have generally overlapped with those of the Soviet Union. See Peter Bender, *East Europe in Search of Security* (London: Chatto & Windus, 1972); Robert R. King and Robert W. Dean, eds., *East European Perspectives on European Security and Cooperation* (New York: Praeger, 1974); and Karl E. Birnbaum, "The Members of the Warsaw Treaty Organization and the Conference on Security and Cooperation in Europe," *Cooperation and Conflict*, 9, no. 1 (1974): 29-34.

4. See, for example, "Manifesto Charging Rights Violations in Czechoslovakia," *New York Times*, January 27, 1977; Ellen Lentz, "East Germany Tightening Curbs, But Dissidents Say They'll Fight On," ibid., November 30, 1976; Malcolm W. Browne, "9 Rumanians Appeal to Signers of Helsinki Accord over Rights," ibid., February 15, 1977; and Michael Getler, "East Bloc Dissent Tests Pledges Given at Helsinki," *Washington Post*, February 6, 1977.

5. Ellen Lentz, "East German Leaders Seem Certain That Unrest Is Now under Control," *New York Times*, May 10, 1977.

6. Paul Hofmann, "Czech Leaders Are Reported Split on How to Deal with Rights Issues," ibid., February 7, 1977. For a discussion on Soviet efforts to promote the consolidation of the Eastern bloc during this period see J. F. Brown, "Détente and Soviet Policy in Eastern Europe," *Survey*, 20 (Spring-Summer 1974): 46-58.

7. *Evropa Archiv*, no. 30 (1975): Z187-188.

8. *L'Humanité*, November 18, 1975; *Pravda*, March 2, 1976; *New York Times*, July 1, 1976.

9. *L'Unità*, June 12, 1969; ibid., March 14, 1972.

10. The Eurocommunist parties' insistence on "internationalism" also enabled them, for example, to criticize policies of the Portuguese Communists. See K. S. Karol, "The Portuguese Obsession," *Le Nouvel Observateur*, June 2, 1975.

11. For examples of recent critical Italian Communist party assessments of the situation in Eastern Europe see Franco Bertone, "Poland: The Cost of 'Truth' Pricing," *Rinascita*, July 2, 1976; and Lucio Lombardo Radice, "Czechoslovakia: But Why Life Is Elsewhere," ibid., August 27, 1976.

12. See, for example, *L'Humanité*, December 13, 1975; ibid., October 22, 1976.

13. Ibid., February 28, 1976.

14. Data extrapolated from *Statistisches Jahrbuch der Deutschen Demokratischen Republik* (Berlin: VEB Deutscher Zentralverlag, 1976); *Statisticka rocenka* (Praha: Státní nakl. technické literatury, 1976); *Statisztika evkonyv* (Budapest: Statisztikai Hivatal, 1975); *Anuaarul Statistic al RSR* (Bucharest: Direcţia Centrală de Statistică, 1975); and *Economic Bulletin for Europe* (New York: United Nations, 1976), 28: 66-68.

15. Hans-Hermann Hohmann, Michael Kaser, and Karl C. Talheim, eds., *The Economic Systems of Eastern Europe* (Berkeley: University of California Press, 1975), especially pp. 36-38, 71-73, 207-214.

16. Ota Sik, "The Economic Imperialism of Stalinism," *Problems of Communism*, 20 (May-June 1971): 10.

17. Arpad A. Kadarkay, "Hungary: An Experiment in Communism," *Western Political Quarterly*, 26 (June 1973): 280-301.

18. This estimate was made by Chase Manhattan Bank. It was reported in *Business Week*, no. 2473 (March 7, 1977): 40.

19. The 1975 oil hike corresponded to an increase from $2.80 per barrel to $7.15 per barrel. See Danilo A. Rigassi, "USSR Becomes World's Leading Oil Producer," *World Oil*, August 15, 1975.

20. "Hungarian Leader Says Energy Prices Cause Problems," *New York Times*, March 18, 1975.

21. Erich Honecker, *Neues Deutschland*, May 18, 1977.

22. Michael Kaser, "Eastern Europe's economies in 1976-80," *The World Today*, September 1976.

23. Similar social discontent was in evidence in several key areas of Bulgaria and Rumania in February and September 1972, respectively. See F. Stephen

Larrabee, "Bulgaria's Politics of Conformity," *Problems of Communism,* 21 (July–August 1971): 51. Also see Trond Gilberg, "Ceausescu's Romania," ibid., 23 (July–August 1974): 29–43.

24. See, for example, "Polish Primate Appeals for Truth and Mercy," *New York Times,* November 22, 1976.

25. "Making the Dissidents Pay the Price," *Time,* December 20, 1976; Browne, "9 Rumanians Appeal."

26. Thomas E. Haneghan, "Human Rights Protests in Eastern Europe," *The World Today,* March 1977, pp. 91–100.

27. Charles Gati, "The Kadar Mystique," *Problems of Communism,* 23 (May–June 1974): 28–33.

28. William F. Robinson, *The Pattern of Reforms in Hungary* (New York: Praeger, 1973), pp. 216–220.

29. Cited in Gati, "The Kadar Mystique," p. 15.

30. "Kadar Says He Sees No Anti-Soviet Stand among Reds in West," *New York Times,* December 8, 1976.

31. Alex Pravda, "Czechoslovakia: The Legacy of 1968," *The World Today,* August 1976, pp. 282–286.

32. *World Strength of the Communist Party Organizations* (Washington, D.C.: U.S. Dept. of State, Bureau of Intelligence and Research, Government Printing Office, 1972), p. 147.

33. See, for example, Paul Hofmann, "Czech Hard-Liners Said to Lose Round in Dispute on Rights," *New York Times,* February 12, 1977. Although Vasil Bilak, a hard-line party secretary, declared that the dissidents will face "serious consequences" for their activities, nothing "serious" has so far happened to them. For Bilak's speech see *Rudé právo* (Prague) February 7, 1977.

34. Peter C. Ludz, "The SED Leadership in Transition," *Problems of Communism,* 19 (May–June 1970): 23–31, and "Continuity and Change since Ulbricht," ibid., 21 (March–April 1972): 46–55.

35. "East German Prime Minister Names New Council of Ministers," *New York Times,* November 4, 1977.

36. *Europa Archiv,* no. 30 (1975): Z187–188.

37. Adam Bromke, "A New Political Style," *Problems of Communism,* 21 (September–October 1972): 1–3.

38. Flora Lewis, "Poland Softens Stand on Critics," *New York Times,* January 16, 1977, and "Many Poles Term Unrest Far Deeper Than Economic," ibid., January 26, 1977.

39. Jan Szcepanski, *Polish Society* (New York: Random House, 1970), p. 75.

40. Flora Lewis, "Poland Is Shifting Priorities to Increase Consumer Goods and Keep Food Prices Down," *New York Times,* January 15, 1977; see also Malcolm W. Browne, "Seeds of Capitalism Are Sprouting in Poland," ibid., April 10, 1977.

41. There are other similarities as well: Italy has been borrowing money from its allies; Poland has been obtaining loans from the Soviet Union. Italy's Communist party and Poland's Catholic church have taken the unpre-

cedented step of appealing to the population to make sacrifices and to give their government a chance to cope with economic problems.

42. *Directory of Bulgarian Officials* (Washington, D.C.: U.S. Department of State, 1976).

43. In April 1965, the Soviet secret police allegedly uncovered a plot to overthrow Zhivkov. Of the ten men implicated, about half were army officers who had fought in guerrilla detachments inside Bulgaria during the Second World War and may therefore have resented Zhivkov's dependence on Moscow. J. F. Brown, "The Bulgarian Plot," *The World Today*, June 1965, pp. 261-268.

44. "Ouster of a Bulgarian Aid Who Held Top Party Posts Seen as Indication of Feud," *New York Times*, May 15, 1977.

45. Trond Gilberg, "Ceausescu's Romania," *Problems of Communism*, 23 (July-August 1974): 29-43.

46. Kevin Devlin, "The Challenge of Eurocommunism," ibid., 25 (January-February 1977): 1-20.

47. See, for example, Christopher S. Wren, "Italian Reds in Visit to Soviet Dissident," *New York Times*, January 30, 1977; Paul Hofmann, "Italian Communist Party Offering a Key Position to Czech Dissident," ibid., May 7, 1977.

48. For a similar view see Charles Gati, "The 'Europeanization' of Communism?," *Foreign Affairs*, 55 (April 1977): 539-553.

49. There is a precedent for this: in the course of the Prague spring a revived "Little Entente" of Czechoslovakia, Rumania, and Yugoslavia seemed to be in formation.

50. The Soviet Union gave "emergency aid" in the form of credit to Poland in 1957, 1971, and 1976 and to Czechoslovakia in 1969. Although details of the 1976 loan to Poland are unclear, it has been established that the Soviets provided up to $1.4 billion through 1980. The reason for the secrecy is generally believed to be that Moscow does not want such financial assistance to be known because of the fear that other bloc countries would make similar demands. For articles on Soviet aid to these countries see the *New York Times*, January 2, March 29, December 19 and 25, 1957; September 11, November 21, December 23, 1968; February 8, October 21 and 29, 1969; February 16, 1971; and *The Economist*, December 11, 1976.

51. This analysis was made by Chase Manhattan Bank. It was reported in *Business Week*, no. 2473 (March 7, 1977): 40.

52. Andrzej Korbonski, "Détente, East-West Trade, and the Future of Economic Integration in Eastern Europe," *World Politics*, 28 (July 1976): 568-589.

53. For the full text see *Ekonomicheskaya gazeta*, no. 33 (Moscow, August 1971).

54. Hertha Heiss, "The Council for Mutual Economic Assistance: Developments since the Mid-1960s," *Economic Developments in Countries of Eastern Europe* (Washington, D.C.: U.S. Congress, Joint Economic Committee, 1970), pp. 528-542.

55. Data extrapolated from *Comecon Statistical Yearbook* (Moscow, 1976).

56. Trade of other Eastern European countries with the Soviet Union as a proportion of their total foreign trade: Bulgaria, 48%; Czechoslovakia, 28%; East Germany, 32%; Hungary, 31%; and Poland, 26%. See ibid.

57. It should be pointed out that the Czechoslovak leadership intended to keep reforms within the context of a Marxist-Leninist system in which party rule, would remain dominant. However, intellectuals outside the top party apparatus, with perhaps some allies within it, apparently hoped for an embodiment of the liberal, pluralistic ethos. See Richard V. Burks, *The Decline of Communism in Czechoslovakia* (Santa Monica: RAND Corporation, September 1968), pp. 18-20.

7

Yugoslavia's Crucial
Place in
World Politics

Nenad D. Popovic

Characteristics of Détente

Détente is the dominant feature in the global political picture today. In the case of the United States and the Soviet Union, détente characterizes their mutual relations or, rather, their hopes. To the extent that it is successful, détente may fundamentally improve prospects for a more lasting global peace. After all, the U.S. and the USSR are *the* contemporary superpowers and therefore are responsible to and for all.

A détente situation is vague since it cannot be specifically stated in any binding international document, nor has it a precise formulation. Détente taken in its active form represents a search for an acceptable mutual accommodation. Otherwise, it is mostly an attitude expressed in the conduct of foreign policies, actually a process in which the U.S. and the USSR treat their mutual conflicts not as an exercise of escalating application of their power but in terms of seeking ways of resolving disagreements through other than military means, especially nuclear confrontation. The stress is on avoiding dangerous confrontations and on easing dangerous frictions.

The present détente situation, like every détente, is not static but ever changing. And its logic is not directed at establishing friendship between the U.S. and the USSR. The differences between the United States and the Soviet Union go far beyond the relationship between two states or even superstates. Soviet-American differences concern their fundamental identities of a communist and a democratic system, respectively.

Détente's main aim is to prevent a global nuclear war. Under such circumstances ad hoc alliances or coalitions may form in the face of common dangers that for the time being override basic differences. There can be bilateral arrangements (e.g., about fishing, disease prevention, or environmental pollution). Yet, paradoxically, détente tends to shift underlying basic differences into other areas. It is necessary always to keep in mind that a profound qualitative dissimilarity separates the U.S. and the USSR that on this side of the fence is termed democracy versus totalitarianism, civil rights versus state needs, due process versus subversion, etc. On the other side, the problem is seen as the struggle of socialism versus capitalism, revolution versus counterrevolution, progress versus reaction, etc. Because each side sees its own efforts as social progress, and because each is an actual global superpower, their competition is fraught with peril.

Détente and Yugoslavia

The fundamental Soviet-American confrontation is being asserted in an infinite number of concrete issues and problems. The majority of them are small and routine but even they tend to function as the vehicles of the entire U.S.-USSR disagreement. Some of the issues are naturally important and acute (e.g., the SALT talks and the Middle East conflict). And, of course, there are many other issues that are latent and consequently have great potential importance. Although the latter are no problem while they are quiescent, they may suddenly erupt, with large-scale ramifications. The purpose of this study is to consider Yugoslavia, one such potentially dangerous zone.

Yugoslavia could easily trigger a chain reaction of events that would frustrate all hopes for détente and that could have consequences of such proportions that the emerging "Yugoslavia" would be as difficult to relate to the existing state as the latter is difficult to connect with pre-World War I Serbia. In other words, Yugoslavia may be the most critical spot in Europe today and thereby in the world.

Historically the Balkan peninsula, in which Yugoslavia is located, has been a troubled area. Critical episodes of European and even world history have been brewed in the Balkans. It is here that East meets West and that the Roman empire split in two and Christianity was divided along a path of anathemas thrown from Rome and Constantinople. The European and the Christian world collided in the Balkan peninsula with the Islamic and Oriental. Belgrade, the capital of Yugoslavia, for almost five centuries carried the name Dar-ul-Jihad ("gate of holy war"). Battlefields whereon Austro-Hungarians fought Turks and later on Russians are to be found in Yugoslavia. And here Great Britain also confronted Russia. It was in Sarajevo that an internal Yugoslav national issue led to the assassination of Archduke Franz Ferdinand and sparked World War I.

After World War I the U.S. isolated itself and Russia insulated itself. The German, Turkish, and Austro-Hungarian empires simply vanished. In the Balkan peninsula a vacuum was created. With the specific purpose of filling that vacuum Yugoslavia, first known as the Kingdom of the Serbs, Croats, and Slovenes, was established. It internalized and therefore localized those smoldering Balkan issues that could start new fires.

In this way, indeed, a number of international issues were naturalized as the never ending domestic Yugoslav crises, ferments, and conflicts that shaped Yugoslav history from 1918 to 1941. Concretely, the problems surfaced in Yugoslavia as permanent misunderstandings between the eastern and western sectors and concepts of that nation: opposing religions, confusion of nationalistic pressures, or divisions over adhesion to the French centralistic or the Swiss federalistic organizational pattern. Yugoslavs were unable to agree even about how many nations they were. And in the background there were economic problems of rich versus poor and peasant versus urban society—amidst the violent social changes shaking all of Central Europe.

Such a constellation of features hastened Yugoslavia's entry into World War II (1941). The war was fought in Yugoslavia—with the exception of a few weeks—as a confused, domestic war in which the sides were many and the bedfellows strange. In addition to widespread and intense enmity complicating the essentially civil war were the deployment of troops of the London based and Soviet recognized Royal Yugoslav Government fighting "objectively" as the allies of the Nazis and the Fascists and the supply by the United States and Great Britain of arms and other matériel to Communist partisans, who were praised but in fact ignored by the Soviets. As a result, the end of the war found Yugoslavia as ravaged as were the areas of scorched land in the Soviet Union. In the 1941-1945 period Yugoslavia lost about 11% of its prewar population.

The Postwar Compromise

There were two different, yet concurrent, developments that determined the outcome of World War II in Yugoslavia. The first was the fact that almost all domestic actors in the Yugoslav part of the war were fighting for either the partition or the dissolution of Yugoslavia. Only the Communist party of Yugoslavia (CPY), led by Marshall Tito, fought for a unified but federated Yugoslavia. This fact not only strengthened the CPY but also enabled it ultimately to impose its rule over Yugoslavia in 1945.

The other development was the agreement between Stalin and Churchill to make Yugoslavia a fifty-fifty proposition not in the sense of splitting the state but rather in the sense of leaving it alone. Under the circumstances related in the preceding paragraph, this meant that the Tito led, ruling Communist team in Belgrade was recognized internationally as the only legal government in Yugoslavia.

The 1945 solution was in both form and substance a repetition of 1918: Yugoslavia was considered an anomaly that was to be left to stew in its own sauce. It internalized a number of international political issues and strains and left Yugoslavs to wrestle with their own indigenous problems, including, most importantly, the reconciliation of various nationalities and national minorities—Albanians, Hungarians, Rumanians, Bulgarians, and Italians—that made up its population.

Thus, Yugoslavia was quite different from the other Central European countries. Consequently, its internal developments were peculiar. In the other Central European countries the fundamental issue was how the people would accept foreign (Soviet) occupation or a totalitarian regime. In Yugoslavia the rupture with the Soviet Union in 1948 eventually gave rise to a different and conflicting understanding of what communism is in general and by which paths to move toward socialism in particular. A Yugoslav variety of communism, known as Titoism, was created. So much has been written about the latter that attention here will be given mostly to how its development has influenced or even has determined the present international détente situation.

The Current International Situation and Yugoslavia

In light of post-World War II developments in Yugoslavia, it is useful to appraise generally the present international determinants of the status and role of that state. I suggest that Yugoslavian issues are not allowed to spill over into U.S.-USSR relations not because they lack international implications but because their eruption into the international arena would be inconsistent with détente. Moreover, both the U.S. and the USSR might be expected, deliberately or fortuitously, not to involve themselves in Yugoslav problems and issues. Since such involvement would only amplify internal Yugoslav

strains, the unavoidable result would be both an escalation of conflicts and their immediate reexport to the international scene.

The two preceding points make it improbable that either the
United States or the Soviet Union would be inclined even discreetly
to support contending Yugoslav factions, much less directly to intervene in that state's domestic affairs (assuming that détente truly
represents Soviet-American attitudes). However, if the existing international setup could be evaluated optimistically, the contrary is the
case regarding the Yugoslav internal situation. Namely, it is the
stability of Tito's regime that has contained domestic problems and
ruled out foreign interference. The question is whether upon Tito's
death or retirement Yugoslav conflicts would be deliberately thrown
into the international arena or whether the U.S. or the USSR would
step in?

Reasons for Tito's Success

So far Tito has succeeded by reacting flexibly to domestic
tensions. Regarding the nationalities issue, his method has been not
to challenge Montenegrin, Macedonian, Croatian, or Slovenian assertions of national identity (even to the point of sedition—Croatians)
or to deny the existence of other national minority problems (Albanians, Hungarians, etc.). On the whole, Tito has given more autonomous rights to Yugoslav nationalities and extended recognition and
equality to the national minorities. He has used the same approach
with workers disappointed with socialist achievements, introducing
self-management techniques to involve both workers in issues of
production costs, management of socialized enterprises, and wages
and average citizens directly in the running of local government
(people's committees).

Yet, it would be erroneous to think that Tito's job has been easy.
On the contrary, it has necessitated hard compromises in which
contending parties often have gained in form while sacrificing in
substance. Thus, Yugoslav nationalities were given almost full self-
rule provided they accepted national unity and the regime. Minorities
sometimes were given more than they had had in their mother
countries (e.g., Albanians) provided they would really become an
integral part of the Yugoslav community. Workers have their councils
provided they duly fulfill their obligations to "society." Local governments can decide on all issues provided they act in keeping with
federal laws and policies. Even some political movements are allowed
provided they accept the basic tenets of the Communist party and
incorporate themselves in it. Churches can stay open provided that

they keep their profile low and that the clergy, led by patriarchs, archbishops, ulemas, etc., remain loyal. Yugoslavs are free to make jokes except about President Tito. Citizens are free to profess various kinds of philosophic and scientific views provided they are not political, and so on. To sum up, in Yugoslavia groups and individuals are given a part of what they need and want as long as they unreservedly accept the regime, which is communist in its philosophy, totalitarian in its practice, and embodied in Tito and his team.

The same tactic of active, and even aggressive, defense is applied in foreign policymaking. Yugoslavia has remained a fairly minor source of international conflict; yet it has generated much irritation abroad by discouraging uninvited foreign interests. In general, Yugoslavia has tended to defuse dangerous confrontations and to stabilize international affairs. Yugoslavia perhaps even contributed something to détente. And it possibly has strengthened world peace by affirming the concept of neutral nonalignment. Yugoslavia also has made clear American and Soviet responsibility in preventing World War III.

Tito is aware that the international profile of Yugoslavia is highly dependent on his unique style of leadership. Thus, he asked, "What will happen after me? . . . We have a collective leadership at all levels . . . and I may leave any day and nothing would change. . . . The [Communist] party is stabilized . . . Marxism is returned into schools. . . . Communist discipline will have to be strengthened." He also pointed to dangers such as "liberalism . . . and the so-called federalism [which] endanger the unity of the Yugoslav nation and socialist state."[1] These words sound like a final message and instructions. They also indicate that after Tito, efforts will be made in Yugoslavia to continue the present course.

Indeed, preparations for "the great change without any change" in Yugoslavia are many and systematic.

1. Thus, the constitution carefully regulates the collective leadership not only as an institution but also as a set of policies that are to be implemented.

2. Ideologically, Marxism is reasserted in its more orthodox form, mostly as Leninism, though much adjusted during the last thirty years to Central European conditions. Therefore, Yugoslavia provides inspiration if not guidance to the Eurocommunist movements.

3. Methodologically, the leadership has stressed the disadvantages of dogmatism and emphasized a pragmatic approach.

4. The most complex issue in Yugoslavia, that of nationalities and national minorities, has been molded by the federalist organization and has been handled by recognizing and meeting the needs of the various population groups.

5. Organizationally, three basic complexes have been created. The real power is given to the army, designed not principally to be a barrier to invasion, which is correctly deemed a matter of total national involvement. The army has been made into a modern, centralized, well-organized, politically indoctrinated, professionally drilled, and disciplined force that is able to deal quickly and effectively with internal dangers and possibly also with external problems.

Although the army is the most politicized part of Yugoslav society, being the keeper and the carrier of the communist spirit, politics is not the business of the army but rather that of the LCY (League of Communists of Yugoslavia, i.e., the Communist party), which is the second power center charged with maintaining the Yugoslav system, with guiding and consolidating major political processes, and with shaping public opinion. To be on the safe side, the LCY also has a political monopoly: other political parties, movements, or organizations are illegal.

The third center of power is the system of local autonomy that rests on the republics, autonomous areas, and peoples' councils and that overshadows the federal administration. Another part of this system is the tight connection with the workers councils, which are in charge of economic processes (but not policies).

6. So far as foreign policies are concerned, nonalignment prevails, its method of implementation being that of *Realpolitik:* always suspect those strong and near, be ever ready to join in strong, popular, international movements such as the Third World, less developed countries (UNCTAD), act through the United Nations, endorse collective security, support disarmament, etc. In this respect Yugoslavia promises, even after Tito, to be just as much a catalyst of détente in the future as it has been.

Here one might note that the Yugoslav understanding of détente is different from that of either the U.S. or the USSR. Yugoslavia wants primarily a world in which there are no wars nearby, a situation in which the existing state of affairs in Europe is maintained because of a dislike for rocking the boat. Yugoslavia believes that a nuclear Soviet-American confrontation would inevitably and fatally involve their country. On the other hand, the Yugoslavs would not like to see the two superpowers drawing too close and becoming too deft in resolving their differences by dividing the world into spheres of interest.

Yugoslavia after Tito

Tito's efforts and the Yugoslavs' desires notwithstanding, after his death there may be a power vacuum that will encourage foreign meddling in Yugoslav affairs. Although Yugoslavs may now agree that they will be united and strive to maintain the national structure Tito has created, nevertheless different interpretations of the same views if not actual differences are inevitable. Such a state of affairs will tend to precipitate several developments.

Differing interpretations and views that initially will seem to be mere personal quirks or quarrels (over honor or power) ultimately will reveal themselves to be the banners of contending social and political forces rather than of ambitious personalities. The latter will be nothing but agencies for contending policies and forces, internal and foreign, not all of which will fit into the present or intended setup. In addition to domestic problems, of which there will be too many, strong and complex international interests, pressures, and jealousies will have to be faced by the Yugoslavs.

By and large, it can be assumed that under détente domestic conditions complicating foreign influences might be either absent or played down. Yet, one has to keep in mind that détente is a strange business that neither creates a world of friendship nor eliminates fundamental conflicts between the superpowers. Détente only averts the use of the ultimate means of destruction as an instrument of foreign policy. Furthermore, détente shifts existing cardinal contradictions into other, less dangerous areas. Therefore, there certainly would be both pressures and opportunities for intercession in the Yugoslav domestic whirlpool.

What specific course developments will take in Yugoslavia is a matter of speculation, but there are some points that appear to be almost certain. One of them is that sooner or later the question of who actually will control power in Yugoslavia will surface. One cannot ignore the fact that the regime is Communist and that dictatorship of the proletariat has been and is considered a nonnegotiable item. Unless the regime changes, the post-Tito system will not be able to avoid the issue of how to allot power in the absence of legitimizing elections; yet, if the regime starts changing it will open all the fractious issues that otherwise would be dormant.

Whichever contingency one considers regarding future Yugoslav developments, increasing difficulties and complications are indicated. The impact of such developments will be substantial because during Tito's successful dictatorship the greatest effort has gone into containing domestic problems and preventing their being in any way connected or involved with foreign issues or pressures. On the other hand, after Tito's departure there will be lures and pressures to externalize and export Yugoslav problems and to seek foreign participation, even perhaps intervention, in order to swing solutions one way or another.

Therefore, it cannot be expected that the Yugoslav contribution to détente policies will be constructive in the future. On the con-

trary, it is much more likely that Yugoslavia will represent a dis-
turbing factor in the international context of U.S.-USSR détente.
One might add that in the foreseeable future Yugoslav developments
in other areas do not promise to be favorable either. The economy
seems to be in disarray: high, chronic inflation, massive unemployment, erosion of national wealth and capital, degradation of cost and
productivity structures, and many other related economic issues
together indicate substantial economic deterioration, which will ag-
gravate political problems. Thus, if Yugoslavia thus far has been a
benefit to détente, in the not too distant future it threatens to
become an active danger spot.

A Yugoslavia beset by internal struggles and processes of dissolution could easily involve one or another (or even worse both)
superpower. Intervention in such a contest could appear to be
attractive since the initial stakes may appear to be relatively low as
compared to desired or imagined gains. Yet, on the other hand, even
gains under the conditions of the nuclear age are not as attractive or
strategically valuable as they would once have been. In July 1914 the
main immediate aim of the Austro-Hungarian war against Serbia was
to cauterize a trouble spot: the dual monarchy's restless Slavic
minorities. The stake, however, was control of the Balkan peninsula.
The latter was taken by Russia in 1914 as a challenge worth a world
war. In November 1940 conflicts over the Balkan area played a role
in Germany's decision to start Operation Barbarossa against the
Soviet Union. It is more than likely that under present circumstances, détente or not, the Soviet Union would react to any foreign
military intervention in Yugoslavia.

Who from the West might intervene in Yugoslavia? No single
European country could measure up to the Yugoslav defense potential, and, in addition, such an attack would fortify Yugoslav unity.
NATO has the material capability; the U.S. alone or with a few allies
could do it. However, such a move would most probably serve only
as the opening gambit in a war with the USSR.

Of course, politics is not mathematics and things could develop
differently since there is an infinite number of events that could take
place. It would be idle and confusing to entertain numerous possibilities at this point. One scenario is that both superpowers would
intervene in minor ways and without fully committing themselves. In
such a case one would predict a protracted Yugoslav civil war. In its
partisan form such a war would be an international free-for-all with
different irons in the fire, substantial foreign material and moral
support, etc. Such a war would turn a new bloody page in Yugoslav
history. It would help no one and it would thoroughly disrupt the
global foreign political picture. In addition, such a war would
strongly affect Yugoslavs, almost all of them U.S. citizens, in Amer-

ica. The other possibility, perhaps more tangible, is that the intervention would come not from the West but from the East: another Hungary in 1956 or Czechoslovakia in 1968. Militarily, those Soviet operations worked but they were traumatic political experiences that harmed the cause of communism just as much as the 1939 Nazi-Soviet agreement. Anyway, as in the case of the United States, a Soviet move would mean the end of détente. The Soviets could also be very much tempted to act through one of their allies on the border of Yugoslavia. Such a course of events would be possible but hardly probable since it would involve both the Warsaw and NATO mechanisms and definitely would mean the end of détente. More likely would be disguised Eastern interventions that used "volunteers," open borders, etc., which would badly strain détente and would confuse the issues. If of short duration, however, this type of tactic might not end détente.

Eastern intervention in Yugoslavia from the inside is even more probable. One should not forget that the actual carriers of power in Yugoslavia are the army, the LCY, and the autonomous self-management networks, which are all profoundly Communist. Though not enthusiastic supporters of the Soviets, most of these sectors are more inclined to the East than to the West. Even if such domestic intervention were to make a substantial majority of Yugoslavs anti-Soviet, there remains the hard fact that Yugoslavia is thoroughly socialized (nationalized capital, collectivized agriculture, and socialized public services). This creates a major prosocialist inertia, which in substance is opposed to the West.

There are a variety of ways in which events could turn; yet they are all inconsistent with détente. For that reason it is enough to state here that any internationalization of domestic Yugoslav problems would be incompatible with détente and with joint U.S.-USSR projects. There is no external solution to Yugoslav problems. They can be settled only and exclusively by the Yugoslavs themselves.

Yugoslavia and Eurocommunism

The issue of Yugoslavia could be also considered from the point of view of Eurocommunism, especially of the French and Italian varieties. Eurocommunists undoubtedly would be against any Soviet occupation of Yugoslavia or Yugoslavia's joining the Soviet bloc. The reason for this is that the Soviets in a strange way defy the laws of physics: they are more attractive when they are further away; their impact is greater when more theoretical or academic and much smaller when tangible. Thus, for Eurocommunism there is no need or desire to have the Soviets move West, particularly not into Yugoslavia.

Eurocommunists would certainly like to see Yugoslavia, especially as depicted in the LCY program, a politically free country according to Western European standards. However, Eurocommunists are on all counts against Western intervention in Yugoslavia, excluding naturally their own manifestations of moral and possibly material support. Otherwise a Western military intervention in Yugoslavia would have only one doubtful advantage: supplying fuel for a furious anti-Western and procommunist political campaign.

One should not forget, either, that the Eurocommunist parties are highly indebted to the Yugoslav Communists, who were the first—on their own initiative and at their peril—to raise the banner of what today is the substance of Eurocommunism. For all these and other reasons one could assume that Eurocommunists would have some irons of their own in the fire if Yugoslav problems become confused and are exported. Yet, the main dangers remain, such as Soviet or Western interference or intervention or political reaction in the West (in the United States, a red scare; in Italy, fascism; in Germany, nazism, etc.). These are the possibilities that in my opinion far outweigh any Eurocommunist readiness to approve or welcome the internationalization of Yugoslav issues or any kind of foreign intervention in Yugoslavia by either the West or the East.

Yugoslavia and American Foreign Policy

Finally, there is the most important point: what is the meaning of Yugoslav developments for American foreign policy? There is no doubt that the U.S. has necessarily to be involved in any issue anywhere in the world where human rights and democratic values and practices are at stake. American sympathies and inclinations, therefore, are clear regarding Yugoslav problems. The same is the case with the main current of American public opinion. However, how can such views be translated into official American foreign policy in general and détente policy in particular, all as related to the case of Yugoslavia.

Principles of human rights are universally accepted by all nations, and they are particularly emphasized by the Carter administration. It seems only natural to expect to find, on such issues, a common ground between the United States and socialist Yugoslavia. Yet, Vice-President Mondale ran into trouble on this issue when meeting with Tito in Belgrade on May 20, 1977. In order to understand the nature of the problem, it is necessary to clarify how each side sees the issue. Namely, the human rights question has both positive and negative impact on détente policies because this issue points to a basic difference that might lead to more conflict. On the international ground it is advantageous for the United States to show the importance of providing such rights to all people in American society, or communist society, or any other type of society. For a communist country, nevertheless, the issue is highly sensitive because there such rights are conditionally accorded to individuals provided they go along with the regime. Therefore, communist countries cannot accept the human rights issue as a part of the détente package.

It follows that the human rights issue is potentially dangerous for the policy of détente. It uncovers the irrevocable differences between democratic and communist societies. President Tito's strong reaction against the inclusion of human rights issues in discussions at international conferences confirms the depth of the general conflict since Yugoslavia though a Communist state is considered to be more liberal than most other communist countries. The Yugoslav reaction only stresses the need for more sophistication and skill in the American foreign policy process.

If one assumes that detente attitudes are a recognized need and that détente is a valid component of U.S. foreign policy today, then the Yugoslav problem comes more clearly into focus. It is evident that Yugoslavia with the passing of time, and of Tito, will tend to be less an asset and more a liability for détente. On that count it would be preferable for the United States to contain the Yugoslav problem and to keep it internalized. Any exacerbation of Yugoslav problems, for instance a dissolution of Yugoslavia into two or more states, would dangerously overload the still fragile détente. On the other hand, it seems that an American military intervention certainly, and a Soviet intervention possibly, would produce a European war.

Under present circumstances, so far as the issue of Yugoslavia's independence is concerned, the practical conclusion could be summarized as follows: (1) to recognize that Yugoslavia is an increasing danger for détente; and (2) consequently, there is greater need for containment of Yugoslav problems, keeping them national and preventing their internationalization. Under Tito's leadership Yugoslavia has been contained from the inside. However, in the future exactly the opposite will be the case: Yugoslavian containment, after Tito, cannot be taken for granted but must be worked out with external assistance—this means the need to consider and formulate foreign policy guidelines on how to prevent deterioration of the global détente situation.

Notes

1. *Nedeljne novosti* (Belgrade), 2 February 1976, supp., pp. 3, 4- 5.

8

The Japanese
Communist Party:
The Miyamoto Line
and Its Problems

Haruhiro Fukui

With the exception of the Komeito, the Clean Government party (CGP), all the contemporary Japanese political parties have long prewar lineages and carry the marks of generally sad and inglorious experiences under the harsh authoritarian regime of the militarist era. This is particularly true of the Japan Communist party, the Nihon kyosanto (JCP), which spent the first two decades following its foundation in 1922 as an illegal, forlorn outpost of the Comintern in a most inhospital land of divine emperors and their fanatically loyal subjects. To this day the party continues to be haunted by memories and myths of bygone days—constant police harassment, mass arrests and torture, forced confessions, apostasy, and a succession of defections among imprisoned leaders. Worst of all, the JCP has not yet succeeded in shaking off its popular image of a conspiratorial, violence-prone, and subversive clique intent on the overthrow and destruction of the existing order, an image systematically and effectively nurtured by its opponents both before and after the Second World War.

In 1976 a long article in a popular magazine touched off a minor political upheaval in Tokyo by insisting that the JCP chairman, Kenji Miyamoto, had been unlawfully released from prison in October 1945 in the midst of postwar confusion and trauma. According to the author, the imperial ordinance responsible for Miyamoto's release at the time had applied only to political prisoners, whereas he had been convicted on five criminal counts involving the illegal confinement and manslaughter of a police informant in 1932 (Tachibana*). No sooner had the article been published than the issue was taken up by the chairman of the Democratic Socialist party, or Minshu shakaito (DSP), in the Diet, becoming a cause célèbre of the party's opponents. However, the ensuing controversy soon was defused by the explosion of another and bigger political scandal involving Lockheed Corporation and Japanese recipients of bribe money paid by the company. The first issue may nevertheless have significantly contributed to the disastrous performance of JCP candidates in the December 1976 House of Representatives elections. Whether or not it made any real difference to the election results, the event highlighted the weight of history, which continues to burden the JCP thirty years after it won recognition as a legal political organization under the postwar constitution.

As its violent and somewhat paranoiac reaction to the charges against Miyamoto suggests, the psychology and behavior of the JCP can be fully understood only if one takes into account the impact of its unique historical experience. It is not possible, however, to include in this chapter a review of the party's misfortunes in prewar and wartime Japan. There are at least two excellent English language books on the subject (Beckmann and Okubo; Scalapino). On more recent developments, on the other hand, there is little available in languages other than Japanese, except press reports, a few journal articles, and a 1972 monograph (Langer). I will therefore begin with a brief discussion of the evolution of the JCP's current orthodoxy, referred to here as the Miyamoto line, to provide the minimum historical background necessary for the examination of the party's present state, strategy, and options in the sections that will follow.

The Rise and Development of the Miyamoto Line

Despite its vicissitudes and complexity of details, the evolution of the JCP's contemporary ideological orientation and political strategy has been relatively simple and straightforward. It has passed through four distinctive phases. During the first few years following Japan's surrender in 1945 the party followed a line of moderation and accommodation with the policies and programs of the American occupation, a line vigorously advocated by Sanzo Nosaka, a veteran

*See alphabetical references list for this chapter, pp. 328–32.—ED

Communist who returned to Tokyo in January 1946 after fourteen year exile in Moscow and Yenan (Scalapino, pp. 53- 55). Following Nosaka's return, the JCP set out to make itself respectable and "lovable" by downplaying its revolutionary intentions and emphasizing its patriotic commitments. The declaration of the February 1946 JCP congress called for the abolition of the emperor system and the establishment of a "people's republic" (JCP 3, pp. 101- 105). It also argued, however, that following the completion of a bourgeois, democratic revolution, the party would lead the nation toward a social system more advanced and better than capitalism, "in keeping with the stage of development of the society, with the approval and support of the majority of the people, through the efforts of the people themselves, and by peaceful and democratic means." It went on to say that the JCP "had never advocated a general denunciation of private property" and that, in fact, the private ownership of property would exist in any type of society, including one under socialism (JCP 3, p. 104). The theory and practice of the lovable party apparently won the JCP some support and confidence among the nation's voters. The party managed to win 7.5% of the vote and thirty-five seats in the 1949 House of Representatives elections, an impressive performance not to be repeated until 1972 (*Asahi nenkan*, 1973, p. 247).

The Nosaka theory thus set the baseline of postwar Japanese communism to which the JCP would revert a decade later. In early 1950, however, that theory was suddenly thrown overboard by an anonymous article in the Cominform organ, *For a Lasting Peace, For a People's Democracy*, criticizing Nosaka's perversion of the Marxist-Leninist theory of revolution and his muddleheaded view of the American occupation and its "progressive" role (Kobayashi, pp. 53- 80; Koyama, pp. 71 ff.; Scalapino, pp. 60- 67). The Cominform's criticisms, which clearly reflected the views of the Soviet (CPSU) and Chinese (CCP) parties, split the JCP's politburo between a majority group (the Mainstream) led by General Secretary Kyuichi Tokuda and including Nosaka and a minority (the Internationalists), including Miyamoto. The latter pressed for immediate acceptance of the Cominform's position and renunciation of the Nosaka theory; the former for a while resisted the combined pressures of the international communist movement and the Internationalists within the party but eventually capitulated. Within a few months the party, under Tokuda's leadership, embarked on what soon proved to be a certain road to disaster.

As the notorious 1951 program declared, the JCP was now committed to the inflexible and impractical theory that violent (armed) revolution alone would liberate the Japanese people from the oppressive rule of American imperialists and Japanese monopoly capitalists, leading to the creation of a free society without class exploitation or distinctions. A blanket purge of the party's top leaders in June 1950, which resulted from a directive of the supreme commander for the Allied powers, had further complicated the situation, driving them either underground or to China. During the following several years the JCP engaged in a futile and self-defeating exercise in "Maoist" extremism, both verbally and in the form of sporadic attacks on government offices and personnel. As the superficial militancy mounted, the popularity of the party plummeted until it became no more than a quixotic political nonentity. In the four House of Representatives elections held during the 1950s the party managed to win 2.6% (1952), 1.9% (1953), 2.0% (1955), and 2.6% (1958) of the vote and zero, one, two, and one seat, respectively (Asahi nenkan, 1973, p. 247). Meanwhile, throughout the decade the JCP continued to be plagued by factional strife spawned by the 1950 split and compounded by the hardships of underground life and activities in the following years.

It was in the process of the JCP's political resurrection and rehabilitation from the ruins left by the adventurism of the early 1950s that Miyamoto began to rise to a position of undisputed power and prestige. He was elected to the standing committee of the presidium at the watershed all-party consultative conference of June 1955. The occasion was set for a general critique and denunciation of the Left's adventurism, factionalism, and political impotence, which were blamed on the misguided decisions and actions of the Mainstream group led by Tokuda until his death in China in 1953 (Koyama, pp. 171- 193; Scalapino, pp. 88- 96). The conference was, however, also an occasion for compromise between the Mainstreamers and the Internationalists; the latter still formed a minority among the newly elected top leaders. In 1950 Miyamoto had led the Internationalists in their pro-Cominform attacks on Nosaka and the Mainstreamers, but he had by 1955 shifted his position to what amounted to a replica of the pre-1950 Nosaka theory. He may well have wanted the 1955 conference to renounce the 1951 program, but he did not press prematurely for such a radical step, waiting until he was assured of certain success. It was not until the 1958 JCP congress that the 1951 document was finally and officially repudiated. Even then, the survivors of the leaderless Tokuda group were still powerful enough to block the adoption of a new program drafted by Miyamoto. On the other hand, Miyamoto achieved a notable success during this congress by winning the key post of general secretary and immediately set out to build a new and invincible Mainstream coalition of central committee members by promoting his loyal followers and either silencing or, more frequently, simply expelling from the party recalcitrant opponents

(Koyama, pp. 224-293; Scalapino, pp. 100-109). By 1961, when the next congress was convened, Miyamoto had established himself as the undisputed leader and had gotten his new party program (the 1961 program) adopted unanimously. The third phase of the JCP's postwar history came to an end and the fourth and last phase—one of consolidation and expansion of the Miyamoto line—was about to begin.

The 1961 program remains the basic guideline for the JCP's ideological and policy commitments, but by the standards of the party's more contemporary pronouncements and behavior, the document sounds oddly traditional and doctrinaire. It begins with a reminder that the party had been founded in the midst of a worldwide struggle of the proletariat for its own liberation in the wake of the great October Revolution (JCP 3, pp. 5-23). Reminiscent of the 1951 program, which it replaced, the document then defines American imperialism and Japanese monopoly capital as the twin rulers of Japan and therefore the main enemies of a JCP led "people's democratic" revolution. The central task of the party is "to develop the demands and struggle of all [Japanese] people . . . against the comprador forces of reaction, of which American imperialism and Japanese monopoly capital constitute the hard core, against their policies of war, against national oppression, against the revival of militarism and imperialism, against political reaction, against exploitation and robbery" (JCP 3, p. 15). The program also calls, however, for the formation of a "national, democratic united front" against the enemies mentioned earlier, led by workers, based on a worker-peasant alliance, and rallying for the cause of the struggle "all working citizens, intellectuals, women, youth, students, small businessmen, and those who love peace and the fatherland and will defend democracy" (JCP 3, p. 19). Even more significant, it emphasizes the importance of the Diet as a tool by which to promote the interests of the people; it also promises to "pay careful attention to the problem of government" and to seek to establish a united front even for such limited purposes as all the democratic forces can provisionally agree on (JCP 3: 20). The 1961 program is thus a curious mixture of a reiteration of the classic two-stage revolution theory and a timid and cautious call for reversion to the old Nosaka theory of the lovable, patriotic party dedicated to the achievement of revolution through peaceful, democratic, and parliamentary means. The messages of the document are incongruous, but they share an emphasis on the theme of nationalism, one directed against the external enemy—"American imperialism"—the other addressed to all patriotic and democratic forces in the country.

In the years since its adoption in 1961, this nationalist orientation of the program and therefore Miyamoto's new line was seriously challenged first by a pro-CPSU and then by a pro-CCP group. These challenges were met with stiff rebuffs and ruthless counterattacks resulting in mass expulsions and defections of the challengers, in 1964 and 1967 respectively (Koyama, pp. 342- 370, 403- 408).

Meanwhile, Miyamoto and his new Mainstream shifted their public posture on the "problem of government" to an increasingly liberal and moderate position until a whole new set of propositions on "socialism in an advanced capitalist country" has evolved outside and far beyond the language of the 1961 program. It is hard to judge whether Miyamoto intended in 1961, much less in 1955, to take the party under his leadership so far afield into the backwaters of the original Nosaka theory. This road has proved, however, to be an eminently successful and productive one in terms of dividends more tangible than ideological propriety or theoretical consistency. The worldly successes in turn greatly have helped Miyamoto win the confidence and loyalty of the party's rank and file members and further consolidate his tight grip on the top leadership group.

REEMERGENCE OF THE JCP AS A POLITICAL FORCE

The rise of Miyamoto and his new Mainstream in the faction politics of the JCP has been paralleled by an impressive rise of the party in the politics of Japan. During the first phase of its postwar history the JCP grew rapidly, from less than 7000 in early 1946 to well over 150,000 in 1949, the year the party won 35 seats in the House of Representatives (Morita, p. 65). During the period of the Left's adventurism that followed, however, the party suffered debilitating losses not only in leadership personnel and Diet representation but also in grass-roots membership. At the time of the 1955 consultative conference it reputedly had no more than 20,000 members; in 1958, when the 1951 program was officially renounced, JCP membership was about 35,000 (Iizuka 1, p. 190; *Yomiuri shimbun*, July 19, 1976). During the following decade, however, the membership figures quoted by JCP leaders at party congresses increased by leaps and bounds—over 80,000 in 1961, nearly 150,000 in 1964, and 300,000 in 1970 (*Yomiuri shimbun*, July 19, 1976). By 1975 the JCP boasted of 350,000 members, roughly equal to the number of bona fide members of the Liberal Democratic party, or Jiyuminshuto (LDP)—346,000—and far surpassing the stagnant 50,000 of the Socialist party, the Nihon shakaito (JSP); the 40,000 of the DSP; and even the 120,000 of the CGP (*Asahi nenkan*, 1976, pp. 260- 269).

The more dues paying members, the more abundant party funds. And in fact the growth of the JCP's revenue has been even more spectacular than that of its membership. According to one estimate, the JCP headquarters received about 132 million yen ($1.00 to ¥360.00) in 1958, but the figure jumped to 1.271 billion in 1965, 4.107 billion in 1970, and 11.958 billion in 1975 (Morita, pp. 69- 70). In the last year mentioned, the JCP was the richest of the five Japanese parties, surpassing the LDP (11.493 billion yen), not to speak of the JSP (1.714 billion), the DSP (779 million), and the CGP (6.536 billion) (Morita, p. 55). The bulk of the JCP's revenue did not come, however, from membership dues collected from its swelling ranks of new members. In fact, it has been the official policy of the party to keep membership receipts at the level of about 1% of its total revenue (JCP 7, p. 34). In practice, membership receipts and contributions from external sources have never accounted for more than a small percentage of the party's total income. Furthermore, even these declined over the years, from 4% in 1958 to .8% in 1975 for the former and 21% in 1958 to 5.8% in 1975 for the latter (Morita, pp. 55- 56, 69). The remaining 75% and 93% in the respective years, and similar percentages in the years between, represented gross profits from sales of the party's numerous publications, especially the well-selling *Akahata* (*Red Flag*).

The JCP publishes nearly a dozen periodicals and some of them have quite respectable circulations, such as the monthly *Zen'ei* (*Vanguard*: 150,000) and *Gekkan gakushu* (*Monthly Study*: 70,000) (Iizuka, p. 213; Langer, p. 34). None, however, approaches *Akahata* as a regular and dependable source of funds as well as a tool of mass proselytization. In 1958 the daily paper had a relatively modest circulation of about 50,000. The following year a special Sunday edition was added and since then both editions have rapidly expanded their circulations—100,000 and 200,000, respectively, in 1961, 200,000 and 900,000 in 1965, over 400,000 and 1.5 million in 1970, and 650,000 and 2.35 million in 1976 (Nagata, p. 30; *Yomiuri shimbun*, July 19, 1976). As one observer has remarked, the JCP has become one of the most successful publishers in the country and *Akahata* is by far the most successful and profitable of its products.

The success of the party paper to some extent is the result of a substantial number of captive readers, probably nearly all of the 350,000 members. Apart from that, however, many nonmembers apparently find its articles readable, interesting, and informative. Especially since 1968, when the daily edition became a twelve-page paper, *Akahata*'s editorial staff has made very substantial efforts to make it attractive by expunging the more obviously propagandistic materials and abandoning the polemical and academic style of writing, by devoting much space to practical problems of daily life, such as comparative prices of merchandise, by providing television listings, sports news, and movie reviews, and so forth. In 1973 the paper had a 300-member editorial staff, including about 30 correspondents based in major cities throughout the country and 7 at overseas bureaus in Pyongyang, Hanoi, Moscow, Bucharest, Prague, and Berlin (Nagata, pp. 89-90). In addition, some 13,000 party members scattered over the country were registered as regular contributors of local news, daily sending several hundred articles to the editorial staff at *Akahata* headquarters. Moreover, the paper is home-delivered daily by some 50,000 members and their families (Nagata, p. 184). At a subscription price of 1000 yen per month for the daily edition and 330 yen for the Sunday edition only (November 1976), the paper was apparently competitive with the major commercial papers. More important, according to a party source, the collection of subscription fees was about 70% in the early 1960s but improved to nearly 100% during the next ten years (JCP 7, p. 59). There is no good way to authenticate this or any other claim made by the party, but assuming that half of the amount suggested by these statistics is spent by local outlets of the paper, a quick calculation would show that some 9 billion yen per year should be available to JCP headquarters from this single source in recent years (Morita, p. 72). This conclusion is consistent with the widely shared impression of the party's affluence at election time.

Whether or not Miyamoto's entrepreneurial acumen and the success of the *"Akahata* strategy" were the most important factors in the JCP's performance at the polls, the party did achieve some notable results in both national and local elections during the last decade and a half. As Miyamoto proudly pointed out to a guest from France, Georges Marchais, in the spring of 1976, the party had at the time ten times as many of its representatives in the Diet and four times as many in local assemblies as it had had in 1958 (JCP 4, p. 53). In the House of Representatives alone, it had only one seat in 1958 but three by 1960, five by 1963, fourteen by 1969, and thirty-five by 1972 (*Asahi nenkan*, 1973, p. 247). On the local political scene the JCP was conspicuous in the 1950s for its nearly complete absence among administrative heads of prefectural and city governments. In 1972, however, governors of six prefectures, including Tokyo, Osaka, and Kyoto, had been elected with the joint endorsement and support of the JCP and one or more of the other opposition parties. More than one-fifth of the 643 cities of the country had "progressive" mayors elected similarly (*Asahi nenkan*, 1973, p. 245).

Under Miyamoto's leadership the JCP thus has gained a considerable amount of political respectability and influence. Assisted by a dozen or so well-organized "front" groups of shopkeepers, doctors, scientists, young workers, students, women, and so forth, the party has managed to establish an effective network of communications and mobilization capable of reaching nearly every community and neighborhood in the nation (Tamura; Suzuki, p. 69). As I shall argue in a later section, the party is by no means about to attain government power even in alliance with another opposition party or parties, much less by itself. The foregoing brief historical account should convince the reader that the JCP is no longer a miniscule group of quixotic, fanatical, old-fashioned ideologues. If the party was that twenty years ago, it has become something very different and far more formidable as a factor in contemporary Japanese politics.

The JCP Leadership

COMPOSITION AND BACKGROUND

According to the rules of the JCP, chapter 3, the party congress is the highest decisionmaking organ of the party and appoints members of the central committee, which in turn appoints members of the presidium (*Zen'ei*, September 1976, pp. 322- 333). The last body establishes a standing committee (standing presidium) and appoints members of both the secretariat and the editorial committee for the central party publications. The party congress has to be convened, however, only once every three years to hear and approve reports of the central committee, "determine" policies of the party, and, if necessary, revise the party program and rules. Similarly, the central committee must meet no more frequently than twice a year unless one-third or more of its members demand a special session or sessions. In effect, these two bodies are not designed to watch and direct the party's day-to-day activities; the presidium and, more accurately, the presidium standing committee have primary responsibility for the actual management and control of party affairs (Iizuka 1, p. 222; Ueda and Iizuka, p. 140). One may look at the profiles of the presidium members in order to identify and describe the types of men who run and lead the JCP.

Table 1 is a list of the presidium members as of January 1977. Of the seventeen standing committee members, Chairman Miyamoto is beyond any doubt the most powerful and respected. As one author puts it, the JCP today is very much a "Miyamoto party" (Iizuka 1, pp. 2- 3). At the age of sixty-nine, however, he is getting old and is known to have been eager for some time to hand over the reins of party leadership to a younger man. As a step in that direction Miyamoto picked forty-six-year-old Tetsuzo Fuwa during the July 1976 party congress as acting chairman, i.e., his heir apparent, and added three new vice-chairmen—Hiroshi Murakami (fifty-five), Tomio Nishizawa (sixty-three), and Koichiro Ueda (forty-nine)—to

T A B L E 1. JCP presidium members as of January 1, 1977.

NAME	OFFICE
Standing Committee Members (17)	
Ebisudani, Shunsho	Head, control committee
Fuwa, Tetsuzo (Ueda, Kenjiro)	Acting chairman, presidium; director, secretariat; member, House of Representatives
Hakamada, Satomi	Vice-chairman, presidium
Ichikawa, Shoichi	Deputy director, secretariat; director, election policy bureau
Iwabayashi, Toranosuke	(None)
Kaneko, Michihiro	Deputy director, secretariat; director, united front bureau
Kurahara, Korehito	Head, intellectuals, culture, and education committee; head, religion committee
Matsushima, Harushige	(None)
Miyamoto, Kenji	Chairman, presidium
Murakami, Hiroshi	Vice-chairman, presidium
Nishizawa, Tomio	Vice-chairman, presidium; head, international affairs committee
Oka, Masayoshi	Vice-chairman, presidium
Okamoto, Hiroyuki	Director, education bureau, head, publications planning committee; principal, party school
Senaga, Kamejiro	Vice-chairman, presidium; chairman, Okinawa prefectural committee; member, House of Representatives
Suwa, Shigeru	Director, organization bureau
Takahara, Shinichi	Director, business bureau; head, finance and business committee
Ueda, Koichiro	Vice-chairman, presidium; chairman, policy committee; director, propaganda bureau; member, House of Councillors
Other Members (24)	
Akeda, Yoshio	Chairman, Osaka prefectural committee
Furukata, Saneyoshi	Acting chairman, Okinawa prefectural committee
Gesu, Junkichi	(None)
Hama, Takeji	Chairman, Tokyo prefectural committee
Hoshino, Tsutomu	Member, House of Councillors
Ibaraki, Yoshikazu	Director, local government and residents bureau
Ida, Makoto	Chairman, Aichi prefectural committee
Kasuga, Shoichi	Member, House of Councillors
Kawada, Kenji	Member, House of Councillors
Kobayashi, Eizo	Deputy head, theory committee
Kojima, Masaru	Acting chairman, Tokyo prefectural committee
Konno, Yojiro	Member, House of Representatives
Kudo, Akira	Chairman, economic policy committee; member, House of Representatives

TABLE 1. *(Cont.)*

NAME	OFFICE
Nakajima, Taketoshi	Member, House of Representatives
Nirasawa, Tadao	Director, Akahata editorial bureau
Ofuchi, Masaki	(None)
Omura, Shinjiro	Chairman, Fukuoka prefectural committee
Sakaki, Toshio	Head, theory committee
Sunama, Kazuyoshi	Head, appeals committee
Tada, Ryuji	Chairman, Hyogo prefectural committee
Uchino, Takechiyo	Head, audit committee
Yasui, Shinzo	Chairman, Kyoto prefectural committee
Yonehara, Itaru	Head, pollution and disaster policy committee
Yoshida, Motoharu	Head, human rights protection office

Source: Asahi shimbun, December 7, 1976; Suzuki, pp. 78-79.

the three who were reappointed—Satomi Hakamada (seventy-two), Masayoshi Oka (sixty-two), and Kamejiro Senaga (sixty-nine). (See Table 2, p. 294) Of the newly appointed, Nishizawa is not much younger than Miyamoto, but Murakami and Ueda are. Incidentally, Ueda is Fuwa's elder brother and both have apparently been groomed by Miyamoto to carry on his ideas and policies in the post-Miyamoto period to come (Tawara, pp. 318-324). The rejuvenation of the leadership group was not only desirable from the point of view of Miyamoto's personal comfort and well-being but necessary for keeping the top leadership in tune with younger members, who constitute the bulk of the party's new recruits during the last two decades. According to Miyamoto's report to the 1970 congress, 90% of the current members were under fifty in that year and 54% between eighteen and thirty (Iizuka 1, p. 184). And it is these new and young members who have been most enthusiastically pushing the Miyamoto line, sometimes against the wishes of older cadres entrenched in local party organizations.

Apart from Miyamoto, Fuwa, and the six vice-chairmen mentioned earlier, the standing committee consists of the heads of seven party bureaus and committees and two members without formal offices. The latter, Harushige Matsushima and Toranosuke Iwabayashi, have been involved, as head and deputy head, respectively, in the work of an ad hoc committee on party construction since about 1970 (Mizushima, pp. 33, 48). The committee was appointed to cope with the problems the party began to face in the early 1970s in further expanding its membership, promoting sales of party publications, sending more party members to the Diet and local assemblies, and so forth. Committee members presumably continue to work in these areas, but relevant information is not available. In any event, the presidium standing committee, as it is currently composed, includes heads of key party bureaus and committees. The secretariat is said to be dominated by members of the Diet (Iizuka 1, p. 224), but this is not true of the standing committee. Fuwa and Senaga have seats in the House of Representatives and Ueda in the House of Councillors, but none of them can be said to owe his membership on the presidium standing committee to his membership in the national legislature.

Among the remaining members of the presidium, on the other hand, Diet members are numerically more prominent. There are six of them, evenly divided between the two chambers. Even here, however, the nine party officeholders, including one who combines membership in the Diet, clearly predominate. They are followed by eight who head the most powerful prefectural committees of the party, including those in Tokyo, Osaka, Kyoto, Aichi, and Fukuoka. Not surprisingly, the JCP presidium thus represents, above all, the key party offices; it is effectively plugged into party groups in major urban centers through the representatives of the prefectural committees; and it hears from and controls the actions of the party's representatives in the Diet.

For an ambitious JCP member to make the presidium it is thus essential first to attain chairmanship of an important party office at the headquarters or, alternatively, a top position in one of the JCP prefectural committees. Once he attains either position, he is within shooting distance of a seat on the powerful, decisionmaking body. He may then be invited to run for a Diet seat on the party's ticket with all the necessary financial and organizational support provided by the party. How, then, does one get into a high office at either the headquarters or in a local committee? In both cases what matters is apparently one's work as a party activist, i.e., one's record of activities in programs and campaigns organized by the party. One may begin at the headquarters and climb the ladder of the established hierarchy there on the strength of one's native intelligence or acquired skill to contribute to the party's cause. The orthodox route for a member who chooses to try his luck in this way is the party secretariat. A secretariat staffer is at obvious and great advantage in his bid for a seat on the presidium, with which the office is constantly kept in contact and for which it serves as the primary source of information and advice. Among the 1977 presidium members Fuwa, Ichikawa, Murakami, Suwa, Gesu, Hoshino, Ibaraki, Kaneko, Kojima, Kudo, Nirasawa, Ofuchi, and Sakaki took this route. A local aspirant, on the other hand, must contend with his competitors much more on his own and in a much less organized arena of competition. One promising way to advance one's chance of success would be to form or join a strong faction of local party leaders and ride its support to the top prefectural committee post. In both cases proven loyalty to Miyamoto and his line is a prerequisite of ultimate success; in neither case is educational or occupational background of crucial importance. A closer look at the profiles of the presidium members will be helpful in elucidating these last two points.

GROUPINGS OF JCP PRESIDIUM MEMBERS

No group of forty-one individuals, not to speak of a group of experts in ideological struggle and verbal battles, is likely to be completely free of occasional disagreements and disputes. If they persist over a significant period of time, such disagreements and disputes will give rise to mutually antagonistic and exclusive groups with more or less stable and identifiable affiliates and interests, i.e., factions. Whether the JCP has fallen victim to this general rule is hard to judge; reliable information is almost totally unavailable to an outsider. Even so, some observers believe that factions exist among the current JCP leaders. On the occasion of the 1976 party congress the JCP made public for the first time special issues of its "internal circulation only" newsletter, *Party News (Toho)*, which contained readers' letters critical of some recent policy changes undertaken by the top leadership. Some questioned, for example, what they regarded as signs of opportunistic conformism in those changes; others took issue with Miyamoto's excessive preoccupation with election results; still others expressed concern that the party might have abandoned the essentials of Marxism-Leninism (*Mainichi shimbun*, July 25, 1976; *Yomiuri shimbun*, July 19, 1976). These comments in an important party document lend credence to the view that the JCP is faction ridden just like the LDP and the JSP. Tsuyoshi Mizushima, the author of the book on which my discussion in this section heavily draws, has identified seven factional groups among top JCP leaders: Tokyo University alumni, recruits from the JCP secretariat, former local cadres from the Osaka-Kyoto district, local party bosses from other areas, labor union leaders, former officers of the postal workers union, and the survivors of the Tokuda faction (Mizushima, pp. 240–243).

A careful check on the backgrounds, current party positions, and ideological tendencies of presidium members leads me to believe that it is much too risky to assume the presence of well-defined factional groups in the JCP presidium and to assign its members to one or another of such groups. If one were to choose between the assumption that there are established factions and the opposite assumption that there are no such factions, one would do well to choose the latter assumption to be on the safe side. One good argument for such a choice would be that at least the most articulate of Miyamoto's opponents and critics have all been systematically and successfully eliminated from the party during the last two decades.

To backtrack a bit, the factional struggle following the 1950 Cominform criticism was fought between, on the one hand, the Mainstream, led by Tokuda and joined among others by Ritsu Ito, Yojiro Konno, Nosaka, and Shigeo Shida, and, on the other, the Internationalists, led by Miyamoto and joined by Satomi Hakamada, Kozo Kameyama, Shigeo Kamiyama, Shojiro Kasuga, Korehito Kurahara, and Yoshio Shiga (Iizuka 1, pp. 227–236). Of these protagonists of the early fifties, Tokuda died in 1953; Tokuda's confidant, Ito, was expelled from the party in 1952 as a "spy" and "antiparty provocateur" and has not been heard from since. Shida was charged with "corruption" and embezzlement of party funds and fled the party's inquisitors in 1957. Then, following the 1961 congress, Kameyama and Kasuga, both originally Internationalists, were expelled on charges of "structural reformist" tendencies and, more directly, because they opposed the new party program of 1961, drafted and defended by Miyamoto. Then went Shiga and Kamiyama in 1964, when the former voted in the Diet for ratification of the 1963 partial nuclear test ban treaty and the latter supported Shiga's action. With them left many who shared their pro-Moscow sympathies, leaving the party in the hands of a precarious alliance between Miyamoto style nationalists and pro-Peking leaders. The latter included none of the major actors of the 1950 controversy; they were entrenched in a dozen prefectural party committees, most prominently in Yamaguchi prefecture (JCP 1, pp. 12–14, 20, 25). In any event, the pro-China group in the JCP, too, was eliminated, through either expulsions or defections, after the JCP-CCP confrontation of 1966.

Thus, only five of the original protagonists survived the successive purges of the fifties and sixties—Konno and Nosaka on the Mainstream side and Miyamoto, Hakamada, and Kurahara on the Internationalist side. Nosaka served as chairman of the presidium standing committee until 1970 but has since been relegated to the honorary position of central committee chairman. Konno has stayed on the presidium and plays an inconspicuous role as a member of the House of Representatives.

In addition to Konno there are now fourteen members of the presidium closely associated with the Tokuda faction. Four of them held important party posts during Tokuda's reign. They and Konno may still be somewhat suspect; none of them has managed to get elected to the standing committee. On the other hand, those ten who were minor functionaries in Tokuda's days have apparently not been disadvantaged in any obvious way. If the more prominent survivors of the Tokuda faction are in fact regarded by Miyamoto's men as less than fully trustworthy, their guilt does not seem to extend to the less prominent among their former associates. And the backgrounds of the rest of the present presidium members do not reveal anything suggestive of anti-Miyamoto proclivities in terms either of past associations or of known ideological preferences. It seems reasonable to regard the entire group currently constituting the JCP presidium as an enlarged Miyamoto faction, assuming that there are dissidents and malcontents outside the group, especially in some prefectural and local party committees.

It is nevertheless both possible and useful to distinguish among several types of presidium members. Table 2 offers one possible classification. The groups identified there are not factions in the ordinary sense of the word. Nor are the assignments of individual members to the five groups based on better criteria than my own subjective and arbitrary judgments. A few could have been placed in a different group for reasons at least as good as those guiding the placements I selected. For example, Murakami is found in the fourth group, but he would sit just as comfortably in the second group. Fuwa could likewise be moved from the first to the second group. The procedure I followed in constructing the table was, first, to separate out persons formerly associated with the Tokuda (Mainstream) faction; second, to divide them into the more prominent and the less prominent in terms of party offices they held during the first half of the 1950s; and, last, to divide the remainder into three groups—those who have clearly made it to the top, those who have been up-and-coming since about the 1970 JCP congress, and those who have been associated with the old Internationalist faction but do not seem to have advanced in rank and position as far or fast as the first two groups. I was not able to track down the records of the three grouped as "unclassifiable."

Table 2 suggests several interesting facts about the five types of JCP top leaders. First, their ages vary from forty-six (Fuwa) to seventy-six (Kawada), as of January 1, 1977. Collectively, the fifth group is the oldest, with an average age of 71.6, followed by the third group (68.5) and the first group (64.1). Conversely, the second group is the youngest (50.6), followed by the fourth group (58.2). It is not surprising that the former Tokuda faction leaders should be old; it is significant that they are collectively older than the top leadership group, all except Konno being older than Miyamoto. It is also interesting that those old guard Miyamoto men who have been passed over in promotion decisions are several years older on the average than those who have already made it to the top and, more significant, they are eighteen years older than the up-and-comers

TABLE 2. Groups among JCP presidium members.

NAME	YEAR BIRTH	YEAR MEMBER	YEAR PRESIDIUM	EDUCATION	FORMER OCCUPATION
1. *Top Leaders* (7)					
(S) Fuwa	1930	1947	1970	Tokyo U (economics)	Student activist
(S) Hakamada	1904	1925 (?)	1958*	KUTV (Moscow)	Worker
(S) Kurahara	1902	1927	1958*	Language school	Culture movement activist
(S) Matsushima	1912	1947	1961	Teachers college	Journalist
(S) Miayamoto	1908	1931	1958*	Tokyo U (economics)	Writer
(S) Nishizawa	1913	1939 (?)	1964**	High school (Harbin)	Researcher
(S) Oka	1914	1948	1964	Tokyo U (economics)	Teacher
2. *Up-and-comers* (10)					
(S) Ibaraki	1924	1946	1970	Technical school	Labor unionist
(S) Kaneko	1924	1946	1970	Vocational school	Labor unionist
Kojima	1927	1947 (?)	1973	High school	Student activist
Kudo	1926	1947 (?)	1973	Tokyo U (science)	Student activist
Nakajima	1928	1949	1976	Tokyo U (literature)	Student activist
Nirasawa	1922	1948	1976	Business school	Student activist
Omura	1921	1947 (?)	1973	Keio U (dropout)	Family business
Sakaki	1929	1947	1973	Waseda U	Student activist
(S) Suwa	1926	1946	1973	Technical school	Labor unionist
(S) Ueda	1927	1946	1970	Tokyo U (economics)	Student activist
3. *Veteran Party Bureaucrats: Miyamoto Loyalists* (6)					
(S) Ebisudani	1908	1931 (?)	1970	Elementary school	Worker
Gesu	1912	1931	1966**	High school (dropout)	Clerk
Hoshino	1906	1945	1976	Kyoto U (literature)	Journalist
(S) Okamoto	1909	1949	1966**	Tohoku U (economics)	Professor
Sunama	1903	1927 (?)	1966**	Tokyo U (economics)	Clerk
Tada	1907	1929	1970	Elementary school	Worker

4. *Veteran Party Bureaucrats: Tokuda Loyalists* (10)

Akeda	1925	1948 (?)	1973	Wakayama U (dropout)	Labor unionist
Hama	1921	1947	1970	Vocational school	Union leader
(S) Ichikawa	1923	1946	1970	Technical school	Labor unionist
Ida	1914	1948	1970	Kyoto U (science)	Labor unionist
(S) Iwabayashi	1908	1931	1966**	Middle school	Union leader
(S) Murakami	1921	1947	1970	Vocational school	Union leader
Ofuchi	1913	1945	1964**	Vocational school	Labor unionist
(S) Takahara	1917	1947	1966**	Technical college	Union leader
Yasui	1917	1948	1970	Teachers college	Union leader
Yonehara	1909	1946	1964	High school (dropout)	Worker

5. *Reformed Tokuda Faction Leaders* (5)

Kasuga	1907	1928	1958*	Technical school	Labor unionist
Kawada	1900	1922	1964	Elementary school	Union leader
Konno	1910	1929	1964**	High school (dropout)	Labor unionist
Uchino	1901	1928	1966**	Elementary school	Labor unionist
Yoshida	1904	1928	1966**	Vocational school	Labor unionist

6. *Unclassifiable*

Furukata	(?)	1972 (?)	1973	(?)	(?)
Kobayashi	(?)	(?)	1976	(?)	(?)
Senaga	1908	1972 (?)	1973	High school (dropout)	Okinawa People's party leader

Legend: (S) before name indicates standing committee membership. One asterisk (*) indicates in or before the year given. Relevant information for the period before 1958 was not available. Two asterisks (**) indicates first elected as candidate member in the year given and promoted to full member rank in a later year.

Source: Tawara, pp. 304-315; Mizushima, passim; Koyama, pp. 287, 280; Kamiyama, p. 429; *Zen' ei*, December 1966, p. 208; ibid., August 1970, p. 272; ibid., January 1973, p. 366; Beckmann and Okubo, pp. 362-389.

about to join or replace the top group. Not surprisingly, all five men in the fifth group joined the party before the beginning of the Second World War. So did a majority in the third group (four out of six) and in the first group (four of seven). In contrast, all in the second group and all but one in the fourth joined after the war. These facts lead me to believe that the fifth group has little or no growth potential left and the third group is in a position only marginally better. On the other hand, the second group is obviously the wave of the future; the fourth group has a pretty good chance provided that its members continue to demonstrate their loyalty to the Miyamoto line, as well as their ingenuity and skill in the management of important party affairs.

Second, the date and manner of the first election to the presidium tend to reinforce the impressions about the relative growth potentials of the several groups. With the exception of Fuwa, who is very much an up-and-comer by most standards, the top leaders were all elected to the body in 1964 or before, three of them in 1958 or before. On the other hand, two of the five Tokuda faction leaders in the fifth group were elected as late as 1966. Furthermore, both of these two, and Konno, who was elected in 1964, were made only candidate members in the first instance. The case of the third group is similar; none won a seat on the presidium before 1966, two of the six not until 1970. Three were elected candidate members the first time around. At the other extreme, all the up-and-comers were elected in or after 1970—three in 1970, five in 1973, and two as late as 1976. When they were elected, however, they were all made full members at the initial appointment. The fourth group again presents an intermediate case; four were elected either in 1964 or 1966, but three, with the exception of Yonehara, originally had the candidate title. All the rest, except one, made it in 1970 as full members without a period of probation. If the future belongs to the up-and-comers, as I have suggested, it belongs to those who were born in the 1920s, joined the party during the second half of the 1940s, and were admitted to the presidium in the seventies. By these criteria, all but one (again Fuwa) in the first group will soon be gone; those in the third and especially in the fifth are almost gone; the second group is fasting coming; and four in the fourth group may join the comers and the remainder the goners.

The educational and occupation backgrounds of the current presidium members also show some interesting differences across the five groupings. Those in the first three Miyamoto groups are considerably better educated than the last two Tokuda line groups in terms of formal schooling. Whereas none among the five cadres and only one among the minor functionaries of the defunct Tokuda faction graduated from a university, three in seven, five in ten, and three in five, respectively, of the first three groups come from the most prestigious, formerly imperial universities (Tokyo, Kyoto, and Tohoku) or private universities (Waseda and Keio). It is, however, equally interesting and important that all are mixed groups, representing varied types and levels of formal educational background and experience. The top leaders group—the front-line carriers of Miyamoto's "self-reliance and independence" banner—includes three "Russian specialists": Hakamada, who attended the KUTV (the Eastern Workers Communist University) in Moscow; Kurahara, who specialized in Russian at Tokyo Foreign Language School and then spent twenty months in Moscow; and Nishizawa, who attended Harbin High School in Manchuria under Japanese occupation. The up-and-comers are as a whole at least as well educated as the top leaders, but they, too, include technical and vocational school graduates. Two among the older Miyamoto followers in the third group finished only elementary school. A university diploma may make some difference; it is obviously not a determining factor in one's success or failure at the top echelon of the JCP hierarchy.

The careers of the presidium members prior to their entry into the "party life" present a somewhat neater pattern of differentiation among the five groups. For those with "working class" backgrounds I made distinctions among factory or mine workers who were apparently uninvolved in union activities (worker), those actively involved in such activities (labor unionist), and those who held union office (union leader). Table 2 shows that all the leaders (the fifth group) and all but one of the minor functionaries (the fourth group) of the old Tokuda faction come from the ranks of unionists and union leaders. In contrast, the top leaders in the first group and the veteran Miyamoto men in the third have much more heterogeneous backgrounds, a majority issuing from the professional and white-collar classes. Miyamoto himself was a writer of some distinction who at the age of twenty won an award from a left-wing but respectable literary magazine (Mizushima, p. 15; Beckmann and Okubo, p. 374).

The members of the first, third, fourth, and fifth groups had lived, in one way or another, in the "real world" outside the confines of the party before they became full-time revolutionaries. On the other hand, a majority of the up-and-comers joined the party straight from the somewhat artificially secluded world of students. Six of the ten, including all four university graduates, entered party life while still students and have stayed active in the party without interruption since graduation. They are a purebred, pedigreed, new species of party member. Untainted by, if also untested against, the corrupting influences of the "real world," they are talented and sophisticated word artists of modern revolutionary theory. In their academic training, elitist outlook on society and politics, pragmatic bent, and

298   THE MANY FACES OF COMMUNISM

flair for abstract theorizing, they resemble most closely their university alumni in the nation's government bureaucracy and in academia. Collectively, they comprise the think-tank of the party, to defend and fortify the evolving orthodoxy of Miyamoto style national communism against attacks and criticisms from outside or inside the party. In a battle of words and ideas none of the other groups could match or challenge the skill and ingenuity of these young theoreticians. Miyamoto has recognized the special ability of this group and effectively has harnessed it to the consolidation and development of his power and ideological line.

As late as 1972 Miyamoto spoke at some length of the continuing danger of factional tendencies in the party and attacked anonymous "neo-opportunists of the left and the right" for their alleged attempts to fan such tendencies (JCP 7, pp. 16–17). It is possible that factionalism still exists in the presidium and, especially, the larger central committee. If so, it has apparently been kept under control and has so far failed to become a serious problem. As a result of successive expulsions of Miyamoto's most vocal opponents and critics during the last twenty years, the JCP leadership today has few enemies within the party. The main enemies are all outside—Shiga's pro-Moscow Voice of Japan group, the pro-Peking JCP Left, the radical students of the Revolutionary Communist League and their offshoots, the New Left antiwar youth committee affiliates in several large public service unions and in the locomotive engineers union. It is mainly at these groups of the Left and the Right as well as the reactionary and middle-of-the-road parties that the guns of the JCP's young and able theoreticians have been aimed in recent years. And for good reason. Twenty years after they began to take shape at the 1958 congress, the ideological and programmatic contents of the Miyamoto line are still very much in flux and vulnerable to assaults from the party's numerous enemies.

THE IDEOLOGY OF SCIENTIFIC SOCIALISM

Nationalism and pragmatism blend and reinforce each other in the ideology of socialism as it has evolved under Miyamoto's leadership. The disastrous consequences of his and his party's acceptance of the 1950 Cominform criticisms taught him a lesson; neither the Soviet nor the Chinese nor for that matter any foreign party could or should be permitted to criticize, much less dictate, the policies and strategies of the JCP. As a result of its capitulation to pressure from Moscow and Peking, the party's loyalty to the Japanese working class and its interests lost credibility. Even its opposition to "American imperialism" became suspect; it sounded like the refrain of a slave harking to his foreign master's orders. The exercise in "armed revolution" not only impressed the Japanese public with the incredible naivete of the "guerrilla fighters" but also bred lasting suspicion and hostility among the very people for whose sake the revolution was supposed to have been undertaken. The pragmatism of the Nosaka theory was nowhere in evidence and the party managed nearly to obliterate itself from the arena of real world politics.

As I suggested previously, the JCP retained opposition to American imperialism as one of the two major planks in the 1961 program. The thrust of its new nationalism since the 1955 consultative conference has been, however, independence from Moscow and Peking and, more important, winning back the confidence and support of the general public in Japan itself. The first has been justified as the practice of "true proletarian internationalism"; the latter, presumably as "true patriotism." The resolution of the 1966 congress thus said,

> Our party's position of self-reliance and independence is a most principled position that integrates true patriotism with true proletarian internationalism so that [we may] take full responsibility for the liberation struggle of the Japanese people and, at the same time, contribute most effectively to the advance of the international revolutionary movement. It is based on the lessons of an important historical experience of the Japanese and world communist movement (*Zen'ei*, December 1966, p. 49).

The two emphases of the process, which one author has called the "naturalization" of the JCP (Langer), progressed sequentially; the establishment of self-reliance and independence vis-à-vis the CPSU and the CCP during the 1960s and the adaptation of the official party policy and practice to Japan's existing political order and social norms during the early 1970s. The 1963-1964 dispute with the CPSU and the 1966 confrontation with the CCP were the watersheds in the process on the international front. In the first instance the apparent issue was whether the 1963 partial nuclear test ban treaty was good or bad; the real issue was whether the CPSU could dictate endorsement of the treaty to the JCP. Miyamoto's answer was an emphatic "no." When the CPSU put pressure on him and the JCP, through pro-Soviet groups in the JSP, and Shiga and a minority in the JCP central committee led by him, Miyamoto sent a four-man negotiating team to Moscow not to seek a reconciliation but to protest against and defy the CPSU's "great power chauvinism" (Scalapino, pp. 161 ff.; Suzuki, p. 165; Toki). Finally, when Shiga and another central committee member with a seat in the House of Councillors, Ichizo Suzuki, voted in the Diet for ratification of the treaty, they and their sympathizers were kicked out of the party.

In the second instance, the prima facie cause of the break was the issue of the involvement of the CPSU in a proposed international united front against American imperialism in support of Ho Chi Minh and his Vietnamese party; the real issue was Mao's insisting to the visiting JCP delegation led by Miyamoto that the Japanese comrades abandon their wishy-washy, "peaceful" revolution line and adopt Maoist style guerrilla warfare strategy. The CCP's meddling in the "internal affairs" of the Japanese party was no more acceptable to Miyamoto than the CPSU's. Gesu argued during the October 1966 JCP congress in defense of the party's decision to refuse to listen to Mao:

> The Selected Works of Mao Tse-tung refers to the special circumstances of the Chinese Revolution. For example, China was then a semicolonial, agricultural country in which new and old military cliques had long been entrenched throughout the land and engaged in perpetual fighting. The imperialist powers were behind their pet cliques to keep the country in a permanent and extremely complex state of internal conflicts and war. . . . Unlike a highly advanced capitalist nation, such as present-day Japan, China was an agrarian society in which rural villages were not completely dependant on cities. Despite the obvious and numerous difficulties, it was feasible for rural bases of revolutionary activities economically to sustain themselves. In addition, [the CCP] had a vast land area to use to its advantage. Do similar conditions exist in today's Japan? No. . . . Even an elementary school pupil would understand that the experience of the Chinese Revolution cannot be mechanically applied to this country. Unfortunately, the anti-JCP dogmatists do not seem to understand this simple fact (JCP 1, pp. 138–139).

Like Shiga and his pro-CPSU group in 1964, the CCP's allies and sympathizers, prominent in several JCP prefectural committees and front organizations, received stiff treatment from the central leadership and the incident ended in mass expulsions and defections. By the late 1960s the international thrust of the Miyamoto line was well established in the JCP's evolving new orthodoxy.

Conscious and systematic efforts to adapt the party's domestic policies and activities to the circumstances of a "highly advanced capitalist country" began in the sixties. The 1966 JCP-CCP dispute concerned, indirectly but importantly, the role of parliamentary institutions and the value of a multiparty system in the building of socialism in a developed capitalist country, i.e., Japan. Thus, Gesu's address quoted earlier was entitled "The Revolutionary Significance of Parliamentary Activities" and an article in Akahata dwelled on the potential of the Diet and local assemblies dominated by progressive majorities to serve as tools of "peaceful revolution" (JCP 1, pp. 136–144; Akahata, December 10, 1966). The efforts have become, however, far more obvious and bolder since the middle of 1969, when the JCP announced, for the first time publicly, that if and when the party came to power it would not ban any party or its activities even if that party was opposed to the JCP and its programs (Suzuki, p. 64). The 1970 JCP congress not only confirmed this commitment to uphold the competitive multiparty system under Communist rule, with an explicit pledge to allow change of government through free elections, but went a step further to undertake preservation and strengthening of all the existing constitutional guarantees for political freedoms and civil liberties (*Zen'ei*, August 1970, pp. 147-149).

From 1970 to 1977 the JCP leadership expended its time and energy mainly to develop and formalize the party's program for "socialism in Japan." By 1974 the commitment on democratic freedoms and civil rights became a pledge to defend three rather hard to define types of freedom—freedom to life, civil and political freedom, and freedom of the nation (*Zen'ei*, August 1974, pp. 207-214). These were presumed to include all the freedoms guaranteed by the present constitution of Japan and more (JCP 13, pp. 47-48). The contents and extent of the specific freedoms involved were explained in some detail in the "Declaration on Freedom and Democracy" adopted at the 1976 JCP congress. Thus, the private ownership of property, including a home and land, would be guaranteed to a working person, major means of production owned by big businesses alone being liable to nationalization; the sovereign rights and freedoms of the people would be fully protected; the Diet would become the "supreme organ of state" both in name and in practice and universal suffrage would continue; all political parties would be guaranteed free and unrestricted activity and there would be changes of government through elections; and the inherent right of every nation to choose its own social and political system and to exercise its sovereign powers in conducting its diplomatic, military, and economic affairs would be upheld (*Zen'ei*, September 1976, pp. 52-71; *Yomiuri shimbun*, July 18, 1976). And Miyamoto assured that the declaration was not just a ploy but a statement of the party's solemn pledge to the nation (*Yomiuri shimbun*, July 31, 1976; Fuwa 1, vol. 1, pp. 170-175; ibid., vol. 2, pp. 123 ff.; idem 2, pp. 113-114; *Zen'ei*, September 1976, pp. 6-37).

The spirited campaign on the theme of democracy and freedom has been accompanied by a veritable semantic revolution in the JCP lexicon. The revolution was inconspicuously launched at the 1970 congress when a few minor changes in the established terminology of the party were quietly made—the central committee "candidate" member was renamed "associate" member, the party's "cell" became "branch." These were purely cosmetic changes of no substantive significance, at least in the short run. "Associate" members of the central committee continued to be accorded the same status and to play the same role as "candidate" members. Likewise, the "branch" remained, like the "cell," the basic unit of grass-roots organization and activity. It consists of three or more members residing in the same neighborhood or employed at the same place of work. Party life and activity at this lowest level continue to emphasize above all discipline and solidarity among the members, thus inevitably perpetuating the conspiratorial image associated with the traditional "cell," which it replaced. The 1970 congress also established a social science institute to study problems of "scientific socialism," including the adequacy of conventional translations of foreign words (Iizuka 1, pp. 162 ff.). Presumably as a result of the new institute's work, "proletarian dictatorship" (*puroretaria dokusai*), as the term was used in the 1961 program, became "proletarian rule" (*puroretaria shikken*) in 1973 and then the "power of the working class" (*rodoshakaikyu no kenkryoku*) in 1976 (*Zen'ei*, January 1974, pp. 253-259; ibid., September 1976, pp. 46-50; Miyamoto 4, pp. 33-34). In 1976 the term "Marxism-Leninism" was replaced by "scientific socialism" in both the program and the rules of the party (*Zen'ei*, September 1976, pp. 50-51).

The two-step semantic change and reinterpretation of "proletarian dictatorship" was explained and justified essentially by the contemporary and practical needs of the party operating in present-day Japan. It was thus argued that the original term was mistakenly associated with the notion of violent revolution, which might have been appropriate in the age of the Russian Revolution but which was inappropriate to the present tasks of the Japanese party. The JCP theoreticians took pains, however, to point out that the "power of the working class" is synonymous with "proletarian dictatorship" as Marx and Engels used that term in their writings; that the connotations of force and violence were added later by Lenin to suit the special circumstances of his work in tsarist Russia; and, in effect, that the changes in the Japanese translation of the term did not in any way modify or distort its original meaning (Fuwa 2; idem 4, pp. 123-182; Miyamoto 4, p. 34; Ueda and Iizuka, pp. 151-154).

In expunging the other and more popular term "Marxism-Leninism" from basic party documents, however, the JCP clearly went one step further than merely returning to the original words and ideas of Marx and Engels. The change was not justified by the plausible argument that, following the logic presented in the preceding paragraph, "Marxism-Leninism" is "Marxism" contaminated and corrupted by "Leninism." It was argued instead that the contemporary theory of socialism had been built on the ideas of Marx, Engels, and Lenin but had been vastly enriched thereafter by the cumulative experience of the worldwide communist movement

(*Zen'ei*, September 1976, p. 51). The JCP was to be guided by this newer and better version of Marxism, which could best be called "scientific socialism." Needless to say, this brand of socialism has all the trappings of parliamentary, democratic government and is suitable to the circumstances of an advanced capitalist country like Japan.

The process of "naturalization" of the JCP is not yet over. It has been suggested somewhat facetiously that the Japan Communist party (*Nihon kyosanto*) may someday be renamed the Japan Communal party (*Nihon kyodoto*). But what concerns us here is not how far the process is going to reach but rather what effects it has had on the prospects of the JCP for attaining the power of government.

The JCP and Prospects for a Coalition Government

THE JCP'S COALITION GOVERNMENT PLANS

The JCP program adopted in 1961 and amended in July 1976 envisages a three-step approach to socialist government in Japan: first, the building of a "national, democratic, united front"; second, the establishment of a united front (coalition) government; third and last, the development of the coalition government into a socialist (JCP) government (*Zen'ei*, September 1976, pp. 314- 315). Socialist society, i.e., society with a socialist government, is the first stage of a communist society. For practical purposes, therefore, the mission of the party is to be accomplished when a socialist government comes into being. Before that happens, however, a national, democratic, united front must be established and an interim government supported by that front. The JCP leadership has understandably been concerned so far mainly with problems of the first two stages.

In the afterglow of its impressive performance in the House of Representatives elections of the previous year, when it had managed to win fourteen seats compared to five in 1967, the 1970 JCP congress confidently, if prematurely, resolved to establish a democratic coalition government during the second half of the 1970s (Suzuki, p. 49). Meeting a year after an even more impressive victory (thirty-eight seats) in the 1972 House of Representatives elections, the party announced a draft program for the coalition government. Entitled "The Proposal of the JCP Concerning the Program of Democratic Coalition Government," the document consists of three parts. Part 1 proposes to terminate the United States- Japanese military alliance and to safeguard Japan's security by a foreign policy of peace and neutralism (JCP 8; *Zen'ei*, January 1974, pp. 160–252; Iizuka 2, pp. 20–28, 119–163). The existing United States–Japan mutual security treaty would be terminated by the unilateral action of the Japanese government, with the approval of the Diet and in accordance with the procedure provided for in the treaty itself. Japan would then establish peaceful and friendly relationships with nations regardless of differences in social systems, including the United States. The Japanese government would negotiate with the Soviet Union the return of not only the few northern offshore islands but the entire Kuriles group. As for the Japanese Self-Defense Forces, which the JCP regards as unconstitutional, they would be gradually abolished in several steps: the suspension of the current defense force buildup plan, the reduction of defense expenditures, the suspension of equipment and manpower increases, the closing of bases, and the retraining of troops and personnel.

Part 2 of the program envisages an end to economic policies geared to the exclusive interests of big business, the protection of the people's livelihood, and a better balanced development of the nation's economy. For the benefits of the working masses, social welfare and security programs would be vastly expanded, inexpensive housing provided, wages raised, farmers guaranteed fair and adequate prices for their produce, a new land reform undertaken, and pollution and natural disasters brought under control. The taxation and fiscal systems would be democratized, but nationalization would be limited to the key industries, especially those operating in the energy field. "Democratic control" would be applied to all large and monopolistic firms in all industries; it would consist of investigations by the Diet, administrative guidance from the government, inspections and restraints by employee unions, the same by pollution control committees and committees of residents to be established for the purpose, and so forth. The government would aim at self-sufficiency in foodstuffs and keep down foreign agricultural imports to a minimum. However, trade would be promoted with all nations on the basis of the principles of peaceful coexistence. Economic and technical assistance to developing nations would be expanded.

Part 3 promises to prevent revisions of the constitution, the strengthening of democratic institutions, and the promotion of education and culture. Significantly, the party committed itself for the first time to uphold the entire text of the present constitution, including the provisions relating to the emperor and not just the "democratic" parts of it as previously. Diet seats would be reapportioned among the election districts so as to eliminate existing inequities. Civil liberties and political freedoms would be fully protected. The system of justice would be democratized, and local autonomy would be strengthened. Finally, school and university education, arts and sciences, and sports would be promoted along democratic lines. Thus, a better and happier nation would emerge under the guidance of the coalition government.

The draft program is obviously very ambitious but also diffuse and somewhat incoherent. As soon as it was published, it was subjected to criticism and denunciation from diverse quarters. An anonymous group leveled particularly savage criticism at the entire document, arguing that if the program were ever implemented Japan would be reduced to a militarily untenable, economically bankrupt state (Gurupu 1984-nen). The JCP's replies to these and other criticisms have not added much to what the 1973 document already states (Ueda and Kudo; JCP 13, pp. 53 ff.). One may therefore assume that the major points of the program summarized here represent the current JCP blueprint for the policy program of the interim coalition government. In terms of the politics of Japan, however, the real issue is not whether the specifics of the program are theoretically sound or even feasible; it is whether there is basic trust and will to work with each other between the JCP and its potential coalition partners. It is this question on which the success and failure of Miyamoto's work during the last twenty years ultimately depend.

THE JCP VERSUS THE DSP AND THE CGP

Among the four Japanese parties with which the JCP contends for power, the ruling LDP naturally falls outside the range of the party's potential coalition partners. The Liberal Democrats are, as Ueda has put it, "agents of the American and Japanese forces of reaction, that is, a party that depends on American imperialism and represents the interests of the Japanese monopoly capital, which also depends on American imperialism" (Ueda and Iizuka, p. 110). The DSP comes close to the LDP in the JCP's list of enemies. The mutual enmity between the two parties has been evident since the DSP's foundation in 1961, but it has intensified considerably during the last ten years. The reason is simple and obvious. Unlike their former partners in the JSP, leaders of the DSP are and always have been consistently and inflexibly anticommunist and anti-JCP. As a 1968 JCP book pointed out, the party's "middle-of-the roadism" had a distinct tilt against the JCP and toward the LDP (JCP 2, part II). As the JCP steadily increased its share of seats in the national legislature and in local assemblies during the late 1960s and early 1970s and especially as it began to announce plans for a coalition government centered around itself, the DSP naturally hardened its anti-JCP posture. In 1970 the then DSP chairman, Eiichi Nishimura, revealed at a press conference his counterplan for the establishment of a "democratic, progressive, coalition government." The idea was to build a coalition of two parties (the DSP and the CGP) and one faction (the anti-JCP faction in the JSP led by Eda) to overthrow LDP rule and, more important, to arrest the advance of the JCP (Takahashi, pp. 150-164; *Mainichi shimbun seijibu*, pp. 39-41). If the plan succeeded, a new party based on a grand coalition of anti-JCP "progressives" was to be formed in 1972 and ascend to power in 1975. The JCP condemned Nishimura's proposal as a restatement of the "three anti-isms" of the prewar Democratic Socialists—anticapitalism, antifascism, and anticommunism (*Akahata*, January 20, 1971; ibid., May 16, 1971). In a sense it would have been more accurate to call it a replica of the 1926 "three-anti program" of the Social Mass party rather than of the 1931 "three anti-isms" of the Japan Workers Club (Takahashi, pp. 18-27), but the point was well taken, Nishimura was obviously talking about a united front against the JCP.

The DSP subsequently made it known even more clearly that it had no intention at all of cooperating, much less sharing government power, with the JCP. Nishimura's successor, Ikko Kasuga, has called it absolutely out of the question for the party to work with the Communists; another DSP spokesman dismissed the JCP's coalition government program as totally unrealistic and expedient, reiterating the party's call for a different kind of coalition excluding the JCP (*Mainichi shimbun*, December 7, 1976; Ouchi, pp. 98-120, 340-342) The party's official "People's Progressive Coalition Government Plan" announced in 1974 promised to "exclude groups that intend to amend the Constitution in its essentials and aim at revolution and one-party dictatorship on the basis of Marxism-Leninism incompatible with parliamentary democracy" (Iizuka, pp. 47-48, 187; Mainichi shimbun, December 7, 1976) In early 1976 Kasuga provoked the JCP's wrath by taking to the Diet floor the "lynching murder" case and raising questions about Miyamoto's status in connection with the case (which was discussed earlier) JCP reacted strongly with charges of the DSP's collusion with the LDP and big business, even branding the party chant of death" (Hiron to Seisaku, March 1976, pp. 9-44-55; Asahi shimbun, January 21, 1976). But probably odd from the point of view of the JCP's drive for power increasing evidence that the DSP actually collaborates in elections. Thus in the 1975 gubernatorial and local two parties entered into arrangements to endorse dates and campaign jointly for them, with substantial several key contests (*Nihon keizai shimbun*, April shimbun, April 29, 1976). This practice has

JCP-DSP rift and made any future compromise and reconciliation most unlikely.

The JCP's view of the CGP was less rigid and marginally more positive until early 1972. Thus, some CGP leaders were judged to be "reasonable" and some possibility was said to exist for cooperation between the two parties (*Akahata*, May 16, 1971). As long as the "reasonable" men continued to behave themselves, the JCP would "not close its doors" to the possibility of fruitful, if limited, cooperation (*Akahata*, February 6, 1972). In the next few years, however, the good men in the CGP leadership apparently either changed their minds or chose to stop pressing their views against their bad comrades and the possibility of JCP-CGP cooperation quickly waned.

The CGP announced in 1973 its own "Plan for a Middle-of-the-Road Progressive Coalition Government," which asserts the party's opposition to the LDP, authoritarian power, and big capital and expresses its determination to defend the constitution and the parliamentary system of government (Iizuka 2, pp. 45- 46, 165- 172). The plan also warns against the danger of "forces intent on abrogating the principles of the present constitution and establishing dictatorship," meaning the JCP. There ensued an intense public debate between the two parties on the problem of the constitution and the nature and tasks of the coalition government to be established. By the time the debate ended inconclusively in early 1974, the JCP apparently had come to the realization that the CGP was essentially as "reactionary" and anti-JCP as the DSP (JCP 10, p. 35 et passim). In recent years JCP pronouncements on the CGP have increasingly lumped the party together with the DSP and the JSP rightist faction led by Saburo Eda in what it contemptuously calls the "E-Ko-Min" alliance ("E" for Eda, "Ko" for *Komeito*, or the CGP, and "Min" for *Minshu shakaito*, or the DSP) (JCP 13, pp. 31- 33; idem 14, p. 62; *Yomiuri shimbun*, July 31, 1976). In some ways the CGP outranks even the DSP in the JCP's enemies list; for example, it is said to be the self-professed promoter of the E-Ko-Min machinations (JCP 13, p. 34) and its "intellectual criminality" is contrasted to the DSP's "primitivism" (*Akahata*, October 11, 1976).

The CGP has responded in kind. In its 1974 publication the party piled on the JCP numerous charges of proclivity toward violence and duplicity—of well-camouflaged plans to subvert the constitution, to destroy the system of democratic government and then establish a one-party dictatorship with the facade of a multiparty system, and so forth (CGP). The CGP chairman, Yoshikatsu Takeiri, has suggested that the JCP may be called a "totalitarian" party (*Komei shimbun*, July 9, 1975) and promised to stick to his decision not to share government power with it (*Mainichi shimbun*, December 7, 1976). The party's newspaper has condemned the JCP's profession of democracy and freedom as purely deceptive (*Komei shimbun*, September 28, 1976).

The intensity of mutual animosity that today prevails between the JCP and the CGP leads me to believe that the chances of reconciliation between them in the immediate future are not much better than those for reconciliation between the JCP and the DSP. For practical purposes, and short of a miracle, one may thus eliminate both as serious candidates for JCP's coalition partners. The latter's only hope lies with the JSP.

THE JCP AND THE JSP

For various reasons discussed previously, the JSP is the only party with which the JCP appears to have some chance of entering into a durable relationship of cooperation in order to implement its united front government plan. The JCP leaders no doubt know this very well and have tried to woo the JSP to their side, alternately by appeasement and by threat. Apart from the anti-security treaty joint struggle of 1959-1960, however, they have not yet managed to work out a mutually acceptable formula for effective cooperation and joint efforts to build an anti-LDP united front. There are several difficult problems that are likely to continue to foil the JCP's attempts to improve the situation.

The most obvious problem arises from the JSP's own concept of and plan for an interim, potentially coalition based government. The first official JSP plan for the establishment of a socialist government, entitled "The Road to Socialism in Japan" and adopted at the 1966 JSP congress after several revisions, envisages three types of interim government: first, a one-party JSP government based on a JSP majority in the Diet; second, a JSP government with a JSP plurality in the Diet and the collaboration of other party or parties; and, third, a coalition with other progressive parties, excluding the LDP (JSP, pp. 48-50). The trouble is that in all cases the JSP has to be the dominant party and the collaborating groups, if any, would hold subordinate and, presumably minority, positions in the government. As the party's numerical strength in the Diet declined in the following years and the high hopes of the mid-1960s waned, the plan was drastically modified to provide for a more flexible coalition formula. The "National Coalition Government Plan" of 1971, which is commonly referred to in party circles as the "New Medium-Term Line," represents this modified approach. The basic goals of this program are essentially the same as those of the 1973 JCP program: the termination of the United States-Japan mutual security treaty and the neutralization of Japan; the reorientation of economic policies partial to big business; the protection and enrichment of the people's lives; the defense of the democratic rights of the people guaranteed by the constitution; and additional social, educational, and cultural reforms (Iizuka 2, pp. 31–35). The program retains, however, the assumption of the 1966 document that the prospective coalition government would be led and dominated by the JSP. The problem is further compounded from the JCP's point of view by the commitment of the new JSP approach to a four-party coalition, involving all the opposition parties. Considering the JCP's recent and current disputes with the DSP and the CGP, this poses a formidable difficulty for cooperation between the JCP and the JSP.

Behind the four-party coalition formula put out by the JSP lies another and more fundamental difficulty for JCP-JSP cooperation. The root problem is the tradition of factionalism in the JSP, which breeds perpetual ideological, programmatic, and tactical disputes and maneuverings among the party's influential members. At present there are five major factions, two mini-factions, and independents. A complex game of faction politics is played among these groupings with the lines of competition and alignment constantly shifting depending on the nature of the issue in dispute. Among the major factions the Socialism Association (the Sakisaka faction) stands at the left end of the ideological spectrum, followed by the Katsumata and Sasaki factions. The Eda faction is at the other end of the spectrum, closely followed by the Associates of the New Current. The Comrades of the Peasant and the Comrades against the United States–Japan Security Treaty are small clusters of individuals bound by common interest in the problems suggested by their groups' names. The independents include some bona fide independents and many fence sitters, swinging one way or another depending on which way the wind blows. [The Eda faction has since split with the JSP.—M.A.K.]

The Socialism Association is pro-Soviet, in addition to being the most committed and doctrinaire Marxist-Leninist among the JSP factions. The Katsumata faction is much less committed either to Moscow or to Marxism-Leninism but usually cooperates with the association in interfaction disputes, especially over personnel matters. On the other side, the anti–security treaty group is fervently pro-China and the Sasaki faction only marginally less so. Both are ideologically left by most criteria, but they cooperate with the right Eda faction and the New Current in opposing the Socialism Association–Katsumata faction alliance ("Kuno suru shakaito"). The present JSP chairman, Tomomi Narita, is an independent and General Secretary Masatsugu Ishibashi is a Katsumata faction affiliate. They and the rest of the party's current executives sit precariously on a shifting balance of power among the factions.

The factionalized state of the JSP presents the JCP with an almost insoluble problem. Assuming that Narita and the executives of the party could somehow be persuaded to accept partnership with the JCP as an unavoidable, if distasteful, fact of life, they would be opposed by most of the major factions for diverse and contradictory reasons. The Eda faction is nearly as anti-JCP as the DSP and the CGP and would no doubt oppose any conciliatory move on the part of the party leadership even, perhaps, to the extent of threatening to bolt the party if its views were ignored. The New Current would take a similar position. The Sasaki faction would certainly object on the ground, if nothing better, of the JCP's "unfriendly" attitude toward Peking. The same would be true of the anti-security treaty group. The Katsumata group would prefer to follow the Association in any major interfaction showdown.

The Socialism Association is superficially the most likely reservoir of goodwill and support for JCP-JSP cooperation because of its ideological affinity with the JCP leadership. Ironically, however, the fact is that it is the group in the JSP most consistently and fanatically anti-JCP. Alternatively called the Sakisaka faction, in deference to the charismatic veteran polemicist on the economics faculty of Kyushu University, Itsuro Sakisaka, who leads the group, the association was formed in 1951 by the survivors of the prewar worker-peasant faction (*Rono-ha*) of academic Marxists. In the late 1920s and throughout the thirties this group fought a bitter, if mostly unproductive, running battle of words with another group of academic Marxists called the Lecturers (*Koza-ha*), thus called not because they were university lecturers but because they contributed to a series of treatises on the history of Japanese capitalism under the general title of *Lectures on the Developmental History of Japanese Capitalism* (Iwanami shoten, 1932-1933). The central issue of the dispute was whether Japanese capitalism was fully mature to the extent of having reached the stage of full-fledged imperialism, as defined by Lenin, and therefore called for a one-stage socialist revolution; or, alternatively, was it still overshadowed by the remnants of medieval feudalism—the archaic emperor institution, biglandlordism, underdeveloped bourgeoisie, and so forth—and therefore required a two-stage revolution—a bourgeois democratic revolution in the first instance, followed by a socialist revolution. In those days the first group worked through the Worker-Peasant party and the latter group through the prewar JCP. After the Second World War the first group joined the JSP, continuing to argue for a one-stage socialist revolution; the latter reestablished the JCP, seeking to apply the two-stage revolution theory to the changed circumstances (which soon led them to replace feudal remnants by American imperialism as justification for the first stage "bourgeois democratic" revolution).

Today the JSP is still committed to its classic formula at least as faithfully as is the JCP to its own version. It is, however, the Socialism Association and, more specifically, Sakisaka, who sustain this remarkable tradition in the JSP (Sakisaka 1, pp. 218- 227). And it is in this historical context that the present and future relationship between the two parties is debated by theoreticians on both sides. Unfortunately for the JCP, the Sakisaka group can still make or break the JSP. Since its foundation in 1951, it has been a party within a party for all practical purposes. It has its own platform (the "Thesis of the Socialism Association"), its own organ (*Socialism*), an active youth group (the Socialist Youth League), and, above all, its own will to act—in defiance of the party leadership if necessary ("Kuno suru shakaito").

For reasons that should be fairly clear already, the JCP has directed its attacks mainly at the Eda faction on the right and the Socialism Association on the left in its coercive approach to the JSP. It has condemned the former as following a program totally irrelevant to true socialism and practicing a policy of "exclusion" as opposed to the policy of "unity" essential to the creation of a workable united front (*Zen'ei*, September 1976, p. 33; Ishida). In the meantime, Sakaki has declared the "historical bankruptcy" of Sakisaka's theory (Sakaki); Ueda has counted seventy anti-JCP articles in the association's *Socialism* in the period between 1970 and 1973 and charged the group with incorrigible Moscow worship and JCP phobia inherited from its prewar mentors (Ueda and Iizuka, p. 161). Sakisaka's judgment that through the semantic revolution the JCP had in effect abandoned the vitally important concept of dictatorship of the proletariat provoked an immediate and forceful retort from Fuwa (*Asahi shimbun*, May 18, 1976; ibid., June 1, 1976).

Even while these harsh exchanges were going on with its principal opponents in the JSP, the JCP continued its conciliatory approach to the party's leadership. Thus, Ueda pointed out the obvious fact that the basic goals of the JSP coalition government program are virtually identical with those of the JCP's similar program and asked, "Is it not evident that the parties on which the people pin their hopes for the arrival of a united front and which, therefore, share the greatest responsibility for fulfilling their hopes are the JCP and the JSP?" (Ueda and Iizuka, pp. 157- 158). Then, too, an official JCP publication expressed the party's resolve to continue to do its best to promote cooperation and joint struggle with a broad range of democratic forces, specifically including the JSP (JCP 13, pp. 159- 160). Miyamoto referred to an increasing number of labor unions that had publicly called for a closer relationship between the two parties, proposing the creation of new and more permanent organizational machinery to extend the JCP-JSP joint efforts, which had so far been limited to election times (Miyamoto 4, p. 29). As I have already pointed out, given the JCP's recent relationships with the three other parties, cooperation with the JSP, leading to a coalition government dominated by, if not exclusively of, the two parties, is the only hope left to the Communists of ever sharing the power of government in the foreseeable future. The party's carrot-and-stick approach is perhaps most logical and unavoidable. The chances of its ultimate success are not nil—anything is possible in politics!—but rather dim, to say the least. Yet does there exist voter support for the JCP powerful enough to carry it to power regardless and in spite of the party's failure to win the sympathy and cooperation of the other opposition parties?

THE JCP AND THE GENERAL PUBLIC

We have seen that the JCP was the rising star on the horizon of Japanese election politics in the late 1960s and early seventies. There are now indications, however, that the steady upward trend of its popularity at the polls may well have come to an end. Table 3 gives the comparative percentages of votes and numbers of seats won by the five parties in the House of Representatives elections held from 1967 to 1976. The table shows that the 1976 fall of the JCP's percentage of the vote was not nearly as precipitous as the fall of JCP seats, the discrepancy suggesting a problem with the party's election strategy rather than with the basic pattern of voter support, i.e., the same problem the CGP had in 1972. It is nevertheless important to note that the JCP's share of the vote failed to show any increase for the first time since the early 1960s. It is equally significant that this disappointing performance followed the most spirited and best publicized preelection campaign the party had ever put up.

TABLE 3. **Percentages of vote and numbers of seats by party, 1967-1976.**

| | 1967 | | 1969 | | 1972 | | 1976 | |
	Vote %	Seat	Vote %	Seat	Vote %	Seat	Vote %	Seat
JCP	4.8	5	6.8	14	10.5	38	10.4	17
LDP	48.8	277	47.6	288	46.9	271	41.8	249
NLC*							4.2	17
JSP	27.9	140	21.4	90	21.9	118	20.7	123
CGP	5.4	25	7.7	47	8.5	29	10.9	55
DSP	7.4	30	10.9	31	7.0	19	6.3	29

*The New Liberal Club was formed in 1976 by defectors from the LDP.
Source: Asahi nenkan, 1973, p. 247; *Asahi shimbun,* December 8, 1976.

The resolution of the July 1976 JCP congress underlined the importance of the elections scheduled for later in the year.

> The forthcoming general elections [of the House of Representatives] will be an occasion of great nationwide political battles that will determine the direction of the country's politics in the second half of the seventies. In these important political battles, which are bound to prove to be counted among the "fiercest contests in history," our party carries a historic mission to enrich and strengthen its policy line and programs through investment of all the available intellectual resources of its entire membership and through utilization of its total capability to the fullest extent possible (*Zen'ei*, September 1976, p. 38).

The historic significance of the elections made it an "absolute imperative" for the JCP to improve on its performance during the 1969 and 1972 elections (Miyamoto 2, pp. 22-23). Despite all the hyperbole and the heroic battle cries, however, there was a nagging premonition of impending disaster even among the party's leaders. The presidium report that followed the presentation of the Congress resolution just quoted warned that the target of fifty-one seats might prove unattainable and that the CGP might overtake the JCP to regain its 1969 position as the third largest party in the House (*Zen'ei*, September 1976, p. 87). As Table 3 shows, the premonition materialized in December, with a resounding impact.

Despite, and to some extent because of, the bold program of democratization and liberalization the JCP had followed in recent years and the series of well-publicized successes it had achieved, the JCP had come under increased attack from both the Right and the Left. The criticisms of the 1973 coalition government program by the anonymous group were a good example and so was the controversy (sparked by the 1976 magazine article) over Miyamoto's role in the 1932 lynching incident. At least as troublesome were criticisms of the party's continuing adherence to the doctrine of democratic centralism in the management of its internal affairs. Many, including those who were generally sympathetic to the party and its liberalization program, questioned the sincerity and authenticity of Miyamoto's professed good intentions on account of this doctrine (*Asahi shimbun*, July 25, 1976; *Yomiuri shimbun*, July 31, 1976). So far, however, the JCP leadership has categorically denied any intention to give up the principle explicitly provided for in the party's rules (*Zen'ei*, September 1976, pp. 317, 320; Miyamoto 4, p. 40).

Despite the great publicity given to its recent achievements at the polls, by both friends and foes, the JCP has never managed to win the confidence and support of more than a small minority of the Japanese public. The sharpened criticisms and attacks leveled at the party in the press and in popular magazines during the last few years have further lowered its standing with the average voter. Thus, in an

Asahi shimbun public opinion poll of June 1975 (a national sample of 3000 adults) only 8% of the respondents preferred the JCP to any other party, as compared to 45% and 24% who preferred the LDP and the JSP, respectively (*Asahi shimbun*, July 6, 1975). In describing the JCP 10% praised it either as a good performer in general (7%) or as a defender of the working man's interests (3%); on the other hand, 15% positively disliked the party, 13% thought it much too extreme, and 8% felt it was unrealistic and impractical. Subsequent polls by the same paper (with similar samples) indicated further decline in the JCP's popularity during 1976, as shown on Table 4.

Public opinion in Japan is no more stable or logical than that in any other country. It does seem beyond much doubt, however, that the JCP's popularity has been anything but overwhelming. And this absence of strong, sustained public support for the party is in the final analysis the most troublesome obstacle to the arrival of a JCP dominated government.

The JCP's performance in the 1976 House of Representatives elections was an unsurprising consequence of the widespread public antipathy that the Miyamoto line has so far failed to overcome. No more surprisingly, the overall achievements of the party in prefectural and local elections have not been quite as impressive as the rather spectacular improvement in the late 1960s and early seventies might have led one to believe. It is true that the party has captured, jointly with the JSP, the mayoralties and governorships of several key cities and prefectures, including Tokyo, Osaka, and Kyoto. Elsewhere, however, it has not done nearly as well. In discussing any party's performance in local elections, one must keep in mind the important fact that many elections are still fought basically on a nonpartisan basis. This is particularly true of town and village level elections; about 95% of town and village mayors and 90% of town and village assemblymen are independents. But so are also nearly 90% of city mayors and 60% of city assemblymen (councillors) and prefectural governors. It is only in prefectural and Tokyo special ward assembly elections that nearly all candidates run on party tickets. Bearing this fact in mind, one may still ponder the relevant

T A B L E 4. Party preferences in *Asahi shimbun* polls.

	MARCH 1976	OCTOBER 1976	FEBRUARY 1977
JCP	7%	6%	4%
LDP	41	45	21
JSP	27	24	21
CGP	5	5	6
DSP	6	5	6

Source: Asahi shimbun, February 17, 1977.

statistics: as of the end of 1975 the JCP's share of *partisan* seats was 16.6% in city assemblies, 15.4% in the Tokyo special ward assemblies, and 4.8% in prefectural assemblies (Sorifu tokeikyoku, p. 242). According to the plans announced at the 1970 JCP congress, by late 1973 the party was to have its members elected to "every prefectural and local assembly," as well as several dozen representatives to the Diet, the latter meaning at least forty (Iizuka 1, pp. 22-23). Three years after the target date, JCP members were found in only slightly more than a half (55.7%) of prefectural and local assemblies, whereas its parliamentarian group consisted of seventeen members in the House of Representatives and twenty in the House of Councillors (at least three short of the 1970 projection).

Even the size of the JCP's party membership appears to have peaked in the early 1970s. The 1970 plan projected a total membership of several hundred thousand, meaning over 400,000, by 1973. In the summer of 1976, however, the actual membership size was estimated to be about 380,000, still a respectable figure compared to the other opposition parties but substantially below the projected level (*Yomiuri shimbun*, July 19, 1976; *Nihon keizai shimbun*, August 1, 1976). And this was in spite of a significant relaxation of the JCP code of behavior that was recently adopted obviously in the hope that the alarming dropout rate among younger members might be cut down. The code of behavior sets out four "standards": a member must conscientiously engage in the learning of the party's policies, including the regular reading of the decisions and resolutions of the party congresses and *Akahata*; he must regularly attend branch meetings and participate in the discussion of the policies of the party and in the activity programs of the branch; he must actually engage in party activities in accordance with the policies of the party and the branch; and he must be punctual in the payment of membership dues and subscriptions to party publications. In 1971, however, it was made clear that these rules were no more than "standards" to guide a member's activities and that they could not be used in determining eligibility for continued membership (*Akahata*, November 26, 1971; ibid., December 18, 1971). When voluntary membership terminations were increasing at a high rate, especially among newer and younger members, the party obviously could not afford to add to the losses by forced resignations through the strict application and enforcement of the standards. And now the priority went clearly to the quantity, not the quality, of the membership.

It is ironic but perfectly logical that the JCP's "phenomenal" growth should have taken place simultaneously with the "miraculous" growth of the Japanese economy during the 1960s and the first part of the seventies. The former was to a large extent a by-product of the economic and social "evils" begotten by the latter—the surging inflation of commodity and land prices, the spreading pollution of the air, water, and soil, the congestion of cities, with housing shortages, inadequate transportation systems, crowded schools, and so on. It is then perhaps also logical that the beginning of the party's woes should have coincided with the halt of the country's rapid economic growth and with the beginning of serious interest among conservative politicians and bureaucrats in coping with the aggravated economic and social problems. This is not to suggest that the "naturalization" and liberalization of the party did not help it win greater public support than previously. Nor has the party ceased to push the process. Far from it. It has in fact begun even to extol bourgeois values and virtues, as when, to everyone's surprise, its leaders spoke of the special moral obligations of the schoolteacher to society and the duty of the civil servant to work selflessly for the general good of all (Fuwa 2, p. 258). The party's approach to mass media, especially the press, became markedly more liberal in the late 1960s; Miyamoto began to meet regularly with reporters in 1967 and the following year a JCP reporters club, representing all the major papers, opened up shop in the party's headquarters (Suzuki, pp. 28–29; Iizuka 1, pp. 16–17). Since then the JCP Central Party School has been opened to visits by the public. And, finally, since 1970 the party has begun to permit the press to attend the triennial party congresses.

All these deliberate steps to create a better image of the party among the public have no doubt helped to bring the JCP to where it is today in the nation's politics—a small minority without a means of translating its philosophy and ideas into government policies but strong enough to worry and frighten its opponents and competitors. What these steps have failed to achieve, at least so far, is to bring the JCP much closer to governmental power. As I have already suggested, and as most careful observers of the party's performance would agree, there is not much chance that it will even join a coalition government in the immediate future (Tawara, pp. 325-327).

The International Politics of the JCP

INTER-COMMUNIST PARTY RELATIONS

As I mentioned earlier, the Miyamoto line came with a barb in its international application, first used against the CPSU and then against the CCP. The JCP's disputes with these two parties are no longer as intense as they were during the 1960s, but the principle of "self-reliance" and "independence" has further hardened and there is no likelihood that it will ever be significantly modified, much less abandoned. The JCP rules give a prominent place to the principle in the preamble.

> The JCP and all its members firmly uphold their position that theirs is a party self-reliant and independent, alone responsible for revolution in Japan; they will carry on the revolutionary tradition and militant spirit of the party, advance always together with the people of Japan, perpetuate the superior historical heritage of the Japanese nation, fight to create a new Japan with independence, democracy, neutralism, and improved living conditions and to bring about a shining socialist and communist society (*Zen'ei*, September 1976, p. 318).

As Miyamoto has said recently, the party is interested neither in exporting its ideas to another country nor in importing another party's policies; the JCP policies shall be "determined in Tokyo" (*Yomiuri shimbun*, July 18, 1976).

Since their showdown of 1964 the JCP and the CPSU have tried on several occasions to come to terms with each other. In 1968 and again in 1971 formal talks were held between representatives of the two parties, the first in Tokyo between Miyamoto and Suslov and the second in Moscow between Miyamoto and Brezhnev (Iizuka 1, p. 128; Akiyama 2). Neither talk succeeded in ending the dispute and in 1974 the parties fought another war of words over criticisms of the JCP first published in the Argentine Communist party organ, *Nueva era*, and later reprinted in the CPSU journal *Party Life* (*Akahata*, September 15, 1974). The relationship has recently somewhat improved; the CPSU central committee sent a delegation to Tokyo in early 1976 to meet and discuss the "normalization" of relations with JCP executives. Later in the year the Soviet ambassador to Tokyo, Polyansky, began to call at JCP headquarters, something his immediate predecessors had not done for years (Akiyama 2, pp. 15-16). Despite these signs of a gradual thaw, there is no apparent enthusiasm on the JCP's part for anything like the close relationship it had with Moscow during the forties and fifties, especially if that means compromising the basic principle of independence enshrined in the party's rules.

Apart from Miyamoto's nationalist line in the politics of inter-communist party relations in general, there are a few other obstacles to an early and speedy compromise between the JCP and the CPSU. An important sore point since 1964 has been the latter's support, allegedly financial as well as moral, of Shiga and his Voice of Japan group. The CPSU has gained little, except the aggravated resentment of the JCP, from its relationship with Shiga's group. It may now have finally decided to terminate the unprofitable relationship in order to mend fences with Miyamoto's party. A less obvious problem arises from the CPSU's friendship with the pro-Soviet groups in the JSP, especially the Socialism Association. Exchanges of official delega-

tions have been made regularly and frequently in recent years between the two parties themselves and with labor union groups
affiliated with them (Saiki, p. 22). This poses a problem for the JCP
analogous to but far more difficult to handle than the CPSU's
support of Shiga's group. On the policy side, the JCP's public
position on the northern territory issue complicates the situation. In
the July 1976 "Declaration on Freedom and Democracy" the JCP
reaffirmed its promise to seek the return of the two offshore islands
Habomai and Shikotan on conclusion of a peace treaty between the
two countries and the reversion of all the Kuriles following the
termination of the United States-Japan security treaty (*Zen'ei*, September 1976, p. 70; Toki). None of these problems is by any means
insoluble; they are troublesome enough to make it unlikely that the
two parties will reestablish a relationship of genuine mutual trust and
affection in the immediate future.

The JCP-CCP relations have evolved along similar lines. Following
the 1966 break, the CCP for a while kept up a ruthless campaign
against the JCP, publicly renouncing the latter as "Miyamoto's revisionist clique" and counting it among the CCP's four major enemies
alongside American imperialists, Soviet revisionists, and the reactionary government of Japan. It also gave both public recognition and
support to the pro-CCP defectors, the so-called JCP Left, receiving,
in the fall of 1971, the group's representatives in Peking with great
fanfare and publicity. The JCP responded in kind and the verbal
warfare between the two at one time nearly overshadowed the
JCP-CPSU exchanges (Iizuka 1, pp. 121-124).

During the last few years, however, the dispute has lost much of
its earlier heat and stabilized at a level of animosity and recriminations roughly comparable to that between the JCP and the CPSU.
With Mao gone and the ascendancy of the moderates in Peking
increasingly in evidence, it is possible that the two parties will find it
expedient to patch up their longtime quarrel and work out a relationship less offensive to both. Here again, however, the JCP is unlikely
to do anything that might damage its carefully cultivated reputation
as an independent national party. It has made this point quite clear
by opposing the inclusion of an antihegemony clause, implicitly
aimed at Moscow and vigorously pushed by Peking, in the Sino-
Japanese treaty of peace and friendship being negotiated by the two
governments. As a JCP publication has put it, such a clause would
compel Japan to conform to Peking's particular foreign policy line
and thus compromise Japan's diplomatic independence (JCP 13, p.
141).

Although it has forcefully and successfully asserted its independence from the CPSU and the CCP, the JCP has gradually developed
close and friendly ties with several West European and Southeast
Asian communist parties. In fact, the party's drift away from the

former and toward the latter has been the most conspicuous aspect of its interparty diplomacy in recent years. The current geographical distribution of the JCP's friends can be inferred from a comparison of space devoted to news relating to various parties in the JCP's semimonthly international affairs journal, *Sekai seiji shiryo* (*Documents on World Politics*), which publishes translations of foreign language articles, mainly from communist party publications in other countries. Table 5 summarizes the country-by-country breakdown of space allotment, measured in the number of pages—less than half a page is counted as zero and more than half as one page—in the twenty-four issues of the journal from December 1975 to November 1976. (Conveniently, each issue consists of sixty-four pages. Inconveniently, back issues of the journal more than two years old were unavailable, making diachronic comparison impossible. The most recent issue available was November 1976—hence, the cutoff point.)

As Table 5 suggests, the JCP has shown special interest in recent years in the work of the Vietnamese Workers party. During the period studied it not only devoted a larger space in the journal to this party than to any other foreign communist party but Miyamoto and other JCP leaders have gone out of their way to speak of their solidarity with the comrades in Indochina (*Akahata*, November 8, 1975; *Zen'ei*, September 1976, pp. 19-20). In comparison to the prominence given to the Vietnamese party, the neglect of the other Asian parties is striking. It is rather surprising that the North Korean Workers party should not have been represented at all. By all indications the relationship between the JCP and the Korean party has been generally good (*Riron to Seisaku*, March 1976, p. 42; Iizuka 1, p. 38). However, Miyamoto apparently takes strong exception to the notorious Kim Il-sung cult, and the presence and activities of the militantly nationalist (North) Korean group in Japan, the General Association of Korean Residents in Japan, may have complicated interparty relations (Tawara, pp. 190-193). Whatever circumstances may explain the conspicuous absence of news on the Korean party, it is both surprising and interesting.

Much less surprising yet also revealing is the nearly complete neglect of the CCP and the CPSU. Among the Asian parties listed in Table 5, the CCP is not accorded even as much space as the miniscule anti-Indonesian National Liberation Front of Timor; the entire space allotted to the CPSU concerned the single event of its twenty-fifth party congress. This suggests that the self-reliance and independence line recently has taken the form of studied neglect and indifference rather than active campaigning against the two great power communist parties.

Far more interesting and significant is the JCP's tilt toward a few West European parties. Over one-third of the entire relevant space of

T A B L E 5. Space allotment in *Sekai seiji shiryo* by region and country, December 1975-November 1976.

REGION AND COUNTRY	PAGES
Western Europe	*513 (36.2%)*
France	162
Italy	160
France and Italy*	27
Spain	144**
United Kingdom	15
Portugal	5
Asia	*319 (22.5%)*
Vietnam	238
Laos	35
Timor	21
Cambodia	18
People's Republic of China	7
Americas	*141 (9.9%)*
Chile	81†
Cuba	55
Honduras	5
Middle East and Africa	*137 (9.7%)*
Algeria	71
Angola	19
Lebanon	15
South Africa	9
Other	23
Eastern Europe	*100 (7.0%)*
USSR	49††
Rumania	46
Yugoslavia	5
Miscellaneous	*209 (14.7%)*
European communist party conference, Berlin, June 1976	62
Conference of nonaligned nations, August 1976	58
U.S. Senate, Pike Committee report on CIA activities	53
Latin American conference of Christians for socialism, April 1972	22
United Nations reform	14
Total	1419 (100%)

Note: From the total of 1536 pages those devoted to brief news entitled "Spot Foreign News," reports and statements on Japan by foreign visitors, etc., were excluded.

*Includes both joint communiqués of the two parties and articles relating to both countries.

**Of this number seventy pages were given to the translation of Santiago Carrillo's recent writing.

†This includes forty-four pages of excerpts from the report of the U.S. Senate special committee on CIA activities in Chile.

††The relevant articles related exclusively to the twenty-fifth CPSU congress, February 24-March 5, 1976.

the journal was devoted, roughly equally, to the parties of France, Italy, and Spain. This tilt represents, in fact, an aspect of the JCP's current interparty diplomacy as prominent as its rift with the CPSU and the CCP.

The close collaboration between the JCP and the West European parties began in the late 1960s in the wake, and to a large extent as a consequence, of the JCP's disputes with the CPSU and the CCP. The disputes cost Miyamoto's party its two most important traditional allies, which began to work with the JCP's domestic enemies against it, rather than with the JCP against its domestic enemies. The JCP also faced a distinct possibility of increasing isolation in the international communist fraternity.

The 1967 visit to Tokyo of a PCF (French Communist party) delegation was the beginning of a series of increasingly frequent mutual visits resulting, as a rule, in joint statements and pledges of cooperation and solidarity. In the 1970s the exchanges considerably picked up pace: in 1971 a JCP mission led by Miyamoto held talks and issued joint statements en route to Moscow with leaders of the Italian, Spanish, and Rumanian parties led, respectively, by Berlinguer, Carrillo, and Ceausescu (JCP 14, p. 12; Iizuka 1, pp. 38, 125-126). A second PCF group visited Tokyo in the same year. The international theory conference that the JCP held in 1972 on the occasion of its fiftieth anniversary was attended by representatives of the three European parties, as well as those of the Australian, West German, and British parties (Taguchi, p. 6). In 1973 a third PCF delegation went to Tokyo, and a JCP group led by Fuwa visited Paris and issued a joint statement with the PCF leadership (JCP 14, p. 50; Iizuka 2, p. 16). In 1974 another JCP mission, led this time by Nishizawa, attended the eleventh Rumanian party congress in Bucharest and while there held talks with PCI (Italian Communist party) representatives (*Akahata*, December 21, 1974). In 1975 the PCI sent its first official mission to Tokyo and the PCF its fourth, along with groups from the Rumanian and Yugoslavian parties (JCP 14, p. 1; *Koan Joho*, October 1975, pp. 59-64). The *Akahata* correspondent in Bucharest attended and reported on the fourteenth PCI congress in the spring of the same year (Onuma). Finally, in 1976 the Spanish party sent Santiago Carrillo and the French party Georges Marchais to Tokyo and both participated in well-publicized mass rallies organized by the JCP, in addition to engaging in more professional talks with Miyamoto and other JCP theoreticians (JCP 14).

The record of the JCP's growing camaraderie with West European parties is thus quite impressive. And there is no doubt that a genuine sense of common interests and destiny underlies and animates this relationship. The joint communiqués that Miyamoto issued with Carrillo in March and with Marchais in April 1976 both emphasized the need for the international communist movement to establish and respect certain basic principles governing interparty relations: the independence and equality of all national parties; noninterference in the internal affairs of one another; and recognition and acceptance of the diversity of circumstances facing communist parties in different countries and the resulting diversification of methods chosen to cope with such circumstances (*Akahata*, April 1, 1976; ibid., April 11, 1976). The two communiqués also reaffirmed the commitment of the parties to support and defend democratic freedoms and civil rights both before and after the establishment of socialism. As Fuwa told the JCP central committee meeting shortly after Marchais and his wife left Japan, these were the points of central interest and importance on which the JCP and not only the French and Spanish but also the Italian party had come to complete agreement (JCP 14, p. 1).

The close similarity of approach and language used by the JCP and the West European parties specifically in reference to the problems of the independence of each national communist party and the value of democratic, parliamentary institutions naturally raises a question about the impact of the interparty communications and interactions on the JCP's ideological and tactical posture. When the JCP abandoned the term "proletarian dictatorship" in favor of the "power of the working class" at its July 1976 congress, the Japanese press asked whether the party had not taken a cue from the PCF, which had taken a similar step in February at its twenty-second congress (*Yomiuri shimbun*, July 31, 1976). When Fuwa spoke at the same JCP congress of a "stable majority" in the Diet being needed for the establishment of a viable coalition government, the press similarly wondered whether Berlinguer's warning against his party's participation in a coalition regime supported by a bare 51% parliamentary majority had not given him the idea. It is difficult, however, to attribute the JCP's initiatives unilaterally to cues from Paris or Rome. For one thing, as we saw earlier, the JCP had embarked on the process of naturalization and liberalization by the early 1960s, if not much earlier, largely in reaction to its own experience during the period of the leftist adventurism. After all, the party had broken with the CPSU and the CCP in the mid-1960s precisely over the issue of independence and the parliamentary path to socialism. For another, the Miyamoto line is as incompatible with dependence on a West European party as it is with subordination to the Soviet or the Chinese party. The truth is probably that the mutually supportive contacts with the West European parties have substantially reinforced the direction and accelerated the speed of the so-called naturalization process in the JCP (Miyamoto 4, p. 44; Ueda and Iizuka, pp. 175, 268).

It is important to note the commonality of interests and views that the JCP apparently finds in the West European communist parties. It should not lead us, however, to forget or underestimate the even more fundamental importance the JCP attaches to the idea and practice of national independence, whether in the sense of the independence and integrity of a nation in international politics or in the sense of the independence and autonomy of a national communist party in inter-communist party relations. That this question of national independence is a much more basic problem to the JCP than democracy and the parliamentary road to socialism in an advanced capitalist country is evident from the degree of attention and respect paid to the parties of Vietnam, Algeria, Cuba, Laos, and even Timor and Angola. The extensive coverage in the party's journal of alleged CIA activities in general and in Chile in particular makes sense when one takes into account the party's overriding preoccupation with the issue of national sovereignty and independence. And so does the modest space given to the affairs of such countries as Lebanon, South Africa, and Honduras. For the same reason, Rumania and Yugoslavia attract some degree of JCP interest and sympathy. And the same concern with national independence colors the party's attitude toward the capitalist world.

THE JCP ON JAPANESE FOREIGN RELATIONS AND POLICY

As I mentioned previously, the 1961 JCP program defined American imperialism and Japanese monopoly capital as the two main enemies of Japanese revolution. The document said: "At the present time, Japan is ruled basically by American imperialism and Japanese monopoly capital, the latter being dependent on and allied with the former. Ours is a highly advanced capitalist country, but it is also a de facto dependency partially occupied by American imperialists" (JCP 3, p. 9). This basic view of the paramount power and position of American imperialism as a force of reaction and counterrevolution in Japan has survived all the semantic and practical changes in the JCP's theory and practice that have taken place during the last decade and a half. It still comprises the main body of the program and an essential and prominent part of the rules of the party (*Zen'ei*, September 1976, pp. 305-316). According to this view, American imperialism not only keeps Japanese people in bondage but has been preparing war against the socialist bloc and using its military bases in Japan to repress the national liberation struggles of other Asian nations and to extend its rule over their people and territory (*Zen'ei*, September 1976, p. 305). Miyamoto and other leaders of the party continue to reaffirm their commitment to the original 1961 program and to avow their determination to keep fighting on the two fronts defined by the position (Miyamoto 4, p. 30; JCP 14, p. 10; *Zen'ei*, September 1976, p. 97; Fuwa 2, pp. 253-254).

The JCP's call for the termination of the United States-Japan mutual security treaty and subsequent declaration of Japan's neutrality naturally and logically flow from its view of American imperialism. The termination of the treaty would be followed by the dismantling of the more than 100 bases and installations currently maintained by the U.S. military in Japanese territory and the withdrawal of all the troops and other personnel manning them (JCP 13, pp. 133-136, 157). I have already pointed out that this plan was incorporated in the first part of the 1972 draft program of the proposed democratic coalition government. The JCP's position on Japanese-American relations thus appears quite firm and inflexible. It also seems consistent with the party's obsessive interest in the problem of national independence, which, as we have seen, characterizes its posture in inter-communist party relations in general.

The impression may not be completely accurate, however. The view of American imperialism dominating and enslaving Japan, which underlies and justifies the JCP's objections to the security treaty and, inferentially, to the cooperation between the two nations in matters of defense and security in general, no longer sounds very plausible to the Japanese public in the mid-1970s, if it ever did in earlier years. Given the overriding importance the Miyamoto line attaches to making the party respectable in the eyes of the average voter, the continuing commitment to and publicity over what appears to the voter an outdated and irrelevant plank in an otherwise innovative and interesting program inevitably becomes increasingly burdensome. JCP leaders know this and have begun, with a great deal of caution and subtlety, to shift their public position on the issue.

Miyamoto argued recently that by terminating the "chain" of military alliance that binds Japan to the American imperialists' policy, it would become possible for the peoples of Japan and the United States to enter into and develop "truly" friendly relations (Miyamoto 2, p. 21). During an interview with me in 1975 a member of the party's central committee argued that the party is not "anti-American," that it is fully aware and respectful of the democratic traditions of the American people, that the opposition to imperialism and colonialism, whichever nation practices it, is in the interest of the American people as well as that of Japanese and other Asian peoples, and that the JCP hopes to see the friendly relationship further develop between the two nations, especially in the economic and cultural fields (Toki; JCP 8, p. 38). These are still a few straws in the wind. It will undoubtedly be some time before the shift of gear becomes sufficiently clear and official to lead to a revision of the program. But when that happens, the revision will probably amount to a rewriting of the entire text of the document. Considering the speed and facility with which the party has accomplished revisions of nearly equal importance and difficulty in many other areas of its theory and practice, one should not be greatly surprised if a new program is announced sooner than one might like to predict at the moment.

Apart from its attacks on the United States-Japan military alliance, the JCP has not developed well-defined positions on the country's relationships with capitalist nations in general. Its 1972 coalition government program promises to promote relationships of equality, reciprocity, and friendship with "all capitalist nations" (JCP 8, p. 28). The only exceptions would be those nations that are ruled by military juntas or fascist regimes established by coup. Beyond that, the party would implement measures to control and regulate unlawful activities of multinational corporations through, for example, revision and strengthening of Japanese antimonopoly laws (JCP 13, p. 90). The JCP's view of multinationals is basically negative: it regards them not only as the major sources of political corruption in countries in which they operate but also as a prime cause of dependency of the smaller and weaker nations upon the bigger and stronger ones (Miyamoto 2, p. 9). Here again the party's concern with the question of national independence is in evidence.

Still highly tentative and incomplete as they are, the JCP's positions on several other topics are also strongly colored by the same concern. For example, Ueda has spoken on behalf of the party's leadership in opposition to the liberalization of restrictions on foreign agricultural imports, especially foodstuffs (Ueda and Iizuka, p. 203). Similar protectionist considerations have been extended even to Japanese economic assistance to developing countries and, as a result, the party has nearly managed to drive itself to a position of self-contradiction. On the one hand, it calls for the provision of government loans and free gifts with no strings attached, designed solely to help recipient nations cope with their economic problems and establish viable and independent economic systems of their own choice; on the other, it promises to promote economic and technical assistance programs that would contribute to the "autonomous and democratic development of Japan's own economy" (JCP 13, pp. 90, 96).

Apparently also for reasons relating to its preoccupation with Japan's national interests and sovereign rights, the JCP opposed ratification of the nuclear nonproliferation treaty by the Diet. The treaty was designed, according to the JCP, to legitimize and perpetuate the nuclear monopoly of the great powers and the dependence of nonnuclear nations, such as Japan, upon the "nuclear umbrellas" allegedly provided by the great powers; such a state of affairs would be patently inequitable and even dangerous (Nishizawa; JCP 13, p. 140).

Given the sparseness of relevant JCP statements on the subject, it is difficult to say much about the specific directions and emphases of Japan's foreign relations in general as envisaged by the party leadership. On the role and activities of the United Nations, for example, the party has been virtually silent; the 1972 coalition government program merely undertook to make the world organization function as it was originally intended, i.e., to "maintain international peace and security" (JCP 8, p. 29). It has called for ratification of the 1966 U.N. conventions on human rights, which the Japanese government has signed but so far not ratified (JCP 13, p. 105). No further elaborations of its views on these and other international issues are found in current party publications. From these fragmentary and very incomplete pieces of evidence, one may suggest two conclusions. First, the JCP has not yet given much thought to issues of Japan's foreign relations, apart from the one problem of the United States–Japan military alliance. Second, to the extent that it has given thought to such issues, the party prefers, as one would have expected, an international economic and political system of controlled freedom and managed competition rather than one based on principles such as guide the General Agreement on Tariffs and Trade and capitalist-oriented international organizations.

Some Implications for U.S. Policy

It is not the purpose of this chapter to counsel the government of the United States, or for that matter any other government, as to how it should conduct itself toward the JCP. Policies of a government result from and reflect complex sets of values, interests, and calculations. Considerations of impact on the politics of a foreign country are unlikely to be a major factor of policymaking in any government. Considerations of the probable or possible reactions of a nonruling party in a foreign country and their effects on the attitude and policies of that country's government are even less likely to enter significantly into the governmental policymaking process. With these caveats, however, the discussion of the JCP presented in this chapter does suggest a few things that an interested observer of contemporary Japanese politics and foreign policy, whether he is in government in Washington or not, may find useful to keep in mind in thinking about Japanese politics in general and the JCP in particular.

First of all, the foregoing discussion has shown that the JCP has indeed come a long way since the mid-1950s in transforming and "naturalizing" itself in some very important and lasting ways. It would obviously be wrong to describe the party and its policies in old and outdated shibboleths and clichés. It is no longer a small, conspiratorial group of dedicated Marxists intent on overthrowing the established order of society and government by force; it is a mass party of nearly 400,000 members publicly committed to upholding the existing system of parliamentary democracy. It is a party perhaps not widely respected, much less "loved," but accepted by the Japanese public as a fully legitimate group contending for power within the framework of the country's multiparty system. The JCP should and does deserve to be treated as such a group by anybody who believes in the virtues of democratic politics as they are practiced in contemporary Japan.

Second, the JCP has been led by a group of intelligent and capable leaders, all loyal to Chairman Miyamoto and his ideas. Collectively, they represent and promote the line of national communism, domestically with its emphasis on democracy and freedom and internationally on independence and self-reliance. This is a leadership group of great internal coherence and solidarity, willing and able, as it has proved time and again, to dispose of any serious dissident or offender among its own ranks with ruthless efficiency. Whether by design or by accident, the nationalistic proclivities that the group displays with remarkable consistency and tenacity evidently appeal to a segment of Japanese public opinion and help the party hold a position of power, limited and fluctuating yet by no means negligible, in the politics of the country. Any policy of a foreign government that ignores or offends the nationalistic sensitivities of the Japanese would contribute to the party's credibility and influence among Japanese voters.

Third, the JCP has not managed to grow into a major political party likely to come to power in the foreseeable future, even by way of coalition government. Despite its well-publicized and real electoral achievements during the 1960s and the early seventies, the party has not come much closer to assuming the power of government. By itself, the party has been far too weak to mount an effective challenge to the ruling LDP; vis-à-vis the other opposition parties, it has maintained relationships of mutual and open distrust and hostility with the DSP and the CGP and the major factions in the JSP, which guarantee continuing difficulties in the JCP's attempts to bring about a durable anti-LDP united front. Either way, chances are slim, if not nil, that a JCP dominated government will come into being within the next decade or so. It therefore would be quite premature to start rejoicing or mourning over the specter of such an eventuality.

Fourth and last, good understanding and diagnosis of the problem is a prerequisite of a sound prescription for its solution or correction. In my opinion, the JCP has not been well understood outside of a very small group of specialists, mostly Japanese journalists. My hope is that this chapter will contribute to the understanding of the problem as much by revealing gaps in our information and pockets of ignorance as by describing and analyzing known facts about the subject.

References

AKIYAMA, JUN'ICHI (1), "Nihon kyosanto no aratana shiren: Tokyo tochijisen wo megutte" (A new test for the JCP: The Tokyo metropolitan gubernatorial election), *Koan Joho*, February 1975, pp. 1 – 26.

—— (2), "Yuko kaifuku wo mezashite ugokidashita nisso ryoto" (The communist parties of Japan and the Soviet Union move toward the restoration of friendly relations), *Koan Joho*, November 1975, pp. 15– 30.

BECKMANN, GEORGE M., and GENJI OKUBO, *The Japanese Communist Party 1922–1945*, Stanford University Press, 1969.

CGP, Publications Department (Komeito kikanshikyoku), ed., *Kempo sangensoku wo meguru nihon kyosanto hihan* (A critique of the JCP's views of the three principles of the constitution), 1974.

DEN, HIDEO, and SHIMAZAKI YUZURU, "Shakaito taikai wa nani wo nasubeki dattaka" (What ought the JSP congress to have done), *Shakaishugi*, February 1975, pp. 35–46.

FUWA, TETSUZO (1), *Jinminteki gikaishugi* (People's parliamentarism), 2 vols., Shin nihon shuppansha, 1974.

—— (2), *Kagakuteki shakaishugi kenkyu* (A study of scientific socialism), Shin nihon shuppansha, 1976.

—— (3), "Zenkoku katsudosha kaigi de no Fuwa shokicho no hokoku" (General Secretary Fuwa's report to the national conference of party activists), *Riron to Seisaku*, March 1976, pp. 13–27.

—— (4), "Kagakuteki shakaishugi to shikken mondai: Marukusu Engerusu kenkyu" (Scientific socialism and the problem of dictatorship: A study of Marx and Engels), *Zen'ei*, July 1976, pp. 123–182.

Gurupu 1984-nen, *Nihon kyosanto minshu rengoseifu koryo hihan* (A critique of the JCP democratic coalition government program), Takagi shoten, 1975.

IIZUKA, SHIGETARO (1), *Miyamoto Kenji no nihon kyosanto* (Kenji Miyamoto's JCP), Ikkosha, 1973.

—— (2), *Rengo seiken koryo ronso* (The controversy over the coalition government program), Gendaishi shuppankai, 1974.

ISHIDA, TSUTOMU, "Toitsu no ronri to haijo no ronri" (The logic of unity versus the logic of exclusion), *Zen'ei*, November 1976, pp. 142–155.

JCP, Central Committee, Publications Department (Nihon kyosanto chuoiinkai shuppankyoku) (1), *Nihon kyosanto to futatsu no sensen de no toso* (The JCP and the struggle on two fronts), 1967.

—— (2), *Nihon no chukan seito* (The middle-of-the-road parties in Japan), 1968.

—— (3), *Nihon kyosanto koryo mondai bunkenshu* (Collected documents on the JCP platform), 1970.

—— (4), *Komeito no taishitsu wo kyumei suru: genron shuppan bogai wo megutte* (An inquiry into the character of the CGP: The obstruction of the freedoms of speech and publication), 1970.

—— (5), *Nihon kyosanto no gojunen* (Fifty years of the JCP), 1972.

—— (6), *Minshato: sono riron to kodo* (The DSP: Its theory and action), 1972.

—— (7), *Nihon kyosanto no soshiki katsudo* (The organizational activities of the JCP), 1973.

—— (8), *Minshu rengo seifu koryo ni tsuite no nihon kyosanto no teian* (The JCP's proposals for a democratic coalition government), 1973.

—— (9), *Kakushin toitsu sensen no tankyu* (In search of a progressive united front), 1973.

—— 10), *Kempo kyoto mondai to komeito: nihon kyosanto no komeito e no shitsumon to hihan* (The issues of the constitution and joint struggle: The JCP's questions to and criticisms of the CGP), 1974.

—— (11), *Komeito hihan* (Criticisms of the CGP), 1974.

—— (12), *Zoku komeito hihan* (Additional criticisms of the CGP), 1975.

—— (13), *Nihon kyosanto no uttae, kihon seisaku, seiken koso* (The JCP's appeal, basic policies, and plans for forming a government), 1976.

—— (14), *Rekishi wo hiraku atarashii chikara: Nihon kyosanto to supein furansu ryo kyosanto no rentai to goi* (A new force to turn history: Solidarity and agreements between the JCP and the Communist parties of Spain and France), 1976.

JSP, Committee on the Theory of Socialism, and JSP, Central Party School, (Nihon shakaito shakaishugi riron iinkai, nihon shakaito chuo to-gakko), *Nihon ni okeru shakaishugi e no michi: gakushu tekisuto 1* (Road to socialism in Japan: Study text, 1), 1966.

KAMIYAMA, SHIGEO, ed., *Nihon kyosanto sengo juyo shiryoshu* (Collected important documents on the postwar JCP), San'ichi Shobo, 1971.

KATSUBE, GEN, "Uchigawa kara mita seiiki" (Inside the sanctuary), *Shokun*, November 1976, pp. 90–101.

KAYA, OKINORI, *Kono mamade wa kanarazu okiru nihon kyosanto kakumeii* (A JCP led revolution would be inevitable if present conditions continue), Roman, 1973.

KINOSHITA, HIROSHI, "Itaria tsushin" (Reports from Italy), *Zen'ei*, April 1976, and subsequent issues.

KINUGASA, TETSUO, "Gendai kakumei no shutai wo ikani keisei subeki ka" (How should we build an active force for a modern revolution), *Shakai-shugi*, November 1975, pp. 14–50.

KOBAYASHI, TOSHIAKI, *Sengo kakumei undo ronsoshi* (A history of polemics on the postwar revolutionary movement), San'ichi shobo, 1971.

KOYAMA, HIROTAKE, *Zoho sengo nihon kyosantoshi* (A history of the postwar JCP), rev. ed. Haga shoten, 1972.

"Kuno suru shakaito" (The troubled JSP), *Sekai*, March 1976, pp. 207-210.

LANGER, PAUL F., *Communism in Japan*, Hoover Institution Press, 1972.

MAINICHI SHIMBUN SEIJIBU, *Seihen* (Change of government), Mainichi Shimbunsha, 1975.

MIYAMOTO, KENJI (1), *Nihon kakumei no tembo* (Prospects for a Japanese revolution), Shin nihon shuppansha, 1968.

—— (2), "Zenkoku katsudosha kaigi de no Miyamoto iincho aisatsu" (Chairman Miyamoto's address at the national conference of activists), *Riron to Seisaku*, March 1976, pp. 8-12.

—— (3), "Senpan ankoku seiryoku no jidai gyakko no inbo wo yurusazu" (We shall not let the dark, war criminal forces conspire to turn the course of history back), *Riron to Seisaku*, March 1976, pp. 44-55.

—— (4), "Nihon no fudo ni fusawashii kagakuteki shakaishugi no michi" (The road of scientific socialism suitable to the climate of Japan), *Bunka Hyoron*, October 1976, pp. 18-49.

MIZUSHIMA, TSUYOSHI, *Shokugyo kakumeika: nikkyo 160-mei no rirekisho* (The professional revolutionaries: The curricula vitae of 160 JCP leaders), Zembosha, 1970.

MORITA, MINORU, "Nihon Kyosanto no kinmyaku" (The JCP's funding sources), *Shokun*, November 1976, pp. 54-74.

NAGATA, HISAMITSU, *Akahata senryaku: nani ga kyosanto to zenshin saseta ka* (The Akahata strategy: What accounts for the JCP's advance), Kodansha, 1973.

NAKAMURA, KENJI, "Nikkyo ga futatabi kawaru no wa itsu ka: shakaishugi kyokai to no toso no kanata ni" (When will the JCP change once again? Beyond the current dispute with the Socialism Association), *Kaikakusha*, September 1976, pp. 23-31.

NAKANISHI, YOSHIO, "Asada ippa no muho na riken tsuikyu to boryoku no ronri" (The Asada clique's unlawful quest for interests and the logic of violence), *Zen'ei*, January 1975, pp. 109-123.

NAKANO, SHIGEHARU, and ISAMU MIYAUCHI, "Nihon kyosanto no rekishi ni tsuite omou" (Some thoughts on the history of the JCP), *Asahi Janaru*, 1 October 1976, pp. 28-41.

NISHIZAWA, MASARU, "Kaku-kakusan boshi joyaku to Miki naikaku" (The NPT and the Miki cabinet), *Zen'ei*, August 1975, pp. 21-37.

OKAZAKI, MASUHIDE, "Sakisaka-ha no toitsu sensen ron wo hihan suru: toitsu sensen no na ni yoru hankyo bunretsushugi" (A critique of the Sakisaka faction's united front theory: An exercise in anticommunist maneuvers to divide our ranks in the name of a united front), *Zen'ei*, February 1974, pp. 140-156.

ONUMA, SAKUNDO, "Itarii kyosanto taikai" (The PCI congress), *Zen'ei*, June 1975, pp. 149-155.

OUCHI, KEIGO, *Ashita no konai yoru wa nai: hokaku hakuchu kara rengo jidai e* (There is no night but that is followed by a morning: From a neck-and-neck race between the conservative and the progressive party to an era of coalitions), Fuji kyoiku senta shuppankyoku, 1975.

SAIKI, KUNIO, "Soren no tai-nichi shisei" (The Soviet attitude toward Japan), *Koan Joho*, January 1975, pp. 12–23.

SAKAKI, TOSHIO, "Sakisaka riron no rekishiteki hasan" (The historical bankruptcy of the Sakisaka theory), *Zen'ei*, October 1974, pp. 73–103.

SAKISAKA, ITSURO (1), *Watakushi no shakaishugi* (My socialism), Shiseido, 1959.

—— (2), *Zoku nihon kyosanto ron* (Discourse on the JCP: Part two), Shakaishugi kyokai, 1974.

SASAKI, ICHIRO, "Senmei na komeito no hankyo no kiseki" (The indelible tracks of the CGP's anticommunism), *Zen'ei*, January 1976, pp. 14–86.

SATO, HIROYUKI, "Zen yato ka shakyo chujiku ka kyosan nuki ka" (A coalition of all the opposition parties, or one centered on the JSP and JCP, or one without the JCP?), *Kaikakusha*, September 1976, pp. 90–98.

SCALAPINO, ROBERT A., *The Japanese Communist Movement, 1920–1966*, University of California Press, 1966.

SORIFU TOKEIKYOKU (Office of the Prime Minister, Bureau of Statistics), *Nihon no tokei* (Japanese statistics), Okurasho insatsukyoku, 1976.

SUZUKI, TAKURO, *Kyosanto shuzai 30-nen* (Thirty years on the JCP beat), Keizai orai sha, 1976.

TACHIBANA, TAKASHI, "Nihon kyosanto no kenkyu" (A study of the JCP), *Bungei Shunju*, January 1976, pp. 94–150.

TACHIBANA, TAKASHI, and TAKASHI ITO, "Shinwa no hokai" (The collapsed myth), *Shokun*, November 1976, pp. 38–53.

TAGUCHI, FUKUJI, *Gendai nihon no seiji to toitsu sensen* (Contemporary Japanese politics and united front), Aoki shoten, 1973.

TAKAHASHI, HIKOHIRO, *Minshato ron: sono rinen to taishitsu* (The DSP: Its ideals and characteristics), Shin nihon shuppansha, 1972.

TAMURA, RYUJI, ed., *Zukai nihon sayoku seiryoku shiryo shusei* (Collected documents with graphic illustrations on the left-wing forces of Japan), Chuo chosakai, 1970.

TANAKA, JOJI, "Shakaito taikai to kaido Asada-ha no mondai" (The JSP congress and the problem of the Asada faction in the "village" liberation league), *Zen'ei*, March 1975, pp. 157–160.

TAWARA, KOTARO, *Hadaka no nihon kyosanto* (The JCP undressed), Nisshin hodo, 1972.

TOKI, TSUYOSHI (member, JCP central committee), interview 16 August 1975 with the author.

TOMINOMORI, EIJI (editorial writer, *Asahi shimbun*), interview 18 October 1976 with the author.

UEDA, KOICHIRO, and AKIRA KUDO, *Minshu rengo seifu de nihon wa kou naru: fukumen hihan e no hanron* (This is what would become of Japan under a democratic coalition government: Rejoinder to the anonymous critics), Shin nihon shuppansha, 1974.

UEDA, KOICHIRO, and SHIGETARO IIZUKA, *Gendai kiki to henkaku no riron* (The current crisis and the theory of change), Gendaishi shuppankai, 1975.

WATANABE, TSUNEO, *Hokaku renritsu seiken ron: 1970-nendai kohan no seiji tembo* (Conservative-progressive coalition government: Political prospects in the latter half of the 1970s), Daiyamondosha, 1974.

YOSHIDA, YOSHINORI, "Komeito no kamen wo hagu" (Unmasking the CGP), *Zen'ei*, October 1976, pp. 111-142.

9

China and the World
in the Mao and
Post-Mao Eras

Tang Tsou

The Post-Mao Era

This essay represents an attempt to lay down certain interpretive themes to be tested by further historical research. They are tentatively held and are intended to provoke debate.

The post-Mao era began on September 9, 1976, with the long expected and repeatedly predicted death of Mao Tse-tung, the last giant of the twentieth century, a period of world wars and of revolutionary upheavals. For the Chinese—and particularly their leaders—this period has been a time of despair and a time of hope; a time of brutal, self-defeating *Realpolitik* and a time of noble, boundless idealism; a time of egoism and a time of selfless dedication to noble causes. Extraordinary political leaders with unusual combinations of idealism and realism have engaged in political struggle to the bitter end, seeking the victory of their cause while taking the risk of being devoured by the struggle. Man's fate in twentieth-century China has been an unfolding of political triumphs and personal tragedies, glorious deeds and ignominious acts, uncanny wisdom and blind folly. It has been a history written with the blood and tears of myriad individuals—illiterate soldiers fighting for a cause or merely for their daily ration, ruthless politicians and far-sighted statesmen, martyrs and renegades, the victors and the vanquished, who are

333

separated only by a thin, unpredictable, and imperceptible line of personal fortune, momentary decision, and historical accident. But all have one thing in common. They have left their chosen tasks unfinished and their hopes unfulfilled. Their place in history, individually and collectively, depends on those who come after them and on future events at home and abroad that they can neither anticipate nor control.

After less than one month of uncertainty, events in post-Mao China have unfolded dramatically, decisively, and yet with a controlled and steady pace that has so far confounded most outside observers. Contrary to the expectations of those writers who tend to analyze Chinese affairs explicitly or implicitly on the basis of Soviet experiences, there are as yet no signs that an eventual process of de-Maoization will occur—at least not in the form that de-Stalinization took in the Soviet Union. Instead of a period of indecisive political struggle, turmoil, or even civil war, the political power of the "gang of four" was demolished at one stroke, and their leverage in various localities and governmental units has been destroyed. Systematic plans have been made to eliminate their political and ideological influence. The Maoist legacy has been assimilated by the post-Mao leadership. It has glorified Mao's memory, made selective use of his thought, and given differential emphasis to its sometimes contradictory tenets.

The post-Mao leadership has formulated a program that combines modernization and "liberalization" with selective preservation of revolutionary changes already achieved and with the rebuilding of a badly damaged political system. The program of modernizing agriculture, industry, defense, and science and technology has been set within the general framework of "continuing the revolution." Basic research in science and technology, which had been sadly neglected, has been raised to a high level of priority in an attempt to overcome the most serious obstacles to, and to eliminate the bottleneck in, the modernization of agriculture, industry, and defense. In turn, the need to build up national defense and the constant stress on the danger of a Soviet attack have been used to legitimize further the priority given to basic research and rapid economic growth.

Most official statements have reflected the desire to preserve a pattern of development in which economic growth is accompanied by achievement of a greater degree of economic equality and by expansion of participation, although the balance among these three desiderata may fluctuate from time to time. The doctrine of the dictatorship of the proletariat, which has been rejected by Eurocommunism, has been retained so that the centrifugal social and political forces in a vast country with a huge population can be kept under control. The necessity of a measure of decentralization has been recognized by reviving the division of the nation into six major areas for the purpose of economic reconstruction. In the ideological realm, the notion of the unity of theory and practice has been given renewed prominence, as in the early days of the revolutionary movement, so that it can underscore the need for realism and prudence in the formulation and implementation of programs and policies. The heavy emphasis on superstructure and revolutionary theory to the neglect of the economic base and the real need of the people in their daily life has been corrected.

Since 1949 all sorts of social experiments have been tried. Some succeeded, others failed, and many produced mixed results. A period of consolidating the successful experiments and of rectifying the excesses of others is at hand. Stability and unity have been given top priority. A broad consensus seems to have been formed around these new trends. It finds expression in the results of the third plenum of the tenth central committee, which reaffirmed the selection by the political bureau of Hua Kuo-feng as chairman of the party, the reinstatement of Teng Hsiao-ping to all his former positions, including that of chief of staff of the People's Liberation Army, and the purge of the "gang of four."

As is the case in politics at the highest level in China, political struggles and personal disagreements over questions of both policy and power are inevitable. But it is unlikely that these will lead to political upheavals similar to those in the years since the start of the Cultural Revolution in 1966. Moreover, in the long run, even serious internal disruptions are not likely to reverse the process of economic development or bring it to a complete halt. Naturally, objective conditions such as insufficiency of readily arable land and a huge population will set a limit to the rate and level of economic growth.

China's relations with the two superpowers will be the decisive factor in its future development. Although its relations with the superpowers will determine China's level of defense expenditure, the availability of advanced technology, and the expansion of trade, these are not the major factors in this assessment. Internal political factors are the most important. A rapid deterioration of relations with either or both superpowers from the present unsatisfactory level would produce serious internal political divisions over foreign policies and over the question of war and peace. Deep and prolonged frustrations in foreign affairs might lead to psychological trauma and repressed hostility that would then be displaced to internal targets. It is generally believed that there were serious differences over policy toward the Soviet Union, particularly on the question of how to deal with American escalation in Vietnam in 1965. Even if this belief turns out to be wrong, it is clear that Mao's ideological dispute with the Soviet Union—particularly his analysis of the source of Soviet revisionism—played a part in his appraisal of China's own political development. It was no accident that Liu Shao-ch'i was designated "China's Khrushchev." One can also suggest that in their ideological attack on the Soviet Union, the ultraleftist ideologues, notably Chang Chun-chiao and Yao Wen-yuan, developed or adopted a series of propositions on the "new class" and on the "bureaucratic monopoly of state capitalism" that also became part of their "theory" regarding the emergence of "a bourgeois class right within the Chinese Communist party."[1]

Similarly, the Sino-American military confrontation in the Korean War in late 1950 contributed to the adoption of a policy of eliminating American influence in China. One aspect of this policy was to curb drastically the influence and role of Western trained Chinese intellectuals. The dissatisfaction and disaffection of the intellectuals turned into overt demands and opinions during the Hundred Flower period that the regime found impossible to accept. After the antirightist campaign in the second half of 1955, the political influence of the Western trained intellectuals, including some scientists, declined dramatically and progressively until recently. Although their loss of political influence was primarily a product of internal political development, the heightened Sino-American hostility and the desire of the Soviet Union to reduce and eliminate other foreign influence in China accelerated this process and magnified its results. The impact of China's foreign relations, particularly with the two superpowers, on internal Chinese politics deserves much greater attention and research effort than it has so far received.

There is another and perhaps more basic reason why adverse developments in foreign relations might more effectively reverse, halt, and slow down the present course of Chinese development than any purely internal problems. Despite their rich and varied experience in Chinese internal affairs accumulated during the twenty-odd years of revolution, the Chinese Communist leaders, with a few notable exceptions, had relatively little direct and personal experience in foreign affairs. Under the guidance of Chou En-lai, a new corps of foreign service personnel was built up almost completely from scratch. Limited contact with Western nations, including most importantly the U.S., deprived them of a chance to learn directly the intricacies and complexities of Western societies. The clear break with the Soviet Union and the opening of a dialogue with the U.S. represented a much more drastic reversal of policies than any shift in internal program. These decisive changes in foreign policy were made personally by Mao and Chou. Their theoretical assumptions are of relatively recent origin and are more likely to become subjects of dispute now that both of their originators have passed from the scene. Moreover, the results produced thus far are far from satisfactory. Therefore, the ultimate outcome hangs in the balance. Although the post-Mao programs in internal affairs hold out promise of great success, the fate of post-Mao China may very well hinge on China's conduct of foreign affairs. It is to this difficult problem that we now shall address ourselves.

Problems of Chinese Foreign Policy

From 1949, when Mao proclaimed the success of the revolution—that China, which had been supine, had at last "stood up"—China has been able to act as a regional power and also has begun to project its influence outside of Asia. China has surmounted a series of crises that posed real threats to its national security. This is no mean achievement for a nation that had good reason to fear constantly for its very survival—a nation whose army was soundly defeated in all major battles from 1937 to 1944 and whose major cities, communication lines, and richest areas had been occupied until Japan succumbed to the military might of the United States.

But each success in overcoming a crisis is generally accompanied by the emergence of new problems that are caused by the measures of other nations. China's spectacular military performance first in defeating MacArthur's armies and then in stalemating the U.N. forces was followed by the transformation of America's emergency measure of neutralizing the Formosa Strait into a long-term policy. Chou En-lai's conciliatory and masterly diplomacy at the Geneva conference in the settlement of the first Vietnam crisis was followed by a treaty of mutual defense with Taiwan and the SEATO treaty, which formalized the U.S. policy of containment. The bombardment of Quemoy and the liberation of a few offshore islands to the north were accompanied by the conclusion of the United States- Republic of China defense treaty of December 1954 and a congressional resolution giving the president the discretion to defend Quemoy and Matsu islands. The Bandung conference brought about the ambassadorial talks between China and the U.S. that served only to highlight American unwillingness to make even minor concessions and that proved the inability of Chou's conciliatory diplomacy to yield concrete results. The near success of the tactic of capturing the offshore islands and the Nationalist troops there by cutting off their supply through bombardment and small craft operations merely brought about a demonstration of American naval strength that extricated the U.S. and her Nationalist clients. It also revealed to Peking that China's Soviet ally was more interested in obtaining control over the

Chinese navy and coastal defense than in helping that nation move toward a solution of the problem of Taiwan.

China's determination to continue to pursue its independent course in both internal and foreign affairs and to have a voice in settling the common policy of "the socialist camp" led to an open break in the Sino-Soviet alliance and left China almost completely isolated in international politics. China's masterly and controlled use of armed forces in the limited border war with India in 1962 was followed by an enhanced Soviet presence in the South Asian subcontinent. The border clashes along the Amur River successfully demonstrated China's resolve to resist any territorial encroachment. But they also revealed Chinese military vulnerability and weakness, which was further underscored by subsequent Soviet public hints and unpublicized threats to use nuclear weapons against China.

The establishment of a Sino-American dialogue through Kissinger's secret trip and Nixon's public visit, the signing of the Shanghai Communiqué, and the establishment of formal diplomatic relations with Japan represented great triumphs in the personal diplomacy of Mao and Chou and the high watermark of Chinese success in world affairs since 1949. But the Watergate affair and the triumph of North Vietnam, aided by sophisticated Soviet weapons, over the Thieu regime twice blocked the normalization of Sino-American relations and frustrated Peking's expectations that were based on American hints and promises. China's generous support for North Vietnam and the Vietcong in their most difficult years and during their approaching victory produced a united Vietnam that is a strong military power and a rival claimant to islands and possible oil research in the South Sea and that has been tilting toward the Soviet Union. Having normalized relations with China while enjoying a rising trade and deriving increasing economic benefits from Taiwan, influential figures in both public and private spheres in Japan endeavor to block the normalization of Sino-American relations so that Japan can have the best of both worlds as the United States becomes the target of Peking's wrath. Meanwhile, American loans and investments have flooded Taiwan, and trade has jumped to a new high level in response to Taiwan's strategy of making American economic interests the hostage or guarantee of continuing American diplomatic relations and defense commitments. A small portion of the economic benefit derived from American economic policy, and yet a substantial sum in absolute terms, has been spent by Taiwan in a campaign to prevent the U.S. from normalizing relations with Peking. Up to late June 1977, Washington-Peking relations rapidly deteriorated and the prospect of normalization receded perceptibly.

There cannot be a solution to the problem of Taiwan for many years to come. It will periodically cause serious conflicts between the

United States and China. It will set an upper limit to the improvement in Sino-American relations and slow down or even reverse that process.

It is unlikely that the Soviet Union will make any substantial concessions, as distinguished from empty gestures, to Peking, if for no other reason than not to frighten the U.S. into making concessions to China on the question of Taiwan. So long as the question of Taiwan remains unresolved, the Soviet Union will have adequate room for maneuver in the triangular relationship. Hence, Chiang Ching-kuo's government on Taiwan is an important informal ally of the Soviet Union not only against Peking but also in global diplomacy. The historic distrust of the Chinese toward the Russians and the Chinese Communist leaders' memory of Soviet "betrayals" will not make their dealings with the Soviet Union any easier. Thus, Peking must constantly entertain the possibility that American-Soviet relations will improve faster than Sino-American or Sino-Soviet relations or that the United States and the Soviet Union will work out their differences to such an extent that China can play no significant role in global politics.

The one bright spot for China in this picture is that although China can be dealt a devastating military blow, it cannot be subjugated. China's strength will grow if its leaders can prevent frustrations in foreign affairs from producing open and debilitating internal splits. In this context, the Chinese ability to take a long view of history, to accept setbacks without counterproductive overreactions, to make the best of unfavorable international situations, and to adjust operational policies to present capabilities and current reality without forsaking national purpose will have a crucial bearing on China's ultimate success in both internal reconstruction and the achievement of a favorable position in the global balance of power between the two superpowers. But the theoretically and historically interesting question is why the Chinese still find themselves in a very difficult position in world politics despite the tremendous efforts and sacrifices they have made, ranging from the military confrontation with the U.S. in Korea to the large program of economic aid to the Third World countries relative to the Chinese GNP and China's own needs for capital, resources, and manpower, and despite China's tactical and strategic dexterity in its diplomatic and political policies and moves, particularly since 1969.

The Chinese/Russian/American Triangle

The explanation offered in this chapter is an extremely simple and obvious one although it is one that is not generally accepted. In oversimplified terms, this explanation runs as follows: In a triangular relationship of two strong powers and a weak power, conflicts of interest between the two strong powers are generally more numerous, more intense, and less easily reconcilable than those between the weak power and either of the two strong powers. Hence, the weakest of the three powers will ally itself or lean toward the weaker of the two strong powers or against the one of the two strong powers that is in ascendency or on the offensive so as to prevent that strong power from achieving hegemony or predominance in world politics. The weakest of the three powers will generally place itself in the middle position to take advantage of struggles between the two strong powers, refrain from taking actions or making pronouncements that would create sharp conflicts with either of them, and avoid the assumption of burdens and commitments that one of the two strong powers would be forced to assume in virtue of its interests and position in the international system.

Occasionally the weak power might find it necessary to exercise its influence to urge one of the two stronger powers to make greater exertions in opposition to the other stronger power, or to refrain from relaxing its efforts, or to prevent an imprudent relaxation of tensions between them. The weak power could do that by threatening to assume a more neutral position or by leaning to the other side. But except for a real threat to its national security, the weak power should not take direct actions that would create sharp and irreconcilable conflicts with the other strong power. Under these circumstances, the weak power could take advantage of the political equilibrium to develop its national strength to approximately the same level as that of the two strong powers so that its political influence would increase. Japan's rise from total defeat to world power in less than a generation conforms to this pattern. Ultimately, the erstwhile weaker power may hold the balance of power between the two former stronger powers. This is the course that Japan may follow in the years to come.

In the case of China, a series of historic circumstances so far have prevented China from assuming a middle position between the two superpowers. These historic circumstances found expression in the inability of the United States to withdraw quickly and completely from intervention in the Chinese civil war, in the American decision to cross the thirty-eighth parallel, and in the disastrous advance toward the Yalu River. They were reflected also in the CCP's decision to lean to one side (the USSR) and to try for a total military victory in Korea in late 1950 without making an attempt to recover Taiwan through negotiation on the basis of the initial triumph over MacArthur's army or without an ironclad Soviet guarantee of military support for the eventual unification of China. Up to the Sino-Soviet split, these historic circumstances were shrewdly exploited by the Soviet Union to gain the middle position and to intensify hostility and conflict between the U.S. and China. Mao's receptivity to the opening of a dialogue with the United States in 1969 and his theory of "three worlds" represented an endeavor to regain the middle position. But to be successful, this policy must overcome many extremely difficult handicaps left over from the loss of the middle position in the past. The future of this grand design still hangs in the balance.

The historic circumstances that prevented China from occupying a middle position between the two superpowers are well known. But it is necessary to connect these circumstances with perceptions and policy decisions in Peking, Washington, and Moscow. In 1949, China emerged from a century of defeats and humiliations that in turn had followed centuries of political hegemony and cultural preeminence in East Asia. The reversal of China's national fortunes was accompanied by a protracted, violent revolution that completely altered the class structure and the political system. In achieving victory in a protracted struggle within China, Marxist-Leninist ideology was subject to the constant test of reality. It was Sinicized to fit Chinese conditions, and this process of Sinification was facilitated and justified by the notion of the unity of theory and practice.

The CCP had little direct dealing with noncommunist powers prior to 1949 with the exception of a brief but intense period of contacts and negotiations with Americans from 1944 to the end of the Marshall mission. This period of reality testing merely reconfirmed the international communist theory of two camps, which the CCP had accepted from the very beginning. This theory of two camps fitted the Chinese tendency to seek universal solutions to all problems—a mentality developed when China was a universal empire. The events that reconfirmed this theory of two camps were, of course, the continued American intervention in the Chinese civil war on the side of the Kuomintang, General Marshall's inability or unwillingness to restrain the Kuomintang, and the deep-rooted anti-communism of the American Congress and people. The United States followed a policy of intervening in Chinese internal politics and civil war almost as a matter of course because foreign intervention in Chinese politics had been the normal state of affairs since 1911. Thus, the U.S. superseded Russia, Great Britain, and Japan as the last imperialist power to occupy a predominant position in China. Although the United States did decide in 1949 and 1950 to withdraw completely from Chinese affairs, it reverted once more to the pattern of intervention in the Chinese civil war by neutralizing the Formosa Strait almost as a reflex reaction to events to which China was only indirectly related and without giving serious thought to the consequences for long-term Sino-American relations.

Most interpreters of China's policy of leaning to one side argue that continued American support of Chiang Kai-shek and the anti-communism of Congress and the American people gave China no alternative. Moreover, they point out that by allying with the Soviet Union, the CCP found it easier to gain Soviet concessions concerning rights and privileges in Manchuria and Sinkiang that had been granted to it by the Nationalists. Theoretically, it is also true that it was in China's interest to ally itself with the weaker of the two superpowers to preserve the balance.

But what these interpreters overlook is that the pattern of Sino-Soviet relations under the alliance need not have taken the specific form it did. Under this specific form, China gave up without any serious thought the possibility of occupying the middle position that had been opened up by American policies and pronouncements from late 1948 to the outbreak of the Korean War. China did not even use this possibility as a bargaining lever to obtain a better deal from the Soviet Union in forming the alliance. China also tended to take the lead in attacking Western policies rather than play a role secondary to that of the Soviet Union, as in the recognition of the Democratic Republic of Vietnam. In spite of their difficult experience in dealing with Stalin before and after the conclusion of the alliance, the Chinese Communist leaders undoubtedly set their policies within a broad idealistic framework in which the two Communist allies would cooperate closely in defining and pushing their common goal and in which the Soviet leader of the bloc would reciprocate the wholehearted support of the Chinese junior partner by upholding the latter's minimum interests.

The significance of the theory of the two camps—and its corollary that communist states and parties have a duty to support Soviet policies and defend the motherland of socialism—lies in the ideological inhibition that it imposes with respect to occupying an advantageous middle position between the Soviet Union and the United States. To that extent, it facilitates the Soviet effort to use its allies as a spearhead in attacking the West. It enables the Soviet Union to stay in the second line or middle position while its allies take the offensive or defend the first line, thus raising the level of conflict and tension between them and the United States. It opens up for the Soviet Union the alternatives of either backing up its allies when they are winning or working for a settlement of the conflict when they are losing or stalemated, or, more generally, of seeking a détente with the United States on terms advantageous to the Soviet Union at a time when the U.S. is entangled or losing in a series of troubled spots.

This pattern of Soviet policy remains unchanged from the North Korean confrontation with the South Korean and American armies through the Chinese intervention in the Korean War to the victory of Cuban troops in Angola. It has given the Soviet Union local victories or at least stalemates even when its forces are uncommitted and held in reserve. It even enabled the USSR to advance its global influence when its strategic and conventional forces were inferior to those of the U.S. and when its economic power and science and technology lagged far behind the American. It has contributed to the decline of American political power while gaining time for the Soviet Union to catch up in military, economic, and political strength.

After the conclusion of the Sino-Soviet treaty of alliance, the Chinese adhered to the theory of two camps whatever their inner reservations may have been. At the same time, they were testing this theory, as well as the policies derived from or justified by it, against international reality, just as they had tested the "doctrine of proletarian hegemony" against Chinese reality from 1927 to 1933. Ultimately, they found it wanting. But before they departed from it in actions, broke with the Soviet Union openly, and formally rejected it as a doctrine, a series of events had occurred that placed China in sharp conflict with the U.S., that solidified the middle position occupied by the Soviet Union, and that enabled the Soviet Union to play China and the United States against each other, promoting anti-American sentiments and views within China and encouraging anti-Chinese sentiments and views within the United States, particularly the belief that China wanted to promote war and that China is expansionist.

The concept of a bipolar world was the Western counterpart to the theory of two camps. But a major difference set apart the application of the two concepts. Whereas the theory of two camps helped the Soviet Union to occupy the middle position, the concept of a bipolar world paid little attention to the middle power. It did not discourage the United States from jumping into crisis situations and using its military forces on the first line in many local encounters between the two camps. The result was the development of sharp and almost unmanageable conflicts between the U.S. and the formal or informal allies of the Soviet Union, leading in some cases to the direct use of American military forces.

In the case of China, historic circumstances contributed to this confrontation or the creation of still unresolved problems. We have already mentioned that the glaring weakness of China in the nineteenth and twentieth centuries and the habitual pattern of intervention by foreign powers in Chinese politics and China's civil wars constitute one set of background factors that should be taken into account in understanding the American tendency to opt readily for intervention rather than complete withdrawal in the period between, say, 1945 and June 27, 1950. But the neutralization of the Formosa

Strait need not have led to the crystallization of an American policy of utter hostility toward China and twenty-one years of complete separation between the two countries—had the American forces not crossed the thirty-eighth parallel or raced toward the Yalu. From a larger historical perspective, these American actions were based not only on the assumption of Chinese weakness shared by all Western nations in the first half of the twentieth century but also on an inability to understand China in the light of the latter's understanding of itself as a nation that had "stood up" and that was in ascendancy in Asia.

A general understanding of diplomatic history should have told us that a nation in ascendancy generally will seek a zone of political influence and a ring of friendly states along its boundaries so as to strengthen security along the borders. It should also have informed us that a proud nation that has succeeded in becoming strong after a period of weakness, defeat, and humiliation will react strenuously to a threat to its newly found image. Conversely, if China had been a strong power for some time and its national interests outside Chinese borders clearly defined, the United States would have long hesitated and carefully weighed the risks of military confrontation with the Chinese before sending American forces across the Yalu and permitting them to reach the Chinese border.

As it was, China succeeded in defining its national interests in areas along the border only at the huge cost of a military contest with the U.S. that made the problem of Formosa difficult to resolve, even to this very day. Although China's success in defining its interests along the border had the salutary effect of deterring the United States from invading North Vietnam, a situation was created in which the conflict of interests between the United States and China over the question of Taiwan and Sino-American hostility reached a much higher level than the conflict and hostility between the Soviet Union and the United States. A conjunction of historic circumstances together with the sad miscalculations or shrewd manipulations on the part of the three major actors caused China to lose the chance to move to the middle position up to the present time. It enabled the Soviet Union to play the two ends against the middle until 1969. Although historic circumstances and the national interests of China constituted the major set of factors motivating China's intervention in Korea, one should not overlook the Chinese justification of their military action in Korea: they voluntarily stood on the first line so that the Soviet Union could stay on the second line.

Although the Soviet Union occupied the advantageous middle position from 1949 to 1963, it did make a historic mistake. It apparently believed that American hostility toward China and the insoluble question of Taiwan gave China no place to go and no other role to play except to serve as the irreconcilable antagonist of the U.S. and to work within the framework of global policies laid down by the Soviet Union. The USSR sought détente with the United States while doing nothing decisive to help China solve the Taiwan question and even while urging China to leave the question of Taiwan aside. The Soviet Union realized that as long as there was no movement toward solving the question of Taiwan, Sino-American relations could not improve beyond a certain limit. It placed relations with India and other countries ahead of relations with China in its program of foreign aid and its calculations concerning global politics. However, the USSR did not take into account the boldness of the Chinese leadership and its willingness to opt for a total break with the Soviet Union. It miscalculated the Chinese ability to survive and to recover from three years of partly manmade and partly natural disasters and apparently believed that withdrawal of all Soviet aid, including experts and blueprints of uncompleted Soviet aid projects, would deal a crippling blow to China and perhaps lead to the downfall of Mao. In short, the USSR underestimated China's potential as a factor in global politics.

The Nixon-Kissinger overtures to China in 1969 following the Sino-Soviet military clashes in Chengpo Island enabled the United States to supersede the Soviet Union in the middle position. This fundamental change in world politics helped the U.S., to whatever small extent, in limiting the consequences of the total defeat in Vietnam, the achievement by the Soviet Union of nuclear parity, the continued superiority of Soviet conventional armies, the rapid expansion of the Soviet fleets, the weakening of the economic position of the West as a result of the oil embargo and rise in prices, the deteriorating situation in Africa, and the unsatisfactory situation in Korea. It also contributed to the materialization of the summit meeting between Nixon and Brezhnev that initiated a new period of détente. It has enabled the United States to use the threat of further improvement in Sino-American relations as leverage against the Soviet Union. China, on the other hand, succeeded in eliminating a perceived American threat from the sea while at the same time confronting forty-five Soviet divisions along the northern border. China also has opened up the possibility of some kind of American support if the Soviet Union attacks. But as we noted earlier, China remains in the unfavorable position of a nation that has extremely hostile relations with one of the two superpowers and an unresolved but essential problem (Taiwan) confounding relations with the other. The relations between the Soviet Union and the United States are easier than this.

The Three Worlds Theory

In his speech before the sixth special session of the U.N. General Assembly, Vice-Premier Teng Hsiao-ping declared on April 10, 1974, that "as a result of the emergence of social-imperialism, the socialist camp which existed for a time after World War II is no longer in existence."[2] With this statement, the theory of the two camps, which had died a violent death a long time ago, was given official burial. In its place, Teng formally outlined a theory of "three worlds." This doctrine also expanded, modified, and synthesized the theory of the intermediate zone outlined by Mao to Anna Louise Strong in 1946, the idea of the second intermediate zone developed in 1964, and the concept of surrounding the cities of the world from the countryside of the world that was contained in an article published under the by-line of Lin Piao in 1965. More fundamentally, it can be considered a synthesis of Mao's ideas of the united front that were developed during the Sino-Japanese War and the newly acquired Chinese knowledge of international politics, particularly the importance and advantage of occupying the middle position in a series of triangular relationships.

For the Chinese leaders, it was something quite new. It is the core of "Chairman Mao's revolutionary foreign policy," to use their own words. As usually has been the case in Chinese doctrine from time immemorial, this theory is an intricate and inseparable mixture of descriptive generalizations, programmatic prescriptions, and general principles in which reality and hope, facts and fears, forecasts and plans are utterly fused. In this scheme of things, the Third World and the nations in the Third World, including China, stand collectively and individually in a middle position between the two superpowers. Although the nations of the Third World are in conflict with either or both of the superpowers, the conflict between the superpowers is even sharper. As Teng has put it in speaking at the United Nations, "Since the two superpowers are contending for world hegemony, the contradiction between them is irreconcilable; one either overpowers the other, or is overpowered. Their compromise and collusion can only be partial, temporary and relative, while their contention is all-embracing, permanent and absolute." Hence, the Third World and the nations in it can exploit the differences between the two superpowers in order to advance their own interests.

Of the two superpowers, Teng said in his United Nations talk, the Soviet Union is "especially vicious" in its attempts to subject "other countries to its control, subversion, interference or aggression." The implication is clear that although the Third World countries should resist and attack both superpowers, individually and collectively, their main target of attack should be the Soviet Union. William Hinton made the point explicit, on the basis of his conversations with top leaders in Peking in September and October 1975.

> There was a shift in the slogans in Peking's foreign policy. Some time ago, the slogan had been: "Mobilize the Third World, unite with all those forces of the Second World willing to struggle and oppose the two superpowers." Now the slogan was "Mobilize the Third World, unite all the forces of the Second World willing to struggle, neutralize the U.S. and strike the main blow at the Soviet Union."[3]

Speaking to "progressive elements" in the United States, Hinton failed to mention the parallelism in American and Chinese policies in various parts of the world. Thus, China has pursued a policy of strongly supporting America's presence in Japan, telling "our Japanese friends" that their relationship with the U.S. should have priority over "their relationship with us." Similarly, China established close political and economic ties with Western European countries and the European Economic Community and strongly supported the strengthening of NATO. It also opposed the Soviet supported Cuban intervention in Angola, while applauding the Moroccan-French support for the Zairian forces that resisted the invasion of "mercenaries" from outside. China has attacked Soviet policy and "exposed" Soviet designs everywhere. It approved the Egyptian dispute with the Soviet Union and received a high level delegation from Somalia after Soviet-Somalian relations became very strained. Moreover, since the Soviet Union is the main enemy, China has found it possible and justifiable to cultivate good relationships with Third World countries regardless of the nature of their regime so long as they pursue a policy of opposing Soviet "hegemonism." Thus, China has maintained smooth relations with Iran while adopting a low posture in Dhofar.

The other Third World countries and China should and can occupy a middle position between the First World and the Second World, which consists of the developed countries between the First and Third Worlds. As Teng noted in addressing the U.N.,

> The hegemonism and power politics of the two superpowers have also aroused strong dissatisfaction among the developed countries of the Second World. The struggles of these countries against superpower control, interference, intimidation, exploitation and shifting of economic crises are growing day by day. Their struggles also have a significant impact on the development of the international situation.

However inaccurate it may be, this analysis of the relationship between the countries in the Second World and the superpowers serves to justify policies of cultivating profitable economic relations and good political relations with the former while waiting for an opportunity to exploit the contradictions between them.

The successful execution of this policy of trying to move to the middle position depends on the intensification of conflicts between the U.S. and the USSR, on the emergence of sharp differences between the superpowers and the countries of the Second World, and finally on the development of a united bloc of Third World countries. Hence, the Chinese forecast a situation of "great disorder under heaven" in which "all the political forces in the world have undergone drastic division and realignment through prolonged trial of strength." Again, "So long as imperialism and social-imperialism exist, there definitely will be no tranquility in the world, nor will there be lasting peace."

Thus, as the Chinese see it, war is an ever present possibility. For themselves, they urge constant vigilance against surprise attack by the Soviet Union. But they assign a much higher probability to conventional war between the two superpowers than to nuclear war, which they give only a low probability. They rate the probability of local wars indirectly involving the superpowers higher than direct military confrontation between them. They believe that the political use of military power is a fact of international life and can produce important shifts in the power balance. But above all, they feel that political changes and developments within nations will ultimately decide the power configuration of the world. They profess to believe that these changes will be in their favor. Thus, in his United Nations talk, Teng quoted Mao as having said that "the danger of a new world war still exists and the people of all countries must get prepared. But revolution is the main trend in the world today."

The parallels between this theory of the three worlds and the CCP's strategy and tactics of the united front during the Sino-Japanese War are obvious. Just as the CCP divided the political forces in China into the reactionary and die-hard forces, the middle-of-the-road forces, and the progressive forces, Peking is now dividing the world into three parts. Just as the CCP's strategy is to develop the progressive forces, win over the middle-of-the-road forces, and isolate the die-hard forces, Peking now is endeavoring to develop the friendly forces in the Third World, to win over some of the nations in the Second World, and to isolate the superpowers in the First World.

But there are new elements that are integrated with these familiar notions from the days of the united front. Although the CCP made fine distinctions among the various political groups within the reactionary camp and adopted different tactics in dealing with them during the united front period, it did not draw a sharp distinction between them. Now in the new doctrine of the three worlds, a sharp distinction is drawn between the two superpowers. The Soviet Union is designated the main target of attack. To use the phraseology of the united front, there is only "struggle" against the Soviet Union but very little "unity" with it. In China's relations with the United States, there is both "struggle and unity": "unity" with the U.S. on most of the global questions; "struggle" with the U.S. mainly on the question of Taiwan. In the strategy and tactics of the united front, the CCP was the leader of the progressive forces and took a strong position in opposition to the die-hard forces. In the doctrine of the three worlds, the main antagonists are the two superpowers; China and the other Third World forces occupy the middle position, from which they can exploit the contradictions between them, although in reality China finds itself opposite the Soviet Union and the United States occupies the middle position. Similarly, the doctrine posits sharp conflicts among the various nations in the Second World and the two superpowers that can and should be exploited by China and the rest of the Third World. It is in this sense that the doctrine of three worlds is a synthesis of the traditional strategy and tactics of the united front, with a new insight into the advantage of occupying the middle position in world affairs. It represents an abandonment of the many unrealistic aspects of the theory of two camps. It injects an additional measure of moderation, maturity, and flexibility into Peking's foreign policies.

Mao's death so far has brought about no change in Peking's theory and general framework of foreign policy. After China rejected Brezhnev's empty gestures concerning an improvement of relationships, Sino-Soviet polemics have reached a new level of intensity, with China characterizing "Soviet social-imperialism" as "the most dangerous source of world war." To be sure, the post-Mao leadership also has escalated its attack on the United States and has expressed extreme impatience over the lack of movement toward normalization of Sino-American relations, particularly with respect to the question of Taiwan. Total lack of an American response to Chinese expressions of dissatisfaction may lead to some improvement in the Sino-Soviet relationship. In the long run, it possibly might even force China to make the U.S. the main target of attack. But even if this should turn out to be the case, this development could still be encompassed within Mao's theory of the three worlds.

In other words, Mao's doctrine of the three worlds provides the flexibility that the Chinese need in the conduct of their foreign policy in the near future. It permits the adoption of a wide range of alternatives within a very broad general orientation. The major fixed points in this orientation are as follows. First, try to recapture the middle position between the two superpowers that was lost after the Chinese military encounter with the United States. Second, organize the broadest possible "united front" against one of the two superpowers, which is designated the main target of attack at a particular time, and work out policies parallel to those of the other superpower while maintaining the principle of "independence and autonomy" in this united front. Third, cultivate good economic and political relations with nations of the Second World as an element in this broad united front. Use these good relations to develop policies that work mainly against the principal enemy but, when the occasion demands it, against the secondary enemy as well. Also use these good relations to gain access to advanced technology and industrial goods and to increase China's bargaining power vis-à-vis one or both of the superpowers in trade and in diplomacy. Fourth, help and encourage the nations of the Third World to become more independent of the superpowers and to organize regional systems of power and order. Deny these areas and regions to the superpowers.

In comparison with the concepts developed in the past, this theory of the three worlds is much more comprehensive. It provides a general orientation for perceiving and dealing with a very complex, always changing international environment. When it is considered as a description of world politics, many of its elements are neither realistic nor accurate. But when viewed as a programmatic statement, it is sophisticated and subtle. It is basically different from the theory of the intermediate zone of the 1940s because the latter was insepatable from the theory of the two camps. It also marks an advance on the concept of the second intermediate zone of the mid 1960s because the latter was not linked to an explicit framework of the world in which the contention of the two superpowers was viewed as the dominant feature and in which the other developed countries were considered important partners in a broad united front. In comparison with the concept of surrounding the cities of the world from the countryside of the world, it gives diplomatic and political moves much greater prominence and deemphasizes the explicit m itory analogy.

Notwithstanding the utility and sophistication of the doctr the application of its general principles and the achievement of specific aim of recapturing the middle position entail many diffi ties. This is so primarily because the policy of leaning to one si theory of two camps, a series of concrete events, and the h complications surrounding the reunification of China as a great have placed China in the most unfavorable position China-Soviet Union-United States triangle. The success foreign policy in the short and middle range depends on th cation of the American-Soviet conflict to such an ext overshadows the specific conflict of interest between States and China over the question of Taiwan or the distrust and ideological differences between China an Union. Hence, in their propaganda, the Chinese have up Soviet designs on Western Europe, Africa, the M

Far East, South Asia, and the Indian Ocean while playing down their own fear of a Soviet attack. According to this propaganda, the Soviet Union is making a feint in the East as it prepares for an attack in the West. A series of setbacks would occur if the world does not move in the direction forecast by the theory and described in the propaganda, if American-Soviet relations improve, and if the Soviet Union betters its relations with Japan and Western Europe. China has no control and very little influence over these events. Although the conflicts of economic interests and the differences of view between the United States and the Second World sometimes work out to the advantage of China, on certain crucial issues, they also may work against China. For example, Japan does not want Sino-American relations to be normalized soon partly because Japan wants to preserve and develop her economic interest in Taiwan and partly because the normalization of Sino-American relations might result in a marked increase in Chinese imports of American technology and plants and a corresponding decrease in trade with Japan. There are indications that Great Britain is at most lukewarm toward the prospect of normalization.

As noted at the beginning of this chapter, the immediate question of normalization and the long-term problem of Taiwan would put a limit on the possibility of lowering the conflict with the United States. Even if normalization occurs in the near future, the question of Taiwan remains. In the short run there is little inducement or sanction that China can use to obtain substantive as distinguished from symbolic concessions from the United States. Trade, cultural exchange, etc., are minor matters. Presumably, China could respond to signals from certain powerful groups and individuals in the U.S. that the latter is willing to sell arms to China. Acceptance of the proposal would greatly strengthen Chinese armed forces in a very short time. China then might pose more of a threat to the Soviet Union in the East, thereby decreasing the Soviet threat to Western Europe. Obsessed by its experience in obtaining arms from the Soviet Union, China so far has rejected such signals. China fears that the purchase of arms from the United States would tie it to American apron strings, and would give the U.S. undue influence over Chinese policies. Ultimately, China would be used by the United States in a military confrontation with the Soviet Union. A military connection with the U.S. could jeopardize China's influence in the Third World and in leftist groups around the world. It would put a serious obstacle in the path of China's long-term design to move toward the middle position in the triangle.

Thus, the short-term alternatives open to China in the implementation of its grand design as revealed in the doctrine of the three worlds are very limited. But in the long run, the prospects are by no means totally hopeless. Conceivably, China views the complete solution of the Taiwan question as a long-term problem. If normalization should occur or even if normalization does not occur, continuation of the present policy, perhaps with a less pronounced tilt toward the U.S. and a greater willingness to improve relations with the Soviet Union on a state-to-state basis, will enable China to take advantage of the advanced technology and industrial know-how of all nations. In the next ten or twenty years, China's national power is bound to increase quite rapidly. China's weight in international affairs will become much more substantial and will become too great for anyone to ignore.

In other words, a period of intensive devotion to internal reconstruction in all aspects of its social and political life and a determined refusal to allow the ebbs and flows of foreign relations to interrupt this process will ultimately enable China to play out the role envisaged in the theory of three worlds. But the implementation of this program puts the utmost demands on China's capacity for self-restraint, prudence, perseverance, and long-term calculation in the face of an apparent lack of success in the international arena, the provocations of China's adversaries, and various specific setbacks. If this task appears almost impossible to accomplish, so was the task that the Chinese leaders envisaged for themselves in their revolution in the 1920s. In any event, it is a task that is implicit in Mao's doctrine of the three worlds, which Mao bequeathed to his successors.

Notes

1. Their views on this subject are revealed, among other places, in a most interesting article by Chih Feng in *Kuang-ming jih-pao*, 9 May 1977, p. 2.
2. *Peking Review*, 19 April 1974, p. 6.
3. Interview with William Hinton, *The Guardian* (New York), May 5, 1976, p. 15.

Appendix:
Center for Strategic and Foreign Policy Studies, The University of Chicago

Advisory Board

Peter B. Clark
President and Publisher
The Evening News Association
Detroit, Michigan

Clyde Dickey, Jr.
Partner
Arthur Andersen & Company
Chicago, Illinois

John Golden
President
Quarry Hill, Inc.
Arlington, Virginia

Alexander Hehmeyer
Counsel
Isham, Lincoln & Beale
Chicago, Illinois

James H. Ingersoll
Vice-President
Borg-Warner Corporation
Chicago, Illinois

Morris I. Leibman
Partner
Sidley & Austin
Chicago, Illinois

William J. McDonough
Executive Vice-President
First National Bank of Chicago
Chicago, Illinois

Samuel W. Sax, Chairman of
    Advisory Board
Chicago, Illinois

Alex R. Seith
Partner
Lord, Bissell & Brook
Chicago, Illinois

Sydney Stein, Jr.
Chicago, Illinois

Core Group

Robert Z. Aliber
University of Chicago
Graduate School of Business

Jeremy R. Azrael
University of Chicago

M. Cherif Bassiouni
De Paul University
College of Law

George I. Blanksten
Northwestern University

353

Core Group *(Cont.)*

Gerhard Casper
University of Chicago
Law School

Kenneth W. Dam
University of Chicago
Law School

Peter F. Dembowski
University of Chicago

Alan Dowty
University of Notre Dame

Edwin H. Fedder
University of Missouri at
St. Louis

Lawrence Finkelstein
Northern Illinois University

Hellmut Fritzsche
University of Chicago

Betty Glad
University of Illinois at
Urbana-Champaign

Gidon A. G. Gottlieb
University of Chicago
Law School

Robert T. Holt
University of Minnesota

Gene T. Hsiao
Southern Illinois University

Akira Iriye
University of Chicago

Morris Janowitz
University of Chicago

D. Gale Johnson
University of Chicago

Morton A. Kaplan
University of Chicago

Walter H. C. Laves
Indiana University at
Bloomington

David A. Rosenberg
University of Wisconsin at
Milwaukee

Sam C. Sarkesian
Loyola University

Edward Shils
University of Chicago

Stuart A. Solin
University of Chicago

Harvey Starr
Indiana University at
Bloomington

Frank Tachau
University of Illinois at
Chicago Circle

David Tarr
University of Wisconsin at
Madison

Tang Tsou
University of Chicago

Other Free Press Publications

Isolation or Interdependence: Today's Choices for Tomorrow's World, edited by Morton A. Kaplan.

ISBN 0-02-916940-0 254 pages

> *These original essays focus on the major choices facing America in its role as a world power—choices concerning economics, resources, technology, science, military policy, culture, and national and international politics. The book poses alternative solutions to world problems, comparing a policy of interdependence to the concept of "Fortress America" (isolationism).*

"This book asks all the right questions. . . . It illuminates many of the major issues of our time."

U.S. Senator Charles Percy

"This book represents an innovative undertaking which will help provide the focus we need in determining the future course of American leadership and policy."

U.S. Senator Sam Nunn

"An incisive collection. . . . The essays are well written and the arguments are lucid and lively. They are also very timely. . . . They all raise important issues . . . deserve close sifting and weighing by American decision makers."

Perspective

"This volume makes an important contribution toward clarifying the vital choices [concerning] the future peace and welfare of this nation and the world."

U.S. Representative Clement Zablocki

Japan, America, and the Future World Order, edited by Morton A. Kaplan and Kinhide Mushokoji.

ISBN 0-02-916910-0 369 pages

"In a period in which we will be moving either into a world of increasing interdependence and cooperation or retreating into competitive nationalism, relations between Japan and the United States will play a major role in the development of the international system and, in turn, will respond to these developments."

-from the Introduction

"It is regrettable that anthologies are so difficult to review. When they are done poorly the reviewer loses zest at so many easy targets; when they are done exceptionally well, as is this one, there is not room for the just measure of praise."

Foreign Service Journal

"Well-informed report . . . with unusually good input from the Japanese side."

Orbis

"An ambitious effort . . . shifts from the international stage to the domestic stage, from political to economic environmental questions with different experts putting their own intellectual stamp on the issues discussed . . . well integrated. . . ."

The Asian Student

Publications with Other Publishers

The Military-Industrial Complex: A Reassessment, edited by Sam C. Sarkesian. Sage Research Progress Series on War, Revolution, and Peacemaking, Volume II, 1972.

Military Rule in Latin America: Function, Consequences, and Perspectives, edited by Philippe C. Schmitter. Sage Publications, 1973.

SALT: Problems and Prospects, edited by Morton A. Kaplan. General Learning Press, 1973.

Strategic Thinking and Its Moral Implications, edited by Morton A. Kaplan. University of Chicago: Center for Policy Study, 1973.

NATO & Dissuasion, edited by Morton A. Kaplan. University of Chicago: Center for Policy Study, 1974.

Index